D1015652

*Energy
Unbound*

Energy Unbound

A FABLE FOR AMERICA'S FUTURE

L. Hunter Lovins
Amory B. Lovins
Seth Zuckerman

Illustrations by Mark Wilson
with a contribution by PAUL CONRAD

SIERRA CLUB BOOKS   SAN FRANCISCO

The Sierra Club, founded in 1892 by John Muir, has devoted itself
to the study and protection of the earth's scenic and ecological
resources—mountains, wetlands, woodlands, wild shores and rivers,
deserts and plains. The publishing program of the Sierra Club offers
books to the public as a nonprofit educational service in the hope
that they may enlarge the public's understanding of the Club's
basic concerns. The point of view expressed in each book, however,
does not necessarily represent that of the Club. The Sierra Club
has some sixty chapters coast to coast, in Canada, Hawaii, and Alaska.
For information about how you may participate in its programs to
preserve wilderness and the quality of life, please address inquiries
to Sierra Club, 730 Polk Street, San Francisco, CA 94109.

Jacket design by Paul Bacon
Book design by Abigail Johnston
Illustrations by Mark Wilson and Paul Conrad. Paul Conrad cartoon reprinted
by permission of Paul Conrad and the Los Angeles Times.

LIBRARY OF CONGRESS CATALOGING IN PUBLICATION DATA
Lovins, L. Hunter, 1950–
    Energy unbound.   Bibliography: p. 357
    Includes index.
      1. Renewable energy sources—United States.
2. Energy conservation—United States. 3. Energy
policy—United States. I. Lovins, Amory B., 1947–
II. Title.
TJ807.9.U6L68 1986   333.79   85-8199
ISBN 0-87156-820-9

Printed in the United States of America

10 9 8 7 6 5 4 3 2 1

Dedicated to the millions of people around
the world
who are making the vision a reality.

—LHL, ABL, and SZ

Contents

Contents

*Energy
Unbound*

1 Eunice Goes to Washington

*E*UNICE BUNNYHUT shook her head and ran her hands over the silver crushed-velour seat of the sleek, grey limousine. It was so amazing, she thought to herself: me, a housewife, here. She closed her eyes and remembered. She had first seen the ad in the *Dubuque Telegraph-Herald*. What had it said? "Person with common sense and good judgment sought to manage small team," or something like that. Well, she hadn't thought too much of the ad, but she had sent off her résumé to the post office box in Des Moines. Eunice had been a homemaker for twenty-four years, and now that her youngest, Jimmy, was a senior in high school, she wanted to make some money instead of just volunteering for the PTA. She smiled again at the job descriptions she had written. "Fast-food concession manager" was the time she had brought in five hundred dollars with a bake sale for her daughter's rugby team. "Neighborhood services coordinator" was the time she had arranged a carpool with the other parents on the block so they could get their kids to the day camp, the swimming pool, and the Grant Wood exhibit in Cedar Rapids. At the time, she hadn't thought of herself as anything special. Those were things that anyone could have done, and it had been pretty obvious that they had needed doing. But they did look good on paper.

All that seemed very far away now. Actually, when several months had passed after applying, Eunice had forgotten about the matter. Then the phone had rung: Mrs. Eunice Bunnyhut, please. That had led to an interview, a security check—Eunice still bristled at some of the questions on the form—and finally a meeting with the President's right-hand man, the Special Assistant to the *President of the United States!* Even now Eunice's eyes grew big at the thought. The assistant, a nondescript pudgy-faced man in a dark blue suit—she could never remember his name—had explained that the President was tired of energy policies that didn't make sense to him. He wanted another layperson to take a stab at it. And Eunice seemed to fit the bill. "Me?" she remembered herself bleating. "But what do I know about energy?" Nevertheless, Mr. Blue Suit had insisted and had rather flattered her. And her husband, Joe, had been wonderfully understanding. He was between jobs just then and told Eunice he wouldn't mind seeing Washington, D.C., for a while. So she took the post.

Now here she was in a limousine, for crying out loud, gliding past the silhouette of the Washington Monument, on her way to her new job. This was her second day. She had spent the first day with the President's man, being briefed and getting used to the idea that "Secretary of Energy" was really not a typing and stenography job. Last night, returning to her newly leased Georgetown town house and soaking her feet in the tub, she had turned to her husband with a sigh. "Joe," she had said, "I have a feeling we're not in Iowa anymore."

For her first working day, she had scheduled a nine-thirty meeting with her top aides. Each had prepared a briefing book for her, which she had received the day before, but she could make neither head nor tail of what the books said. They were full of bureaucratese—such phrases as "expected sectoral electric demand to be met thermally is projected to be in the vicinity of seven exajoules primary fuel, though probabilistic analysis may evoke lower forecasts." Pure gobbledegook. Perhaps her assistants would be more lucid in person. She feared, however, that they might not be.

The limo arrived at the Forrestal Building, one of the new monuments to Portland cement that clustered around the Capital Mall. This one was a concrete box on concrete stilts that seemed to Eunice not unlike a giant spaceship. Blinking up at it, she wondered if it might still overcome its tremendous bulk and soar out past the stratosphere if things ever got too hairy in Washington . . . perhaps her office came with a command console like that of the *Enterprise* . . . ? She began to feel a mite unnerved.

Eunice shook herself sharply. This would never do. Holding herself primly, she took the quick elevator ride and walked to her office to meet Barb, her secretary, (small *s*, she noted to herself with a twinge of pride) and to exchange her purse for a legal pad and pen. Then she and Barb headed for the seventh-floor conference room.

She walked in—only a few minutes past nine-thirty—and saw that all eight of her Assistant Secretaries were already there, chewing away on the fat. When she entered, they quieted down suddenly. Hmm, she thought happily, now if only I could get my children to behave that well. But the pleasure was short-lived. There's business to attend to, she reminded herself, and as her secretary had warned, she had better get her assistants firmly in hand from the very beginning.

So, deliberately setting her pad and pen down she settled into the leather-backed chair that awaited her at the head of the table, and took a deep breath. "Good morning, gentlemen," she began in her best businesslike tone. "I'm Eunice Bunnyhut, and I'm looking forward to the opportunity of working with all of you. We're all busy people; so let's get right to business. First, let me thank you for the briefing books. They must represent a lot of work, um, but I'm sure you'll all agree that they were rather one-dimensional. So, could one of you please tell me in somewhat simpler terms what's really going on in energy?"

The assistants exchanged glances. First to speak was the Assistant Secretary for Policy. "Actually, ma'am, things are going very well," he said. "Gasoline prices have been stable or dropping for a couple of years now. There are no lines at the pumps. The energy crisis is over, and we're reentering an era of plenty."

The Assistant Secretary for Emergency Planning looked pained. "Well," he began, "I'm not so sure I'd agree. Things do look pretty stable now, but the oil coming out of the Persian Gulf could be cut off at almost any moment. That would be about six percent of the oil we use, turned off like a light—and it could send the international price through the roof. And you know, domestic supplies aren't that secure, either. Refineries, ports, and pipelines all make great targets for terrorist attacks."

Eunice was puzzled. The two men worked in the same department and read the same information. Why didn't they agree? "Wait," she asked, "what are you saying? Is energy a problem or not? And by the way, why am I still paying so much for it?"

The Assistant Secretary for Petroleum, a stately grey-haired man, rose to reply. "Madam Secretary, please understand the complexity of the oil markets. At the exchanges in Europe where oil is traded, the prices can plummet, but that may only translate into a penny a gallon less at the pump. You understand, one must remember the strong dollar, the refiners' margins, and the tilt to the light side of the barrel."

Eunice began to feel that she was losing control. The Assistant Secretary for Pricing caught her nervous glances and chimed in: "And some of the prices are rising. Heating oil is still creeping up. Natural gas—one of our most plentiful domestic resources—is ratcheting up in price, too."

"But if natural gas is so abundant," Eunice objected, "how come it's getting more expensive?"

"Oh, that's an easy one," said the Assistant Secretary for Petroleum. "Natural gas prices were held down by government order for a long time, and now they're rising to market levels just like oil."

Eunice's feeling of being in the wrong pew was overshadowed by a growing frustration. No wonder the President couldn't understand DOE policy; the Department's top officials couldn't, either. She shook her head and said, "I'm sorry, gentlemen, but none of this makes any sense. Prices are going up, prices are going down, no one can guarantee supplies from one day to the next, but there's lots of energy. And why is my utility bill going up?"

"We needed electricity to ensure our continued economic growth," said the Assistant Secretary for Utilities, "so we built lots of power plants. We should have plenty of electricity for a while."

By this point, Eunice's hopes that her Assistant Secretaries might actually be able to explain official policy were evaporating in a cloud of contradictions. She braced herself, though, and decided to ask at least one more question, even though it was probably not going to help. "But if we have plenty of electricity," she persisted, "why was my bill last month so outrageous?"

The Assistant Secretaries exchanged glances again. A bad sign.

"Well, funny you should mention it, Madam Secretary," said the Assistant Secretary for Utilities. "The utilities built lots of expensive plants to meet that ever-growing demand. But to pay for the plants they had to raise the rates. Now people have to pay so much for electricity that they're not buying as much of it as we thought they would; so the utilities can't afford to build more plants. In fact, some of them can't even afford to pay for the plants they've *already* built. And the guys who are trying to finish plants now are in real deep . . . uh . . ." he hunted for another word. "Anyway, hardly anyone has ordered any big plants since 1981. But our experts think that if we could just get more responsive rate regulation—you know, higher prices—the utilities won't have much trouble building another trillion dollars' worth of power plants by the year 2000. And, in fact, we project that to keep the lights on and America working, they'll *have* to build that many. We *must* have another four hundred thirty-eight thousand megawatts of power plants on line by the year 2000. You see, there's not a moment to lose."

Eunice sighed. "I'm sorry I asked," she said. "But this all seems absurd. Utilities build lots of plants and can't pay for them. People use less power, but we need more—and maybe they'll use more if we charge more for it. Oil prices are dropping even though no one knows whether, um, Texas refineries and Saudi oil fields will still be there tomorrow." She paused briefly to mentally check that those were the locations mentioned in the briefing books. Yes, that was right. "And," she continued a bit more confidently," the government is letting the price of natural gas rise even though some people can't afford it already. Does any of this make sense to you? What can we do?"

The Assistant Secretary for Policy had been fidgeting for some time and seized his opportunity. "We're already doing just what is needed. If you'll just look at this easel over here, Madam Secretary, I've prepared a few charts to give you an idea of how we've got the situation under control. For one thing, we're putting a lot of money into synthetic fuels, a great new technology to turn coal and oil shale into substitutes for foreign oil. We've spent a few billion on synfuels over the last five years . . ."

Suddenly the Assistant Secretary for Nuclear Power interjected, "Yeah? And nearly all the oil companies have pulled out, in case you haven't noticed."

The Assistant Secretary for Policy resumed unruffled, ". . . and the other main focus of our budget has been our nuclear program, with a total of nearly nine billion dollars directly spent on it in the past five years. In fact, nuclear accounts for sixty-two percent of this department's 1985 budget request for civilian energy technologies—nearly twice its 1981 share. We're quite proud of our efforts to free this promising technology from the strait jacket the eco-freaks had it wrapped in."

Again there was an outburst, this time from the Assistant Secretary for Synfuels. "Yeah, and have you noticed that no new reactors have been ordered by U.S. utilities since 1978? Utilities had to write off fifteen billion dollars in nuclear plants in 1983–84. This department sank three billion into an Ohio enrichment plant, then cancelled it. And when the Washington Public Power Supply System killed two of its nukes, it defaulted on two point two billion dollars in top-rated bonds."

Eunice had had it. "Boys! Boys! Stop fighting. Is this any way to run a national policy? You men can't even agree on the basic facts, and besides, it seems that your solutions keep turning into new problems. What problem were you trying to solve in the first place?"

"There's not enough energy to go around," lamented the Assistant Secretary for Nuclear Power.

Eunice indulged herself. "If you keep carrying on like this, I know that'll certainly be true of me," she said tiredly.

"Yeah, there's not enough energy to go around," added the Assistant Secretary for Policy, "and a lot of it is too expensive. But unless we can get our hands on a lot more energy, this country and the civilized world will grind to a halt. We have to use more and more energy—our quality of life depends on it."

Eunice thought for a moment. "Is that really true?" she asked. "I'm not sure it is. Wait, wait! Let me think this through. There's not enough energy to go around; so we could raise the price to make people use less. But it's already too expensive; so we should lower the price. But if we lower the price, then people would want to use more, which would only aggravate the first problem. Is that what you're trying to say?"

"See, you understand already," the Assistant Secretary for Policy said brightly.

Now Eunice was getting mad. "What do you mean, I 'understand'?" she said, her voice coming dangerously close to squeaking. "That was all nonsense. It led us right around in a circle." Eunice paused a moment to regain her composure. She hoped she looked calmer than she felt. Were grown men really spending all this time on such silliness and thinking that it made sense? "There's got to be a more sensible way of thinking about energy issues," she finally said.

"Good luck," said the Assistant Secretary for Policy. "We've been working on it for a dozen years and *we* still haven't come up with one."

Eunice thought out loud. "When the price of beef went up, and I still had to feed my family, of course, what did we do? We ate chicken and fish; we ate things like lasagne that had very little meat in them. We found ways to eat well without having so much beef in our diets. If we apply that to energy . . ."

The Assistant Secretary for Policy cut her off. "You can't. That's conservation, and as the President said, it means being colder in the winter and hotter in the summer. The American people won't stand for it. They know that this nation didn't conserve its way to greatness; it produced its way there."

"Hmph. Well, let's try another approach," Eunice retreated. "What do we really want the energy for, anyway? I wouldn't want just the energy, after all. I want to be comfortable, and be able to make weekend trips to visit my brother. I suppose I also want power for my sewing machine and heat in the stove. And the factories have to operate."

The Assistant Secretary for Nuclear Power jumped in. "Right, and all those things take energy. That's why we're all here: to get the energy for all those services."

"I know," said Eunice, tiring of the interruptions. "But be

patient. I'm just learning. It seems to me that we've fallen into the middle of all this and gotten lost. If you'll just bear with me a bit, I'm going to try to find the beginning. Now—if my family is hungry, I need to get food for them. So I go shopping, but I don't try to buy out the store to get all the food I can find regardless of prices, do I? And I don't buy my everyday food at a gourmet deli. I've always had to watch my budget. So I make lists—how much of what kind of food I want. Then I shop carefully for the best buys. Oh yes, I'll buy a special treat for each of my children, and Joe—he's my husband—loves fresh strawberries. But I'm still pretty careful about giving my family the best nutrition I can, at the best buy. It seems to me what you guys are doing is like going into the store and grabbing several of everything and then trying to figure out how to pay for it all. And you haven't even thought about who's going to eat it."

"But, ma'am," objected the Assistant Secretary for Utilities, "this is the nation's energy we're talking about, not your grocery allowance. We simply can't afford to run out. The nation will just have to pay the price, even if we have, er, leftovers, or extra items sitting on the pantry shelf." He nodded curtly to Eunice, as if to punctuate his little speech, and folded his arms. Then in a loudish whisper he expressed the group's feeling to the Assistant Secretary for Nuclear Power, who sat beside him: "God, first a dentist, now a housewife. This democracy thing is getting out of hand."

Eunice bristled, and ignoring their exasperation, she retorted, "The nation *won't* pay. My neighbors, the Fitzsimmonses, just insulated their attic and caulked and weather-stripped last year, and their heating bills have dropped by half. They're using less energy, and they're still as warm as they were before—or warmer, they say. It seems to me that people may *not* want to buy more energy as long as they can be sure that their houses stay warm in the winter, they have lights to read by at night, and they can take a hot bath when they want to."

"Our synfuel plants, nuclear power stations, and coal mines will provide them with all the energy they need for that," said the Assistant Secretary for Policy.

"Yes," said Eunice, "but look how much they cost. How State Power and Light is ever going to be able to pay for its unfinished nuclear plant—Mausoleum One, I think they call it—is beyond me. I think it's beyond them, too. The plant's bigger than the utility is—it's like being pregnant with a three-hundred-pound baby. And you know who ends up paying for those things—people like me who get two- or three-hundred-dollar utility bills in January. Mary and Bob Fitzsimmons paid only a thousand dollars to have their house insulated and caulked, and they already saved half that cost last winter. If everyone did that, maybe we wouldn't *need* to finish all those expensive plants."

The Assistant Secretary for Nuclear Power was aghast. "Do you realize what you're saying? Do you know how expensive it is to cancel the reactors that are still under construction? We've invested one hundred twenty-five billion dollars, and we'd get nothing back."

"Well," said Eunice, startled by such a magnitude, "I don't have all the figures on that. The answer—whether finishing Mausoleum One is worth it—probably depends on a lot of things. But I'm sure the topic will come up again, after I've had a chance to find out more. Remember, I'm new to this job. But," she ventured, regaining a sense that something had to change, "do you know how many homes you could insulate for a hundred billion dollars? At the rate things are going, it'll be cheaper to buy the solar cells I just read about in the newspaper than to buy a utility's electricity. Then everyone will just unplug from the electric company. I must say," she added cheerily, "that sounds sort of neat."

The Assistant Secretaries stared at Eunice in horror. As the roomful of middle-aged men glared at her, Eunice realized that she just might have called into question some cherished beliefs. Maybe, she thought, we'd better wrap up the meeting—we clearly aren't going to get much further today. So she brightened her face, as she used to do when her kids were little and they pouted or sulked in a corner.

"Oh come, come! Don't mope like that," she said. "I'm sure there are still lots of things that the Department of Energy could do to help people use energy better and get energy in ways they can afford. And I'm sure I don't understand enough about the problems yet. I mean, knowing what the Fitzsimmonses did is fine, but there are a lot of other things out there that I still need to find out. So let's end the meeting for now and get back together at the same time next week. In the meantime, I have a lot of homework to do."

With that, Eunice picked up her legal pad and pen and walked out of the room. The Assistant Secretaries sat as though shell-shocked. Walking down the hall, her secretary squeezed her hand. "Oh, Madam Secretary, that was wonderful!" said Barb, her soft Texas accent ringing with pride. "You really showed them."

"Showed them?" said Eunice in disbelief. "If anything, I showed them my ignorance. "Oh, dear," she sighed. "I need some time to collect myself. Why don't you go on back to the office? I'll just go for a short walk or something. I think I need to powder my nose."

2 *Enter Duncan*

*E*UNICE WALKED PENSIVELY through the corridors of the seventh floor, wandering aimlessly down mazelike hallways. She poked around discreetly, realizing with a touch of inadequacy that the vast warren of bureaucrats' hutches was now under her nominal control. Unaware that she was passing an open office, she pondered aloud, "How did we ever get into this mess? Energy never used to be such a problem . . ."

Behind her came the soft thump of a book closing. A tanned face with strikingly blue eyes emerged from the office she'd just passed and inquired after her, "Would you really like to know?"

Eunice turned to regard a man in his late thirties, dressed in an oxford shirt, tie, and faded blue jeans that stood out amidst the Department's conformity like a Sherman button at a Georgia picnic. "You're new around here, aren't you?" the man observed, leaning an arm against his door frame. "You must be—you're still asking questions. Well, I could probably enlighten you a bit—if you'd like me to." His face crinkled a bit beneath his tan as he smiled. "Who knows?" he added. "You might even have an open mind, and that really would be a treat to discover around here."

Eunice, realizing she was staring at the man, recovered her manners enough to stop staring and ask, "But who are you?"

"Duncan. Duncan Jefferson Holt," the man said. "Here, do come in," he invited, sweeping the day's mail from a government-issue chair and setting the stack in a corner with its predecessors.

"Mr. Holt, I really must be . . ." Eunice began.

"Duncan. Call me Duncan. Your question is very important," he said, sitting and wagging his finger playfully at her. "Those who do not remember the past are condemned to repeat it."

"Condemned? To repeat it?" Eunice echoed, tentatively entering the office and seating herself. "Like those Assistant Secretaries I'll have to face again? Oh, no, that discussion was straight out of *Alice in Wonderland*. I definitely don't want to repeat that." She shivered, then finished primly, "But I do want to know my facts better before I talk to them again."

Duncan's brows knit briefly behind his aviator glasses as he mentally filed the reference to "Assistant Secretaries." Eunice watched him, wondering about his accent. Eastern prep school, but with a hint of . . . Texas? Gentle, too.

" 'Crisis,' they called it," he began. "A 'great surprise.' But anyone who'd been following history could have told them it was inevitable. Although when one is comfortable," Duncan stretched back in his chair, "why imagine that the era of wealth might ever end? Circumstances in the 1960s were very much like they seem now. Energy? Why worry about energy? You know, the whole problem really comes from thinking that all energy is alike—that one source can and should do all kinds of tasks.

"Take oil, for example. When the first gusher was struck in Pennsylvania in 1859, it sparked a period of unprecedented growth in the use of energy. For the first time since humans had discovered fire, energy was abundant and easy to obtain, at least for those nations with big deposits of oil. Not only that, but it came in a form that could be used in applications as different as an automobile and an electric power plant. It could be trucked and piped and tanked. After World War II, the first war fueled mainly by oil, energy use doubled in twenty years. Between 1950 and 1973, the United States enjoyed an era of unparalleled material abundance; energy and other natural resources seemed cheap and available as never before. In fact, the efficiency of many industrial and commercial processes actually declined in those years because it seemed silly to worry about how energy was used when it was so cheap."

Duncan sat forward intently. "But those easy days were just what caused the crises. Much of the petroleum that fueled the worldwide boom of the fifties and sixties came from countries halfway around the globe from the eventual consumers. Remember, most of the world still depends on firewood and dung. But the booming United States and the rebuilt Europe and Japan lusted after oil. So, like the raiding corsairs of the Middle Ages, large, politically adept corporations searched the globe for oil fields to feed the growing appetites back home.

"But the people in the oil-rich nations were not included in the resulting wealth. Eventually, those countries began to wise up. In 1960 these nations, led by their Harvard- and Oxford-trained economists and MBA oil ministers, formed the Organization of Petroleum Exporting Countries, in the hope of getting some fair bargaining power with such giants as ARAMCO, the Arabian-American Oil Company.

"By 1970 other problems were on the horizon. Yields at some of the richest American oil fields—in California, Oklahoma, and Texas—were beginning to drop. American oil extraction began to decline for the first time ever. And the United States became a net importer of oil, dependent on foreign crude to sustain our growing addiction. But we avoided a basic truth: It's a round earth, and, as with any finite container, there can be only so much oil in the ground. When it's all used up, all of Shell's horses and all of Shell's men won't be able to find any more." Duncan paused for breath.

"So what happened then? All I remember is that suddenly you couldn't find thirty-cent gasoline anymore," Eunice said.

"Matters indeed came to a head in 1973," Duncan continued, "when the members of OPEC voted to raise their prices by what seemed then an unthinkable amount: from under two dollars per barrel to about four. Later that year, when the Arabs raised the price of a barrel of crude to eleven dollars and imposed an oil embargo on the United States and most of Western Europe, energy zoomed to the top of the political agenda. For the first time, people realized how precious energy was, particularly imported energy.

"Suddenly, energy independence was a vital national goal. But, of course, having believed the future to be limitless, we responded to our new-found awareness of shortage in a rather child-ish way: 'We're running out of energy?' we said. 'Well, let's get some more.' Worse, no one had thought very much about why we wanted the oil in the first place. The policy, simply put, was: First, let's find more oil—offshore, in the Arctic, in the oceans off Viet-nam, in the Atlantic—wherever, never mind the price. Huh? Oil is getting harder to find? Well, oil is energy—let's just get more energy—any kind will do. But we must have more energy, of any kind, from anywhere."

"But that's just what those Assistant Secretaries were saying," interrupted Eunice, startled. "Do you mean to say that they're right?"

"Hardly. But this definition of the problem has, in fact, under-lain national policy for four successive administrations. Let's re-member a little history. President Nixon took the first try, since he had the dubious fortune to be in office when the Arabs brought the energy issue to international prominence. He was forced by circumstances, as his successors also would be, to say something. His response, Project Independence, called for a policy of expand-ing domestic supplies of energy by any and every means possible. That would have meant reliance on coal, mostly to be strip-mined and converted into electricity and synthetic fuels; on oil and gas, increasingly from Arctic and offshore wells; and on nuclear fission, eventually in fast-breeder reactors. But the major goal of Project Independence was to subsidize energy prices, because it was feared that higher prices would 'constrain economic growth.' Perhaps fortunately, Nixon's preoccupation with other matters in 1973–74 got in the way of his administration's execution of energy policy.

"The preoccupation with 'supply side' energy policy re-emerged, though, in President Ford's State of the Union message. The plan was slightly less grandiose than Nixon's. Still, the year 2000 was supposed to see four hundred fifty to eight hundred new reactors, five hundred to eight hundred huge new coal plants, and more than a thousand new coal mines. The massive electrification that was to have been part of the package was described by one expert as 'the most important attempt to modify the infrastructure of industrial society since the railroads.' Running such a program just from 1976 to 1985 would have cost more than one *trillion* dollars—that's in 1976 dollars—a sum amounting to well over three-fourths of all available domestic investment in the entire economy during that period."

"A trillion dollars?" squeaked Eunice. "But that's the program the Assistant Secretaries just tried to talk me into! No, wait, that was just for the power plants—they weren't even counting all the oil and gas and coal. But those Nixon and Ford proposals never made it off the ground, did they?"

"Ford's program," agreed Duncan, "like Nixon's, succumbed to economic realities. The money to finance the megaprojects simply wasn't available. Wall Street found the investments too risky, and their attitude didn't encourage Congress to step into the gap. However, no one was sure what the alternative should be. Although the old policy was visibly failing, as rising costs and nuclear plant cancellations showed, few people believed that the newly popular solar and other renewable technologies could run a major industrial society. Critics pointed out the economic and environmental risks of official policy, but nobody had a coherent alternative."

Eunice was confused again. "But, if all those huge programs failed, shouldn't we be running out of energy now? You're not saying that, are you?" Duncan was about to clarify, but Eunice's enlightenment cut him short. "So we may not ever need the huge projects they were pushing on me this morning."

"Ah," Duncan said, grinning. But as he smiled, one eye narrowed, almost winked. Something Eunice had said was bothering him. He couldn't quite identify it, though; so he continued. "Wait until you hear the rest of this history—it gets better," he chuckled. "President Carter's 1977 National Energy Program came with lots of bells and whistles, but it wasn't too different. It was certainly more dramatic, complete with a declaration that the energy crisis constituted the moral equivalent of war for the nation. When I heard that phrase," he said, wincing at the memory, "I immediately noticed that it abbreviated to MEOW, and tried to get a message back to Carter. But he was already set on the wording. Anyway, his plan would have invoked all kinds of emergency measures that were supposed to speed the United States on the path toward energy independence. An Energy Mobilization Board and an Energy Security Corporation were to be created to put 'high priority' energy projects on the fast track to completion, thereby bypassing the checks and balances of our democracy and the common sense of the marketplace.

"Conservation was portrayed not as using energy more efficiently, but rather as sacrificing comfort and convenience. Carter even insisted on announcing this policy while he sat in front of his fireplace wearing a sweater. Imagine," Duncan scowled, "imposing a national dress code of cardigan sweaters! Worse, eighty-eight billion dollars was to be spent on synthetic-fuel projects, which, if they worked, would have provided 'oil' from coal and shale. But the 'oil' would have cost three to five times the oil price then prevailing. Even so, those projects might perhaps have succeeded if the price of energy kept rising; but in that case all sorts of energy-saving measures would have made even better economic sense. Anyway, costly oil means costly money, and since synthetic-fuel plants are made mainly of the money invested in them, they can probably *never* compete."

Eunice was lost again. "But then how come those guys still want to do that?" she asked, somewhat bewildered.

Duncan gave a wry smile and shrugged. "Some folks just won't read their history," he said.

"However," he continued, "perhaps the worst aspect of the Carter plan, and the one that guaranteed failure, was its lack of necessity. If the huge, 'hard' energy projects, the risky investments, and the mandatory curtailments of energy services had been the *only* possible alternatives, the assault on democratic institutions might have been excusable. But, in fact, the policy was economically unsound as well as politically unacceptable. And Congress, while it fluttered in the gale of claims of national urgency, eventually and sensibly did very little. Unfortunately, the various portions that *were* enacted after the political horse-trading lacked any logical coherence. For instance, the poor were to survive the deregulation of oil and gas prices with the help of federal programs to insulate their houses so they could stay warm while conserving energy. But those programs were inadequately funded, leaving only the fuel assistance programs that paid heating bills for the poor—in effect, doing nothing more than lining the pockets of the oil companies."

Eunice sat forward, shocked. "But that way, the poor would continue to need that assistance forever, without ever being able to get up on their own two feet. What a short-sighted handout!" she exclaimed.

"Exactly," said Duncan, shaking his head sadly. "Now, things might have had a chance to work themselves out, but, again, circumstances conspired against that. In 1979 the Iranian revolution cut off the oil coming out of that country and caused yet another round of price rises and panic buying. You'd think that two oil crises in one decade would convince the nation of the need for an energy policy that would not deplete our bank account, our national resources, or our security. However, the makers of U.S. foreign policy reacted instead by declaring the Persian Gulf an area of strategic importance to the nation, and thus was the Rapid Deployment Force born." Duncan sighed. "I'm still amazed how people can talk about 'our' oil fields over there, as if the world owed us our luxury. Say," he digressed, "did you realize that what it costs each year to maintain the Rapid Deployment Force, if invested in weatherizing American buildings, would enable us to save enough oil to eliminate all our oil imports and thus the need for the Force?" He grinned as Eunice sorted through what that meant and then blinked in amazement.

"Anyway," he continued, "in 1980 Ronald Reagan rode to power on a platform of getting the federal government off the backs of the people—and, coincidentally, off the backs of the utilities, the oil companies, and other energy firms. His programs may have been couched in the terms of the free market and decentralization, but the Reagan administration, perhaps mindful of the interests that paid for its election, took steps to ensure how the market would decide." Duncan cast a cynical eye at Eunice, effectively shutting off any protest. "Look," he argued, "the administration's energy budget called for the elimination of federal programs that gave consumers and businesses energy information, and thus enabled the market to work. The 1983 budget proposals called for cutting the conservation programs by ninety-eight percent from the 1980 level, and those for renewable resources by eighty-seven percent. Lest this seem odd, the administration stated that solar energy and conservation were mature technologies that should meet the test of the market.

"Nuclear power, on the other hand," Duncan let some irony into his voice, "was essential for our energy future. Despite thirty years of development and sixty-five-odd billion dollars in federal subsidies, lately increasing by some fifteen-plus billion dollars per year, nuclear power wasn't yet ready to brave the chill winds of the marketplace. Reagan insisted that nuclear power therefore required continued federal assistance and pledged, in October 1981, a major federal effort to revive the nuclear industry. He called for the rapid elimination of 'unnecessary government barriers to efficient utilization of our abundant, economical resources of coal and uranium.' Economical! With utilities going broke right and left trying to build nuclear plants." Even Duncan seemed incredulous. "Under this program, the feds boosted direct spending on nuclear energy to more than two billion dollars a year in 1985. Nuclear research and other 'commercial' nuclear-related programs account for about three-quarters of DOE's civilian research and development funds, not counting the roughly sixteen billion dollars in annual tax subsidies given to electric utilities generally. In fact, the last time the senior advisory board reviewed DOE's budget, they found that ninety-six percent of the energy-supply research and development budget requested in 1983 was earmarked for electrical supply, and ninety-nine point two percent of *that* ninety-six percent was for nuclear electricity. They simply tried to starve competing options."

Eunice knew better than to interrupt a voice with such determination. Besides, these were just the kind of numbers she'd wanted this morning. Duncan was happy to give her more. "Reagan's Department of Energy, presided over by strongly pronuclear administrators, stated its purpose to be the promotion of large, centralized electric power plants, especially reactors. Upon arrival, Reagan's first Secretary of Energy ordered all DOE publications reviewed to assure conformity with this position. At the same time, the Department was busy eradicating the programs and publications that had actually fostered decentralization and individual choice, such as the monthly *Energy Consumer*, one of the few DOE publications that helped the common people solve their energy problems on their own. Reagan's DOE even impounded and destroyed informational booklets that had already been printed, simply to try to prevent the word from spreading about renewable energy. Sort of silly and sad," Duncan mused, "especially because the nuclear industry that we're still subsidizing so heavily is dying anyway. Fewer nuclear plants are operating or are on order today than there were in 1972. They just cost too much.

"Anyway," continued Duncan, "all four of those Presidents' plans went nowhere. It's kind of funny, because while they weren't looking, the energy problem was actually beginning to solve itself. But our Presidents and other officials couldn't see that because all of them had been asking the wrong question. They were all stuck in the crisis-management mode of how to get *more energy*, of any kind, at any price, because they thought the problem was only how to replace increasingly scarce, vulnerable, and expensive foreign oil."

"Yes," interjected Eunice, "I was going to ask you that. What will the price of oil be two years from now?"

"You know the truth? No one knows. Some people guess ten dollars a barrel, but it could just as easily be a hundred dollars. People guess anywhere in between, but not even the Saudi Arabian oil minister or the Chairman of Exxon can say what it *will* be. That depends on too many things—volatile international situations, improvements in energy efficiency, economic growth, interest and exchange rates, to name just a few. But more importantly, that's not the right question to be asking at all. If we ask and answer the right questions, over time we'll hardly care what the price of oil is. And the first question is so simple that almost everyone has overlooked it: What do we need energy for? Just asking that question ought to remind us that we don't need energy for its own sake. You, for example, wouldn't know what to do with a barrel of oil. That's about as much oil as the average American uses, directly and indirectly, every seventeen days—but what we want is the use, not the oil. Energy is only useful as a means to an end—to keep our houses warm, get from place to place, to run our electric appliances. Rather than asking only where to get more energy, we should instead ask: How much energy do we need to satisfy our needs in the cheapest, most efficient ways? What kinds of energy do we need? And how best can we get that energy?"

"Yes, yes," said Eunice. "But that's just what I was trying to say to . . ."

Eunice was interrupted by a knock at the door, and before Duncan could respond, the door burst open and a short, distinctly gnomish young man scurried in. "You won't believe whom the President just appointed Secretary of Energy!" he exclaimed with gerbil-like anxiety, batting at some wisps of hair that seemed to elude him. "As if giving us an oral surgeon to lead the Department in '81 wasn't enough, now the White House had to give us a housewife." He fiddled with a tufty beard that seemed as out of sorts as he did. In fact, Eunice had the feeling he was actually unraveling around the edges.

Duncan regarded the scruffy creature in the doorway, his eyes narrowing. As a growing mirth began to play across his face, he raised a hand to silence the gnome. Then, aware that Eunice had turned scarlet, Duncan cradled his chin between thumb and forefinger and grinned engagingly. "Oh, I don't know, Hobart," he mused, appearing to ignore Eunice. "I think a housewife's common sense just might be handier in this job than all the so-called expertise of a James Schlesinger or some nuclear engineer." Then he turned and accorded Eunice his full attention and grinned again. "Please excuse the interruption, . . ." he offered in his most courtly manner, ". . . Madame Secretary. Shall we continue?" He smiled blandly at Hobart.

Hobart suddenly realized that Duncan was not alone. He stood gaping at Eunice for a moment before taking a sudden interest in the calculator holster hanging from his belt. Then he glanced piteously at Duncan as though he wanted nothing more than to crawl into that calculator case, emitted a bleat that could have meant "Oh, no," turned, and fled.

As the door slammed shut behind him, Eunice and Duncan both burst out laughing. When Eunice calmed down enough to speak, she asked between giggles, "But what was that?"

"Oh, a member of the species *Bureaucraticus scientificus,*" choked Duncan, blinking back tears of laughter himself. "They're nocturnal creatures who live in small, dark holes in various Washington offices. Not carnivorous, though; so don't worry. Hobart's MIT, you know. He wasn't ready for graduate school so I talked him into coming on as my assistant. He's a whiz with numbers, but some folks think that the only one who communicates with him is his computer. He did used to enjoy breaking into various government computers, but I think I've broken him of that." He smiled at Eunice as she wrinkled her nose and chuckled. "You'll get used to him. Now, where were we? Ah, yes," he continued, "deciding what we need energy for, or what a few of us here in the Department call 'end-use thinking.' " He chuckled once more, shaking his head again at Hobart's sudden departure before resuming his lecture.

"End use?" Eunice asked blankly.

"Right," Duncan said, "once we ask the question that way— how much energy, of what kind, do we need to do the jobs we want done—we're in a position to begin framing a national policy about where to get that energy."

"Mr. Holt," Eunice began timidly.

"Duncan," he corrected.

"Uh, Duncan . . . but where would you go from there? I mean, I guess I'm supposed to do just that—develop a policy that works. But I honestly don't even know where to start." The weight of her responsibility suddenly overcame Eunice in a rush.

"Well," Duncan offered, "if you'd like to talk more about all this, I'd be happy to try to be of service."

"Oh, please, I'd like that very much," she almost pleaded. "That would be wonderful." She felt rather discombobulated after all that had happened, and a guide seemed quite in order. "But what will we talk about? Where will we begin?"

"Well, for starters, I don't think we should begin today. You've had a pretty full one already," said Duncan. "But tomorrow, starting won't be hard—we've already done that. The next step is to explore the three crucial questions that energy policy most often ignores:

¶How much energy do we need?

¶What kinds of energy do we need?

¶Where can we get it?

Then perhaps I can help you explore how to move from our current situation toward an energy policy that will really meet our needs. But more important than any of the specifics of a prescription, I hope I can offer you something else—a perspective on energy issues, a way of analyzing them that can lead to a sound energy policy today or twenty years from now. Now, why don't I expect you tomorrow morning? Would nine-thirty be convenient? You just tell Barb where you'll be, and she'll cover as need be."

Duncan rose and inclined his head in ever-so-slight a bow as he showed Eunice back into the hall. She looked at him one last bewildered time, then turned. As he watched Eunice trundle off toward her gold-carpeted sanctum, Duncan Jefferson Holt mused to himself, "My, my, we've got a live one." Then he grinned and, turning across the hall, bellowed, "Hobart! . . ."

3 Doing More With Less

*E*UNICE HAD SPENT a gloomy night. Efforts to explain the previous day to her husband seemed only to have given him, too, the impression that none of the experts at the Department knew what they were talking about. However, as she rode the elevator from the dank, subterranean Department parking lot, Eunice felt her spirits lifting. After all, Duncan *had* promised to explain it all to her.

As she walked into her office, Barb grinned wryly. "I hear you ran into Duncan yesterday," she said.

"Why, yes," Eunice said, a bit surprised. "He certainly knows a great deal. But who *is* he?"

"Oh, he's quite a character," Barb drawled. "He spent some years at Los Alamos designing bombs. But it got to him after a while—he got to feeling bad about his work, so he took a transfer to Washington back in '75."

"Bombs?" Eunice asked, fingering her pendant.

"Oh, sure," said Barb. "You know, all of that nuclear stuff is under the auspices of our department. Besides, it was a logical career for him, given his prankster nature. He's the kind who used to explode cherry bombs when he was a teenager, so a nuclear bomb was just a bigger challenge." She grinned conspiratorially. "And he's still a joker at heart. Back in '77, when Consolidated Edison was called on the carpet for the big New York blackout, he arranged with his friends in the maintenance department to kill the lights in the middle of their presentation."

Eunice tried a bit unsuccessfully to suppress a chuckle. Then, noting Barb's broad grin, she asked, "You seem to know him rather well. How . . . ?"

"We're, uh, good friends," Barb said. "You run along now. I'll hold all calls. And don't go worrying your pretty head. Ol' Duncan Jefferson Holt will do you proud."

Eunice blinked and nodded obediently as she gathered her things. "Well," she acknowledged. "I must say I am looking forward to this morning. And you're sure you'll . . . ? Of course. Yes. Well then, I'll be going," she said and left, as Barb turned to catch the phone.

Duncan's cheery greeting brought Eunice's mood to a positive glow. As she settled into a truly comfortable armchair (Eunice guessed that its source was better left unknown) and sipped a mug of freshly ground coffee, she wondered why all those Assistant Secretaries settled for Styrofoam cups, instant coffee, and the powdered "whitener" that appeared to be a byproduct of petrochemical manufacture. Thus absorbed, all she heard of Duncan's first comment was "refrigerators."

"Refrigerators?" She blinked.

"Yes, the Parable of the Refrigerator," he repeated imperturbably. "Do you remember the pre–World War II refrigerators, the kind with the motors on top?" Duncan grinned at Eunice's start of recognition. Before she could launch a reminiscence, he continued: "Those motors were about ninety percent efficient. These days, most refrigerator motors are only about sixty percent efficient. And the manufacturers have moved them underneath; so the heat from the motor rises up into the food compartment. Thus, with the blessings of modern technology, we have refrigerators that can easily spend half their effort taking away the heat of their own motors!"

Duncan chuckled. "In the meantime, the manufacturers have been trying to make the inside of refrigerators bigger without making the outside bigger. Indeed, given time, they might have made the inside bigger than the outside. What they were doing, of course, was making the walls thinner and putting in less insula-

tion. But that lets warmth from the kitchen straight in through the sides. In fact, only a few percent of the energy you put into your refrigerator ends up actually keeping food cold; the rest of the energy gets lost.

"The manufacturers also designed refrigerators so that when you open the door, the cold air falls out and the walls frost up. So most refrigerators now have electric heaters inside that go on now and then to melt the frost. Many also have electric strip heaters around the doors to keep the gaskets from sticking, instead of using a nonstick coating like you find on a frying pan. Many even have electric heaters in their outer skin to keep moisture from condensing on it!" Duncan grinned wryly. "You can try if you like, but it's hard to come up with a dumber way of using electricity than trying to heat and cool the inside of your refrigerator simultaneously. By the way," he added, "that's also exactly what we do in a lot of big office buildings."

Eunice's giggles erupted into incredulous embarrassment. "Oh, but you can't be serious!" she said. "Does *my* refrigerator do that, too?"

Duncan shrugged, "I expect so. And that refrigerator, if you don't use electric space or water heating, is probably the costliest single part of your household electric bill—about one hundred twenty-five dollars a year. Nationally, refrigerators use the equivalent of about half the output of all nuclear power plants."

Eunice's laughter chilled to concern. "Oh, no! But what can I do? I have to have a refrigerator."

Duncan raised a soothing hand. "Of course you do. Fortunately, the knowledge of how to build a good refrigerator was not lost at the end of World War II. It's just that electricity became five times cheaper between 1940 and 1970; so the engineers simply substituted electricity for copper and brains. But there are still some smart engineers on the job.

"For example, consider how many kilowatt-hours it takes to run a standard American refrigerator for a year. Say, about a thirteen-cubic-foot model with a top freezer." Duncan paused, seeing a blank look come over Eunice's face. "Yes?" he inquired.

"Uh, I feel sort of silly . . ." Eunice reddened.

"No, no. Don't. That's why we're here," Duncan reminded her.

"Well," she began, "what's a kill a watt?"

Duncan laughed merrily. "Ah, my dear Eunice, you truly are a gem. Do you know that most people in this office don't know that either? But they'd never dream of asking. One kilowatt is the amount of electricity it takes to run a toaster, or ten bright incandescent light bulbs. A kilowatt-hour is how much electricity we use if we run something like a toaster at the rate of one kilowatt for an hour. Let's see, at average 1985 prices one kilowatt-hour cost about eight cents. It's about the amount of electricity it takes to keep a big, fairly old color television on all evening, or to lift a ton a thousand feet in the air, or to take a ten-minute electrically heated shower with one of the newer, more efficient showerheads or a four-minute shower with an older, more wasteful one.

"Anyway, in 1975, it took eighteen hundred kilowatt-hours to run that refrigerator-freezer I described, nearly triple what it took in 1950. Then, in 1976, California passed a law saying that you couldn't sell a refrigerator in that state that used more than about fourteen hundred kilowatt-hours per year. Within four years, virtually every refrigerator on the market met that standard, and the best—made by Amana—did a third better. Meanwhile, in 1980, a government consultant—A. D. Little—said that better motors, gaskets, insulation, and so on could reduce the demand to six hundred fifty kilowatt-hours per year. By 1981, the typical model on the Japanese market used seven hundred, and Toshiba's best used only five hundred fifty. Noting that whatever exists is possible, the consultants went back to the drawing boards and concluded that, by pulling out all the stops, they could get it down to four hundred twenty. Meanwhile, a Danish engineer showed that improvements that lowered consumption to two hundred sixty—for a refrigerator of the same performance—would be highly cost-effective. Such refrigerators are now being marketed in Denmark. In 1984, behind the best technologies but ahead of most governments, California stiffened its future 1992 standard to about seven hundred kilowatt-hours per year.

"Furthermore, in 1979 an engineering graduate student in California built a refrigerator that performed at two hundred eighty-eight kilowatt-hours per year. His first commercial model used about one hundred eighty. He is currently selling one that performs just like that prototype, and if you live in the Frostbelt and use a little outdoor cooling fin, consumption drops to about half that—or less than a tenth of what was typical just ten years earlier. He even thinks he can cut that by another half to two-thirds! And various do-it-yourselfers have built home-brew experimental types of seasonal-storage refrigerators that are cooled by ice stored over the winter for use the whole year through. Such schemes can even work in some milder climates by radiating heat to the clear night sky. The only electricity these ice-boxes would use would be for the light that goes on when you open the door, about half a kilowatt-hour per year."

Eunice recovered her once-again-fallen jaw. "Do you really mean that I could get a refrigerator that uses *no* electricity? Except for the light, I mean. How wonderful! My milk would never spoil because of a blackout. Oh, Mr. Holt, where can I get one? Will it cost much more than the one I have now?"

Duncan frowned. These details of implementation always annoyed him. "It's Duncan, please," he insisted, "and, well, right now these superefficient refrigerators are handmade by a few inventors living back in the woods. They're too simple for this Department's engineers to be interested in. No, don't chicken out now," he said, noticing the look of doubt growing on Eunice's face, "they're just as convenient as the one you have at home, more attractive, and you can even get them trimmed in hardwood. And if some manufacturer would build them in mass production, they'd be about as cheap as an energy-hog model—maybe cheaper. At this point, for a handmade refrigerator using only a few percent the electricity of a commercial model—and thus saving you upwards of a hundred dollars a year—you do have to pay about twice as much. But, remember, that's really an investment. The thing pays off in, say, five to eight years, and then it's making *you* money on its savings." Duncan stopped. He could tell Eunice was lost in thoughts about how this marvel would fit into her house.

"But I didn't tell you all this to sell you a fridge," he said, drawing her back from a kitchen somewhere in Iowa. "It's really a parable of how we use energy throughout our society. In refrigerators, textbook-simple improvements in engineering can cut the energy use by twentyfold or more, even without the kind of basic redesign that can cut energy use to near zero. Just using 'smart' refrigerators will cost-effectively eliminate the need for more than twenty giant power plants. And similar kinds of smarter design can be applied to almost every energy-using device we have. In fact, we could cut our household electric bills for appliances by three-quarters and displace dozens of additional power plants just by using very efficient appliances."

Eunice began to picture a mass program to change every appliance in the country, and stammered, "How . . .?"

Duncan nodded sympathetically. "Price," he announced.

"Excuse me?" said Eunice, blinking.

"As the price of oil has quadrupled to sextupled in real terms since 1973, the incentive has grown for good old Yankee ingenuity to be applied to the problem of saving energy. It has also spurred good old Japanese and German and international ingenuity generally, as we've seen with refrigerators. As keen minds and tinkering hands applied themselves to the problem, new energy-saving technologies have emerged rapidly. Typically, a good idea in this field is superseded by something better in about six months. Now, you haven't heard very much about this because the research undertaken after 1973 has only lately begun to bear fruit. But just you watch. These innovations are popping up like mushrooms after a rain: here, there, bunches of them all of a sudden. What are those things Hobart told me about?" He frowned in recollection. "Oh, yes. Dehumidifying clothes dryers that save two-thirds the electricity and water-driven dishwashers that use no electricity at all. Now, this year, next year, as they all come on the market, people will start buying them, one by one, just in the normal commercial course of things. You don't have to have a 'kill a watt' patrol," he grinned at Eunice, to credit the borrowing, "going into everyone's house, kidnapping inefficient refrigerators. In time people will just get rid of the clunkers and buy more efficient models because it saves them money."

Duncan thought a moment and then said, "Throughout the energy field, we are in the position of someone who hasn't been able to keep the bathtub full of water because the water keeps running out. This Department has mostly been trying to sell America bigger water heaters. But what we really needed was a plug. Now, finally, people are realizing that given how much the water heaters cost, it's worth investing in plugs of all sorts.

"And," he added, "some very impressive plugs are coming on the market these days. For example, the best available technologies that already make economic sense can double the energy efficiency of jet aircraft and can double the efficiency of electric motors and their drivetrains as presently used in industry. You know," said Duncan, "that last saving alone would more than displace every nuclear power plant in the country. Furthermore, we can triple the efficiency of steel mills, quadruple the efficiency of household appliances and light bulbs, and quintuple the efficiency of cars. In fact, in 1981, Volkswagen tested a Rabbit that got eighty miles a gallon in the city and one hundred miles on the highway. And the best new buildings going up today use about a tenth to a hundredth as much energy per unit of floor space as do older buildings in the same climate; so, if you put up a new building that requires a significant amount of energy for heating and cooling the air, you haven't used the best state of the art."

"Wait, please," Eunice broke in. "Aren't all those things you're calling 'efficiency' the same things that used to be called 'conservation'?"

"Well, it's *part* of what used to be called that," said Duncan. "But 'conservation' is an easily misunderstood word. People muddled different kinds of energy savings together, when there really are two very distinct main kinds. What we're talking about are efficiency improvements made by using 'technical fixes,' changes that are basically unnoticeable to the end user. But 'conservation' got a bad rap because when you used that word, people thought of turning down their thermostats, wearing a sweater in the house, or driving less. Now, I call all those measures 'curtailment,' which is altogether a different beast from efficiency improvements. And that's why I keep saying efficiency—to make sure there's no confusion."

"You know," Eunice said, dredging up a memory from one of the last oil shocks, "that reminds me of something else I used to hear about conservation. People used to say that it was a good thing we hadn't conserved yet, because if we had, we wouldn't have any more notches left to tighten on our belts. Isn't that true?"

"On the contrary," Duncan said, "that's another result of the same confusion between efficiency improvements and curtailment. If you improve the efficiency with which you use energy, you don't need to worry as much about a temporary cutoff of your supplies. If you're turned down the thermostat and you run out of oil, yes, then you're in trouble; however, if you insulate your house so that it needs virtually no heating energy, then it's a very different story. Superinsulated houses are not just less vulnerable to a cutoff of Mideast oil; they really couldn't care less about it. They will stay more comfortable without oil or gas than most old houses will be with all of their regular supplies in place." Duncan pondered whether to pursue that idea and decided against it. "We should talk more about this later on," he said, "but rest assured that using energy more efficiently makes you *less* vulnerable to emergencies and, by stretching your supplies, makes emergencies less likely to happen in the first place."

"But surely," objected Eunice, "even if everyone gets efficient, our energy supplies won't really be stretched all that far. We're still going to need an awful lot of energy to run all our buildings, factories, and vehicles."

"Less than you might think," Duncan rejoined. "A lot less, in fact, than anyone in this building, except Hobart and me, has dared think. The energy that people can save is much greater than the energy they would get from *all* the supply programs this Department has ever proposed."

"Can you prove that?" Eunice challenged. "I mean, I don't want to be drowned in numbers—you must have reams of them." Her gaze wandered over the piles of paper overflowing from every shelf and cranny onto the floor. "But I'd like to know where you get such a big total for the savings you say are worthwhile. Let's start right here. This is a big, modern office building. How could you save energy here?"

"I'd start with the lights," said Duncan instantly.

"What about the lights?" asked Eunice, a little startled. "They look fine to me."

"Inside each of these light fixtures," Duncan began, "is a ballast."

"I thought ballasts were in ships," said Eunice.

"These ballasts," explained Duncan, "are little metal boxes that condition the electric current to make the fluorescent tubes go on and stay on. They also buzz and make the lights flicker and drive me nuts. Listen . . ." Eunice became aware of a pervasive humming sound, like a giant hive of faraway bees. "And so the first thing I'd do," Duncan continued, "would be to replace these ballasts with a new kind that uses solid-state electronics. They run at such a high frequency that there's no flicker or hum, and the lamps put out the same light with about forty percent less power. In fact, in the offices that have windows, I'd set up those electronic ballasts to dim the lights automatically according to how much daylight is coming in through the windows. Then my electricity savings would rise to probably seventy or even ninety percent."

"Won't those fancy ballasts cost more?" asked Eunice.

"Sure, but you'll get your money back in about a year—two or three years if you pay someone to replace all the old ballasts right away rather than as each one burns out. Part of the saving, you see, is that big buildings like this have to be air-conditioned all the time to take away the heat of the inefficient lights; so better ballasts would save both lighting *and* air conditioning. In all, just that one step should cut this building's electrical use by more than half. And nobody but the clerks who pay the utility bills would know the difference."

"What else would you do?" asked Eunice, interested despite herself.

"I'd finish my lighting improvements by improving the tubes themselves—the best new kinds would save another ten or fifteen percent of the power still being used and give almost perfect color —and by using fixtures that allow more of the light to get out into the room and less to be absorbed by opaque parts and by dead bugs that get trapped inside. Then I'd paint the ceiling a lighter color so the light would bounce around better. And I'd open the curtains," he gestured toward the light flooding in, "and put in switches so that people like me who know there's sunlight out there would be able to turn off their lights." He glared at the uselessly beaming lights. "The nearest switch is four offices away," he explained. "And if people didn't know there was light out there, well, I'd open the curtains and remind them. But I'd put stick-on films on the windows, too, so everyone could have comfortable light without glare. In bigger rooms I'd put in reflective blinds to bounce the light off the ceiling onto desks farther from the windows, or maybe I'd use some of the new holographic windows that can concentrate sunlight on the ceiling to be bounced to where it's needed. In a new building I'd even pipe daylight around in optical fibers or plastic rods or mirrored ducts." Eunice looked startled. "Oh, it's worth it, all right. The alternative, remember, is to have the lights and air conditioners fighting each other."

"And one more thing," added Duncan, "before we leave lighting. There's too much of it. We're a nation of light junkies. In fact, the retired head of the engineering group that sets most lighting standards recently said that he expects eye-health problems from overlighting to start surfacing in the late eighties. He should know," Duncan scowled. "It was his group that accidentally set the standards, I'm told, ten times higher than they meant to. They just misplaced a decimal point in their standards handbook and have been too embarrassed ever since to correct it. Maybe that story is apocryphal, but it does help explain why American office-lighting standards are seven times those of Sweden, for example, which are themselves among the highest in Europe."

"But if we used less light," asked Eunice, "would I still see all right?"

"You'd probably see better," responded Duncan, "and not get so many headaches. Of course, everyone should have enough light to do comfortably whatever task they're doing. Some tasks and some people, especially older people, require more light than others. That's why I'd use the little screwdriver adjustments in the electronic ballasts to set each one to the general lighting level needed in each place—there's no point illuminating brightly enough for fine needlework in closets and hallways—and then add 'task lights' to fill in more light as needed, but only at the places where people are actually working. Like this desk lamp."

"Um," said Eunice, a little confused, "it does seem that there are lots of things you can do to get more light with less electricity. But what does that mean?"

"It means we don't need to build forty or fifty more big power plants," replied Duncan. "And those high-frequency electronic ballasts and efficient fluorescent tubes with great color rendition are also available in a neat little package that screws into the same socket you now use for incandescent light bulbs." He gestured at his desk lamp.

Eunice suddenly realized that the lamp contained a bulb with a funny shape—a bit longer than usual, with a molded plastic housing. "That *is* a different kind of bulb," she agreed. "What does it do?"

"It and its kind will ultimately eliminate another thirty big power plants and save electricity now costing eight billion dollars a year," said Duncan cheerfully. "It uses eighteen watts of electricity but gives the same amount of light as a seventy-five-watt ordinary bulb. It also lasts more than thirteen times as long. It may cost you fifteen-odd bucks at the store—"

Eunice looked at Duncan in shock. "But who on earth would spend that for a light bulb?" she asked.

"You may, when you realize that over its ten-thousand-hour lifetime it'll save you about ten dollars' worth of replacement bulbs, plus the hassle of replacing them—often from the top of a ladder—plus thirty or forty dollars' worth of electricity. So you'll get your money back two or three times over. Of course, it's a good deal not only for you, but also for your utility. It's cheaper for the utility to help you save electricity with the quadrupled-efficiency bulb than to pay for the fuel to make the same amount of electricity in a power plant. So it would be worth the utility's while to finance the bulb, or even to give you one."

"Oh, now you must be pulling my leg," chided Eunice. "A utility pay *me* to use *less* electricity?"

"Absolutely," said Duncan, "because it's cheaper for everyone to save electricity than to make it. But we'll come back to that later. First let's finish what to do about this building. And I've barely started giving you my list of ways to save energy and money right here."

Eunice was already bewildered, but she bravely nodded her agreement.

"Let's see," Duncan said, looking critically around the room. "I might next look at the windows." He nodded to himself. "There are new kinds of windows—and shades, films, and various other attachments—that can help keep us more comfortable—snugger in the winter and more free from glare and heat in the summer. In fact, there are new kinds of windows six or eight times as heat-tight as the single glazing in this window," he waved toward it, "but that look just as clear and cost so little more that you'd recover the extra cost from energy savings in a year or two."

"Can I use those windows in my house?" asked Eunice, remembering the Dubuque winters, cold drafts, and thick sheets of ice on her windows in January.

"Of course," said Duncan, "and in most Frostbelt climates, these superefficient windows can even gain more winter heat—from light scattered by clouds and bounced upward by snow—than they lose, facing in any direction, probably including due north."

Eunice wasn't sure why this mattered, but it sounded impressive. She nodded, but her face gave her away.

Duncan grinned. "That's important because most windows are almost like having holes in your house. Heat streams right out. Unless the windows face south. Then they collect more heat from the sun than they lose. Of course, it's *easier* to get solar heat if you face the sun. But, if you superinsulate better and design more carefully, it hardly matters which way your house faces or what shape it is; you'll still be able to keep it comfortable year-round with just superefficient windows. But you're distracting me again —I haven't even finished with this building." He grinned, and Eunice got the warm feeling that he was enjoying spending his morning with her. "So, once I'd overhauled the two biggest sources of unwanted heat—lights and windows—I'd check for airtightness, check if the roof could be a lighter color or better insulated, and then start rebuilding the mechanical systems."

"What's mechanical about a building?" asked Eunice. "Doesn't it just sit there?"

"That's the name for all the fans, blowers, pumps, and so forth that circulate and condition the air in big buildings," Duncan explained. "Once we reduce the heat generated in, and accidentally admitted into, the building, we'll need a lot less air conditioning—maybe none—to keep us comfortable. You hear that noise?"

Eunice listened. Suddenly she became aware that the building wasn't just sitting there; not only were the lights buzzing, but the whole building reverberated with rumbles and hums, hisses and wheezes. She realized she'd unconsciously been making an effort to speak over the noise.

"All that noise is from mechanical equipment. With efficient lights and windows we'd dispense with a lot of the noise and make the rest much softer. We could adjust the ventilation system, for example, to bring in only as much fresh air, and to circulate only as much air to each part of the building, as is needed at the time. We could even control that ventilation with simple instruments that sense carbon dioxide, exhaled by people, and smoke. That way, everyone would always enjoy plenty of fresh air, but the fans wouldn't be running full blast when the building is almost empty. I'd also make sure that the building brings in outside air whenever that's cool enough to contribute to comfort, and in the summer, I'd recover coolth from the outgoing air to prechill the incoming air. I'd install dampers to control airflow better. I'd insulate ducts. I'd put in better controls—ever notice how many people say their offices are uncomfortably hot or cold?—to improve comfort and reduce energy waste. And I'd clean the equipment more often so that it transfers heat better. I'd even oil the bearings."

Eunice looked surprised. She didn't know what a bearing was, but she knew if you didn't put oil in a car awful things happened. "You mean people forget to do that?" she asked.

"Sure," said Duncan. "For two weeks I've been trying to get maintenance to oil a particular squeaker behind a locked grille down in the basement, but it's so complicated down there that they say they can't find it. Anyway, I'd improve upkeep across the board and reward the technicians with a share of whatever energy they save." Eunice smiled; yes, that would be like him. "I'd pay attention to every detail," he continued. "Why, I just looked at the world's most efficient air conditioner in Florida a couple of months ago. Its designer had imported a special kind of rubber drive belt from Japan just because it would stretch and slip less. That change saves twenty watts. Doesn't sound like much, but in every air conditioner in every home, just that little belt would save another couple of big power plants.

"Anyhow, when I got through handling all these details and doing some other things too technical to bore you with, and maybe even some ridiculously simple ones such as putting in ceiling fans to keep people more comfortable in warm weather, then I'd go through the entire mechanical system from stem to stern and make all the motors smaller and more efficient—everything from the blower fans to the cooling-tower pumps. And I'd put electronic controls on them to make them more efficient when they're running at less than their intended load, such as when the ventilation system is turned down for fewer people indoors."

"It sounds like," said Eunice slowly, "saving energy involves lots of little pieces, many of which help each other. But all the savings add up. I mean, it seems there are so many kinds that even if each of them is small, their total must be very large."

"Exactly!" exclaimed a delighted Duncan. "Nothing I described sounded very dramatic, did it? But in combination they'll reduce the energy needs of a building like this one by sixty to ninety percent—even more in a new building." Eunice's eyes widened. That was a number she could understand. "And if you do it right the first time, these measures save so much in expensive mechanical equipment and duct work that they can make a superefficient office building *cheaper* to build than an inefficient one! This isn't just theory; the best designers and builders have done it. And even far less sophisticated improvements can save a third to a half of the energy in most existing office buildings, repaying their cost in two or three years. The *average*, unsophisticated fixing-up of an office building saves twenty-nine percent of the energy with an eight-*month* payback."

"That's quite a bit," mused Eunice.

"You bet," Duncan nodded emphatically. "In fact, you can save about as much energy in commercial buildings as in houses, even though the technologies may be different. And if you look not only at the basic improvements I mentioned for the buildings themselves, but also for what's inside them, it's possible to save even more. Those superefficient windows we talked about can also be used to keep unwanted heat out of the freezer chests in a supermarket—in fact, one of the factories that makes the high-tech film in the middle of that kind of window is booked up for years ahead for just that purpose. Now computers, a major source of heat in many offices, make a tenth to a hundredth as much heat now as they did five to fifteen years ago, and the latest kinds are two to five times cooler still. Some of the latest models have no cooling fans at all. There's even a kind of photocopier that uses a tenth the usual amount of electricity, simply because it sets the toner powder onto the paper with a cold compression roller instead of a heated drum."

Eunice was getting lost again, but she remembered the blast of hot air that came out of the photocopier in her neighborhood library.

"Also," Duncan continued, "anything that saves paper—less bureaucracy, more electronic mail—can save a lot of energy indirectly, too, not just in the photocopiers but in the paper mills and even the factories that make the photocopier toner. You know, that powder uses several kilowatt-hours per *pound,* just to grind it so fine." He sighed. "You know what's the most energy-intensive product in the whole economy?"

"Aluminum?" Eunice guessed, remembering the television ads about saving energy with recycling.

"Good guess, but no cigar—especially since the best new aluminum smelters use two-fifths less electricity than conventional ones. Not even magnesium or titanium takes the title. Actually, I think it's probably maple syrup, because you have to boil off all that water, maybe forty-odd gallons of it per gallon of syrup. And that's not," he added defiantly, "going to stop me from using that wonderful stuff, but it does help me understand why it costs so much."

"Do most industrial products take a lot of energy to make?" asked Eunice. "I remember those ads saying how much electricity we could save—I think it was ninety-five percent of it—in making aluminum, just by melting down and recycling used aluminum cans, like we did with all kinds of scrap during World War II."

"Quite right," said Duncan, "and we could readily save upwards of a fifth of all our industrial energy by using materials more efficiently and recovering more of them that we now waste. Ultimately, if we really had a smart materials policy, we could save as much as two-thirds of our industrial energy—because, after all, what industry does is to process, transform, and fabricate materials, and there are innumerable ways to do that more efficiently.

Just the substitution of space-age materials will save us scads of energy. Within a few years, for example, we should have graphite fibers cheap enough to displace many structural uses of steel and aluminum. But if you were referring just to the processes that go on in our factories, sure, Eunice, there too we can save more energy than anyone thought possible a few years ago."

"Like how?" said Eunice. "With more new technologies?"

"Some new," Duncan agreed, "and some very old. Among the oldest are such simple good-housekeeping measures as plugging up steam leaks, insulating pipes and boilers, and recovering waste heat from a process to preheat the materials entering that process or a different one. We now have better ways to do these things and much better microcomputers to control industrial processes so that they're always using a minimum of energy and money. These are fancier industrial versions of the new generation of 'smart' household appliances, which optimize their own performance, diagnose their own faults, and even turn themselves off when not in use. In fact, one particular kind of microcomputer control, costing about fifty to a hundred thousand dollars, and made in Iowa, by the way"—Duncan winked at her—"can make huge compressors so much more efficient that it saves upwards of a million dollars' worth of electricity every year, and makes the compressors run longer and more reliably in the bargain.

"Then there are such fundamentally new processes as curing paint with microwaves instead of gas furnaces, or heat-treating metals in fluidized-bed furnaces that transfer heat with amazing speed and uniformity, or forming complex metal parts by pressing and baking metal powders rather than by casting molten metal and then machining much of it away. The chemical industry has developed some amazingly efficient processes. There's one, for example, that saves upwards of three-quarters of the electricity used to make low-density polyethylene, the kind in your kitchen garbage bags. It also makes the film two-fifths stronger; so about a third thinner film will do the same job. Dow Chemical alone has already about doubled its own energy efficiency in the past decade, still has a long way to go, and notes with satisfaction that its competitors lag far behind. New paper-making processes can save upwards of two-thirds of the fuel and forty-odd percent of the electricity used in today's paper mills. In fact, all of Swedish industry—the most energy-efficient in the world today—figures it can save at least half its electricity use through advanced technologies that compete at today's Swedish electricity price. And Sweden's electricity price is less than a third of what you're now paying."

"I can see," said Eunice, "that as with buildings, there are many individual ways to save energy that add up to a huge total saving. But what ties it all together? In houses, the key things seem to be insulation, better windows, and weather-stripping—that is, ways to stop heat from going in or out when you didn't want it to. In offices, you seemed to say that the key to unlocking the whole puzzle was better lights." Duncan nodded, pleased with his quick student. "Is there one key measure like that in industry?"

Duncan reflected. "I suppose," he said, "that recovery and reduced losses of heat might be it; after all, six-sevenths of all our industrial energy goes to make heat. But in industrial use of electricity, as opposed to fuels, there's an unquestioned winner: motors."

"Motors?" asked Eunice. "How much electricity do they use?"

"Sixty-four percent of all electricity used in the whole American economy," answered Duncan. "And most of those motors aren't nearly as efficient as we used to think they were. You see, most of them are big—so big that they use ten or twenty times their own cost's worth of power every year. That's good, because savings can then easily pay for replacement motors, which are usually more efficient than the old ones. Big motors are often said to be about ninety-odd percent efficient. But in practice, a great many motors are old and inefficient. We can do much better with new materials and winding patterns—and almost all motors are bigger than they need to be."

"Why are they too big?" asked Eunice. "Didn't anyone figure out what the right size would be?"

"Usually," said Duncan sadly, "the designer would figure the biggest load the motor could ever possibly need to handle, then add a fat safety margin, then round up to the next commercial motor size. Such laziness was excusable when electricity was cheap, but now it causes American industry to waste many billions of dollars every year—because a motor becomes very inefficient very quickly as its load falls substantially below the full level for which it's designed. You remember I talked about replacing fan and pump motors in more efficient buildings with smaller motors to fit the reduced loads better?"

Eunice nodded.

"Well, the reason for that replacement," said Duncan, "is that the efficiency of a typical fan motor, say, will drop by half at eighty percent of full load and will skid by a disastrous ninety percent at a third of full load. At reduced loads—such as you have most of the time in, say, a machine shop, where equipment is used only part of the time but the motors are always running—most of the motor's power goes into heat, not work.

"Luckily," he added, "there is here, as usual, a technical fix. Several kinds of electronic gadgets—they're called things like 'variable-frequency inverters' or 'power-factor controllers'—can keep the motor running at nearly full efficiency regardless of how its load varies. They're the electrical equivalent of the fuel-injection computer that gives your engine just the right amount of gasoline for its load. And of course it's often worthwhile, while you're replacing the motor with a modern, more efficient model, to make it just the right size, perhaps boosting its normal power, if necessary, with a smaller 'piggyback' motor, or a clutched flywheel that cuts in only when needed, or a special transmission to give you more torque whenever that vat of goo you're stirring becomes especially gunky."

Eunice was completely lost, but she responded bravely, "That sounds simple enough. But what will it save?"

"For a big factory like a paper mill," said Duncan, "where lots of big motors run at mostly constant speeds, you'd save about fifteen to thirty percent. In industries whose motors vary a lot in speed and load, you'd save half or more. Nationally, if you add in some simple improvements in our often medieval drivetrains, the dozen or so kinds of motor and drive-system refinements will more than displace the entire nuclear power program—more than seventy giant power plants' worth. And that'll cost less than half as much as those plants cost just to operate, even if building them were free."

Eunice gasped. "And what about the arguments that those plants are unsafe? No. Wait! All those arguments about whether nuclear power is safe wouldn't be necessary if we just made the motors in our factories as efficient as they should have been in the first place?"

"Yup," Duncan confirmed. "Now you understand why I think efficient energy use is important. It can save us a lot of money and an unbelievable amount of hassle. If nuclear power, or any other controversial technology, is uneconomic and unnecessary, why should we argue about its other problems at all?"

"Wait a minute," Eunice said again. "You've told me a lot about saving heat and electricity, but you haven't talked about how we're going to get around from place to place with a lot less oil. Do you have any, er, rabbits in your transportation hat?"

"Oh, lots," Duncan grinned appreciatively. "They're among the most prolific technological rabbits of all. And I'm not even going to get into such things as mass transit, or carpooling, or corporate vanpooling, or bicycles, or living nearer where we work, or working at home on computers, or walking—as the conservationist David Brower once said, 'All those who believe in individual mass transit, raise your right foot.' But that seems to suggest curtailment, or driving less. No, I'm going to assume that our society will become even more frenetically mobile. Of course, there are limits—nobody can drive more than one car at the same time; some people will always, I hope, be too young to drive; and for that matter, nobody wants to sit in a car for many more hours than they do now. But let's look just at technological ways to get more miles per gallon.

"For starters," he continued, "please take my word for it—there are lots of good technical analyses and experiments in the field—it's pretty easy to make a normal-sized, well-performing car that averages more than eighty miles a gallon. You make use of slick aerodynamics, efficient tires and engines, better lubricants—again, lots of little things that add up to big total savings. For example, General Motors just announced that by using a new kind of magnet they can halve the weight of starter motors. That one improvement can save the country about one or two hundred million gallons of gasoline every year. And if an eighty-mile-a-gallon car would cost extra to build, it'd still pay back that extra cost several times over at today's fuel prices."

"I don't understand," said Eunice, "if such a car is possible, why Detroit isn't knocking my door down to sell me one."

"Because," Duncan replied cynically, "they make more money selling you several big, high-markup cars during the time they hope you'll take to find out it's possible to do better. And probably because they don't think you're smart enough to want to buy such a car anyway. Of course, if Detroit doesn't offer it, you know who will. Sooner or later, you'll get to choose whether you prefer twenty or eighty miles a gallon, and Detroit will get to test its market forecasts in the marketplace. I hope," he added, "the American auto companies live to learn from the experience."

"Is eighty miles a gallon about as far as you can go?" asked Eunice.

"Not at all," said Duncan, "even though it's farther than we might actually want to go—because even if we're less efficient than that, maybe sixty miles a gallon, that's probably all the efficiency we need to fuel the whole transportation system from liquid fuels obtained from farm and forestry wastes. But I'm getting ahead of my story; so let's postpone that talk for another day. To answer your question, if we use, say, infinitely variable transmissions, or what are called 'series hybrid drives'—where a little motor runs an onboard electric generator that charges a small battery bank, which runs motors on the wheels—or several other fancy options, we can probably get well over a hundred miles a gallon with reasonable performance. And we can certainly do that in smaller cars suitable for two-person commuting, one of the specialized uses that accounts for so much of our driving. Alternatively, we could readily break the hundred-mile-per-gallon barrier by using sophisticated lightweight materials."

"Does that mean," asked Eunice suspiciously, "some tinny little box that'll be mashed if a truck runs into me?"

"Not at all," reassured Duncan. "In fact, using modern composite materials or crushable metal foams, a car weighing under a thousand pounds could keep you safer than you are right now in a big American car. Again, the manufacturers just haven't bothered yet. They will when they realize that's what you want."

"How about other kinds of vehicles?" asked Eunice. "Do the technological miracles stop with cars?"

"Not at all," said Duncan. "In fact, they expand. There are even more ways to improve engines, tires, and aerodynamics in trucks than in cars—to say nothing of putting long-haul freight back on the rails. The latest passenger jets use about half as much fuel as the older models, and the next generation will save another forty percent. The best new Japanese freighters are saving half their fuel through better propellers and hull designs; antifouling paints, which keep the barnacles off so the hull stays smoother; and, when the wind's right, the use of computerized airfoils, or, in plain English, modern versions of sails."

"So when you add up all these savings," said Eunice, "throughout our industrial economy—transportation, factories, and buildings—how big are they?"

"The best estimates from analyses in a variety of industrial countries," said Duncan, "range from tripling to more than quintupling our energy efficiency: that is, saving anywhere from two-thirds to more than four-fifths of our total energy use, cost-effectively with today's technologies at today's prices."

A long silence passed as Duncan let this sink in. "So we could be as well off as now," asked Eunice tentatively, "using a small fraction as much energy as we use today, even though it might, I suppose, take us several generations to become quite that efficient?"

"Absolutely," said Duncan, "and we'd save lots of money in the process."

"If it already makes economic sense, and the technologies are improving all the time, then why do we need a Department of Energy?" Eunice continued.

"So that you," replied Duncan with a sardonic gleam in his eye, "can find out what I've just told you, so that you can tell lots of civil servants about what you've discovered, and ultimately, so that you can tell the American people too. Because except for you and me, and of course Hobart, not a soul in this Department, and only a handful in the country, have the remotest idea how much energy saving is possible and worthwhile. It's one of the best-kept secrets in the country."

"Won't my Assistant Secretaries say," Eunice argued, "that you may be right in theory—though I doubt they'd actually admit that—but that it's not practical, or it'll take too long to save that much, or Americans aren't ready for it?"

"Mmm, they'll say all those things and more," Duncan confirmed, "but by the time we're through, you'll know the fallacies in those putdowns. You'll know why huge energy savings are not only practical but are actually being achieved around the country; how it's being done a lot faster than anyone thought possible; how most Americans are far ahead of their leaders; and how you and this Department can help energy efficiency happen faster, more smoothly, and more pleasantly for everyone."

"That," said Eunice, "is a tall order. And I think it's about time for a tall glass of something. I need," she admitted, "some time to digest all this. Because if a tenth of what you're saying is right, then most of what my Department has been doing all these years is . . . is . . . absolutely fish-brained! And it'll be up to me to do something about it." Eunice stopped, then took a very deep breath. It was going to be an interesting job.

4 *Insulate Your Roof or Freeze in the Dark?*

*E*UNICE NEATLY WIPED the last crumbs from her mouth as she gazed at a cartoon on Duncan's wall. She felt completely full —of sandwiches and information.

"Why, then . . . but if . . ." she tried, falling silent as several attempts to verbalize her reaction to Duncan's recitation sputtered.

Duncan smiled comfortingly. "I know," he said. "It's a bit much to grasp on first hearing." He munched a last potato chip. "Maybe," he said, considering, "it would help if I bring it closer to home. Let's assume a pretty standard two-thousand-square-foot house built in a moderately severe climate—say, in Denver or Chicago. Or Albany. Detroit, maybe. Even Dubuque." He grinned.

"In 1976 that average U.S. house would have required twenty-six hundred therms of natural gas to heat for a typical winter." Eunice looked blank. "Never mind what exactly what a therm is; it's a unit of heat—about as much as you'd get by burning a hundred cubic feet of natural gas. Now in those days the average householder was paying about five hundred dollars for that much gas. By 1980, responding to the price shocks of 1973 and 1979, the average gas requirement had dropped slightly. If our standard house were built after the Iranian revolution in 1979, it would have used about twenty-two hundred therms. That's an improvement, but we can do a lot better—and some folks do. A typical

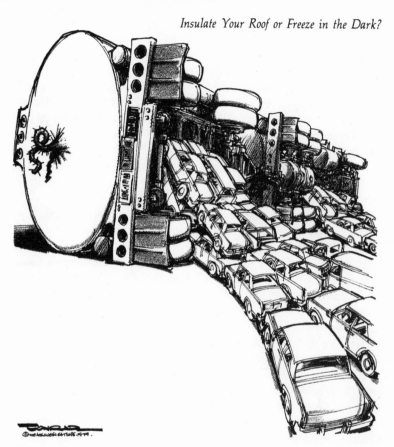

"She gazed at a cartoon on Duncan's wall." (Reprinted by permission of Paul Conrad and the Los Angeles Times.)

Swedish house of that time, transplanted to Denver or Albany, would have used about a thousand therms. But even before that, as the U.S. Department of Energy in 1977 proposed building standards that would limit our typical house to about six hundred therms per year, engineers in the United States were pioneering houses that used about a third that much.

"And in Saskatchewan, Canada, where one popular method of doing what's called 'superinsulation' was born, designers built a house about that same time that would use about a hundred fifty therms a year. Such houses then cost thirty-five hundred dollars more to build than an average house—about seven or eight percent more than normal. Right now, most houses built on the Canadian prairies use that technology, and the contractors have reduced the extra cost to about a couple of thousand dollars, give or take a thousand."

Eunice eyed Duncan suspiciously. "Uh," she wondered how to phrase this, "would I want to live in one of those houses? Would it look nice? Would I be comfortable?"

"Certainly," Duncan replied cheerfully. "An energy-efficient house can look and feel just like the kinds of houses you've always known." He thought a moment and corrected, "Actually, that's not quite true. These houses can have virtually any design from futuristic to Colonial, and indeed most real Colonials can be fixed up to perform almost as well. In fact, in a climate quite similar to Dubuque's, some builders in St. Louis are 'rehabbing' old brownstones with a neat superinsulation technique. The extra cost adds thirty-five dollars a month to the mortgage bill, but the energy savings are seventy-nine dollars a month. Thus the people who live in these buildings come out ahead by forty-four dollars a month, or more than five hundred dollars a year. A building that used to cost nearly eleven hundred dollars a year to heat and cool at 1983 prices now costs just sixty-six dollars a year to heat and seventy-three dollars to cool. And the house is now insulated against future price increases. The economics are even better for houses that are built right the first time.

"But there is one difference between standard houses and this type," said Duncan in mock warning. "The superinsulated ones are really comfortable. Windows that keep the heat in don't get miniature Niagaras of condensation in the early mornings; so windowsills don't get drenched. Doors that are properly weather-stripped don't let jets of wintry air in underneath. Drafts—caused by the circulation of air between the sources of heat and poorly insulated ceilings, walls, and windows—are minimized. And because heating and air-conditioning systems are a major source of noise and dust in a house, the smaller they are and the less often they turn on, the quieter and cleaner the house will be. Indeed, the best-insulated houses don't need any heating or cooling systems at all." Duncan smiled as he watched Eunice's housewife instincts work on that one.

"Good energy efficiency will also help if the electricity goes off or if there's a shortage of natural gas or heating oil. A house that is tightly built and thoroughly insulated will stay warm for a long time, not unlike a Thermos bottle. And if your friends who are freezing in their uninsulated houses come over, just their body heat will keep your place toasty."

Eunice's fascination was overshadowed by concern. "A Thermos bottle? Oh, I couldn't stand the stuffiness. And didn't I hear some report about tightly weatherized houses being dangerous? Something about air pollution? Inside the house?" Eunice asked.

Duncan nodded. "Yeah. That *would* be a problem, all right, *if* you didn't ventilate. Now, most people don't think about ventilating because all the little holes in their walls do that for them. A typical house has about enough little holes and cracks to amount to a square yard or more of unplanned ventilation. That's like leaving a window wide open all year—while you try to keep the place warm or cool, and run up your electric bill."

Duncan paused and grinned. "It's what a friend of mine, Lee Schipper, calls 'space heating' . . . heating outer space."

Eunice smiled despite herself, but persevered. "At least it gives you fresh air, though."

"Ah, but there are much better ways to do that," countered Duncan. "Ways that give plenty of fresh air but that don't lose energy. Wouldn't you prefer to have the ventilation under your control, rather than just letting the wind whistle through your house?"

"How could I do that?" asked Eunice, her doubts showing around the edges.

"Well, of course, you could selectively open and close windows, but that's pretty unsophisticated," Duncan teased her. "No, today's modern householder demands the latest in an air-to-air heat exchanger."

"A what?"

"Heat exchanger. It's really quite a simple gadget," Duncan explained. "It's an exhaust fan, blowing out the stale, inside air and bringing in fresh air from outside. What makes it so clever is that the two airflows pass each other in separate channels, but side by side; so as the inside air goes out, it gives up its warmth to the incoming air that's passing along just beside it. Other designs exist that yield the same results. Of course, that's in the winter, when the air in your home—or factory, or hog barn—is warm, and you want to warm up the fresh air as it comes in. In the summer the exchanger keeps on ventilating, but then it's keeping in the cool air that your air conditioner or window shades work so hard to get you. Meanwhile it's bringing in lots of fresh air, cooling that down, and flushing out any pollutants you may have in your house.

"Actually," Duncan said, frowning, "the indoor pollution issue is mostly used by people—like the nuclear boys—who have a stake in everyone's living in inefficient houses. The best way to guarantee indoor air quality is not to keep houses leaky, but to avoid putting polluting substances in them in the first place. Indoor air pollution in houses can occasionally be a real problem, but it's rather easily solved. It seems to me the real problem is in office buildings with all the plastic carpets, chairs, drapes, copy machines, and such giving off toxic fumes. And the problem is fierce in factories and such places as dry cleaning shops." He shook his head in annoyance. "How can a civilization put up with slowly poisoning itself?" He lapsed into a stony silence, staring out his unopenable window at the red stone turrets of the Smithsonian.

"Duncan?" Eunice interrupted timidly.

"Ah. Right. Sorry," Duncan rejoined, exorcising his gloomier musings. "Yes?"

"Well, it's seemed to me all along that all this saving energy is great for one's self-satisfaction. I mean, after my neighbors weather-stripped their home, they felt snug and virtuous. And Mr. Fitzsimmons dazzled dinner guests by rattling off how much energy he was saving. But it seems to me . . ." Eunice paused to see if Duncan appeared to care at all what her perceptions were. Buoyed by the open look of interest on his face, she concluded, ". . . that what's really important is how much money you can save with all these energy savings."

Eunice suddenly found herself slightly appalled at what she'd said and blushed to her roots. "I mean . . . but . . . I know money's not . . . everything," she sputtered.

Duncan just laughed merrily and nodded at his pupil. "You got it. And don't be embarrassed. Most people in this country— in all countries, I dare say—are powerfully motivated by what can save them money. And that's just what's going to get us out of this mess. Sure, moral exhortations can move a nation, and when Carter called for national sacrifice many people indeed tried to tighten up to help the country. But that only lasts for a while. Then people need a more personal and tangible reason if they're going to change their lifestyles. As a friend of mine from an Arkansas utility says, 'Better to tie the program to people's pocketbooks than to wrap it in the flag.' Happily for solving the energy problem, everything I'll talk about can be done with no significant effect on lifestyle, *and* doing it will save everyone money. That combination is why these changes are coming so fast. Entrepreneurs can make money producing and selling these gadgets. And the public—householders, industrialists, and the guy on the corner—can save money using them.

"For example, a straightforward program of fixing up your house can save fifty percent or more of your utility bill: simple stuff, such as weather-stripping windows and doors, tuning the furnace, and adding more insulation. In fact, a couple of months of that sort of energy saving will easily finance a spectacular dinner party so that you can brag to *your* friends about how low your utility bills are."

"But where do I start?" Eunice ventured, feeling a little intimidated.

"You know the best way to fix up your home?" Duncan declared. "Call a 'house doctor.' "

"Oh, now . . ." began Eunice.

"I kid you not," defended Duncan. "A 'house doctor' is someone who treats the chills and fevers of your house. They do checkups. They even make house calls." Duncan grinned. "The 'doctors' have all sorts of ways of diagnosing where the building is leaking heat. They may use a 'blower door' that fits in your front door; it has a big fan that pressurizes the house so that air tries to escape through all the little leaks. The 'doctor' then goes around blowing little puffs of smoke, which zip out the leaks, showing just where you need to caulk. The 'doctor' then caulks and weather-strips, catching about three times as many leaks as if you'd just looked for them by eye. A good 'doctor' also checks for uninsulated pipes and clogged furnace filters. The 'house doctors' I know charge several hundred dollars, and most of their 'patients' make back that money in only a few months of energy savings."

"But how can I find a good one?" asked Eunice.

"Same as with any new doctor: Ask around. Ask your utility or your local chamber of commerce. If they've never heard of 'house doctors'—it's a pretty new profession—ask some local solar installers. Also try the phone book and your local environmental or safe-energy group. But when you get a name, ask for references. Most 'house doctors' are very good, but as with all craftspeople, you want to assure yourself that they do good work that satisfies your neighbors."

Eunice looked intrigued. "Imagine. A doctor for a house. But it makes good sense. I don't think I'd want to mess around with gooey caulk." She wrinkled her nose.

Duncan laughed. "Aw, c'mon. It's not that bad. And there's really a lot you can do yourself to save money on your energy bills. For instance, new, more efficient showerheads will mean that more people in your family can take showers without draining the hot-water tank, and wrapping insulation around the tank and pipes will hold in the heat longer and help the tank to heat up again more quickly. You can even set the water heater's thermostat so the water is plenty hot, but not so hot that you need to dilute it with cold water to keep from scalding yourself. You can do all these things without being a plumber or an energy-saving expert.

"Efficient showerheads may not sound like much, but they can be important. Here," he said, handing Eunice a page he'd dug out of one of the stacks on his desk. "Here's a memo I did for a local Girl Scout troop."

Eunice read:

TO: The Chevy Chase Girl Scouts
FROM: Duncan J. Holt
ABOUT: Efficient Showerheads

Energy-efficient, water-saving showerheads can save you a lot of money. A good one with an on-off switch costs about five dollars. If you have four people a day taking showers, installing low-flow heads will save you about one hundred five gallons of hot water each day. Let's assume you have two showers, for a total investment, then, of ten dollars. Suppose that you heat your water with natural gas costing sixty cents per therm* (a typical 1983 price) and that your shower water is at one hundred ten degrees Fahrenheit. The one hundred five gallons that you don't use every day would take more than two-thirds of a therm to heat,** at a cost of forty cents. That means that in a month your family will save twelve dollars—two dollars more than the showerheads cost. From then on, the showerheads are making you money. And, if you have electric heat, the payback is usually much faster—a matter of days.

*One therm, a common measure of the heating content of natural gas, equals 100,000 BTUs (British Thermal Units). What is a BTU? See next footnote.

**The calculation is as follows: It takes one BTU to raise the temperature of one pound of water by one degree Fahrenheit. One pound of water weighs $8\frac{1}{3}$ pounds; so 105 gallons weigh $105 \times 8\frac{1}{3} = 875$ pounds. Then we assume that the cold water starts at fifty-five degrees Fahrenheit, and subtract that from one hundred ten degrees (the final temperature of the water) to find that the water has to be heated by fifty-five degrees. (This doesn't count the several degrees by which the water cools off in the pipes between the heater and the shower.) Thus, it will take $55 \times 875 = 48,100$ BTUs to heat 105 gallons of shower water. But since, at most, about seventy percent of the heat content of the gas makes it into the water (the rest goes up the flue, is lost in incomplete combustion, etc.), we must increase that by about 1.4 times, to 67,300 BTUs, or two-thirds of a therm, or about forty cents' worth.

Happy Scouting!

Duncan waited while Eunice read the memo, nodding slowly to herself. As she looked up, he continued, "Let's take another example. Suppose you insulated your attic, raising the R-value—the common measure of insulation performance—from R-11 to R-38 by adding eight inches of fiberglass to the four inches already there. That means that the heat loss through the attic, if you do a thorough job, will drop by seventy-one percent. Such an operation would cost about five hundred or six hundred dollars if a contractor did it, and two hundred or three hundred if you did it yourself. If the house were in a climate like Denver's or Detroit's, the new insulation would save about two hundred fifty therms a year—say, a hundred fifty dollars' worth of gas. In a climate like that of Oakland, California, or Memphis, Tennessee, it would save about half as much. Now, the payback is slower than for the efficient showerheads; so you might want to get the showerheads first. But it's still very worthwhile to go for the longer paybacks, too. In fact, the best use of the money saved by doing the cheapest things first is to finance more costly savings later. With an average house, if you invested anywhere from several thousand to about eight or ten thousand dollars and bought the best buys, your house would need virtually no energy to keep it warm through even a Minnesota winter. Even in Miami, if you used good passive cooling measures—window shades, overhangs, coatings, fans, trees—you would need only a little air conditioning at night, or maybe none at all."

Eunice's common sense staged a protest. "Oh, Duncan, you can't mean that! No heating in Minnesota? In January? And no air conditioning in the summer? What about all those poor people in Dallas? They'd roast." Eunice's face registered the opening sentiments of full revolt.

Again Duncan laughed and raised his hands in placation. "Easy there, whoa now," he soothed. "First of all, if you want to keep your air conditioning, that's fine, too. And there are even much more efficient air conditioners that work better than old-fashioned ones in hot, humid climates and yet use only about three-eighths as much energy. But it *is* possible, even straightforward, to build a house or office building that uses no air conditioning, even in a desert or tropical climate. Several new office buildings in Reno, Nevada, use no heating or refrigerative cooling —and that's no gamble. The best new offices in Sweden are doing the same thing. The best new houses in Houston save about eighty percent—and could easily save ninety percent—of the usual air-conditioning energy. And I've been in a house in northern Australia—a full tropical climate—that was sixty-eight degrees inside while it was a hundred three outside, with *no* active cooling. It *is* possible and it sure does save money, especially if you're building a new house, to build it right in the first place. You see, doing that saves putting in all the duct work, furnace, air conditioner, and such. And that saving usually pays for the energy-saving measures by itself; so often there is no upfront cost. That's why those offices in Reno and Stockholm even cost *less* to build than the old kind.

"But this sort of performance really shouldn't be all that surprising. Many of the best measures have been practiced for centuries. Each part of the world has its traditional building styles that cope with its particular climate, such as verandas and cupola cooling on houses in the South and thick adobe walls in the Southwest. You know, some of the cliff dwellings of the Anasazi in the deserts of New Mexico and Arizona still stay warm in the winter and cool in the summer even though no one has lived in them for thousands of years."

Duncan leaned back and stretched his arms behind his head. "The point is, how much you want to spend on your utility bill is increasingly your choice. There *are* things you can do instead of paying high bills. Lots of things. That's partly why a number of utilities are in danger of going broke. Ah!" he cautioned, holding a stop-sign hand up to stem Eunice's diversionary interest. "That's a story I'll tell in all the gory detail, but not now.

"For now, think of what happens if thousands of individuals, consumers all, choose to become more energy-efficient, one by one, with a light bulb here, a plugged industrial steam leak there, an insulated candy store on Main Street, a new fifty-mile-a-gallon car for the hot-rodders at the high school. What effect does it have on the whole country if individuals save energy? Total use is simply the sum of what everyone uses separately. If everyone saves, say, a quarter of their energy use, the effect on the nation will be dramatic. In fact, we *have* saved a quarter since 1973, and that's why, within a decade, we have gluts of all kinds of fuels, along with stable or falling energy prices.

"There are other, subtler effects of saving energy, too. As it is now, much of the money that people spend on energy in a community drains right out of that community. A 1977 study in a Massachusetts county showed that the amount of money spent on household energy imported from outside the region was equal to the payrolls of the ten largest employers in the county put together. A series of studies in places as diverse as Springfield, Illinois, and Santa Cruz, California, shows that about eighty-five cents of every dollar spent on energy leaves the community. The remaining fifteen cents that stays in the community helps everyone out—because the gas station attendant can take his or her salary and spend it at the grocery store and the local movie theater, and the grocer and usher in turn spend some of their incomes in the community, and so on. This 'multiplier effect' means that if people can cut the amount they spend on energy brought in from outside their locality, they'll have more money to spend within their communities, making everyone better off. You remember the rehab housing example from St. Louis?" Duncan inquired, noting that Eunice was indeed following closely. "Well, those folks found that a dollar spent on energy leaves only fifty cents in the local economy. But on the other hand, a dollar spent on weatherization and solar energy puts two dollars and twenty cents into the local economy.

"And it's equally true when we look at a state or at the nation as a whole. Money that is spent on imported fossil fuel is clearly a drain on the national economy, because U.S. firms have to pay people in foreign countries for that oil. While those firms do invest some of that money back in the United States, that investment may be temporary and can as easily be moved elsewhere. But even money that is spent on domestic oil, coal, or gas is, in many ways, a loss to the economy. For one thing, there are almost always cheaper ways to get the same energy services than by burning the amount of fossil fuels that we do now. For another, money spent on efficiency—especially on fixing up older houses, in which most of the cost is for labor, not materials—creates more jobs than money spent buying fuel. According to government and private-industry economists, a million dollars spent on energy efficiency will directly create fifty jobs, while a million dollars spent in the petroleum industry will create only ten. The difference expands even further when those employees spend their paychecks. And last and most importantly, once the energy leaks are plugged—and hence the cash leaks as well—the money will stay in the community, state, or country, creating more jobs and economic opportunities for the people there."

Eunice thought for a moment. "How big of an effect is this?" she asked.

"It's big," Duncan answered. "According to a 1983 study commissioned by the Coalition of Northeastern Governors, a policy shift toward energy efficiency in New England, New York, and Pennsylvania would create one hundred twenty thousand more jobs than an emphasis on providing new energy supplies, much of which would have to be imported from outside the region and probably from outside the country."

"Gracious!" Eunice explained. "Efficiency sounds better and better. But can we reasonably hope that energy demand will actually decline?"

5 The Follies of Forecasting

DUNCAN SHRUGGED. "Well, let's look at what the experts say. Here, you'll enjoy this!" He shot Eunice a mischievous grin and busied himself rummaging through the papers piled on his desk.

Eunice noticed again how startlingly blue his eyes were. "I shouldn't like to see him angry," she cautioned herself. "Fierce little glints of ice they'd be."

But now they twinkled in amusement as he excavated a sheet showing a matrix of various numbers.

"Here, look at this one," he offered. "An exercise in bureaucratic humility, you might say. There is a favorite game, often played in energy policy circles," he explained, "of trying to guess —'predict,' they call it—how much energy this country will use in the year 2000. The reason that this preoccupation is more than just a silly diversion is that, too often, those 'forecasts' become the basis of national energy policy, to the extent that there is one."

"But why does anyone care?" Eunice looked puzzled. "Why not just let the people in 2000 worry about how much they'll be using?"

"Might be wiser," agreed Duncan. "However, it takes ten years to build a big power plant and a similar lead time to bring on an oil shale program, should anyone want to waste their money that way. Thus, if you believe that fifteen years from now we'll be using twice as much energy as now, then we have no time to lose—we'd better start building now to meet that need."

Eunice looked startled. "Yes, that's just what that silly man was saying in the meeting yesterday."

Duncan could well believe that all sorts of silly things had been said. And he had a pretty good idea of how the argument had run.

"This Department," he told Eunice, "actually ran a study in 1983, the Electricity Policy Project, that said that by the year 2000 we'd need another four hundred-odd giant power plants—a trillion dollars' worth, not counting inflation. To do that, all those new plants would have to be under construction by 1990. But that gives us just four years to order them all. Now, there are fifty-two weeks a year; that's a few hundred weeks between now and the end of the decade. So even counting the plants already under construction, you'd have to order two plants about every week from now till 1990."

Once more Eunice found herself staring open-mouthed at Duncan. "Not really . . ." she disparaged, a giggle beginning. She recovered enough to shake her head.

"And that in a country that has ordered a grand total of two smallish new power plants and no large ones since late '81—and no nuclear plants since '78—while canceling dozens and dozens of power plants. But," he continued, "if, indeed, the use of energy or even just the use of electricity *is* going to grow, then we are going to have to do something, if no more than to acknowledge that our forecast is wrong. If, on the other hand, energy use is going to decline, then new energy-supplying projects are economically risky in the extreme. Which may explain why so many utilities are now in trouble."

Eunice frowned in thought. "You obviously believe that energy use will decline," she observed. "How do you know? What if it grows? How did this . . . my . . . Department conclude it would grow?" Puzzlement showed in her face. "And, uh, I'm almost embarrassed to ask, but how much energy do we use now?"

"Those are all very good questions," Duncan replied. "Taking them in turn: I think energy use will decline for exactly the reasons we've just been through. First, I look at how much energy we're using now to run our society. As of 1984, we were using somewhat over seventy quads of energy per year. A 'quad' is shorthand for a quadrillion BTUs. Never mind for now what that means exactly, just know that it's a lot of energy." Eunice wrinkled her face in concentration, but nodded. Duncan continued, "Then I look at the price: At what price of energy does it become more cost-effective to save energy instead of using it? Then I look at the various energy-saving measures available and how much energy, roughly, they could save by a given date, let's say 2000. I add in population and assume some standard of living—just for grins, I've assumed a growing population and an ever-improving standard of living. That makes it harder on my conclusions, but also makes me more confident of the outcome. At least I won't underestimate. Then, finally, I come up with a rough number for how much energy will be used in 2000.

"Now, if you just look at how much energy we used in 1950, '60, or '70—when, by the way, inflation-corrected prices were falling—and notice that energy use increased, you might be tempted to say that if population should increase, electronic gadgets increase, and industrial growth continue, we'll need more energy. Indeed, under this view, it's not too hard to believe that to *not* supply ever more BTUs would cripple our way of life. Then, on the other side, are the folks like Hobart—bless his beady eyes, hand calculator, and sharp pencils—who actually inventory all the devices throughout the society that use energy. From his numbers, I can know pretty much how much energy is now used to smelt copper, bake bread, run trucks, and such. More important, I can tell what kinds of energy are really needed to do all that, not just what kinds are now used. For instance," he added as Eunice looked puzzled, "many industries use much higher-temperature heat than is really needed for their processes, simply because energy used to be cheap and no one worried about the waste inherent in burning fuel at a couple of thousand degrees to make steam that's needed at only a few hundred degrees. Anyway, when I add up all the energy-saving potential I told you about, I just can't see how we'd want to use more energy in 2000 than we do now. All the economics say the savings are so much cheaper than new supply.

"But here, look at where various 'experts' thought we'd be in 2000. I've arranged the forecasts by when they were made—the vertical axis—and by a little reasonableness ranking. T. H. Huxley said that all knowledge is fated to start as heresy and end up as superstition; so I've got those categories, with a middle stage of 'conventional wisdom.' Then out to the left is a preheretical phase, which I call 'beyond the pale.' Only a dozen years ago, when actual consumption was seventy-five quads per year, the U.S. government forecasters in the Atomic Energy Commission said consumption in 2000 would be one hundred sixty quads. Pretty ambitious, but that was the conventional wisdom about that time."

Eunice tried to imagine what she'd do with more than twice as much energy as she now used, and how she would pay for it. "One hundred ninety quads!" she exclaimed, pointing to 'superstition.' "Who thought we'd use that much?"

"The Department of the Interior, no doubt anticipating James Watt," Duncan teased. "Ah, but Exxon said two hundred thirty," he added. "With a straight face, too. And in those days, national energy policy rested on the blanket assumption that by 2020 or so we'd be using *ten times* as much electricity as we had used in 1972 —who knows for what?" Eunice clapped her hands to her mouth and stared.

"Meanwhile, the Sierra Club's one hundred forty quads was 'heresy,' and when a twenty-five-year-old physicist named Amory Lovins said a hundred twenty-five, well, that was clearly 'beyond the pale.' Serious scholars didn't even bother to read it.

"Then came the Arab oil embargo of 1973. The Ford Foundation released a 'zero energy growth' scenario that said we could use only one hundred quads in 2000. That wasn't taken seriously, but the Foundation's scenario for a series of technical fixes to save energy—meaning the users won't even notice that they are using less—called for one hundred twenty-four quads for the year 2000. That was still 'heresy' at the time, but the 'conventional wisdom' *had* dropped to one hundred forty quads. The utilities, however, still clung to the 'superstition' of one hundred sixty.

"By 1976 a lot had changed. Lovins now had an article in the prestigious magazine *Foreign Affairs* outlining the whole concept of 'end use' in energy. That's the concept I've been explaining: asking what's the job, then what's the right tool for that job. Well, that one article sort of broke open the energy debate. It led to Senate hearings, thousands of pages of debate, and an outcry by the industry, which called Lovins, among other things, 'the nuclear industry's Public Enemy Number One.' Anyway, in *Foreign Affairs*, Lovins claimed that ninety-five quads would be plenty at the turn of the century. In speeches, where he took account of more recent technological progress, he was claiming that seventy-five quads would suffice. Now, that *was* 'beyond the pale.' But the ninety-five —along with estimates out of Princeton that pegged the number at eighty-nine—had already worked their way over into the 'heresy' column. The government had dropped its guess from one hundred forty to one hundred twenty-four—they had discovered that you really *can* weather-strip your house. And the utilities, still in the 'superstition' column, were now saying that we would use one hundred forty, a twenty-quad concession to the realization that if you charge more for energy, people might use less of it.

"It was only two years later that the estimates in each of the categories—'superstition,' 'conventional wisdom,' 'heresy,' and 'beyond the pale'—shifted once again. The Department of Energy said that if the inflation-corrected price of oil were thirty dollars a barrel in the year 2000—roughly the price it actually was, only two years later—the United States would use about ninety-five quads a year. That's exactly the estimate that had been ridiculed two years earlier when Lovins made it. A committee of the National Academy of Sciences issued scenarios ranging from sixty-three to ninety-six quads, even for an economy producing twice as much as ours did in 1975. Lovins, meanwhile, was predicting that consumption could be as low as fifty-five quads, and Professor Steinhart of the University of Wisconsin was suggesting that thirty-three quads would be enough by the year 2050 if people's lifestyles changed somewhat. Meanwhile, the Department of Energy published scenarios that had annual consumption averaging one hundred twenty-three quads in the year 2000, assuming eighteen- to twenty-five-dollar-a-barrel oil—unlikely prices at such a high level of demand.

"Now, notice the pattern: About every two years a new 'beyond the pale' forecast appears and pushes each of the previous

estimates one category to the right, making it one notch more respectable. And sure enough, in 1980, the trend continued. Lovins and colleagues published a study of the West German economy that implied that the United States could get by on fifteen quads in the very long term, by 2080 or so. A National Academy of Sciences committee and some forecasters at Stanford envisioned the possibility of consumption in the high forties to low fifties at the turn of the century. 'Conventional wisdom' had come to rest in the sixties, while Exxon's and the Department of Energy's guesses, pegging consumption at about one hundred quads, began to look sort of lonely out there."

"Uh," Eunice began, "this guy Lovins . . ."

"I thought that might get your attention," Duncan chuckled. "He and his wife are friends of mine; they work as a team on all this energy stuff. Nice folks. Live in a big all-solar house out in Colorado. I'll introduce you the next time they're in D.C. They share my guess, by the way, that even if you assume a new century welcomed by a Gross National Product that has grown by an ambitious two-thirds, our use of nonrenewable fuels would be cut in half—simply by taking advantage of the best buys—with lots more cost-effective savings left to do after that."

Duncan broke off as he realized that Eunice was lost in study of the chart.

"Look at this," she pointed. "According to this chart, the highest official forecast of energy needs in the year 2000 made in 1980 is *lower* than the lowest unofficial forecasts of 1972. How much further can this pattern go? I mean we'll surely use *some* energy in 2000."

Duncan grinned and agreed. "Sure, and the best current predictions are that we'll use sixty to seventy quads. But that is a very significant number. If the administration and this Department let ideology drive their forecasts instead of analysis, and the energy industries are dumb enough to tool up to supply the official forecast ninety-odd to a hundred-odd quads in 2000, but people don't buy that much, the industries will go broke."

"Wouldn't that just serve them right?" Eunice asked.

Duncan laughed and nodded. "But," he added, "it would be kind of hard on the economy to have poured a trillion or so dollars down the drain."

As Eunice nodded, Duncan glanced at his watch. "Um," he broached tentatively, "before I knew I'd be spending some time with you I promised Hobart I'd check over his latest analysis. Heh," Duncan chuckled. "He thinks he's shown that nuclear plants are so heavily subsidized that taxpayers actually finance them at *negative* interest rates. And he's kinda champing at the bit to see if I can find any errors in his calculations. Would you mind if we broke for today?" Duncan looked to Eunice for agreement.

But he needn't have worried. "Oh, of course not," the overwhelmed Secretary cried with only thinly disguised delight. "And I really wouldn't mind some time to review all this. It's rather a lot," she admitted, hastily retrieving her legal pad and disappearing down the hall before Duncan could change his mind.

6 *What's the Energy For?*

BY NOW, Eunice and her secretary, Barb, had settled into a routine. Eunice would arrive early, before most of the Department was in place. Her first task was to go over the previous day's messages with Barb. Barb was the only one who knew where Eunice had been going these last two days, and she approved heartily. Barb had met Duncan not long after she had started working at the Department, back in 1979. What had impressed her the most had been his command of technical facts and his ability to make them comprehensible to people like herself. If anyone could help Eunice understand what was really going on, Barb figured, it would be Duncan. So she and Eunice made a pact: Barb would cover for the new Secretary, inventing meetings at the White House, briefings by key staff, papers that had to be drafted and such, to hold off the curiosity of Eunice's assistants.

For her part, Eunice was happy to leave the day-to-day affairs in Barb's capable hands. Eunice was still bewildered by the bureaucratic jungle gym at the Department and was always surprised when Barb was able to read so much between the lines of the brief memos and phone messages that kept pouring in.

Thus, this morning Eunice had put in her requisite fifteen minutes with her secretary. Then she trudged glumly down the maze of corridors. She was only now beginning to get things figured out, and she walked into Duncan's office looking rather haggard. "What's the matter?" asked Duncan. "You look worn out. Been hopping the Georgetown cocktail-party circuit?"

"Oh, no, I wish it were something as trivial as a party that's to blame. No, I was up most of the night." She sighed and flumped down in the reassuring armchair. "I'm not sure I can handle this job. All the stuff we were discussing was chasing me all night. Oh, thank you." She gratefully sipped on the steaming mug Duncan handed her.

Duncan smiled sympathetically. "Sorry about your nocturnal gremlins," he commiserated, "but welcome to the business. After all, imagine how all those high-paid energy analysts felt when their forecasts and credibility fell to pieces. Why, if those forecasters had had the integrity of 1929 stockbrokers, the sidewalks outside Exxon and the Atomic Energy Commission would have been plastered with bodies." Duncan chuckled at Eunice's horrified expression. "But that didn't happen; so instead of a bunch of dead forecasters, we've got a bunch who don't even know enough to be contrite. A good thing, though. I suppose the life insurance premiums for us energy analysts would have gone through the roof."

Duncan chuckled again. "But let's get on with it. Now, we've talked about *how much* energy we need, but that's not the full story about our energy. We need to know *what kinds* of energy we want, too."

"Why does it matter what kind?" Eunice asked. "Isn't energy energy? That's what the Assistant Secretaries told me."

"Mm," Duncan agreed, "they *would* say that. And, in fact," he added, "that's one of the central problems with this Department. But, no. Energy is not all alike. For one thing, energy does not come packaged as energy; it comes in many different forms, each suited in quality and price to a particular task. It's just like food: You don't just want to feed your kids twenty-five hundred calories a day; you have to make sure that they get the right kinds of food—protein, carbohydrates, fats, and vitamins and minerals."

Eunice perked up, nodding in agreement.

"So it wouldn't do to feed your kids nothing but cantaloupe, or nothing but steak." Duncan grinned at his pretensions of being

a househusband, as Eunice beamed. Perhaps her arguments to the Assistants hadn't been so far off, after all.

"Well," he continued, "energy works the same way. For instance, liquid fuels such as gasoline are especially well suited for transportation because they are comparatively lightweight and compact for the amount of energy they can provide, and they flow well and burn easily. They are, therefore, simpler than, say, coal to carry around in a vehicle's fuel tank. Electricity is a very versatile form of energy that can be used to power complex devices such as television sets, computers, and small motors. You'd be foolish to build a small gasoline engine to drive household appliances such as washing machines and kitchen mixers. Gasoline engines are noisy, smelly, and not always easy to start, all of which make them inferior to electric motors for small household applications." Eunice wrinkled her nose. "Conversely, with the technology now available, rechargeable electric cars would need enormous, cumbersome batteries to attain even half the range or speed of cars with gasoline internal combustion engines. And the infrastructure costs of stringing overhead wires or laying electrified tracks is only justified on high-volume routes such as streetcar lines and main intercity rail corridors.

"Just as you tried to tell those Assistant Secretaries the day before yesterday, people don't want energy for its own sake." Eunice looked shocked. "Mmm," Duncan admitted, "I have my sources. Anyway, as you said, they have no set preferences for one fuel over another, no innate love of kilowatt-hours, lumps of sooty coal, or sticky, sticky black goo. And it's also only the rarest of conspicuous consumers who *enjoy* running up their electric bills or forking over twenty dollars every other day to fill up their gas tanks."

Eunice nodded and shrugged. "But doesn't everyone know that? I mean, it seems perfectly obvious to me."

"Well, Eunice," said Duncan, rubbing his chin and mulling over the problem, "you've got to sympathize with some of the people in this Department. They get so attached to their own particular energy solution that they don't step back and look at the whole picture. As the psychologist Abraham Maslow once said, 'When the only tool you have is a hammer, it's remarkable how everything starts to look like a nail.' Your Assistant Secretaries know so much about their particular kinds of hammers that they forget people just want their houses to be warm in the winter and cool in the summer, to be able to travel easily from home to work and play, and so forth. And people want to do those things in the cheapest, most convenient way. But you're right. An accurate estimate of our energy needs—and, more importantly, an efficient, cost-effective strategy for satisfying those needs—can only begin with a survey of what we will actually need the energy *for.''*

"Oh," said Eunice, her eyes widening, "so the analysts who came up with those ridiculous high numbers on your chart weren't looking at the uses people had for energy."

"Exactly right," said Duncan. "They were just playing a numbers game: How much total energy will we use, and how much of that can my pet technology supply? And they tried to foresee the future just by projecting the past, which is as dangerous as driving fast while looking only in the rear-view mirror. As a result, they overestimated the total amount of energy people will need, and they especially overestimated their needs for electricity."

"But that man Lovins, did he do that, too?" Eunice asked.

"No, that's just the point. Lovins was the one who said that the totals aren't enough; that you have to look at how much of what kind of energy people will actually use, before you can add it all up to get a total."

Duncan rocked back in his chair and drew a long breath. "Well, you ready?" he grinned, sitting forward again.

Eunice blinked, startled. "Excuse me," she blurted. "Ready for what?"

"End uses." Duncan answered, going on as though she were. "As a first cut, we can divide energy needs into three broad categories: heat, transportation, and electric-specific needs such as electronics, motors, lights, smelters, etc. In round numbers, more than half—fifty-eight percent—of our energy needs are for heat, mostly at low temperatures. Another third—thirty-four percent—is needed as liquid fuel for transportation. Only eight percent is needed for those premium uses that can only be satisfied with electricity or that can use it to unique advantage. But right now we're delivering about thirteen percent of our energy in the form of electricity, half again as much as is needed. That percentage would be even higher—about sixteen percent—if some electric plants were not sitting idle, unable to sell their product because it has become so expensive."

"So is this excess of capacity to make electricity part of the reason my electric bills have gone up so much lately?" asked Eunice.

"Ah, very good," said Duncan. "But it's only part of the story. Making electricity is inherently an expensive process, even if you don't overbuild. When electricity is generated in thermal power plants—by burning fuel to make steam, then using the steam to spin the turbines to run the generators—only about a third of the energy fed into the process actually leaves the power plant as electricity. The rest becomes waste heat and is dumped as warm water into the local river or ocean, or decorates the sky as cooling-tower plumes. This inefficiency is an integral part of converting heat into electricity. The two-thirds figure for the wastage is an average; most modern coal plants waste slightly less, and nuclear plants waste somewhat more. These efficiency estimates don't even count losses in the transmission and distribution systems, which amount to about seven percent of the electricity sent out from the power plants. It is chiefly these losses at every step of the process that make electricity a very expensive form of energy.

"Now, it is true that electricity is a very high-quality form of energy, just as brandy is a drink of higher proof than wine. And electricity can do lots of different kinds of work. But to use it, say, just to heat a house is going backward—at a very high cost. Lots of forms of energy can give you heat: oil, coal, solar, weather-stripping . . . I know," he said, waving off Eunice's objections. "Weather-stripping is not strictly a form of energy, but you should get used to seeing all these as being in competition. Using electricity to heat your house directly—say, in a baseboard heater —is like watering down brandy so you can drink it instead of wine. Electric home heating, assuming eight cents per kilowatt-hour and seventy percent furnace efficiency, is roughly equivalent to using oil priced at ninety-odd dollars a barrel, or more than two dollars a gallon—about three times what we now pay. It really makes economic sense to use electricity only for the jobs that actually require it: lighting, electronics, appliances, etc. But those uses are only eight percent of all the energy used in the country."

"Ah," said Eunice, "so that's why our neighbors, the Bowers, pay so much for heating—they have an all-electric home. But if what you say is true, why were those all-electric homes built in the first place?"

"That's a long story," said Duncan, frowning. "We'll get to it in greater detail when we talk about utilities, but to be brief, electricity used to be much cheaper. The costs were different when fuel was cheaper and when electric plants cost less to build. In fact, do you know that it now costs about twice as much for a typical nuclear utility to build the new electric capacity to serve a newly built electrically heated house in the Frostbelt as it costs the contractor to build the entire house?"

Eunice gasped.

"And do you know why a contractor puts in electric heating?" added Duncan. "Because that's the cheapest kind to install. The contractor doesn't care about the heating bills that the new residents will get—only about the purchase price a buyer sees when house shopping. But like I say, let's save that for another day. End use is a big enough subject by itself.

"For now, just remember," Duncan continued, "that we use electricity for lots of jobs that can't justify its high cost. And we have lots more generating facilities than we need, especially if we only use electricity for the jobs that warrant its high cost—those for which a cheaper form of energy can't do what we want."

Eunice thought for a moment. "But then it's sort of silly to argue over which kind of new power plant to build—coal, nuclear, *or* solar. It's like building an addition to your house when you already have three empty rooms that you aren't using."

"Right," congratulated Duncan. "The people who argue about which type of new power plants to build are asking where to get more of a particularly costly form of energy that we already have more of than can give us our money's worth. They are trying to answer the wrong question."

"That's crazy, Duncan," exclaimed Eunice. "I find it hard to believe that reasonable people don't see things the way you just explained them."

"I know it sounds crazy," said Duncan, with the air of a man who has seen so much craziness that a little more wouldn't surprise him. "But let's look at what happened in France, so you can see both how easy it is to fall into that kind of trap and how sticky a trap it can prove to be. Some years back, French planners of energy demand—France, remember, has a centrally planned economy—tried to find out what the largest single energy market was in their country. It turned out that the biggest part of their energy was used for heating buildings. Then, being interested in the efficiency with which the energy would be used, they asked what was the best way to heat buildings. They argued over that a bit, but they found that electricity would be the most *un*economical way to do it. So this particular branch of the French government announced that electric heat should be phased out as a waste of money and fuel. And supposedly they won—that was supposed to be official policy.

"But meanwhile," Duncan went on, leaning back in his chair, "the energy-supply planners took a different tack. They looked at the charts showing how much foreign oil was pouring into France and decided to reduce their nation's vulnerability to another oil embargo. 'We must replace this oil,' they reasoned, 'and oil is energy. All we have to do, then, is find some other source of energy. *Voilà!*' they said. 'Reactors provide energy; we'll build them all over France.' So the two sides of the energy establishment proceeded along a collision course: the market-oriented demand faction, which wanted to heat French buildings as cheaply as possible, and the technology-driven supply faction, which wanted to provide more millions-of-barrels-of-oil equivalent. The problem the reactor-builders ignored, of course, is that these millions-of-barrels-of-oil equivalent exist on all kinds of energy charts and tables, but not in real life. Sure, a hunk of fuel or a given amount of electricity might be the equivalent of a million barrels of oil in its energy content, but not in its price or in how easy it is to obtain or to use. In short, the French nuclear program could produce a million-barrels-of-oil equivalent, but at a far higher cost than a million barrels of *real* oil, let alone of still cheaper substitutes such as roof insulation; so the 'barrels' aren't really equivalent at all."

"What happened?" Eunice asked.

"Sooner or later, these two strategies were bound to crash into each other, and they did." Duncan smacked his hands together graphically. "Both sides realized that the only way to sell all that nuclear electricity would be to heat more buildings with electricity, which the government had supposedly agreed not to do. Now, you could argue that it would still be better to use domestically produced, expensive electricity for heating than cheap, vulnerable oil imported from a volatile region. You would have to ignore the fact that the capital and uranium needed to produce that 'domestic' electricity are also imported, leaving France saddled with a mountainous foreign debt and the French electric company virtually bankrupt," Duncan added parenthetically. "But that again begs the question of the best way to heat a building, or to provide any other type of energy service, for that matter. There are many options besides oil and nuclear, many of which are much cheaper than oil, nuclear power, *or* coal. The disagreement we saw in the case of France's two schools of energy planning comes up again and again in the energy policy of every country. If you start on the supply side, you'll frame the problem as where to get more BTUs, from any source, at any price. And the solutions you find will reflect that: They will be big energy-supply projects. You'll end up needing to sell energy at a high price to pay for those costly supply systems, but people won't use as much energy as you thought unless you sell it for a low price, in which case you won't make enough money to pay off the plants you built. On the other hand, if you start on the demand side, you'll be able to keep down the costs to the consumers, because you'll be buying mainly energy efficiency. You therefore won't be wasting money and energy trying to generate even more electricity—one of the worst buys for most energy uses.

"Of course, the same mismanagement could have occurred with any kind of large, centralized energy planning, whether it was electric or not. The synthetic-fuel program in this country is a prime example. What we need now are not more energy-supply programs or more and smarter bureaucrats to tell us we need them, but a process of distinguishing between means and ends, making sure that the means we use are the best ways to achieve the ends we want. Demand-oriented or 'end-use' approaches to problems can save a lot of money."

"And, I should think, a lot of bother and foolish programs," added Eunice wearily. She sagged a bit and tried inconspicuously to stretch a nagging knot out from between her shoulder blades.

"Aw, Eunice," Duncan teased, "you don't want to get word-bound this early in the job, do you? C'mon, I'll show you how to shake off those shoulder knots, and then we'll look at ways of applying that cost-cutting approach to a number of energy uses and see what it can save."

7 Best Buys First

EUNICE BLUSHED AGAIN. But as she settled down to resume the lesson, she had to admit it had felt good. Imagine, a dignified lady, now a Washington figure, doing stretching exercises in a vacant room of a federal agency. But it had been a pleasant stretch, without a doubt. And, for a man in his late thirties, bound to a desk, Duncan was amazingly limber. He even showed her a couple of stretches that really tugged at the small of her back. Better than Jane Fonda, Eunice giggled to herself. Still, she had felt quite silly in the middle of this concrete tomb, leaning over, touching her toes, and reaching for the ceiling. But she had to admit it was fun. Of course, she probably wouldn't be able to get away with it when people started recognizing her as the Secretary. It would be somewhat unseemly, she thought to herself, and glanced again at Duncan, feeling slightly conspiratorial.

But Duncan was already thinking of the matter at hand. "Well, Eunice," he said, "I promised to tell you how to implement end-use thinking in energy. My only caution to you is that it will sound extraordinarily simple and self-evident. And really it is just a matter of common sense and good judgment, but it is, therefore, foreign to most people in this Department.

"The first question that end-use thinkers must answer is the one we arrived at just before we got up to stretch: What do we want the energy *for?* Once we have listed those uses, we need to figure out how to provide for each of them, and the logical way to go about that is to ask what the cheapest way is of providing each service. Now, you wouldn't think that a very radical notion, but it has played a surprisingly small role in determining energy policy, because energy planners here"—Duncan waved around him at the Department in general—"were obsessed with providing sufficient *supplies of energy* instead of abundant *energy services* as cheaply as possible. Here, let's take a look at an example—say, the case of a newly built house. What are the energy services that a new house and its occupants would need?"

"Let's see," said Eunice, who had just been getting comfortable and ready to listen to another tutorial. She sat up and thought. "They would certainly need to stay warm in the winter and cool in the summer, and they'll need lighting so they don't have to go to bed as soon as it gets dark."

Eunice went on. "And we'll have to give them hot water to wash their clothes, their dishes, and themselves. They'll need heat for cooking, and they'll want the usual range of electrical appliances—television, stereo, refrigerator, kitchen aids, and so on. And you know, Duncan, I've always wanted a heated swimming pool; so let's give them one of those, too. They won't have to become monks just to use energy sensibly, will they?"

"Of course not," said Duncan. He grinned and added, "I know plenty of sensible people who aren't monks." He nodded at Eunice's list. "Good, that'll get us started. Now let's try to figure out the cheapest ways of supplying those services. The best buys will usually be the efficiency measures. We'll want to put lots of insulation in the attic and walls and around the floor slab or under the floor, efficient glazings in the windows, weather-stripping around the doors and windows, and caulking in the cracks and holes. We'll install an efficient refrigerator and showerheads, we'll insulate the pool and keep it covered when we're not using it, and we'll place the windows so as to take advantage of natural light without overheating the house. If the climate is hot, we'll shade the sunny-side windows, maybe vent the attic and walls, have a light-colored roof, and use a very efficient air conditioner or a simpler kind of cooling device, such as a swamp cooler in hot, dry climates. These measures and others tend to be relatively cheap, even in their installation cost. They last a long time and they save large portions of the energy that would otherwise be required. And, as I've said, some of these measures can even *reduce* the initial home-building cost by cutting the size of the required furnace or air conditioner or both, or eliminating one or both of them altogether."

Eunice still had trouble with that one. "Tell me again," she interrupted. "What would keep the house warm in the winter?"

"Just the heat of the people inside, the appliances they would be using, the lights they burn, and so on. It's like wrapping yourself up in a blanket—when you're well-wrapped, it doesn't take very much heat to keep you comfortable."

"So what you're suggesting," said Eunice, "is to wrap every house in America in its own blanket?"

"Precisely, Eunice," Duncan replied. "Now, let's get more sophisticated. Once the house is 'tucked in,' so to speak, other measures begin to make sense, such as greenhouses or sunspaces on the sunny side of the house. A sunspace's contribution to the heating of a house becomes especially significant once the house needs much less heat because the cheaper measures have been taken. Then the air-to-air heat exchangers make sense to provide fresh air. But it would have been silly to spend four hundred dollars on a heat exchanger before blocking up the holes in the shell of the house with caulk and weather-stripping. If you do it this way, cheapest first and then more expensive, you can typically save energy for about a cent and a half per kilowatt-hour of electricity or about fifty cents per gallon of fuel oil." He paused to let the ideas sink in.

"The same idea of starting with the cheapest steps," Duncan continued, "applies to the other energy services we need. Refrigerator manufacturers, for example, should start with sensible amounts of insulation in the walls. Then the motor can be fairly small and will easily tuck in on top of the refrigerator."

"Hmm," Eunice said, "that makes sense. We try to do the cheapest things first, which usually means that we first use energy more efficiently, then see how we can get the little we still need in the cheapest way."

"Bravo," Duncan said. "My star pupil. Let me run through a lesson of what happens if you don't do the cheapest things first. When solar space heating began to become popular in the mid-1970s, engineers would study a house's energy bills, see how much energy the place used, and design a system to collect and deliver that much energy from the sun. The engineers were stuck in the mentality of supplying a certain quantity of energy, instead of examining the house's heating needs as a whole. Often they didn't even weatherize the houses or take steps to save hot water. So they were forced to install systems that were quite large and thus quite expensive. Since the designers' training was usually in the engineering of standard heating devices, their systems resembled oil- or gas-based heating systems in every aspect but the fuel source. The systems even had intricate networks of pipes, tanks, ducts, and collectors. But the complexity of the systems worked against them, and they were often plagued with leaks, thermostat malfunctions, collector freeze-ups, and so on.

"In the past few years," continued Duncan, "the emphasis in solar engineering has shifted dramatically toward insulation and passive systems, in which elements of the house itself collect the sunlight. Good solar installers pay careful attention to reducing the energy needs for heating as part of their design. With the house more tightly sealed against heat leaks, less sun-catching area is needed to keep the house warm, and the systems are cheaper. And since passive systems have fewer or no moving parts, maintenance becomes much simpler and repairs much less frequent. These third- and fourth-generation solar heating systems are almost as far removed from their clumsy, inelegant predecessors as a modern ten-speed bicycle is from the original ungainly Victorian velocipedes."

"You're right, Duncan," Eunice said as he wound down his description. "It does seem pretty simple, once you look at it from that perspective. I suppose it gets more complicated when you start talking about whole countries instead of just one house. But maybe that's one of the roots of all this confusion: People in this

Department keep thinking about the whole country instead of helping people make simple decisions about their homes and businesses. Here, let me see if I can work out how to provide one of the other energy services that the house will need—say, hot water. I guess the first thing to do would be to install those five-dollar showerheads that you keep talking about that give you just as good a shower with less than half the water. And then blankets of insulation around the hot-water tank, and insulation on the hot-water pipes. And by that point, if this all parallels what you said about heating the air in the house, it would make sense to have a simple solar water heater, because you could keep it small enough to be affordable. Is that right?"

"Absolutely," said Duncan with satisfaction at a lesson well taught. "Of course, I can't teach you all of the technologies in one sitting; so there are a few refinements you've left out, such as faucet aerators and demand water heaters that only come on when someone turns on the hot water, so that you don't have to keep a whole tank of water hot. And there's another important consideration: Even if you make your hot-water demand low enough that a solar water heater would make economic sense, it still might not be the best investment decision for you to make next to save money on energy. Adding insulating shutters, or some of the new windows that hold in heat several times better than storm windows, or replacing an old refrigerator with a new, energy-efficient model—all of these might pay off even more quickly than putting solar panels on your roof. You might still install the solar system, but not quite so soon."

"Well, I knew it couldn't be quite that simple," sighed Eunice, "but even these refinements aren't too tough to understand. Let's see if I can pull another guess out of the hat. Take my electric range, for instance. I suppose that using electricity for heat is no better here than in the cases we were discussing this morning, and for all the same reasons: wasting energy in the conversion to electric power, and so on. So I should get a gas range, and not an electric one. And I bet I could turn off the pilot lights and just use a sparker to light the burners. I'm not sure I know what to do past that point, though."

"Enjoy all the money you'd save," Duncan said with a grin. "Now, it's not always possible to get a gas hookup, but if you can, it'll save you half of your energy bill for cooking. You could go even farther, such as making methane from garbage or using steam from solar collectors to cook with. For most people, though, natural or bottled gas will continue to be the best buy, along with more efficient pots and well-insulated ovens. Convection and microwave ovens can save energy, too, if you happen to like them."

"But what about my swimming pool?" asked Eunice. "Oh, I know," she interrupted herself, "you put a pool cover on it and then heat it with solar panels. And the cover keeps down the number of panels you need."

"Got it!" exclaimed Duncan. "Pretty soon I won't be able to tell you anything new. But until that day arrives, let me try out another example on you. We suggested that a household do the cheapest things first; well, the same can apply to a utility company. Consider what happens when a number of factories want to move into the area served by State Power and Light. They will need a certain amount of guaranteed power in order to operate—say, one hundred megawatts. The utility has a number of options. It can build a power plant—coal, nuclear, hydroelectric, solar—to supply the power. Or it can help its other customers cut back on the amount of electricity they need by using it more efficiently, thus freeing that existing power to sell to the new factories. Or it could tell the factories that they should go elsewhere or charge them very high hookup fees. But, if the people in the area want the new industries to come in, the last option is unattractive to everyone; so that leaves the choice of helping existing customers to become more energy-efficient, or building a new power plant. The new plant typically will deliver electricity at anywhere from about four or five cents per kilowatt-hour for a small hydro unit to upwards of twenty cents for the average nuclear plant coming on line now. Construction will make the utility raise its rates to cover the cost of the new plant. Then consumers will pay higher rates, and, as has been demonstrated in many communities, over time they'll start using less electricity—paying smaller bills and making it harder for the utility to pay off its new plants. That rate squeeze, of course, will hurt the new factories, too."

Duncan paused and regarded Eunice. "Sounds like a hopeless fix, doesn't it? On the other hand," he continued, "if the utility insulates people's attics, gives rebates to induce people to buy—and sell—energy-efficient refrigerators, improves industrial motors' controls to make them waste less electricity, and uses a wide array of other measures to stretch its electrical supplies, it can then sell to the new factories the power its old customers will no longer need. In this scenario everyone wins: The utility earns more money at less risk, the consumers get lower electric bills, the utility can run its costliest-to-operate plants less of the time, and the firms that own the new factories will get the electricity they need at less than they would have if the utility had built a new power plant."

"Hold on," said Eunice. "How did that work out so well for everyone?"

"Nothing up my sleeve," replied Duncan, grinning. "We just relied on the common-sense notion that it is best to do those things that cost least. It's a rule of thumb to apply to just about any energy situation: Do the cheapest things first. Applying it to individual houses and to utility companies wasn't that hard, was it?" Duncan shrugged in mock nonchalance as Eunice shook her head. "So—let's apply the same rationale to saving oil. But," he paused, "first things first. I do think it's time for another cup of coffee. Last one to the coffee pot is a gas-guzzler."

8 Over a Barrel?

*E*UNICE AND DUNCAN stood by the coffee pot that Duncan kept in the little cubbyhole of a filing room off his main office. Reaching for the pot that had been sitting on the warmer since the early morning, Duncan swirled the coffee around in it. Eunice smelled the acrid odor of overheated coffee, but resigned herself to a bitter mug; after all, no man she had ever known could tell the difference. But to her great surprise, Duncan grimaced as he sniffed the pot and poured it ceremoniously into the sink. "Just don't tell the toxic waste detail over at EPA," he teased. "They'll have my hide for improper disposal of hazardous chemicals." With that, he began grinding some more beans to brew a fresh pot.

Eunice, though, only half-heard that last sentence. As the evilly brown coffee spilled toward the drain, she remembered a question she had wanted to ask earlier. "Oil!" she said suddenly, making Duncan look at her with puzzlement.

"Oil?" he raised an eyebrow.

"Yes, oil," she repeated. "Everyone, even my Assistant Secretaries, seems to think that oil is The Problem. Or they say, 'Sure, you can have conservation, but you can't change the fact that we're running out of oil.' Isn't that true?"

Duncan, who was loading the coffee into the filter, paused for a moment. "Well, they are right," he said. "We are running out of oil. But that just has to do with the fact that it took millions of years to make the stuff, and we're using up that legacy in about a hundred years—about a hundred thousand times faster than it was created." He poured boiling water over the fresh grind and watched the brew dribble into the pot.

"But you have to understand the historical context," Duncan said, leading Eunice back to their chairs. "The fuel that powered the rise of the new industrial society after World War II was oil —and plenty of it. That oil was priced according to how cheap it was to lift from the underground oil fields, not according to its eventual scarcity. And most of the houses, factories, and cars we have now were designed when oil was very inexpensive. So when the oil embargo of 1973 began," Duncan went on, "oil seemed the only issue. That was what had been cut off. It was the absence of oil that caused the lines at the gas stations and the tremendous hikes in heating bills in the Northeast."

Duncan, like Eunice, smelled the fresh coffee. He disappeared into the "coffee room" and returned with two steaming mugs. "The obsession with finding more oil," he continued, "or making oil out of other things—coal, garbage, shale—was what gave rise to the obsession with finding more energy of any kind, from any source. Luckily, by now, more than a decade after the Arab oil embargo, the importance to the United States of net oil imports has diminished—from seventeen percent to about twelve percent of national energy consumption—and the percentage of our energy that comes from the Middle East has dropped even more sharply, to only a couple of percent. Now, if the price keeps falling, that could change. Nonetheless, U.S. energy policy is in large part shaped by a desire to cut oil imports—and rightly so. Imported oil travels a great distance from wellhead to user and is vulnerable to disruption at any point along the way. And that's as true for British North Sea oil or Canadian or Mexican oil as it is for oil from the Arabian Gulf. Because of the complexity of oil drilling and shipping facilities, the smooth operation of the oil rigs depends on political tranquillity. Yet about three-eighths of the world's oil is extracted in volatile regions such as the Middle East, Latin America, Africa, and Indonesia, leaving the lines of production and transportation at the mercy of the latest coup or act of sabotage."

"But, Duncan," Eunice objected, "isn't that just as true for long supply lines in the United States? I keep hearing about an oil pipeline that crosses Alaska. What about discontented Eskimos or right-wing kooks?"

"You're quite right, Eunice," Duncan agreed. "Oil pipelines are vulnerable, no matter what their citizenship. In fact, we should talk more about those domestic vulnerabilities later on. American oil is only less vulnerable to *political* disruptions, at least once it starts flowing. But let me get back to my story."

Eunice nodded as Duncan continued. "What really makes oil replacement tough is the end uses of that oil. The energy we use for transportation comes almost entirely from oil, because that is an application that requires easily transportable, easily burned liquid fuels. Since mobility is such a critical energy service in this country, our dependence on imported oil is not as small as the twelve percent of our raw energy that comes from oil imports might indicate. In fact, nearly thirty percent of the *oil* we use is still imported."

Duncan warmed to his subject. "We should also not draw a false sense of security from the oil glut that developed countries were experiencing in the early to mid-1980s. A similar calm prevailed between the 1973 Arab oil embargo and the 1979 disruption of oil supplies from Iran. During that period, as now, the real price of oil, corrected for inflation, dropped gradually. Supply then, as now, was plentiful, but that plentitude hid underlying instabilities. As surely as the relaxation in the oil markets in 1976 through 1978 was followed by the oil shock of 1979, the calm of the early 1980s may be followed by another disruption."

Eunice furrowed her brow and fingered the agate pendant she wore around her neck. "Just a minute," she insisted. "It seems like pretty thin evidence to me. I mean, just because one period of plenty was followed by an oil shock doesn't mean that the one we're in will also end unhappily. That's like saying, uh, like saying that the last two cars to pass us were station wagons, so the next one will be a station wagon, too. I'm just not sure you can predict these things at all."

"Um hum," admitted Duncan, smiling at the swiftness with which she had caught him. "You're right, I don't *know* that another oil shock is on its way. But it *might* be; so shouldn't we plan to be safe whether one arrives or not? Or, to put it the other way around, should we stake our prosperity on the hope that more disruptions *won't* happen? But, before I explain how to play safe, let me finish describing how we rolled into this glut. There were two main causes: increasingly efficient ways of using petroleum products, and the competition among oil exporters for a share of the shrinking market in crude oil.

"Remember," he led her, "ever since the first oil embargo in 1973, users have been devising better, less wasteful ways of using energy to obtain the same services. This cut their demand for crude oil, and thus cut the OPEC nations' oil sales by more than half. But many oil-exporting countries have had trouble adjusting to those cutbacks in their revenues. Since 1973 they have grown accustomed to having billions of dollars pour in from their customers. The ones with a lot of oil and not very many people, such as Saudi Arabia or Kuwait, launched grandiose development schemes that needed a continuing influx of cash. Populous, poor nations, such as Nigeria and Indonesia, used the petrodollars as another cash crop to help feed their starving millions and borrowed heavily against anticipated earnings from oil sales. With the market for oil shrinking, many OPEC nations have been forced to compete with each other for a slice of the dwindling market just to get enough money to make their loan payments. These pressures for revenues have made it harder for OPEC members to hold prices high, as they did when it was still a sellers' market."

Eunice found it hard to feel much sympathy for these poor, broke billionaires, and said so. Duncan grinned. "Well," he advised, "remember that little of the oil wealth goes to the shantytowns around Lagos and Mexico City. But, if you still want to stick it to OPEC, the best way is to save energy. It saves us money, and the slack market puts real pressure on them. In fact, the glut will continue while the countries of OPEC feel the pressure to earn more money to buy food and pay off their development loans, while energy-saving technologies continue to be invented, and while the supply from most countries continues uninterrupted. These factors—especially the last one—are hard to predict with any precision. In fact, it would be impossible to state with any certainty whether the price of oil will be $10 or $100 per barrel two years hence—which gets back to your objection a moment ago." Duncan tipped an imaginary hat. "New discoveries of oil that increase supply, international incidents that interrupt it, and a host of other imponderables could shape the price of oil in ways that we cannot foresee. Given that uncertainty, I think we should use energy in ways that make sense no matter how high or low the price of imported oil goes. Simply guzzling oil as we used to do is a strategy that would work only if oil stayed cheap and plentiful. Proceeding with high-cost projects to produce oil substitutes at seventy dollars to one hundred dollars a barrel only makes sense if the price of imported oil will rise to the high end of the likely range. So we need to set a course that will work irrespective of the price of oil."

"Okay, I think I get it," said Eunice. "It's like chocolate chip cookies." Now it was Duncan's turn to blink uncomprehendingly. "You know, cookies . . .? My kids love them, even my husband, Joe. But let's say I didn't know whether a package of them would cost a dollar or ten dollars. What could I do? Well, I could just hope that the price didn't go too high, and then my family would get cross if the price went way up and we could only have them on special occasions. Or I could work out a deal with the bakery down the street that they would always sell me cookies for eight dollars a package—but that's beyond my budget, and I'd be losing out if the price really did stay low. So let's say I want to be a bit sly: I'll make them myself more often, and I'll start making other treats such as lemon bars and fruit tarts and oatmeal chews and peanut butter cookies. And if chocolate chips get too expensive, we can always have more of the other desserts—and not miss the chocolate chippers *too* badly. And I could ask some friends of mine who split up big sacks of flour and rice if they could buy and split a big sack of chocolate chips, too, so we could still get them fairly inexpensively. It's just common sense."

Duncan's mouth had started to water during this soliloquy, but he just swallowed and made a mental note to find out what Eunice's cooking was like. All the nouvelle cuisine in Washington got rather tiresome after a while, and sometimes he wanted nothing more than a good roast chicken or pork chop with mashed potatoes and gravy. But such thoughts were doing him no good at this time of the morning; so he chased away the munchies and returned to the discussion.

"A tasty analogy," he said. "But oil is a bit different. If what your family likes is chocolate chips, cutting back or substituting isn't nearly as good as a steady supply of the cookies they like. But almost nobody wants oil per se. With oil, clearly the best choice, given the economics, is to save as much as we can. This Department has searched for all sorts of oil substitutes, but there are really only two ways to save a *lot* of oil, ways that can significantly curb our oil habit and that make economic sense even if the bottom falls out of the oil market. These ways are: to stop living in houses that leak heat like sieves, and to stop driving petropigs.

"Most of us live in leaky houses. A decent weatherization program in this decade could save two-and-a-half million barrels of oil a day—we've actually saved some of that already—and we could double those savings if we weatherized the same number of houses in the 1990s. Those five million barrels a day exceed our total net oil imports of four-and-a-half million barrels a day. The cost of saving energy in that way would amount to about a quarter of what American oil companies are paying on the international markets."

"All that," asked Eunice, "just from those rubber strips along the door jambs and from those bales and sheets of insulation?"

"Yep," said Duncan, "and the other strategy—to stop driving petropigs—would save oil even cheaper and faster. As anyone who has tried to trade in an old gas-guzzling Oldsmobile or Lincoln can tell you, the trade-in value on those cars is somewhere between chicken feed and a song. In fact, you might have to pay someone to haul it away to the junkyard. Consequently, gas-guzzlers have trickled down to poor people who can't afford to buy a newer, more efficient car. Just at the time when we should be getting those cars off the road, they are lasting longer, in the ownership of people who can least afford them.

"But," Duncan grinned at Eunice, "you like my number tricks —watch this one. Want a much better way to save oil than pouring billions of dollars into synfuels? Take that money and give a *free* high efficiency car to the owners of these petropigs, provided they get their old cars off the road forever. If dealers provided a 'death certificate' to the effect that the old car had been recycled and could not be driven again, the owner would drive away a free forty-mile-a-gallon car. Not only would the owner of the car be better off, but so should the nation. Naturally, a number of implementation problems . . ."

"Oh, come on, Duncan," Eunice cut him off impatiently. "You can't be serious about this. I mean, you wouldn't just give away new cars to people who are driving old clunkers. That's absurd!" He *had* seemed so sane, she thought; but *this* was a real crackpot idea.

"Well, I'm not sure how serious I am about actually doing it," Duncan confessed. "But the economics are totally serious. It really would be cheaper for the nation to displace imported oil by scrapping gas-guzzlers than to build a synfuels plant with government money. But you're right; I can't imagine a program like that making it through Congress, since it would be so good for the common folk." Duncan shrugged.

"But that's a subsidy," Eunice pointed out. "Having the government give people free cars is hardly a typical free-market approach," she protested, "and I thought you didn't like subsidies."

"That's true," Duncan admitted. "Well, let me frame a more free-market solution. Let's say it would cost Detroit one hundred billion dollars extra to retool so that the next fleet of cars and light trucks to be built averages sixty miles a gallon. That's close to five times what I think it would really cost, but let's assume it. The sticker price of each new, efficient vehicle would go up by about eleven hundred dollars, an amount that the owner would recover in a couple of years of average driving."

"There you go again," said Eunice. "Maybe Washington bureaucrats have eleven hundred bucks lying around, but I know most of my neighbors back in Dubuque sure don't."

"You're right, of course." Duncan reddened slightly, acknowledging his inexperience with the finances of ordinary people. "And that's the reason that people start thinking about subsidies —to overcome that sort of barrier to better energy decision making. That was exactly the argument used for taxing oil and then turning around and giving seventeen billion dollars of it back to the oil companies to make synthetic fuels at unaffordable prices. But let's put it differently: An extra eleven hundred dollars on the sticker translates to an extra monthly payment only two-thirds as much as the driver will now *save* in charges at the gas pump. So the driver comes out ahead from the very beginning. Now clearly," he conceded, addressing Eunice's protest, "in time, the market will handle all this. Cars are slowly becoming more efficient. And if they didn't, sooner or later the glut would disappear, there'd be another oil crisis, gasoline prices would rise, and the cars would get efficient. But wouldn't it be nice to avoid another round of shortages?

"It's situations like these," he continued, "that make me wish that government decisions were made on the basis of least-cost economics. The two measures I've just mentioned—plugging the heat holes in houses and getting old, wasteful cars off the road— would more than eliminate America's oil imports in this century, before a power plant or synthetic fuel plant ordered now could provide any energy at all. And these efficiency measures would cost only a tenth as much as the new supply options.

"But," Duncan said, shrugging, "I don't know. Some of these calls aren't easy."

"Well, maybe," Eunice tried, "the role of government is to look ahead, to plan for shortages, and then to tell everyone what to do."

"Oh, no." Duncan laughed. "The government's record of doing that is pretty dismal. Actually, every time I go around this one, I come back to the belief that the government's role is to help the market to operate as freely as it can to pick the least-cost options. Now, understand, markets aren't meant to be fair," he warned, "but only to be efficient. Fairness is the job of the political process—at least if equity is an issue you care about. And, for example, without some government oversight, the environmental problems of energy development would be very difficult to manage. Markets also have very little long-term foresight. However, rather than have the government maintain a military force to cope with the next oil shortage, I'd much rather put some tax dollars into what, in a truly free market, with no institutional barriers, would make an oil cutoff irrelevant."

Eunice nodded thoughtfully. "But it's so hard to be sure," she observed.

"Really," Duncan agreed. "But here, let's look at the opportunities a little differently. Suppose I tell you that underneath Detroit is a giant oil field as large as the biggest field in Saudi Arabia. This oil field can produce more than five million barrels a day for the foreseeable future at only a few dollars per barrel. Interested?" he teased. Then, as Eunice nodded eagerly, he declared, "That is exactly the economic equivalent of retooling the car factories to make the vehicle fleet more efficient.

"Now, doesn't it seem silly that companies would want to go to the ends—and toward the middle—of the earth to find expensive oil, when all that cheap oil is available just by improving our vehicle fleet? Or, to look at it from the oil companies' viewpoint, if they spend billions of dollars looking for more oil, and people can get by with efficiency at a tenth of the cost, Exxon and others will not only look silly, they may lose their shirts.

"But seriously," Duncan posed, "let's look at how much oil we would save if we invested one hundred thousand dollars in five different ways.

"First, we could catalyze a program of door-to-door citizen action to fix up the worst buildings in a community—just basic insulation and weatherization like we've described above. Such a program was tried in Fitchburg, Massachusetts, in 1979 and has since been replicated in many other towns. In the first ten years, that investment saved one hundred seventy thousand barrels of crude oil at a cost of sixty cents a barrel, or one-and-a-half cents a gallon. That's got to be a good deal," Duncan said. Eunice nodded.

"Second," said Duncan, "you could use that hundred thousand dollars to pay the extra cost of making almost four dozen new cars get sixty miles to the gallon, using the highest published cost estimates. Over ten years those cars would save us almost six thousand barrels at about nineteen dollars a barrel."

"That's still pretty good," said Eunice.

"Sure is. Or, third," Duncan resumed, "you could buy several thousand barrels of OPEC oil, stick it in a hole in the ground, and call it a Strategic Petroleum Reserve. After ten years, if you haven't used it, it's still there, and you can probably get most of it back again. It hasn't saved you anything, but it's cost sixty or seventy bucks a barrel to store it and pay the interest on the money spent to buy it, and you can't get *that* money back."

Eunice looked puzzled. "But why," she asked, "would anyone do that?"

"Beats me," Duncan replied, "but that's just what this government has done." He grinned and continued. "Fourth, you could buy a little piece of a Colorado oil-shale plant. After ten years, it will have produced nothing. After that, if it works, it will give us a little under ten thousand barrels per decade, with a retail price of at least ninety dollars a barrel—probably one hundred twenty-odd dollars or more."

"Yes. I keep seeing headlines about oil shale in the papers," said Eunice. "They all say it has problems."

Duncan snorted cynically, "You bet it does. Like how to sell the synthetic 'oil'—if they can even get the plants to work—at several times the price at which the Arabs can't sell *their* oil.

"Last," he continued, "you could have bought a little tiny piece of the late, unlamented Clinch River Breeder Reactor. After ten years it would have produced nothing. After that, it would have given a few hundred barrels of oil-equivalent per decade, if it worked, retailing at hundreds of dollars a barrel. At that price, it couldn't even compete with today's expensive solar cells stuck on your roof."

"That's funny, Duncan," Eunice said. "The only options I've heard of among those five options are the last three, the ones you said are the worst buys."

"Well, sure," Duncan's cynicism was in high gear, "those are the ones the federal government has focused the most money and attention on; so those are the ones that got in the press. Your taxes and mine paid for pursuing them in precisely the wrong order—worst buys first. However," he smiled genuinely, "the sneaky old market is finding a way to tell us that the government has been making the wrong choices. In 1980 alone, Americans spent fifteen billion dollars on efficiency and renewables, and much more since then. Give it enough time and it will all work out."

Duncan sighed and thought for a moment. "You know," he resumed, "so far, we've touched mostly on the potential to improve the efficiency with which we use energy. Next we should talk about the renewable energy sources we could switch to as the oil and gas dwindle, and how quickly and cheaply we can get them. However," Duncan glanced at his watch, "I think we'll be much better disposed for that after we eat. Lunchtime, my dear. Your favorite hot dog stand or mine?"

9 Renewables to the Rescue

*H*OT DOG STAND, INDEED," Eunice grumbled to herself on the way back from lunch. She should have known better than to expect Duncan to take her to a standard, white-bun-and-mustard hot dog stand. No, Duncan had gone and sprung something cosmopolitan on the visitor from Iowa. What were all of those strange foods? Felafel ("feel-awful", she had pronounced it), baba ganoush, humus (she had thought that was the stuff that earthworms improved in your garden). So she had gotten to the front of the line and asked for an all-beef hot dog on a bun, mustard and relish, but hold the onions. Everyone had sort of giggled, and she had had yet another chance to be embarrassed and feel silly. But she had been brave and tried a "feel-awful," and it had tasted, well, unusual, but not too bad.

However, she consoled herself, although this energy stuff might be fairly new to her, she was becoming more comfortable with kilowatts and BTUs. More comfortable at least than she was with the bizarre things Duncan ate for lunch. As she rode up the elevator with Duncan, hoping her felafel would dutifully ride up with her, she happily put lunch behind her to resume where they had left off—renewable energy sources.

"You know, Duncan," Eunice said tentatively, "it seems to me that even if we use energy as efficiently as we can, we're still going to need *some*. I mean, even if my new showerheads use a tenth as much hot water as my old ones, I'll still have to heat that smaller quantity of water somehow. And even if you can sell me a light bulb that uses eighteen watts instead of seventy-five, those eighteen watts will have to come from *somewhere.*"

"Quite right, of course," said Duncan, pleased that she had brought the discussion around to the very topic he intended. "Besides, no matter how much we improve our energy efficiency, we can only stretch our current resources so far; the fuels in the ground will run out several times slower, but they'll still run out, or at least become very scarce and expensive. Sooner or later, existing and new demand is going to collide with dwindling supplies, even at eighteen watts per light bulb; and especially if we want to accommodate growth in population and economic activity —here or abroad—new energy sources will be needed."

"Yes," said Eunice, "that's just what I meant. Except, you know, I'm not so sure that economic activity needs to keep on swelling. I remember growing up during World War II on our family farm, and we didn't have all of these food processors and electric toothbrushes that all the TV ads say are essential. We didn't throw so much away, or buy so many things that we didn't really need. And I don't think we were worse off than people are now. At least we were happy, and our family stayed together."

"Mm, that's sort of what my parents say about the Depression," agreed Duncan. "But," he cautioned, "you and I oughtn't to be the ones to tell people what they should want or what lifestyle to choose. So let's assume, just for the sake of argument, that people will want three cars and a boat in every garage and a helicopter on the roof. That way, if people's values change, and they decide that the older, simpler pleasures are more important to them, then we'll know our analysis will still hold up, because they'll need even less energy than we'll have predicted."

"Great!" Eunice nodded vigorously.

"First," Duncan continued, "let's define some terms. "I'm going to be arguing that in the future, all we will ultimately need will be sustainable sources of energy, and no depletable ones. So, first, let me explain what I mean by that.

"A depletable resource is one that will eventually run out— typically oil, natural gas, and coal; you know, the 'fossil fuels.'

While modern-day peat bogs may eventually be transformed into higher-quality fossil fuels themselves, that process would happen *much* more slowly than the current rates at which we're digging up and burning oil and coal. So for every barrel of oil we use, there's one less barrel of oil in the ground, and thus one barrel fewer for us or our descendants to use in the future."

"Oh," Eunice said brightly, "like the time I went to visit my sister."

"Your sister?" asked Duncan, arching his eyebrows.

Eunice realized that the connection was obvious only to her. She fingered her agate pendant reflectively. "Well, when I went away to visit my sister last year, I left a full cookie jar. And my husband, Joe, bless his heart, he can take care of the kids just fine and make them breakfast and lunch and supper, but he's really not the sort to bake cookies. So the cookies were a kind of depletable resource—the number I put in the jar when I left were as many as there were going to be until I returned. For every one they ate the first few days, there was going to be one less to eat later on."

Duncan chuckled. Simple, he thought, but not a bad analogy. He resumed. "Sustainable resources, on the other hand, are resources that are limited not by how much there is now, but by the amount that flows past us each day—a flow that constantly renews itself. Hydropower—electricity we generate at dams on our rivers and streams—is limited by the rate at which rainfall in the watershed backs up water behind the dam. Windpower is limited by the speed of the wind and how long it blows at that speed. The amount of solar energy we can use each day is limited by the length of time the sun is shining. However, no matter how much solar energy we collect today, it won't affect how much there is to collect tomorrow. The solar radiation won't become scarce, at least not in the time frame bureaucrats worry about. It can't be cut off, and everyone can use it. Think of it this way: Using sustainable resources is like living off our energy salary, our regular income of energy. Every year, we know that we—and everyone else in the world—will receive about that amount of energy. I'll try to persuade you that the salary is plenty to live on if our habits aren't extravagant. Using fossil fuels, on the other hand, is like living off the trust fund that a rich aunt set up for us. As we eat into the trust fund, there's less and less left for us or our children to use in the future. That's not so serious in itself, but if we come to rely on the trust fund for our bread and butter, the danger grows that we'll go hungry when we've finally drawn the balance down to zero."

"Or, if you'll indulge my earlier comparison," said Eunice, smiling as though a trifle embarrassed, "sustainable resources are like the batch of corn muffins I bake twice a week—no matter how quickly they get eaten up, there's going to be more in a couple of days." She paused and frowned. "But which energy sources are sustainable? There are so many of them that they're hard to keep track of."

"Actually, that's one of the greatest strengths of sustainable energy sources," said Duncan. "They are amazingly diverse. And there's an even greater abundance of ways to use the different natural energy flows on this planet appropriately, efficiently, and economically. Besides, more are being discovered all the time. So you shouldn't be too upset if you lose track of them. After all, many of the specialists in the field have a hard enough time themselves. I mean, you can read publications such as *Solar Age, Renewable Energy News, Alternative Sources of Energy, Energy Design Update,* or the specialized newsletters for each technology to stay abreast of some of the new developments, but meanwhile there are legions of inventors and tinkerers out there devising new ways of using renewable energy. The whole field is moving so fast, in so many directions, that nobody can keep up with all of it.

"And," he continued, "that's another of the strengths of renewable energy technologies. Most of them are simple enough that it doesn't take any great technical expertise to design and build a renewable energy system; in fact, there are tens of millions of people in the United States—anyone who's handy with tools—who could set one up. And that means lots more people are able to contribute new ideas. That's why so many good novel ideas for harnessing natural flows of energy are emerging so quickly. Most of the technologies are so simple and accessible that it's easy to generate new ideas, revise designs, and test new prototypes, with no more than days or months between generations. Thus, technical evolution that takes decades with big, lumbering, ten-years-

to-build technologies can be compressed into a year or two. And then there are synergisms—"

"Sinner who?" interrupted a puzzled Eunice.

"Synergisms," Duncan repeated. "It means that the whole is greater than just the sum of its parts. For instance, if you insulate your house really well, you save money not just on heating bills, but also by needing a smaller furnace, or maybe none at all. And you can even use natural air currents to distribute the heat, saving further on duct work and blowers. You can then heat the house by adding a fairly small sunspace, which also lets you grow fresh food year-round. And you can then put a simple solar collector up in the top of the greenhouse to give you hot water. Inside the greenhouse it'll never freeze; so you can save even more money by avoiding the antifreeze loops and other antifrost precautions that make many outdoor solar panels complex and expensive. Anyway, such synergisms between efficiency and sustainable sources —in this example, the heat-tight house, greenhouse, and the solar panel—can be applied soon after they are discovered because the generation time between prototypes is quite short. Compare this to large-scale depletable systems such as a nuclear power plant or a refinery, where the times between generations of ideas is years to decades. This speed of evolution has enabled a wide variety of renewables to come on the market much more quickly than other flavors of technology."

"Can there be sinner-whatever-they-ares between sustainable energy and other uses?" asked Eunice. "Like using the solar greenhouse as a sewing room?"

"Sure," said Duncan, "and that's one of the most important, interesting, and hard-to-analyze features of sustainable energy sources. They can share equipment and functions with everything from a home to a fish farm. For instance, one dairy farm in Pennsylvania converts cow manure into methane gas that runs an engine to generate power to run the farm. The engine also gets hot. That waste heat is used first to make very hot water to wash down the milking parlor. Some other farmers also use waste heat from their own generators to pasteurize the milk. Then the warm water that would otherwise go down the drains is run through pipes that preheat the cows' drinking water. Warm water turns out to help cows give more milk, since they don't have to spend so much of their body energy heating up cold water. The process of digesting the manure yields a virtually germ-free bedding material. That helps keep the cows cleaner, and just the reduction in udder infections pays off the whole system in a few years. Then the used bedding material makes a superb fertilizer, displacing energy-intensive chemicals. Last I heard, that farmer was also planning to use some of the heat from his engine to run a still to produce fuel alcohol from crop wastes. He'd then use that alcohol to run his tractor." Duncan nodded at Eunice, who was grinning broadly. "Clever, huh?" he smiled. "But, you know, the more jobs the same energy system can share, the cheaper all the products become."

Duncan fell silent for a moment. Eunice waited while he thought. "It's interesting," he mused, "most sustainable sources can generally be built very simply or very elaborately or anywhere in between—ranging from shiny stainless-steel commercial equipment to backyard baling-wire rigs. What high technologists can do with a thousand-dollar anemometer—that's a gadget for measuring wind speed—and a piece of digital recording electronics can also be done about as accurately with a five-dollar calculator, the cups from two of those egg-shaped pantyhose containers, and a few bits of commonplace junk."

Eunice found herself wondering how he knew so much about pantyhose. But before she could frame a nonembarrassing way to ask, Duncan was off again.

"In fact," he continued, "a friend of mine was measuring the flow of water through solar panels with a bucket and stopwatch. Some scientists visiting him from this Department were scornful of his primitive arrangement—their labs use fancy digital flow meters costing thousands of dollars—until he told them how the National Bureau of Standards calibrates their flow meters . . . You guessed it—bucket and stopwatch!" Eunice grinned. "That liberty," Duncan added, "to make do with devices at any level of technical sophistication is far more typical of sustainable energy than of 'hard' technologies. You won't find the plans for a do-it-yourself oil-shale plant in *Popular Science.*"

"Does that mean," queried Eunice, "that the 'hard' technologies *have* to be so complicated that they're inherently very expensive?"

"It seems to work that way," Duncan confirmed. "No one has yet come up with a simple nuclear plant. But overcomplexity can be a problem with renewables, too. They can often be cheaper than they're usually designed to be. This Department once paid for an experimental wind machine—it was too big and complex to work very well—" he added parenthetically, "that had tens of thousands of dollars' worth of electronic equipment to shut it down if it started to vibrate too much, so it wouldn't tear itself apart. Later, its designers visited a much better wind machine that had been built decades earlier in Denmark. The clever Danes had a vibration-shutdown device, too: Mounted up in the tower was a saucer with a big steel ball in it. If the tower shook too much, the ball would slop out of the saucer and fall down, and a string attached to it would pull a switch."

Eunice shook with laughter. "And that worked just as well?"

"Better," remarked Duncan wryly. "The DOE/NASA electronic sensors proved unreliable, and the experimenters ended up with a closed-circuit television camera monitoring a painted film can hung from a string, so that if it swayed too much, they could shut down the wind machine manually."

"But that makes it even worse!" exclaimed Eunice. "Why are we spending so much time and money building devices that are not only too complicated, but don't even work?"

"Because many engineers nowadays," replied Duncan sadly, "can't get excited about an energy technology unless it produces a thousand megawatts, is computer-designed, uses exotic materials, takes thousands of people a decade to build, and has brass knobs all over it. Half the engineering profession has forgotten that any fool can make something complicated, but it takes genius to simplify. Backyard tinkerers know this better than most of our space-program hotshots. In fact, I'll bet you that none of our vaunted wind experts could have designed—as Karl Bergey did on an old airstrip in Oklahoma—a wind machine so simple that it could be made in a high-school auto shop, a couple of farmers could take it home in a pickup truck, put it up in a few hours with hand tools, plug it in, and walk away for probably twenty years. That wind machine is designed with an elegant economy of means —the simplest way to do the job. That's what I always thought good engineering was about, but too many engineers these days have been seduced by the sexier, more complex devices, which *they* don't have to pay for."

"But are you saying," asked Eunice, "that we'll all have to make our own wind machines and solar panels? *I* certainly wouldn't know where to start."

"Of course not," Duncan reassured her, "but you could find out how and then do it if you wanted to. On the other hand, if that's not your style, you can buy them in versions ranging from a simple device made down the street, to a slicker one—but not necessarily as clever—made across the city, to the fancy—maybe *too* fancy—one made by an aerospace company across the country. The point is that with sustainable sources, unlike the hard technologies, you can choose what level of complexity, and therefore cost, you want. And if you *want* to get involved yourself, you can. I'll bet your kids would have more fun making a breadbox water heater—especially if you split the savings with them—than regreasing the bearings on their bikes for the eighth time."

"All right," said Eunice. "But let's get down to brass tacks. Could you please tell me about some of the sustainable resources? I still don't have a clear picture of what some of the important ones look like and what they do."

"Absolutely," said Duncan. "Just realize that there are many more of them than I can describe, and even more are being invented all the time; so any list I rattle off will be necessarily incomplete."

"Incomplete or not," Eunice pressed on, "I want some idea of the sustainable options I can choose from. If there are too many for you to know where to start, why don't we just start with our biggest energy needs and work down to the smallest?"

"Admirable suggestion," conceded Duncan. "Of course, you realize that's the opposite of the way things are normally done around here. This Department spends the most effort and money —about two-thirds of its whole civilian research and development budget, in fact—on the kind of energy we use least: electricity. And it spends virtually none on the kinds we need most: heat and liquid fuels. But you're absolutely right that you and I, at least, should do it the right way around—biggest needs first. So, here goes . . . ."

10 *Hot Stuff*

ROLLING HIS SHOULDERS to loosen away the stiffness of sitting so long, Duncan nodded perfunctorily, and began. "Heat, then. That's about fifty-eight percent of all the energy we use. Three-fifths of that need in turn is for low-temperature heat—that is, below the boiling point of water—so let's start there. Most of that heat is used to heat houses when it's cold outside."

"Wait a minute," interjected Eunice. "Do we want to heat houses or the people inside them?"

"Right on!" conceded Duncan again, with some delight. "As a Japanese friend of mine once said when I asked him why he didn't heat his house, 'Why should I? Is the house cold?' You're quite right to go to the *real* end-use of the heat—to make our bodies comfortable. Indeed, often we can do that better by dressing more sensibly, or by plugging up the holes that make cold drafts blow on our feet, than by turning up the thermostat. There's even a whole book called *People Heaters*. But let's suppose we've done all that and still want to make the inside of our house warmer. Did you know that every house in the world is at least ninety-seven percent solar-heated right now?"

"What?" said Eunice. "How can that be? *My* house certainly isn't. Just look at my energy bills in January. I suppose we get a little heat through the windows, although most of it must leak right out again, but . . ." she trailed off in bewilderment.

"Simple," said Duncan. "If the sun never shone, it would be minus four hundred degrees Fahrenheit outside; so every degree above that represents a solar contribution to our heating. What we're arguing about is the last three percent or so of the heat we need. And usually it makes sense to use solar for that, too. Heat at low temperatures—say, around the seventy or so degrees Fahrenheit that makes a sedentary, lightly clothed American comfortable—is the lowest-quality, cheapest kind of energy to provide. You can collect that heat very simply, as kids do whenever they stretch out in the sun on solar-warmed rocks after swimming. You can heat your house by capturing sunlight through your windows and having windows efficient enough that the heat doesn't readily escape again, in just the same way that a closed-up car heats up sitting in the sun. Or you can collect hot air with special windows, or by trapping it between a layer of glass or plastic and a sunlit wall. You can trap heat in a sunlit masonry wall, or in a stack of water-filled drums, or in a greenhouse attached to your house. You can warm water by trickling it down a sunny sheet-metal roof. Or you can use special collecting panels that heat up water—to be used for washing and all the other things we use hot water for—and store extra hot water in an insulated tank for cloudy days. Or—"

"Isn't that the problem with solar energy," Eunice interrupted, "that the sun doesn't shine all the time? Sure, a closed car heats up during the day, but it also gets rather cold at night." Eunice assumed a confident look of having caught out her mentor.

"Not a problem," replied Duncan. "Although it's a fact to design around, just like the fact that power plants and refineries don't always work when you want them to, either. Fortunately," he smiled again at Eunice's challenge, "it's a problem that any good solar designer can solve, even in the cloudiest climates. For example, some of the newer solar collectors, instead of using water or oil or antifreeze to flow through the tubes and collect heat, use fluids like Freon that can actually gather a surprising amount of heat on completely overcast days. Even on a cloudy day, the reduced amount of light that does get through the clouds carries useful energy of high quality. Many collectors nowadays also have special coatings, called 'selective surfaces,' which help them capture solar energy even on fairly cloudy days. You can buy those coatings as paints and stick-on foils and even do pretty well just by brushing a slurry of lampblack onto a metal plate. A slightly better coating has been shown to enable a simple collector in Hamburg, Germany—around the latitude of southern Hudson Bay—to heat water by fifty-four Fahrenheit degrees on a cloudy winter day. In fact, if you built a very special kind of collector, with coatings that absorbed visible light about fifty or sixty times as well as they lost heat, and put it in a very good vacuum to reduce its heat loss, it could capture so much of the potential energy in diffuse light that on a cloudy winter day in Alaska, it could deliver heat at over a thousand degrees—and if the liquid metal you used to cool it ever stopped flowing in those conditions, the metal absorber plate would probably melt!"

Eunice wasn't sure she believed that, but it also didn't seem to matter. "Surely," she chided, "we don't need to get that fancy just to capture and store heat at gentler temperatures for a few days."

"Of course not," Duncan agreed. "I'm just correcting the common misconception that just because we don't get direct rays of strong sunshine on cloudy days, there's no capturable solar energy then at all. Fortunately, very cold days tend to be sunny, while cloudy weather tends to be milder because the clouds trap the earth's heat like a big blanket. But you're right that storage is a cheap solution, and efficiency cheaper yet; because if a house loses heat very slowly, it needs to store very little to carry it over to the next sunny period. In fact, the most efficient houses store enough heat just in their own fabric—you know, the framing, wallboard, plaster, furniture, and so on—to eliminate the need for winter backup heating without using special thermal mass."

"Thermal mess?" exclaimed Eunice. "I don't want any mess in *my* house, thank you!"

"Thermal *mass*," Duncan assured her. "It just means the materials—bricks, concrete, tile, water-filled drums or bottles, rocks, or whatever—that soak up solar heat on sunny days and slowly release it into the building at night or in cloudy periods. It's the same as a cast-iron pot of beans that stays warm for a long time after you turn off the stove. Conversely, the thermal mass of a house will store the cool of the evening through hot summer afternoons."

"Oh," sighed Eunice in some relief. "So it's not messy at all. And in a solar house, can I also get a hot bath after it's been cloudy for a week?"

"If your house is designed to do that, sure," said Duncan. "And the less hot water your showers and other fixtures need to get you wet, the longer a given amount of stored hot water will last. Essentially, every solar water heater stores heat at least overnight, which is why the solar water heaters that were so popular in California and Florida in the 1890s had brand names like 'Day and Night.' "

"The 1890s!" gasped Eunice. "Do you mean people used solar energy back then?"

"Better than that," said Duncan, grinning. "Not only did thirty percent of the houses in, say, Pasadena, California, use excellent solar water heaters in 1897, but most of the solar technologies we think are so new—everything from solar steam engines to solar cells to make electricity directly—are anywhere from a century to millenia old. If you want, I'll get you an amazing book called *A Golden Thread: 2500 Years of Solar Architecture and Technology.* It shows how we're all just reinventing a very old wheel—because, in the rush to burn up all that apparently cheap oil and gas, we forgot about the sun." He scribbled himself a note as he continued. "Even solar dishes to concentrate the sun's rays to make very high temperatures are very old indeed; Archimedes used them to ignite the sails of the enemy fleet at the Battle of Syracuse."

"Uh," Eunice interrupted, noting Duncan's faraway look. "Weren't we talking about my hot bath on a cloudy day?"

"Yes, of course. Sorry. Let's see," he found his place again, "many solar water heaters store only a few days' hot water, and use a small heater—usually gas or electric, but sometimes wood or your old oil furnace—to provide backup. Some solar experts, however, think it's even cheaper to have a *very* big and very well-insulated storage tank that will hold weeks' or even months' worth of heat, because then you'll never need either the fuel or the equipment to provide that backup. Such large tanks lose less heat, cost less per gallon to build, and have other advantages. And some of the niftiest and cheapest solar water heaters have a built-in tank right on top of the solar panel—insulated, of course. These "integral storage" heaters, using that Freon I mentioned to transfer heat from the panel into the water, are freezeproof and can be plumbed right into your existing hot-water system without needing any pumps or controls."

"I don't like pumps and pipes and things that go bump in the night, especially when they stop going bump and start spraying nasty water all over my rugs and I have to call the plumber," grumbled Eunice.

"Well," shrugged Duncan, "that Freon system's your ticket, then."

Eunice thought a moment. "But what if I want something *really* simple?" she asked, "and really cheap?"

"Well, you really might want to get your kids to build you one of those 'breadbox' heaters I mentioned," Duncan suggested. "It's just a drum—like an old water-heater tank rescued from the junkyard, leak-tested, and spray-painted black—installed in an insulated box. You put a clear front of glass or plastic on the box and set it up facing south. It just sits there and heats up, like those first spurts of hot water you get when you start using a garden hose that's been sitting out in the sun. However, breadbox heaters and other types that just heat up a batch of water sitting in a tank in the sun are designed to capture and hold heat, not to water your lawn; so they work much better than a hose. Some people, including millions of Japanese, use an even simpler model—just a big, black plastic bladder that sits up on the roof. You fill up the bladder with a garden hose in the morning and drain it into the bathtub at night. Now, these various 'passive' water heaters may not give you *all* the hot water you need, unless you live in a very sunny climate and use most of your hot water in the afternoons and evenings. But they can certainly put a hefty dent in your hot-water bill, and they're so simple that practically anyone who knows which end of a wrench to use can build one that will work well.

"In fact," Duncan continued reflectively, "there's a way to capture solar heat—up to at least the boiling point of water—while storing it at the same time, and it's so simple you might not believe it . . . unless you fell in."

"Fell into what?" Eunice asked.

"A solar pond," replied Duncan.

"Now you're going to tell me that it's just like a duck pond, only with little suns paddling around in it," objected Eunice.

"No, but it's almost that simple. A solar pond is just a big, waterproofed hole in the ground, filled up with a super salty brine that has somewhat fresher, lighter water floating on top to insulate it. Sunlight heats up the bottom of the pond, and a pipe or two lets you collect the heat stored in the brine."

"Doesn't the hot water rise to the top and lose all its heat, just like happens to my cup of hot coffee?" asked Eunice.

"Good! No!" Duncan nodded in delight at his clever student. "That's the beauty of it. The brine is so full of salt that it's too heavy to rise. And if the pond is designed properly, the hotter the brine gets at the bottom, the more the salt dissolves into it; so the heavier it gets and the more it stays right where it is."

"That's pretty smart," marveled Eunice, "and I suppose it could work out in the desert someplace. But surely it won't work in the winter, or if it's cloudy."

"A lot of people assumed that," Duncan continued, "until the town of Miamisburg, Ohio—which is plenty cold and cloudy in the winter—built a solar pond to heat the municipal swimming pool. To their surprise, even in a very cold and cloudy spell when ice formed on top of the pond, the brine at the bottom stayed at eighty-three degrees. And we now know that a bigger pond, or one designed better, would hold heat even hotter and longer than that."

"And if they can do that in Ohio," Eunice exclaimed, "I'll bet they can do it in Dubuque. Wait till I tell Joe! He's always griping about the trouble they have keeping the pool warm at the 'Y.' "

"As Ohio goes, so goes the nation," Duncan said, grinning.

"Is it anything like that simple," Eunice asked, her interest piqued, "to provide really hot solar heat, say, for an industry?"

"Not quite," admitted Duncan, chuckling a little at her description of heat, "but simpler than you might think. The most common method is to concentrate the sunlight with molded plastic lenses, mirrors, reflective troughs, or reflective dishes that track the sun and focus it onto piping that collects the heat into steam or hot oil. You can then store the heat in materials ranging from synthetic oils to scrap iron and from rocks to molten salt or metal. The principle is just the same as using a magnifying glass for wood burning—"

"Oh, yes, we once started a fire that way when I was in the Brownies," added Eunice helpfully.

"—but of course on a bigger scale. Still, all this needn't be more complex than an ordinary boiler, because although you have to collect the sunlight and get it into some kind of fluid to move the heat around, you don't need to handle a fuel or dispose of ash and flue gas. You can even concentrate sunlight to make temperatures of hundreds of degrees without tracking the sun's path if you design the collector right. Or there are very simple trackers that correct their own position automatically, without even needing electricity for little motors to move them around. Anyway, reliable trackers are common these days—every airport radar uses them—and by following the sun, they can give you the maximum possible energy output as long as the sun's above the horizon."

Eunice was looking a little lost, so Duncan added, "Some effective collectors of high-temperature solar heat are surprisingly easy to build. A little company in Tacoma, Washington, for example, has developed a big, dish-shaped collector with lots of little mirrors arranged on a domelike framework of pipes. The framework comes in a color-coded kit, and anyone, even without being able to read the directions, can assemble it quickly. Such a dish has made very competitive electricity running a steam engine on Washington's cloudy Olympic Peninsula, one of the worst solar climates in the country. And as a source of industrial heat, the dish is cheaper than burning oil in an industrial boiler today. You can also make competitive industrial heat covering solar troughs or little dishes with aluminized plastic film instead of glass mirrors. In fact, there's an Israeli entrepreneur who sells solar heat—not collectors, but heat. If you want steam for your textile mill or whatever, he'll set up solar troughs to make the steam in your factory's backyard. He'll charge you a bit less than you were paying for steam before, and he laughs all the way to the bank—because his solar heat is *much* cheaper."

"How hot can solar heat get?" asked Eunice.

"A lot hotter than you'd have any use for," replied Duncan. "Commercially available collectors go as high as twenty-six hundred degrees Fahrenheit, while experimental solar furnaces—using lots of mirrors all aimed at the same point—can instantly vaporize diamonds, or anything else. So they get much hotter than you'd need, say, to make bricks or ceramics or steel."

"And do they work on cloudy days, too?" Eunice persisted.

"No. Such 'concentrating collectors' need enough direct sunlight to cast a shadow; so they won't work all the daytime hours. That's why you'd want to store the heat, as I said before. On the other hand, if you insist on firing your pottery kiln on a cloudy day, you can always burn fuel to do so." Duncan caught Eunice's puzzled look at the word 'fuel.' "Sustainable fuel, of course—which we'll get to shortly. Don't worry, Madam Secretary, you'll soon be tossing these terms around with the best snow artists in these corridors."

"You know," Eunice said, furrowing her brow at all of these new technologies she hadn't heard of before, "aren't some of the simpler sources of energy sustainable, besides solar? I keep hearing about people who heat their houses with wood. That's a sustainable resource, too, isn't it?"

"Oh, yes, of course," said Duncan. "Sorry for getting carried away with all the technological toys. You know, once upon a time I used to be as much of a technotwit as Hobart."

Eunice gasped slightly. Could this tanned, stylish man have emerged, butterflylike, from the shell of a mere Hobart?

"Um, however," Duncan added quickly, "that's a part of my dim past we can get into later. Anyway, wood. Wood is one of the most ancient of sustainable resources and is getting steadily more popular these days. The paper and pulp industries already get nearly two-thirds of their energy from wood waste, and there are more than ten million iron wood-burning stoves in the United States. Remember, the energy in wood is just another form of solar energy: Trees convert sunlight, water, minerals, and carbon dioxide in the air, through the process of photosynthesis, into the wood we burn. When we burn wood, it's that stored solar energy that we're using; it's just energy that's been left to season for a while, rather than what's shining on us at the instant it's used.

"However," Duncan warned, "wood is not necessarily a sustainable resource. Certainly, it renews at a given rate each year, as trees sprout and grow, and people in many societies harvest the wood from dead, fallen, or old trees without affecting the forests' capacities to rebound and produce more wood. But wood can be used unsustainably, too. When American pioneers cleared the frontier, they cut down and burned old-growth forests, leaving bare ground in its place. In their wake grew smaller forests— or, in some cases, no forests. The pioneers thought the wilderness was almost endless. But in reality they were eating into the 'trust fund' of forest that they found, thus reducing the annual income they could derive from it. A similar change occurred in Great Britain when the great forests were cut and burned during the Industrial Revolution. There actually followed a wood-energy crisis that was part of the cause for switching to coal. Earlier, the Roman Empire had gone through the same thing; they'd even brought in wood from distant lands to heat their baths—until they ran out. You used to be able, Herodotus said, to walk entirely across North Africa without leaving the shade of trees, but deforestation and overgrazing changed it all to desert. The cedars of Lebanon, the whole garden of the Mediterranean, got cut down."

Duncan frowned. "Some of the problems of burning wood faster than it grows up again are more subtle. When forests are clear-cut, the topsoil erodes because there's too little groundcover left to hold it in place. In truth, for most of the world's people, the real energy crisis is not a shortage of oil, but of wood. More than a third of the world's people depend on it for their daily energy, and worldwide, wood provides about as much energy as oil. But the world's forests are disappearing. Many of the tropical rain forests are being destroyed, and some people estimate that in huge areas of Latin America, Africa, and Asia, much of the forest will be gone by the year 2000. Already, there are many areas where people have to walk dozens of miles to find wood for their cooking fires."

"But that's terrible!" Eunice said. "What can those poor people do?"

"It's tough," Duncan replied. "Clearly, they will have to switch to some other fuel, or use their dwindling supplies more efficiently, say with improved clay stoves many times less wasteful than open fire. But overhauling all the stove-related traditions isn't easy, and fuel switching, meanwhile, would put more pressure on limited stocks of oil."

"But couldn't they plant more trees?"

"Yes, and it is truly vital that people do that, especially in firewood-short regions. But even if the trees are replanted by thousands of idealistic Jane and Johnny Appleseeds, in some areas it will be scores of years before the land can again support as lush and productive a forest as it once did, assuming the soil hasn't washed away meanwhile. However, that said, there are some very good reforestation programs around the world. In China and Korea, the area of forested land is increasing. And New England actually has more woods now than it had a hundred years ago when it was heavily farmed."

"So, what you're saying," pondered Eunice, "is that as long as we don't cut down more trees than will grow back, burning wood is okay. I must say, I rather like a roaring blaze in the fireplace on a cold winter night."

"How shall I break this to you, Eunice?" asked Duncan. "A crackling open fire from time to time is great, but it won't heat your house. It'll make you feel all warm and cozy while you sit in front of it, but fireplaces suck drafts up the chimney so that they may actually cool the house that they're meant to warm."

"What?" exclaimed Eunice. "That can't be. It *feels* so warm."

"Here, let me explain how that happens," rejoined Duncan. "A fire needs air to keep burning, right?" Eunice nodded. "And usually, in old fireplaces, the air comes from the room, and it's at room temperature. But when it burns in the fireplace and goes up the chimney, it has to be replaced, or there would soon be no air left in the house. So air starts flowing into the house through all of the cracks along the baseboards, underneath the doors, and so on. This air is at the outside temperature—thirty degrees, say. So the people sitting in front of the fire may feel warm, but the rest of the house will wind up cooler than it was before. And most of the heat from those pretty flames goes up the chimney anyway."

"Are you saying I can't use my fireplace anymore?" asked Eunice, looking alarmed.

"Of course not. You just need to use it wisely. Fireplaces should have holes or pipes leading to the outside, so they can draw their combustion air right from the outdoors without first using it to chill the house. And glass doors in front of the fireplace can keep the drafts out and still preserve that romantic fireplace feeling." Duncan got a dreamy look in his eye for a brief moment. "But of course," he resumed, "the most efficient way to burn wood is in the airtight wood stoves that are on the market now—good, heavy, cast-iron or stone or ceramic stoves that let you stoke up a fire that will last the whole night through. The slow burning gets the most out of the wood, but it can also create a terrible pall of smoke, which has led some communities to limit the number of wood stoves people can have. If these towns were really smart, though, they'd just require superinsulated houses before installing wood stoves, or even the same sort of emission control devices that cars have: catalytic converters for the stovepipes, which not only reduce pollution but actually increase the amount of usable heat at the same time."

"Sounds great. But why doesn't everyone have one, then?" Eunice asked.

"Oh, for the same reason that some people are still driving gas-guzzlers when they could be driving more economical models of the same size and superior styling. It just takes time for word to get around, and it costs money to switch."

"Yes," said Eunice, "maybe we could figure out a way to make energy wisdom a fad, like hula hoops. Then it would really take off. . . . Wait a minute," she continued. "Aren't you tiptoeing around something important? Isn't it possible that the reason people haven't been switching to solar heating in droves is that it costs too much?"

"Well, I *do* call a million American solar buildings, ten million wood stoves, and figures such as twelve percent of water heating in Japan and more than half in Israel done by solar energy today 'switching in droves,' " protested Duncan. "But you've raised the next key point: How much does solar heat really cost, and can it compete? So let me do my best to answer these questions. But before that, you need to know that there's no simple answer."

"Why not?" complained Eunice. "The nuclear boys seem to have simple answers; they just tell me their technology will save everyone pots of money."

"Simple, clear, and wrong," said Duncan. "But let's stick to solar right now. One reason it's hard to quote a single price for, say, solar water heating is that three factors can change that price by about ten- to a thousandfold. One is how smart and simple— or stupid and complicated—the design is. Another is how it's marketed. A solar panel that's made in a factory, sold to a wholesaler, resold to a retailer, and finally sold to you by an installer can have so many markups that it costs two or three times as much as a collector that the same installer assembles from scratch on your roof. It's no wonder that solar prices aren't uniform. Solar collectors, after all, are more diverse in how they're built and sold than, for example, gas water heaters, whose installed price—for exactly the same device, mind you, installed in identical apartments in the same town—can vary by twofold or more, depending on the skill and profit margin of the individual contractor."

"What's the third main source of price variation?" asked Eunice.

"As we've said, efficiency. A superinsulated house can work better with a very small, simple, cheap solar system than a sieve-like house would work with a complex system ten or twenty times the size and cost. Solar systems aren't just black boxes to be plunked down on your roof; they're an integral part of a complete heating system that should start with very efficient use of the energy being supplied."

"I know," said Eunice wearily. "I think I've got that point."

"But at the risk of belaboring it," said Duncan gently, "please remember that it's at the root of solar and indeed all energy economics. Every kind of solar system is *much* cheaper if we buy efficiency first than if we don't. So nobody, including me, can quote you a solar price unless you first tell me how efficiently you're going to use the energy."

"Let's try," said Eunice, "or we'll go around in circles forever. What would it cost me, for example, to use solar heat in my old house, once I've plugged up the obvious leaks and improved the insulation a bit?"

"In *very* round numbers," said Duncan warily, "you can do it, for example, by adding a sunspace, and the heat will cost you perhaps one-and-a-half to about eight dollars per million BTUs. Even the higher end of this range," Duncan moved to answer her blank look, "is generally cheaper than heating with gas, certainly cheaper than oil, and several times cheaper than electric heat."

"But what if it's really cloudy where I live? Does that mean the sunspace will be even more expensive?" asked Eunice. "And will it still work?"

"It certainly will work," Duncan replied. "A cloudy climate just means that the sunspace has to be bigger and better insulated to deliver the same average amount of heat to the rest of the house. The cost would then be near the high end of the range I mentioned —closer to eight dollars than to one-and-a-half. And if you design the sunspace to capture and hold heat really well, to allow for a lot of cloudiness, you may need to open the vents or windows to let excess heat escape on sunny days."

"But you haven't really answered my original question," Eunice persisted. "How do I know if my solar heat will cost me a dollar and a half or eight dollars per million BTUs? That's a pretty big spread."

"Well, it depends on the climate," Duncan said, "on how the sunspace has to be built, on how cheaply you can get the materials, and on whether you do it yourself or hire someone to do it for you. Some farmers in southern Colorado installed those sunspaces for an average of only about two hundred dollars for an entire greenhouse, using a lot of materials they salvaged from the dump. That translated to a cost of less than a dollar per million BTUs. Certainly, having a contractor do the work would cost more. Or you could have it done all in redwood with walnut trim and fancy blinds, and it would be outrageously expensive; but then you'd have to put some of that cost down to interior decorating, not to energy efficiency. You know, you might want to do it anyway. Greenhouses are so fashionable now, and for good reason—it's wonderful to sit there in February munching fresh tomatoes or papayas." Eunice blinked, getting used to the idea of fresh papayas in Dubuque. "I know one guy who asked his architect to design a large greenhouse to add onto his classic New England house. He wanted it two stories high, with a balcony, a hot tub, a spiral staircase, and a jungle. The architect drew it up and hesitatingly said that it would cost twenty thousand dollars. The guy shrugged; he'd expected that. Then the architect added, 'And it'll pay for itself in twelve years from the energy savings.' My friend was dumbfounded. 'You mean I'm even going to make money on this?' he asked. He hadn't even thought about saving energy. He just wanted a greenhouse to improve his quality of life."

"Humph," was Eunice's reaction. Duncan watched as she rolled the thought of a greenhouse around her housewifely brain. "Hmm," she concluded, nodding. "Well, that's pretty straightforward. The costs are sort of fuzzy but reasonable, and it sounds like I can pretty well choose how much I want to pay. How do the costs look for other kinds of solar heat?"

"Let's take water heating for example," Duncan continued. He guessed Joe would soon be pricing greenhouses. "A batch water heater, like the breadbox heater I mentioned, delivers hot water at about two to six dollars per million BTUs, or a fifth to a half of what a gas water heater would cost. In a really cold or cloudy climate, you may do better with flat-plate collectors like the ones you often see on people's roofs—thin boxes with black metal plates inside and glass over the front. Many of those flat-plate systems—by the time you get through with a separate tank, pumps, controls, installation charges, and so forth—cost a hefty ten to thirty dollars per million BTUs. That's not as bad as shale oil or nuclear electricity, but that price might keep you from rushing out and doing it today. Fortunately, some of the simpler models, such as the Freon-filled panels with their own integral storage tank on top, are much cheaper—down to around five to fifteen dollars per million BTUs, depending on how you pay for them. The solar pond in Ohio delivered heat at about nine dollars per million BTUs, which is like . . ." his fingers played over the buttons of his calculator, ". . . let's see, burning oil costing only seventy-five cents a gallon in a pretty efficient furnace. It's hard to find oil that cheap these days."

"How about the higher-temperature collectors you talked about, like those needed for industry?" Eunice inquired.

"Several of the concentrating collectors on the market can deliver heat at four or five hundred degrees at five to ten dollars per million BTUs. That's roughly competitive with most fuels today, and certainly with electricity. A few kinds of concentrators look even cheaper. And even the costlier kinds will become very competitive if they're mass-produced, especially types using inherently cheap materials such as reflective plastic and strong, bright foils. All in all, solar heat at all temperatures isn't necessarily cheap, but it's generally cheaper than using the hard technologies, and many people are able to purchase their systems because of the tax credits."

"Yes," said Eunice, "I keep hearing about these tax credits. But you know, you haven't mentioned them yet in this discussion. Are you just bringing them up now because the numbers won't work out otherwise?"

"Now don't be cynical, Eunice," Duncan teased. "As long as we're comparing costs, these tax credits do deserve mention. Indeed, in the late 1970s the federal government and some states began giving tax credits—not just a deduction from your income, but an outright cut in the taxes you owed—if you bought most kinds of solar systems before the end of 1985. Now, to some people that looks like a subsidy, and it is—it's an incentive to buy solar equipment. Incentives," said Duncan, grinning, "sound nicer than subsidies but cost the same. But," he held up a warning finger, "as we'll see later, every part of the energy industry—coal, oil, nuclear—gets great tax benefits and subsidies of one sort or another. So I would argue that the solar tax credits are just providing a more nearly 'level playing field,' letting all energy technologies compete by the same rules. We'll come back to this point, but for now just take note that with the federal tax credit, the cost of even fancy flat-plate solar systems dropped to six to eighteen dollars per million BTUs—much more competitive. And interestingly enough, even *un*subsidized solar systems, decently designed, compete handily on a cost per BTU basis with *subsidized* but nonetheless even more costly systems such as nuclear power and synthetic fuels."

Eunice nodded as she considered. "I'd like," she said, "to see an analysis of how all the different energy systems are subsidized and how they'd stack up if they all had to compete without subsidies."

Duncan laughed cynically. "Yeah, me too," he said. "But you know, no such analysis exists. I just got the preliminary results of one that—let's see—Rocky Mountain Institute is working on . . ." he rummaged through his desk. ". . . showing that just in fiscal year 1984 the federal subsidy for supplying all kinds of energy exceeded forty-six billion dollars, of which under two billion went to all the renewable sources combined. But those kinds of figures have never been analyzed officially in any detail. The analysts in this Department will be the last to do it because they don't want anyone to know how much energy is paid for by tax dollars—especially the costliest forms of energy, such as nuclear power. It might interest you to know that the tax subsidies for building nuclear plants are already so big that you and I and all the other taxpayers effectively finance their construction at a negative interest rate. Hobart just figured that one out this week."

Eunice recoiled in shock. "You mean *we* pay *them* to build those plants?"

"Yup. But it's one of the best-kept secrets in this town. In fact, if you also count all the money this Department is spending on trying to solve the unsolved problems left after thirty years and more than seventy billion dollars of R&D subsidies already, new nuclear power is subsidized by over seventy percent. If it weren't subsidized, it would cost more than three times as much as it now appears to cost. That's the sort of 'competition' that solar energy, with generally smaller subsidies, is swimming upstream against. To put it less delicately, this country has spent close to two hundred billion dollars—and it'll be twice that before we're through —trying to develop and deploy nuclear energy; and for all that, with some of our best technical talent, we've gotten a source that's uneconomical just to operate, even if building it were free, and that is now delivering only about half as much energy as wood. Rarely has so much been spent by so many for so little. And all solar energy can get is the leftover crumbs from the nuclear feast." Duncan shook his head in some disgust while catching his breath.

"Well, let's carry on anyhow," said Eunice cheerfully, "because it's going to be part of my job to do something about that bias. But let me get this straight. Are you saying that in purely economic terms, the methods of solar heating you've mentioned can work well anywhere in the United States—or, I suppose, abroad too—and that they're already cheaper, even without subsidies, than many sources we're spending billions of tax dollars on right now?"

"You got it," answered Duncan. "Of course, how you design the solar system and what it costs will depend very much on local conditions. Greenhouses heat better, and tend to overheat more readily, in New Mexico than in New Hampshire, and a house in northern Canada may need better windows to keep warm than one in Georgia; but that's a matter of degree, not of impossibility or of basic economics."

"Speaking of Georgia," said Eunice, recalling a sweltering trip to her Aunt Lillian's place one August, "what about cooling? You can't tell me that solar heat can keep us cool, too?" She looked a trifle gleeful, as if she were trumping Duncan's ace.

"Yes, in fact, I can," Duncan replied with equal glee. "And it's not even too difficult," he explained. "For instance, in places where it freezes, like the East Coast, you can dig and insulate an ice pond

—yes, I'm just as serious as I was about the solar pond. You make ice in the winter with a snow machine and then use that to chill air-conditioning water in the summer. They did it at Princeton; my old adviser, Ted Taylor, thought it up. And Prudential, the big insurance company, even built a big office building cooled by an ice pond. The investment is solid as a rock, with an energy cost about one-tenth what a conventional air-conditioning system would be. If Prudential hadn't spent scads of money putting up an unnecessary building around the pond to hide it, it would have been a really good buy.

"And where it doesn't freeze, like in the Southwest," he continued, "the local architecture usually takes care of the problem. The Spanish, you know, didn't build adobes just for the aesthetics. The brick and adobe soak up the coolness of the night air, then keep the house from heating up too much in the daytime. These days you can also achieve the same results with more conventional building materials and designs that are more familiar to easterners. 'Passive cooling,' it's called, and at a fifth or a tenth the price of electricity, it's a lot cheaper than running an air conditioner. For example, you can cut the cooling needs of a Houston home to less than a fifth the usual amount, just by such simple measures as shading the windows, venting the attic, insulating the roof and adding a layer of foil under it to reflect heat away, reducing the leakage of humid air into the house, making the roof a light color, and installing a really efficient air conditioner."

"Wouldn't such a house look odd?" quizzed Eunice.

"Actually, to look at it, you'd never know the difference, except that it might look like an unusually tasteful and well-landscaped home. Passive cooling measures are especially easy to design into a new building or the surrounding landscape. Thermal mass can be a cool concrete or tile floor, and vents can adjust natural air circulation either automatically or manually. Overhangs can block out the sun when it's high in the summer sky, but let it through in the winter when the sun is low. Deciduous trees planted in front will shade the house in summer and lose their leaves when heating season approaches. In general, the more vegetation in an area, the cooler it will stay; conversely, the more asphalt and concrete there is around, the hotter it will get. These common-sense cooling measures, in sum, add so little to the cost of a house that they can sometimes have a *negative* cost of electricity saved, since mechanical air conditioners may not be necessary. Besides, they'll make the house and the neighborhood more liveable."

"What you're describing," Eunice mused, "sounds so simple that I wouldn't call it solar at all."

"You're largely right," Duncan agreed. "In fact, a lot of solar design is just good common sense. We've been so spoiled by cheap energy that many architects and builders forgot that. But they're relearning. And it takes some getting used to. For instance, good solar cooling means *avoiding* solar heat, not courting it. And of course it also means having very efficient lights and appliances—sorry, here comes that efficiency again—to help keep the house from heating up through its internal heat gains. But if you really want active solar cooling, there are gadgets coming on the market to do that, too. The world's most efficient conventional air conditioner is powered largely by solar cells. It's made by a Vietnamese engineer in Florida. Several firms, mainly Japanese, sell some very attractive solar chillers that use solar heat from panels to drive special cooling devices. For example, there are materials that draw water out of the air and thereby chill it, then have the water driven off to the outside air by applying solar heat. These sorts of devices are becoming increasingly competitive, in places ranging from Phoenix to San Antonio to Jamaica."

"Well, all right," said Eunice, "I guess I'm willing to concede that you can heat and cool a house economically, using only renewable resources. And I suppose if it still takes a tiny bit of electricity or fuel, you'll tell me later how to get that from the sun, too?" Duncan nodded his confirmation. "And I suppose you'll say that solar heat for industry either competes with new fuel and power supplies right now or will do so in the next few years, depending on local fuel prices and climate."

"Exactly," said Duncan. "In fact, I wish I'd said that."

"Which means," continued Eunice, "that solar energy can ultimately provide most or all of the heat we need, which you said," she rifled back through her notes, "was more than half of the total energy needs of the United States."

Duncan kept on nodding approvingly.

Eunice gulped, getting used to the novel notion that there is life after oil. "Well, I think in that case," she added defiantly, "we'd better start looking at the other half of the energy we need. Because if you can convince me I can drive a solar car, fly back to Dubuque in a solar airplane, and watch a solar-powered television, I'll be a solar monkey's aunt."

11 On the Road Again

UM, CAREFUL THERE," Duncan warned, chuckling. "You might just be closer to your simian ancestors than you think."

"Oh, Duncan," Eunice chided, "solar cars? Come on!"

"Sure," Duncan shrugged. "And, analytically, you're right to want to consider liquid fuels for vehicles right after heat. Running vehicles is our second-largest energy need—it uses about thirty-four percent of all delivered energy. But if you thought there were too many solar heat technologies to keep convenient track of," he continued with an impish glint in his eye, "you'll think solar-derived liquid fuels are a real zoo. There are just an awful lot of combinations of possibilities. You need to decide what 'feedstock' —sun-grown materials—to start with, how to convert it into a liquid fuel, which kind of liquid fuel to make, and how to use it. Many of the most interesting-looking combinations haven't even been researched yet. But I'll try to give you a summary of what systems are now available. Keep in mind, though, that in this area above all, the best is yet to come; it's still in the labs or in small-scale testing." Duncan shook his head as he thought of possibilities.

Eunice, however, merely looked bewildered. So, lest he lose her, Duncan added, "Yeah, there's lots to come. But we already appear to have enough farm and forestry wastes to make, with presently available processes, enough sustainable liquid fuels to run an efficient transportation system in this country. The cost? Pretty close to today's, and certainly below the cost of the synthetic fuels that are supposed to replace conventional oil in the long run. And it also appears that running our vehicles will become even cheaper and easier with new technologies now well along in development. So prepare to meet thy monkeyhood."

Eunice sat in wide-eyed attention; so Duncan jumped in.

"Let's start with the kinds of liquid fuels that can be made," he said. "Most of the time we hear about ethanol—ethyl alcohol, the kind used in liquor—but of course of a grade that burns well, not one that tastes good. Ethanol has thirty percent less energy per gallon than gasoline, but in return it burns better and cleaner; so it can reduce maintenance and air pollution and make up for its lower energy content by greater efficiency. Ethanol is also, in general, the costliest 'biofuel'—liquid fuel derived from biomass—to make."

"What's biomass?" asked Eunice. "Is it anything like thermal mass?"

"No, no," laughed Duncan. "Not at all. Biomass is a catchall term for anything that grows by photosynthesis and that's available to be converted into fuels. The main kinds are logging wastes and crop wastes. Wood and crops also qualify, although we generally have better uses for them. Some people would also include garbage, since most of it is paper and other organic materials.

"And that brings us to another, cheaper kind of alcohol—namely, methanol, also known as methyl alcohol or wood alcohol," Duncan resumed. "It's made not by fermentation of sugary material like corn, but by chemical reactions that usually involve heating woody materials. It's poisonous; so it has to be handled in ways that control fumes—for example, by using locking couplings on our gas tanks just as commercial aircraft do. Methanol has about half as much energy per gallon as gasoline, but it burns so well, especially in high-compression engines, that the extra efficiency can make up part or all of the difference. Methanol, by the way, is generally cheaper to make than ethanol. And you can use it in your car if you've made sure that the rubber and plastic parts of your fuel system won't dissolve in methanol and if you take some simple precautions against rust."

"Does anyone use methanol or ethanol in cars today?" asked Eunice dubiously.

"Yes—in fact, there's a fair chance you did in Dubuque," he replied. "Five percent of all the gasoline sold in 1984 was blended with biomass ethanol—that turns out to be a better way to boost octane than using lead, which makes us all even stupider than we are already. A ten percent ethanol blend is widely marketed in the Midwest under the trade name Gasohol; Henry Ford was enthusiastic about ethanol in the early days of motorcars, and it's coming back now. In fact, it's such a well-understood technology that around 1937, alcohol blended in the fuel of four million cars was providing eighteen percent of all the motor fuel in Europe. Some cars, today, including nearly all the new ones in Brazil, burn pure ethanol. Methanol is also used in some fleet cars and has been a premium fuel for racing-cars for decades.

"The list of liquid fuels from biomass, however, doesn't stop there. Some more complex kinds of alcohols make a good fuel blend with ethanol or methanol or both. Folks in Brazil and North Dakota have figured out simple solar 'cookers' to make liquids called 'esters,' which can be a better diesel fuel than diesel fuel. You make esters out of ethanol or methanol—even dirty, wet batches that couldn't readily be used directly as fuel—and most kinds of vegetable oil, including inedible kinds." Duncan's eyes really began to twinkle. "Did you know that some farmers burn vegetable oils directly in their tractors, with excellent results? Or that the *copaiba* tree in Brazil can be tapped, just like a rubber tree, to yield a directly usable motor fuel—just like getting gasoline out of a tree? There are many other kinds of plants, such as a huge family called *Euphorbiaeceae,* that yield a variety of big molecules like resins and 'terpenes,' which in turn can be refined into motor fuels. Such plants can grow anywhere from a rain forest to a desert; so they're getting a lot of attention as potential sources of fuel grown on land unsuitable for normal farming. And just cooking most kinds of woody materials with little or no air—a process called 'pyrolysis'—can yield, in the right conditions, a heavy, oily liquid—a mixture of chemical fragments called 'pyrolysates'—that can be used as a fuel in many kinds of engines. It's essentially condensed wood smoke.

"In fact, even my varied menu of biofuel options has left out a lot of exciting possibilities. Just to mention a few, you can run diesel engines on finely ground wood flour, as experimenters in Sweden have been doing for years. You can operate cars, not on liquid fuels, but on compressed natural gas, such as biogas, as hundreds of thousands of drivers are now doing around the world. For instance, Modesto, California, boasts that it is the first city to gain independence from gasoline. It now runs its municipal vehicle fleet on methane from its sewage treatment plant. The methane is produced at a cost equivalent to gasoline at something like fifty cents per gallon. Some scientists believe that a few special feedstocks grown in a few places—Minnesota cattails, for example, or southwestern mesquite, or high-latitude fast-growing trees, or even kelp grown off the California coast in vast floating beds—could satisfy our liquid-fuel needs, assuming efficient use, without needing to use crop wastes at all!"

Eunice sat dumbfounded. "That's quite a rich menu," she finally managed. "Are these fuels compatible with the kinds of vehicles we use today?"

"Generally, yes," Duncan replied. "Some of these biofuels can be used directly in unmodified cars. Some others require minor modifications—to the carburetor, timing, and so on—that can cost up to a few hundred dollars if done to existing cars, or nothing if done at the factory. Many California fleet cars have already been converted to burn pure methanol—usually made from natural gas —because it's cheaper and cleaner than gasoline. And we can even design into new cars the flexibility to burn a variety of fuels. It's well known, for example, how to make carburetors with a little switch that can be set for gasoline, Gasohol, or pure ethanol. In general, diesels need different fuels than gasoline engines, but even alcohols burn very well in spark-ignited diesel engines if a little lubrication is provided."

"How about airplanes?" Eunice asked.

"They can use most of the fuels I've described. In fact, President Reagan's former pilot and an ex-astronaut flew a methanol-powered light plane across the country and found that above ten thousand feet their cheap fuel actually performed better per gallon —because of their piston engine's high compression ratio—than aviation fuel. There are methanol-powered jet aircraft on the drawing boards and even some experimental designs using liquid hydrogen. Hydrogen, by the way, can be made out of water and electricity, and may—if some speculative research pays off—be produced just from water, sunlight, and a catalyst."

"You said ethanol is the best-known biofuel today. How is it made?" asked Eunice.

Duncan grinned and replied, "Well, it's not too different from making moonshine or applejack; the equipment can be bigger or fancier, but the principle is the same. You just ferment any sugary or starchy material, then increase the 'proof' of the ethanol-water mixture. The fermentation can be done on the scale of a backyard moonshiner or that of a big brewery. If you're starting with a woody material, such as logging wastes, you can even use hot acid to break the wood down into a sugary soup that you can then ferment into ethanol. The really interesting technologies are the ones that let us separate the ethanol from most or all of the water without using much energy. Stills have been vastly improved. A few years ago it took fifty or a hundred thousand BTUs to distill a gallon of ethanol to one hundred ninety proof—that is, only five percent water—but the best new stills use only twenty-five thousand BTUs to go to completely dry, or anhydrous, ethanol. Even better processes do the same thing with two-thirds less energy than that, and some even more efficient ones are now in experimental use. So the old belief that making ethanol takes more energy than it delivers is just not true."

"That's good," said Eunice. "It would be sort of silly to lose energy on the deal."

"Yes," replied Duncan, "and some synthetic-fuel processes may do just that. In fact, some experts say we're not too many years from taking more energy to find and extract ordinary oil than it will provide once we've got it."

Eunice thought about that one. That would be dumb, she decided. But if even oil was approaching that situation, perhaps biomass fuels did make sense.

"Does ethanol have any other advantages?" asked Eunice.

"Yes, several," said Duncan. "One nice feature of making ethanol is that the 'distiller's dried grain' left over after distilling the ethanol—a sort of mash—is enriched in protein by the yeast that did the fermentation; so it makes a superior livestock feed. The fermentation also makes carbon dioxide, which can be sold to bottlers or used to grow plants faster in solar greenhouses. In fact, one alcohol plant in Illinois uses both the waste carbon dioxide and waste heat from the alcohol still to grow lettuce. The hydroponic 'factory' is run by handicapped people and produces nearly two dozen crops a year—about enough lettuce for a city of two hundred thousand."

"What about the cost?" Eunice persisted.

"It depends on a lot of assumptions," Duncan began cautiously.

"I knew it," Eunice moaned.

"But it's fair to summarize," he continued, "that biomass ethanol may cost anywhere from a bit less than today's gasoline to a few tens of percent more, depending on how simple and smart the process is and how well the byproducts are used. Methanol can probably be a good deal cheaper, especially if it's made of a waste —such as sawdust at a sawmill or furniture plant, or logging waste in the woods, or garbage—that's essentially free, or even costs extra to dispose of."

"Could you make alcohols and other biofuels in big plants like oil refineries?" asked Eunice.

"Good question," Duncan acknowledged. "There isn't any single answer. Basically, transporting the fuel you produce is relatively cheap, but transporting the much heavier feedstock used to make it is expensive; so you have to balance the possible economic advantages of bigger plants against the extra transportation costs of getting the feedstocks from another area to that plant. My own guess is that we're going to see more decentralized biofuel production—on the scale, say, of a milk-bottling plant, which collects milk from farmers in several counties—perhaps using a little pyro-lyzer in a pickup truck that will go wherever the waste is, even to a logging operation deep in the woods."

"But surely," objected Eunice, "you aren't proposing to run all our cars—there must be, what . . . ?"

"About a hundred thirty million," supplied Duncan.

". . . on liquid fuels produced in little backyard and down-the-street plants," Eunice continued. "I mean, look how many gallons of gasoline Americans use every year. And imagine making that many—I don't know the exact number, but it must be enormous —from the wastes of one dairy here and another forest over there. It would be a mess."

Duncan laughed. "Not all of it should or will come from small plants," he said, "but it could. After all, consider the milk we drink. The United States keeps about eleven million cows in herds averaging sixty cows each. That's an average of just over one hundred eighty thousand dairy herds. But collectively they produce eleven billion gallons of milk a year, and that milk gets to your refrigerator pretty much whenever you want it. That eleven billion gallons is about the same as the number of gallons of gasoline, or ethanol, America's cars would use if they were properly efficient. The same amount of fuel could be produced in the same fairly decentralized way if we wanted to. And because the milk system works, decentralized as it is, nobody's proposing to produce all the milk at a few giant farms in, say, Texas and pipe-line the milk all over the country."

"But milk's not oil," Eunice insisted, still not won over.

"It costs almost twice as much per gallon as gasoline," said Duncan, "but if you insist, let me give you an oil example, too. The average stripper well in the United States—you know, those little rigs you often see with arms bobbing up and down, sucking a little bit of oil out of old oil fields—well, each of those wells lifts fewer than three barrels per day, which is just over a mil-lionth of all the oil we use in the United States. But put together, those dispersed little stripper wells provide a fifth of all American oil—again, more than enough to run a really efficient trans-portation system."

"Humph. So enough of our oil to run really efficient cars, planes, trucks, and pogo sticks is already being provided in a decentralized way?" Eunice admitted.

Duncan nodded. "Of course," he continued, "some biofuel production probably should and will be quite centralized, such as making methanol or pyrolysates at, say, a pulp mill that already has lots of bark and wood wastes left over. I'm just saying that much of the biofuel production will probably be almost as scattered over the landscape as the feedstocks themselves are."

"Speaking of which," Eunice interjected, "I've been itching to ask you what you're going to make all those fuels out of. And don't tell me corn, because I know we have to eat something, and we can't eat our corn and drive on it, too."

"If you're worried about food," Duncan replied, "you might start by asking yourself why eighty-eight percent of all the vegetable protein we grow is fed to livestock, not to people, when those critters are perfectly well equipped to forage for themselves. In fact, cattle were designed to eat grass, which we can't even digest, not corn, which we can. But leaving that aside, the list of nonfood feedstocks we can make biofuels out of is incredibly long and diverse." Duncan paused as he thought. "Let me just give you at least some of the flavor. Traditionally, people studying biofuels assume a vehicle fleet about as inefficient as today's. Then they assume we need enormous amounts of fuel. Thus, they conclude that even using all our corn and other major crops to make ethanol —inefficiently—couldn't do the job. What's the fallacy?"

"First, I suppose," said Eunice, "that they ignored the possibility of becoming efficient."

"Right!" exclaimed Duncan. "If we did that, we wouldn't need the eighteen or so quadrillion BTUs of liquid fuels for vehicles that we now use every year, but only about five or six. And that's for all vehicles, including trucks, aircraft, ships, trains, motorcycles, etc. Furthermore, if we only needed that little liquid fuel, we wouldn't need to grow special 'fuel crops' to make it, nor to intensify production of existing feedstocks; we could almost certainly, in fact, get by with just the farm and forestry wastes we already have and don't know what to do with."

"Like what?" asked Eunice.

"Corn stover, wheat straw and chaff, almond shells, peach pits, coffee grounds, rice hulls, logging slash, citrus pulp, dairy whey, canning wastes, sunflower hulls, peanut shells, apple pomace—"

"Whoa!" pleaded Eunice. "Just what is apple pomace? It sounds volcanic."

"It's what's left over after you squeeze apple cider," Duncan replied with equanimity. "If you aren't from an apple-growing area, you've probably never heard of it—*I* hadn't until I went to visit Three Mile Island last year. But around that part of Pennsylvania and other areas where they make cider, they have a lot of it. And that's typical of how diverse biofuel feedstocks really are. It may be peanut hulls in Georgia, canning wastes in California, lawn trimmings in Dubuque, or cotton-gin trash in Texas, but every place has some characteristic organic waste material that is often a disposal problem. Why, just the cotton-gin trash in Texas —now being burned or thrown into wetlands—could probably make enough liquid fuels to run every vehicle in Texas. Each year, France and Denmark burn enough straw in the fields to run an efficient transportation system. The distressed grain in Nebraska every year—that means it's moldy or otherwise unfit to sell"— Eunice nodded in sad recollection of spoiled Iowa harvests— "could fuel a tenth of Nebraska's cars at sixty miles a gallon. Even Los Angeles County sends to landfills *every day* four to eight thousand *tons* of pure, separated tree material—trimmings, fallen branches, and so forth—not even counting mixed truckloads. That's seventy thousand gallons of gas worth each day being thrown away. The disposal costs continue to rise, but the cost of the liquid fuel would probably work out to about a buck a gallon, give or take a quarter. The huge Boeing plant in Everett, Washington, is even using cartons and other factory wastes as a boiler fuel to make steam and electricity and could probably make liquid fuels economically, too."

"Are you saying," Eunice asked unsteadily, "that if you add up all the little bits of various feedstocks here and there—and some big ones, like logging wastes and, I suppose, the major crop wastes like cobs and stalks from corn—they'd be enough to make five or six quads a year worth of liquid fuels?" She was still unaccustomed to tossing numbers around the way Duncan and Hobart did.

"Yes," said Duncan, "subject to one critical condition." He looked sternly at Eunice and waggled a warning finger. "The land must come first. Right now, much of our farming and forestry are mining operations. They mine soil, water, fuels, genes, farms, and farmers. We simply *must* reform our growing practices to become sustainable. If an alcohol-fuels program serves only to load still more production on an unsustainable system, biofuels could make a lot more deserts."

"Do all the crop wastes need to go back on the soil?" asked Eunice, recalling irrigation water black with lost topsoil, running off the cornfields.

"Maybe," said Duncan. "Some soil scientists think so. But I think what they're really saying is that we need to take every step we can to save our vanishing topsoil. And I agree. At the rate we're going, western Iowa will be out of topsoil before western Nebraska's out of water."

Eunice blinked. "You mean like in that bad storm in 1984?" she asked.

"Yeah," Duncan replied, "when many farmers lost as much soil as they normally do in a year—which is itself an awful lot—in just a couple of days' hard rains."

"But doesn't that mean," said Eunice, "that using crop and logging wastes for fuels would be like trying to have our cake and eat it too?"

"No," Duncan replied, "for three reasons. First, many of the wastes we're talking about are already far removed from the land, or come in such a form that we wouldn't know how to put them back on the land if we tried. Orange peels and apricot pits, for example, don't even compost well. Some of the wastes, if put back on the land, would actually encourage pests. And we can selectively leave, while harvesting, most of the wastes that do the most for the soil. For example, in logging, we can leave the leaves and twigs that contain most of the nutrients, while taking away—for fuel, timber, or whatever—the tree trunk and the larger branches.

"Second," he continued, "many processes for converting farm and forestry wastes into fuels leave behind residues that can and should be put back on the land. We haven't talked yet about 'digesting' feedlot, dairy, chicken, and hog manures into 'biogas,' for example."

"No, we haven't," Eunice agreed. "What's biogas?"

"It's natural gas, just like we put into pipelines," Duncan explained, "but cleaner, and it's made by using bacteria in the absence of air to digest certain rich organic wastes. In fact, some feedlot operators do this right now and sell the gas to pipeline companies, just as if they'd gotten it out of a well. One of the earliest such companies was called Calorific Recovery by Anaerobic Processes, Inc., with the appropriate acronym." Duncan chuckled as Eunice figured it out and blushed. "But the nifty part of the process is that along with the gas, the digester makes a sludge that is a better fertilizer than the original manure. The gas the process produces is mostly hydrogen and a little carbon, both of which can readily be regained by plants out of the air. What's left behind is most of the nitrogen and all the other nutrients, ready to go right back on the fields. Likewise, even pyrolysis can leave a mineral-rich ash, providing trace nutrients for return to the soil. Most conversion processes leave behind the nutrients that are most needed to protect the fertility of the soil, but it is essential that we close the circle by actually getting those nutrients back where they belong.

"And that brings me," he continued, "to the most exciting prospect: using biofuels as a vehicle for reforms that will make farming and forestry more sustainable. Let me give you an example. Some West Kansas wheat farmers I know used to take their combines through the fields, harvesting the wheat and throwing the chaff and straw over the back to be plowed under for tilth. But then, as the price of natural gas to make fertilizer skyrocketed, they found it worth their while to put in rotation crops, or inter-row crops, of legumes—such things as clover, alfalfa, and winter vetch—which could then be plowed under as a 'green manure.' This replaced most of their costly chemicals. But then they found that if they did that, the soil quality could be maintained and even improved without plowing under the wheat straw. So they could bale the straw, right on the combine, at practically no extra cost and use it to make alcohol fuels to run their equipment."

"Nobody lost and everyone was better off," Eunice remarked.

"Exactly," said Duncan. "We need to identify a lot more cases in which biofuels can provide a way to improve the soil, not to deplete it. And I think we're starting to find them. It just means conducting agriculture more in accordance with natural cycles, without leaving so many loose ends in the form of nutrients that we take away and consider to be trash."

"What about Brazil?" Eunice asked. "I've heard about . . . what was it, sugar cane? Doesn't that program have implications for agriculture?"

"Yeah," Duncan grunted. "You bet it has implications. Brazil is a complicated case, though. Like many Third World countries, Brazil has trouble paying for oil," he explained, "so, around 1979, Brazilians launched an ambitious program to replace about three-quarters of the gasoline they were using with pure ethanol within ten years. And, indeed, their 1985 schedule for production of nearly three billion gallons displaces three-fifths of their gasoline. Almost nine out of every ten cars sold in 1983 were capable of using pure ethanol, and there are already more than a million ethanol vehicles on Brazilian roads. Since they're built with higher compression ratios to use ethanol to best advantage, they're a quarter more efficient than the Gasohol cars of a few years ago. Brazilian firms are even starting to make dual-fueled diesel vehicles that can switch between diesel fuel and ethanol. And alcohol fuels are actually improving the efficiency of some diesel engines."

"What does all this cost?" queried Eunice, impressed in spite of herself.

"It's pretty good," replied Duncan. "Even though the ethanol production seldom uses the best new processes, and most of the ethanol is made from specially grown sugar cane, the unsubsidized wholesale cost of ethanol production in 1983 was about ninety-five cents to a dollar thirty per gallon of gasoline equivalent. That looks roughly comparable to the direct cost of gasoline from imported oil, but it's actually cheaper because the oil would have to be financed by borrowing abroad, whereas the ethanol is produced right in Brazil. Growing cane and making ethanol even appears to be no more capital-intensive than finding and refining oil. In fact, Brazil's new five-billion-dollar refinery/petrochemical complex cost nearly as much as the entire alcohol program did, excluding land, up to 1985, but provided only five percent as many jobs as the ethanol program's half-million. The net energy yield of the ethanol program is better than three to one—about the same as for extracting oil and refining gasoline in the United States. It's even better in recently built microdistilleries, which may also cut capital costs by two-thirds and increase labor intensity by fivefold compared with centralized plants. Meeting the 1985 ethanol production goal required about seven million acres of cane fields—about the size of Maryland—but that's only six percent of Brazil's present crop area.

Eunice's original concerns overcame her awe. "But aren't there still problems with the program?" she persisted.

"Yes," said Duncan, "and they're part of the whole fabric of Brazil's economic and social problems—native rights and cultural integrity, cutting down rain forests and destroying ecosystems, the balance of political power between urban elites and peasants, keeping up with rapid population growth. Brazil would have these problems with or without the ethanol program, and the work of some friends of mine at the University of Ceará, in the impoverished Northeast, suggests that with operations the right size, the ethanol program can actually be a creative vehicle for ecological protection and social reform."

"And I suppose," said Eunice, "that making alcohol on farms in America can help farmers make more money and have more reliable supplies of fuel for their tractors?"

"Sure," Duncan confirmed. "In fact, that's one of the reasons that Admiral Thomas Moorer, who was President Nixon's Chairman of the Joint Chiefs of Staff, is excited about on-farm fuel-alcohol production. He's worried that in an oil interruption, farmers—on the end of the supply lines—will face the double whammy of no fuel and no export markets. Already, many farmers in the American heartland, and even such groups as small Black colleges in the South, are turning to renewable fuels as a way of providing both security and economic development.

"And, with the help of such groups as the Small Farm Energy Project in Hardington, Nebraska, many farmers are also drying their crops with solar heat, digesting manures to make fuel gas, recycling crop wastes, and integrating their energy and food production. Why, there's one four-hundred-fifty-cow dairy farm I know where a biogas-run generator has turned a fourteen-hundred-dollar-a-month electric bill into a several-thousand-dollar-a-month profit on sales of surplus power to the utility—never mind the milk and cream.

"However," Duncan interrupted himself, "all this talk of solid wastes reminds me of an engagement." He grinned and rose. "Will you excuse me for a few minutes?"

12 *Power to the People*

*A*FTER DUNCAN LEFT, Eunice slumped in her seat. Truly, there was too much to remember. All of these different ways to capture solar heat and use biomass—how could you tell which one to use? Eunice frowned. Which ones, she wondered, are important, and which ones could you just leave for people like Hobart to worry about? Her frown deepened. Oil sounded so simple, next to this jungle of renewable sources. If only it weren't going to run out, she could ignore this whole thicket, she thought.

By the time Duncan returned from the men's room, Eunice was seriously frustrated, and took it out on her new mentor. "So how was the executive bathroom?" she asked dourly, distracting herself.

"Oh, I didn't go *there*," Duncan laughed. "How could I keep up with all the gossip if I didn't read the graffiti in the men's room that everyone else uses? Why," he said, grinning, "just today, I discovered three plots against the Secretary herself."

Eunice did not laugh. If anything, her countenance turned positively stony. "Hey, what's eating you?" Duncan asked.

"I really don't think I belong here," she confessed. "You threw this long list of energy sources at me just now, and I have no idea what to do with it. What am I supposed to do—choose one from column A and one from column B, like at a Chinese restaurant?"

"Um," Duncan considered, "I know it must be bewildering. But really, you know, you're taking it very well. The last person I explained all this to went slightly off the deep end. He came back the next day with a load of two-by-fours and window frames and started building a solar greenhouse on the Mall to show people how well all this would work."

"What happened?" Eunice asked, her interest returning.

"Oh, someone from the National Park Service called me up and told me what was going on. So I went out and talked him down, so to speak."

"Where did they send him?" Eunice persisted.

"Send him? You mean, like to a mental hospital? Oh no, he just went back to his calculator and his cubicle across the hall-way."

"Oh, no," gasped Eunice. "It was—"

"—yes, Hobart," Duncan laughed. "But, to the matter at hand, let's consider the last and least of our energy needs—electricity—before we wax philosophical about how to sift through all the renewables at our disposal."

"Oh, of course," replied Eunice, more or less revived. "I'd quite forgotten. We still have to find out how the sun can keep the lights on and the motors turning. I should think we would need a great deal of electricity?"

"About eight percent," Duncan reminded her, "of our energy tasks today actually require electricity, if we use it only where it's worthwhile, and not for low-temperature heating and cooling. Really, it's the least of our needs—much less than for heat or liquid fuels. But that's not to say it isn't extremely important to the way we live."

"Well, then," said Eunice, "you'd better have some good answers ready, because I don't see how you can just put a window in the side of your house and let solar electricity shine in."

"We'll see about that," Duncan teased. He rocked back for a moment, collecting his thoughts. "As with heat and biofuels," he began, "there are lots of ways to do the job with solar energy. In fact, there are almost as many ways to make electricity from the sun as there are electric poles between here and the Mississippi.

Different ways are going to be practical in different places; but just as it was with heating, cooling, and liquid fuels, it appears that every location has enough of some combination of solar resources to meet its electric needs. Let's start," he continued, "by remembering that hydroelectric power is solar. It's the sun's heat that evaporates the water to form rain clouds, which let the rain run downhill into the reservoirs and through the turbines. That solar contribution already makes an eighth of our electricity."

"Okay," said Eunice, "but you're not suggesting we build a lot more of those big dams? Or are you? It seems that whenever someone wants to, it's in a place where it would be a bad idea, like the Grand Canyon. Don't the environmentalists say all the acceptable sites for big dams are already used?"

"They're probably right," Duncan agreed, "but a lot of those old, big dams have empty turbine bays, or have generators so old that we could get a lot more electricity out of them—with no extra environmental problems at all—by rewinding them to generate more efficiently." Eunice blinked in surprise. "And then there's small hydro, an opportunity that could add up to be nearly as big as all the hydropower we already have."

"How small is small?" Eunice asked warily.

"Definitions vary," he admitted. "Some are less than a tenth of a megawatt per site; that's about enough for the average use of a hundred homes. On the other hand, some 'small' hydro sites weigh in at as much as twenty-five megawatts. But whatever the size, there's lots of hydro potential waiting to be used. Most of the more attractive small hydro projects would just return to operation the old dams that have fallen into disrepair. Why, just in the past twenty years, more than three thousand perfectly good small hydro plants, equivalent in total to three huge power stations, were simply abandoned—their turbines and generators left to rust or sold for scrap—because the utilities preferred the convenience of a small number of big plants."

Eunice's face showed shock again. "Why didn't someone stop that?"

"Because nobody was paying much attention. Anyway, most folks thought those big plants the utilities wanted to build would be much cheaper than they turned out to be. However, if you add up all the abandoned small dams, most of which can be revived fairly cheaply, you get an inventory of more than ten thousand of them just in New England. New York State alone plans to have the small hydro equivalent to two or three giant power plants back on line by the mid-1990s. Nationally, we have more than fifty thousand unused dams upwards of twenty-five feet high, not even counting some other major power-generating opportunities, such as the locks on canals. In fact, ever since Congress said in 1978 that if you generated your own power, the utilities had to offer to buy it back from you at a fair price, thousands of entrepreneurs have been taking advantage of those small hydro opportunities, contracting to fix up the old dams and sell the power. It's a kind of electric gold rush. There are companies that, if you have flowing water on your land, will offer to make all the arrangements to harness it. They'll finance, license, design, and build the whole thing and just mail you a check for your share of the profits. You put up no money and take no risk."

"What's the catch?" wondered Eunice.

"It only works if the company's competent . . ." Duncan wagged a warning finger, ". . . you do have to check its track record. Otherwise, there really is no catch, provided you can avoid environmental problems," he added. "And that can be a hurdle. At some sites, people have built vacation homes on a lakeshore and don't want the water level to change. Using some sites could destroy fisheries or wildlife or scenic waterfalls. However, we can also afford to be sensitive to these kinds of problems because there are so many small hydro sites, both old and new. In fact, some big utilities are quietly doing so much in this area that they have about ten times as much small hydro underway as they're publicly announcing. At this point, the main barrier to doing small hydro even faster is the huge backlog of permit applications at the Federal Energy Regulatory Commission—and more are piling up, at a rate that's often running about ten per day."

Eunice made a note and drew a big box around it.

"I know you said many of the attractive small hydro dams already exist," she said, "but I don't really like the idea of dams at all. They don't look as nice as free-flowing streams, they must be hard for fish to get around, and sometimes they break and make floods. Is there any alternative to dams?"

"Happily, yes," replied Duncan. "In fact, you can often make cheap power using a 'head'—that's how far the water drops—of only a yard or less. Some of the new devices to collect that energy don't look like turbines at all; they're more like moving ladders or Venetian blinds and apparently let fish pass through unharmed. You can even generate 'run-of-the-river' power just by the force of the water passing by, without needing any dams at all. That doesn't give you any storage; so you get more power in the spring runoff and less in the drier seasons, but it still can be a very useful approach.

"In China it's common to pick off a kilowatt or two of power every fifty or a hundred yards along an irrigation ditch, using little turbines that may even have wooden blades. That may not sound too impressive, but China gets a third of its rural electricity from such small installations—more than ninety thousand of them— and those small Chinese turbines, many of them designed by American engineers half a century ago, are so rugged and cheap that they're now being exported to this country. In fact, if you want proof that an industrial economy can run, not just on hydro —as, say, Canada, Sweden, and Norway largely do—but on *small* hydro, look at Japan. During World War II seventy-eight percent of Japan's electricity came from small hydro plants. And my military friends were fascinated to discover that those plants sustained only one three-hundredth as much total bombing damage as the centralized steam-raising power plants that provided only twenty-two percent of the nation's electricity—simply because the small hydro plants were so dispersed that bombing any one of them would be useless. Thus, they were essentially invulnerable."

"Is most of the small hydro potential in the United States similarly spread out?" asked Eunice.

"Pretty much all over," said Duncan. "Much of it does tend to cluster in the Northeast, Southeast, and Northwest—naturally, there's not a lot in the western deserts—but it's much more evenly distributed than existing big dams are."

"Suppose all the attractive small hydro sites were added up," persisted Eunice. "How much power would they provide?"

"The best guesses are that it could well approach the total capacity of today's big hydropower—equivalent to about eighty giant power stations—especially if you include adding turbines to empty bays and rewinding old generators in existing big dams. So in the next few decades we should be able to come pretty close to doubling our existing hydro capacity, just as we've quietly done over the past twenty-odd years."

"At what cost?" asked Eunice.

Duncan grinned at her growing hardheadedness. "It takes a fair bit of money to build a new dam," he answered, "much more than just fixing up an old one. But once it's built, it costs practically nothing to run. The bottom line is that the power is generally much cheaper than from a new coal or nuclear power plant, and it's inflation-proof to boot."

"Put a round number on it," Eunice pressed.

"It depends very much on the site, but two to eight cents per kilowatt-hour is a reasonable range," replied Duncan, "with five or six being typical. The average American household is paying more than eight cents for power right now, and the nuclear plants now being built will deliver power at about ten to thirty cents—twenty is about average. So compared with them, small hydro is a bargain. The only better bargain, in general—"

"—is using electricity more efficiently," Eunice finished.

Duncan grinned and shrugged. "What can I tell you . . . ?" he teased. "Anyway, there are other sustainable sources of electricity also. Remember all the windmills that used to pump water on the Great Plains?"

Eunice nodded.

"Six million farms once had them, and about a sixth of a million still do. Now, however, there are phenomenally efficient new wind pumpers. One model can reportedly lift water from a three-hundred-foot well in a wind of only five miles per hour."

"But that means you can do it practically anywhere, even in those African countries where they're always having droughts," exclaimed Eunice.

"That's right. Such breezes blow ninety percent of the time over something like ninety-four percent of the earth's surface," Duncan recited. "By the same token, some inventors have developed refrigerators and other devices driven directly by small wind machines. And wind machines don't have to use fiberglass and aluminum; they can be made of local cloth and bamboo."

"But what if we want electricity to use for some other purpose?" asked Eunice.

"That's where windpower really comes into its own," Duncan replied. "There's a lot of energy in the wind, and a typical wind machine can extract thirty percent of it. If the wind blows at eighteen miles an hour, the wind machine will produce nearly twice as much power as the same collecting area of solar cells could generate at, say, ten percent efficiency in bright sunlight. And the wind, unlike the sun, often works at night, too, especially in the poorer solar climates where it's often cloudy and stormy."

"I saw a piece in the *Telegraph-Herald* last year," Eunice recollected, "about all the electricity they're making now on those 'windfarms' in California. The story was amazing. There was a photograph of thousands of wind machines stretching up and down the ridges, like a kind of sculpture garden, with cows grazing underneath."

"By 1986," Duncan confirmed, "there should be the equivalent of several giant power plants' worth of wind machines operating there. But of course the total cost is much less than what those giant power plants would cost, and the windfarms will have been built in a small fraction of the time a power plant would have taken. In fact, windfarms are now competing on the grid in at least six states, and more than two hundred utilities have exploratory windpower programs."

"Who makes all those thousands of machines?" asked Eunice. "Are they turning them out sort of like cars or washing machines?"

"Not quite yet," chuckled Duncan, "but they will, and who'll get the business is a funny story. At first the biggest aerospace and electrical companies thought they could do it best; so they tried building, with government money, wind machines whose blades were as long as jumbo jet wings. Some of us tried to warn them that remaking solar in the image of nuclear—supposing that each machine had to produce lots of megawatts or it wasn't significant —was a serious mistake; we said it'd be cheaper to make lots of smaller machines, which could be mass-produced and would be easier to install and fix. The megawatt brigade answered that we were misinformed ecofreaks and that bigger was always better, amen.

"Well, the big machines did turn out to be very complex and expensive, but most of them didn't work very well. Meanwhile, a few tiny companies were making simpler, much smaller machines that beat the pants off the big ones just on straight economics. Now we're finding that medium-sized machines, each making from tens of kilowatts to a few hundred kilowatts, may even be a little cheaper. Some of them are starting to be mass-produced from standard car and tractor parts. There are now dozens of American wind-machine makers, perhaps two or three dozen of which are commercially viable. But, you know, although some of those machines are very good, they're still not as trouble-free as the best 1930s models, such as the one that worked fine with no maintenance for several decades at the North Pole. So, United States manufacturers are facing stiff competition from some excellent wind machines made in Denmark, Holland, and Germany. The American engineers had better learn to make things as simply as the Europeans can," he sighed, "if we want to keep our own markets."

"But that same article said, as I recall," said Eunice, "that some of those California wind machines didn't even work; they were built as tax shelters."

"Some didn't work, that's true," Duncan agreed, "but the market has been quickly weeding them out, just as it's weeding out lemon nuclear plants. New wind machines are twice as reliable and cost half as much as they those built a couple of years ago. In fact, some of the smartest new designs can profitably produce power without any tax credits, which is more than any coal or nuclear power station can do! That's why the California Energy Commission found that other than small hydro, windpower would be California's cheapest source of new electric generation by 1990. And smaller machines, suitable for a farm or a neighborhood or an isolated house, can be even cheaper, including some do-it-yourself models. First, though, you have to live where there is a good bit of wind. Of course, there are places where the wind just doesn't blow enough to make windpower worthwhile. And even in such windy areas as the Great Plains or the New England coast, it's worth 'prospecting' for the very windiest places, because the amount of power you get from the wind varies as the *cube* of its speed—that is, you'll get almost twice as much windpower at twenty miles an hour as at sixteen. But on the whole, windpower in decent sites is a fine buy—typically about the same as microhydro, around three to eight cents a kilowatt-hour."

"How much windpower can we get altogether?" asked Eunice.

"About as much as we want to build machines to capture," replied Duncan. "In fact, the Dutch government is planning to build eleven hundred big wind machines to make about an eighth of all their electricity by the year 2000. They figure it'll cost just over two cents per kilowatt-hour. We could readily do as well, except that ours would probably be more complicated and cost a bit more."

"Again," said Eunice, "isn't there a catch? For example, didn't I hear somewhere that wind machines make horrible swishing and thumping noises as they go around?"

"Badly built ones are noisy," Duncan agreed, "like the one this Department built in North Carolina. It made such disturbing, low-pitched noises that people griped about everything from an impaired sex life to a minister's not being able to concentrate to write his sermons. And all that was caused by a simple design mistake, which the engineers were even warned about in advance but ignored. The good news, though, is that well-designed, well-built wind machines—which should be all of them—are very quiet, and pretty to watch, too. Aesthetics, of course, is a matter of personal taste, but I think a well-laid-out hillside or ridgeline full of wind machines is rather delightful. In fact, in the Altamont Pass in California, I worry about people driving right off the road because they're so busy gawking at those thousands of dancing machines all around them, like huge lines of airplane propellers and giant eggbeaters."

"Eggbeaters?" asked a startled Eunice.

"So you *were* listening," teased Duncan. "Yes, eggbeaters. There's a kind of wind machine that spins on a vertical axis. It has big, curving, eggbeater-like blades that spin in the wind for the same reason that an airplane wing provides lift. No matter what direction the wind blows from, the whirling blades capture it and turn it into electricity. And the beauty of windpower in states such as California is that the wind is often strongest on the summer afternoons when utilities need the most power to run people's air conditioners."

"What keeps one of those eggbeaters from chopping someone to pieces?" asked Eunice.

"For starters, they're mounted up on towers, well above the ground," Duncan replied. "However, a few badly designed wind machines have suffered broken blades. And you wouldn't want a huge blade hurtling through the air."

Eunice's look said she most certainly did not.

"That's why," Duncan continued, "the European designers start with safety first. They make their machines physically incapable of losing blades. Some blades are also so light—made from foam, for example—that even if they did come loose, they couldn't hurt anyone. The reputable manufacturers in this country use much the same approach. The only danger left, I suppose," Duncan shrugged, "is that of falling off while repairing the machine. You know, one wind-machine designer actually did that. He climbed up one of his machines in a windstorm with no ropes protecting him, to try to fix something. But that's not real bright.

"About the only remaining problems I've heard about," Duncan concluded, "are killing birds—which seems to be much less of a problem than for normal power lines—and interfering with TV reception, but I always thought that might be considered a benefit anyway."

"But I like to watch my favorite shows," Eunice objected.

"Actually, I do, too," Duncan agreed, "so in the rare situations where the rotating blades do garble TV reception for a few homes nearby, either a cable hookup or replacing the metal windmill blades with wood or fiberglass offers a cheap, effective solution."

"So windpower is a very big, and relatively cheap, source of electricity?" Eunice summarized.

"Yes," Duncan replied. "It's not available everywhere, but interestingly enough, it's available in enough places—and those places are different enough from the places with big and small hydropower—that between them, these two sources are quite well distributed over the whole country. And when you add in a likely third source that's rapidly becoming competitive—solar cells— that nationwide coverage is virtually complete."

"What about solar cells?" asked Eunice. "For Christmas, Joe's mother gave Jimmy a little Japanese calculator that works whenever you have enough light to read it by, and it never needs batteries. Is that what you mean?"

"That's one good example," Duncan agreed, "of how some aggressive Japanese companies are building markets for their solar cells so they can make more of them and cut the costs. That particular kind of cell is made of silicon—which is the second most plentiful element in the earth's crust—that's converted into a gas and sprayed on in a thin film. It converts maybe six percent of the light directly into electricity. Those Japanese firms aim to raise that efficiency to about fifteen percent by making cells with several layers, each capturing light of a different color. And U.S. firms can already get that efficiency, but only in costlier kinds of cells that use perfect single crystals of silicon, sliced into very thin wafers. Other materials and manufacturing methods are used for solar cells, too. But what's important is that the prices of most kinds of cells are continuing to drop. They've already fallen by about a hundredfold since the early sixties, and it looks like they'll fall another three- to fivefold during the rest of the eighties. At that rate, they'll become cheaper than the power you and I are buying from the utilities right now."

"Is power from solar cells much more expensive today than what I'm buying from the power company?" asked Eunice.

"Maybe. If there are power lines right on your street, putting solar cells on your roof could be two to five times more expensive than utility power. But that margin shrinks when you compare oranges with oranges—new solar cells with new power plants. Remember, a new central generating station's power will cost up to two or three times as much per kilowatt as you're now paying. Or if you live a quarter- or half-mile from the nearest power line, it's probably cheaper to use solar cells today than to hook up. Or if you used a simple reflector to concentrate more sunlight on a smaller area of costly solar cells, then pulled the resulting heat off the cells and used that extra heat to heat water, you could probably make solar cells pay right now in downtown Dubuque. In fact, one Colorado company's cells concentrate light in this way to make electricity about as cheap—if the proven test cells are mass-produced—as power from a new coal-fired plant today. Also, if you want low-voltage direct current, the sort you get from your car battery, solar cells make that directly; so they're ideal for running electronics or electroplating plants that need that kind of electricity. But if you want higher-voltage alternating current, such as you get when you plug an appliance into the wall socket, you have to pay extra to convert the cells' output to that form— one you can swap back and forth with your utility—and that raises the cost of the whole system. So whether solar cells can compete today depends on how you use them. That can change the price from a few cents to at least thirty-odd cents per kilowatt-hour."

"But are you saying," Eunice continued, "that solar cells are going to get cheaper anyway, so more people will be able to save money by using them?"

"Almost certainly," said Duncan. "The price will continue to fall just as the prices of chips and computers have fallen, and for similar reasons. So many promising developments are happening so fast in so many countries that most experts in the field expect solar cells to be generally competitive by 1990 or so. And from a policy standpoint, notice that timetable. If you order a big power plant, it'll take at least ten years to build. If photovoltaics come on as I think they will, such a plant would be obsolete before it's finished. Several of the biggest utilities have concluded that by 1990, it'll be pretty common for houses in their areas to be net producers of electricity from solar cells on their roofs. In fact, with efficient lights and appliances you'll then be able to become your own utility, meeting your own electrical needs with a cell area only about ten feet on a side. Those cells might even look like shingles; so you'd simply nail them up on your roof."

"You mean I might be able to stop paying electric bills altogether?" Eunice said in amazement.

"Not only that, but your utility could buy back your surplus power—especially on those hot summer afternoons when your cells are cranking out the most electricity and the utility needs it most—and you might therefore end up with your utility paying *you*. Your house could become a tiny but profitable power company." Eunice's look of surprise turned to delight.

"Of course," Duncan admitted, "all the technical advances that make this likely by or in the 1990s were slowed down dramatically in the United States when the Reagan administration cut research on cheaper solar cells. But other countries, such as Japan and Germany, pressed ahead. So we'll probably end up buying a lot of cells from them in the nineties and beyond." He shrugged fatalistically. "The Japanese manufacturers in particular are taking a longer view than ours. They're putting a lot of money now into technologies that could capture the whole market in another twenty years."

"Is anyone using solar cells right now?" asked Eunice.

"Sure," Duncan said, winding up for a recitation. "The Forest Service uses them on wilderness towers, the National Park Service uses them on remote buildings, telephone companies on relay stations and satellites, the military on remote bases and in outer space, state highway departments on signs in the middle of nowhere, the Coast Guard on buoys and lighthouses, thousands of people on their homes, some industries and public buildings on their roofs—"

"Thousands of people?" Eunice interjected. "Where *are* all those people?"

"Mostly far enough from a road that you rarely see their houses," said Duncan. "In fact, I hear that in southern Humboldt County, in the California redwood country, about four house-

holds in five have already left the utility grid—or not hooked up in the first place—and switched to stand-alone solar cells, using batteries for storage."

"Why on earth would they do that?"

"Partly to save money if they're far from a power line," said Duncan. Then he grinned and added, "And probably because some of them are growing illegal crops and don't like meter readers coming to visit them."

"If I wanted to switch to solar cells, how difficult would it be?" asked Eunice. "I mean, is it really a *practical* alternative to my utility hookup?"

"There are some very good little companies nowadays," said Duncan, "that provide a packaged service—they'll fix you up with cells, batteries, and inverters so you can run your old appliances on solar power. Or they'll get you superefficient new appliances if you want. And they'll design, install, and even finance the whole thing."

"I suppose," Eunice hesitated, "that with so many people using solar cells already, we can have some confidence that solar cells really work?"

"Absolutely. They're about the most rugged and reliable power source we know. Military planners like solar cells because they work no matter what, and they need no maintenance. Most kinds of cells look like they should last at least for decades and probably darned near forever. After all," Duncan continued, "there's nothing used up, no chemical reaction inside. There's only a basic physical process—a little like what drives computer chips—that changes sunlight cleanly, silently, instantly, and directly into electricity. And it even works, although at a lower level, on cloudy days, too."

"That's something I've been meaning to ask you about," said Eunice. "I know the sun doesn't shine even as much as half the hours in the day, and I also know the wind doesn't always blow and the rivers are sometimes practically dry. And I suppose all these gadgets can also fail, just like my toaster. So what do I do to keep my lights on or my factory working when these sustainable sources of electricity stop sustaining me? Do I switch to giant flashlight batteries? I mean, it's fine to say that everyone can sell solar power to their utilities, but where does the utility get the power to sell back to them when the sun goes behind a cloud?"

"Oh, a sharp one *you* are," exclaimed Duncan, pleased that someone was keeping him honest. "That's why it's important to use a combination of different sustainable sources of electricity. Actually, a good mix of them will give you a *more* reliable power supply than you have right now."

"Come on," Eunice chided, "I just don't believe that things I *know* don't work a lot of the time, like sun and wind, are going to be more reliable than the big power plants that are now keeping my lights on all but a few hours a year."

"I didn't say that *each* windmill or solar cell or small hydro dam would be as reliable as *each* big power plant, let alone all of them together," Duncan explained. "And what's keeping your lights on isn't a single power plant anyway, but dozens of them spread over hundreds of miles, all hooked together by the grid. If you relied on a single big power plant, your lights would be off as much as half the time. What I said was that a diverse blend of big and small hydro, wind, and, if you want to include them, solar cells—many sources of many kinds in many places, all hooked together by the grid just as big power plants are today—would make your electricity supply even more reliable than it is now."

Eunice thought for a moment as she figured that one out. "Is that like strength in numbers?"

"Yes," Duncan agreed, "and in diversity. For example, stormy weather is bad for direct solar collection but good for wind machines and small hydro plants. Dry, sunny weather is bad for hydropower—at least if the dry spell outlasts the water stored in the reservoirs—but it's great for solar cells."

"I see," said Eunice. "You're saying that at least one or two of your kinds of sustainable power sources should be working no matter what."

"That's right," confirmed Duncan, "when one stops working, another works more to fill in. And if an individual wind machine or hydro turbine is shut down for repairs, we haven't lost much capacity because the others are still likely to be working. It's not like losing a large power plant, which knocks out huge blocks of capacity at once. That's embarrassing. Sort of like having an elephant die in your living room—you need another, equally big elephant to haul the carcass away." Eunice looked puzzled. "Or in electrical terms, you need an equally big source of power standing by all the time ready to take over the load when the first plant fails." Her brow smoothed again.

"And I suppose you'll argue that when a big power plant fails, it takes longer to mend than a smaller, simpler one does, because it's more complicated and its spare parts cost more and are harder to get?" Eunice anticipated.

"Exactly. In fact, failures are briefer for sustainable sources even if they're caused not by mechanical mishaps—such as a broken gear in a wind machine—but by bad weather. For example, imagine a typical array of wind machines spread out on inland ridges along the California coast. The longer the line of wind machines stretches, the more reliably some of them will be working at any given time, since wind, being a flow, is always blowing *someplace.* Now, let's suppose those machines, added together, put out a certain amount of power on an average summer day. Well, you can lay twenty-to-one odds that they won't produce *less* than a third that much power for longer than fifteen hours at a stretch. And you can bet a hundred to one that they won't produce less than a sixth of their average output for as long as ten hours. For comparison, do you know for how long a nuclear plant typically fails when it goes out of action?"

"A week?" Eunice guessed.

"Twice that," said Duncan. "Actually about three hundred hours, during which time it puts out no power at all, instead of the usual thousand megawatts or so. That's why it takes only about ten hours' energy storage for a wind machine in a decent site to be as reliable a power source as a typical American nuclear plant. Furthermore," he continued, "nobody knows when a nuclear mishap is going to happen—or an oil embargo, or a war in the Middle East, or a coal strike, or any of the other outside factors that can disrupt big energy systems. In contrast, the things that make sustainable supplies stop working—night, clouds, calm—are well understood and fairly predictable. Indeed, electric utilities predict weather right now to figure out how much power you're going to need the day after tomorrow for heating or air conditioning. I have a lot more confidence that the sun will rise tomorrow than that someone isn't scheming to blow up the Saudi oil terminals or the Texas pipelines right this minute."

"Hold on," Eunice stopped him. "I remember various times when our power in Dubuque was blacked out. We always heard on my son's transistor radio that it was because the power lines were down, not because the plant wasn't able to generate the power at the other end of the lines. So what if, instead of a few big plants far away, you had lots of smaller ones that were closer to you? Wouldn't that shorten the power lines along which something could go wrong?"

"Bravo!" applauded Duncan. "That's another important reason why dispersed, sustainable sources give more reliable power: It's so simple when you stop to think about it. They're closer to you, and each of them serves fewer people; so if the connecting grid failed, fewer people would lose their power and there would be more ways to reroute power to you."

"And anyway," Eunice added with rising excitement, "don't the big, old hydro dams run essentially all the time?"

"Most of them," Duncan agreed. "They're about the most reliable sources on the grid today, and we already haul their power for up to a thousand miles or so—Pacific Northwest hydropower is shipped to southern California, Churchill Falls power probably down toward the District of Columbia, and so on. Now imagine what the grid would look like if we used electricity really efficiently. We'd need several times less electricity than we now use; so those old, big, cheap hydro dams, instead of providing an eighth of our power as now, would provide nearer to half. Dispersed, small hydro would add another chunk nearly as big. And those two sources are also nicely controllable—if you want less power, you shut the gates and valves on the dams, and if you want more, you open them up. Then, if more intermittent, sustainable sources joined the grid, they'd find free storage—as water behind existing dams—awaiting them. It's only if we keep on building lots of big coal and nuclear plants, and trying to electrify the whole economy, that we have a serious problem of electrical storage.

"In short," he concluded, "by the time today's big power plants retire, they'll probably be mere historical curiosities. Like steam locomotives, which we admire in the museum today, they did their job, but something better came along. In this case, the something better will be a lot of relatively small, sustainable sources of power, backstopped by the big, old dams. Then utilities, rather than making a bulk commodity to sell, will be more of a dispatching and bookkeeping operation, mediating between many dispersed sources and many dispersed users."

"To get to that point," mused Eunice, "you could use big and small hydro, windpower, and the soon-to-be-cheap solar cells. But what if for some reason one of those didn't work? Never mind for now . . ." she forestalled Duncan's move to challenge that premise, ". . . how it wouldn't work—just assume it. What would we do? Return to nuclear? Or are there more sustainable sources of electricity than just those four—no, three; we agreed not to build more big dams."

"Ah," said Duncan slyly, "never fear. Actually, there are lots more solar-electric sources than we really have time to talk about." He glanced apprehensively at his watch.

"Like what?" asked Eunice uneasily.

"For starters, any kind of biofuel, such as the bagasse left over from processing sugar cane in Hawaii and the South, or peach pits and walnut shells, or energy studies—that's my favorite . . ."

"I can see why," snickered Eunice, eyeing the stacks of paper littering every square foot of his office.

". . . can be burned or cooked," continued Duncan imperturbably, "to produce any desired combination of heat, liquid fuels, gaseous fuels, charcoal, and electricity."

"How electricity?" Eunice led him on.

"I can use heat to convert as much of my sawdust, or whatever, to fluid fuels as I like—for example, with a nifty gadget called a 'downdraft gasifier,' one model of which converts about eighty-three percent of the feedstock to methanol, and another model of which can directly convert woody materials into gasoline. If I want, I can take off some extra heat as steam and use it to run a turbine—or, in some designs, even make the hot gases from burning the biofuels turn a turbine directly—then use the turbine to run an electric generator. Or I can simply burn the biofuels to run a boiler and steam turbine, although that's a bit less elegant. Several small companies already make equipment to do all this, in whatever combination you want. In fact, when I mentioned earlier that the forest products industry now gets about three-quarters of its energy from its own wastes, I should have said that many mills make both steam to run the pulping processes *and* electricity—that is, they 'cogenerate' both, which takes only about half as much money and fuel as making heat and electricity separately."

"Is this cogeneration a proven technology?" asked Eunice.

"So much so that decades ago it made more than half the electricity in the country. And no wonder—it uses up to ninety percent of the fuel energy, rather than only a third, as a normal power plant does. It's marvelously efficient, because it uses virtually all the heat in the fuel to do work—and what's left over can even be used to heat the factory, like using the whole pig including the squeal."

"Or," said Eunice, enjoying a reminiscence of her farm girlhood, "finding a use for the hole in the doughnut. But it seems so sensible. Why did we stop?"

"Because many utilities persuaded industrialists to stop cogenerating and let the utility provide the electricity. That made a certain amount of sense for a while—you know, one less piece of equipment for the factory to worry about. But it doesn't make sense anymore now that power plants have become so expensive," explained Duncan. "And the economics are now driving an enormously rapid revival of cogeneration. Just in 1984, it went from five to seven percent of all U.S. power generation, even though this Department," he chided, "stopped keeping tabs on it several years ago; so there's no official way to find out anymore who's cogenerating how much. But by all accounts, it won't be many years before cogeneration is back to the percentage of total generation —upwards of fifteen percent, say—that's common in other major industrial countries. More of that cogeneration can be biofueled without necessarily conflicting with the premium use of biomass feedstocks—making liquid fuels for vehicles. That biofueled cogeneration is extremely reliable: The plants usually run upwards of eighty or ninety percent of the time, much more than a normal large power plant. And as we use electricity more efficiently and need less of it, biofueled cogeneration can make up an even larger percentage of total supply."

"Isn't it messy and awkward," Eunice inquired, "to have to transport and store all that biomass to run what amounts to a small power plant? It's enough bother just to feed my own fireplace."

"Fortunately," replied Duncan, "materials such as wood wastes, sawdust, and peat are now available in pelletized form. It looks sort of like rabbit food, but it's simply compressed biomass. It doesn't soak up water; it's clean and easy to handle; you can store, ship, and burn it at least as well and cheaply as coal. Plants now make it commercially in at least seven states."

"Mm," Eunice said thoughtfully, "so that's your insurance?"

"Oh, there's lots more," teased Duncan. "Let's see, should I spare you the odder ones? Well, let's do a lightning tour. First, there's geothermal energy. Hot rocks in the earth can, in certain places—mainly in the West—release hot water or steam, just like Old Faithful at Yellowstone National Park. You can use this energy to run turbines and electric generators, or industrial processes. You can even use the lower-temperature kinds of geothermal heat to warm buildings or greenhouses or even a whole city. Now, some of the geothermal sites release nasty gases and salts—The Geysers, a big utility-operated geothermal power plant in northern California, makes a pervasive rotten-egg stink—and such byproducts need to be controlled or reinjected into the well, which can also help the site last longer. Some geothermal wells, on the other hand, produce fine, sweet water that can be used for raising crops or shrimp after the heat has been used. Where it's available, geothermal is a potentially large and often cost-effective energy source.

"Then there are solar ponds. Remember those?" Eunice nodded, thinking of solar ducks. "The Israelis generate power with one by using the hot water to run a kind of low-temperature turbine, and a big California utility is planning to do the same. In certain circumstances—for example, if you have cheap, sunny land with a handy supply of the right kinds of salt—it might be a cheap source of steady electricity."

Eunice thought of those bleak, sun-drenched salt and alkali flats she'd flown over when she visited her Aunt Henrietta in San Diego. "But does it make sense," she asked, "to have mile after mile of solar collectors in the desert?"

"I doubt it," Duncan answered. "But that's another concept some people are fond of. They're the same sort of people who've built that enormous array of mirrors in the Mojave Desert all focused on a glowing tower that makes high-temperature steam to drive a turbine to make electricity. And there's another version with clusters of little mirrors, each cluster aimed at its own little boiler on the end of a pole, and all the boilers together making steam to run a turbine."

"Sounds pretty roundabout to me," said Eunice.

"Yeah, kind of a fancy way to boil water," Duncan confirmed. "However, the technology may turn out to be useful for making very high-temperature heat for some industrial processes, such as making glass. I'm not impressed with its economics if all you want is electricity, because we already have so many cheap and sustainable sources of that form of energy. But you did want the list." Eunice nodded; so Duncan continued, "Of course, it's less ridiculous than the solar-power satellite."

"What on earth is that?" asked Eunice.

"It's not on earth at all," Duncan laughed. "It's a nutty idea to put lots of solar cells in orbit—where the sunlight is stronger and available nearly all the time—and then beam their energy down to huge antennas laid on the ground. As you might expect, by the time you pay to get all those solar cells in orbit and build and run the antennas—remember, the cells have to be very cheap for the whole scheme to work—it would actually be a better deal to lay those cheap solar cells on your roof in Seattle."

"Humph," Eunice sniffed. "Who would be silly enough to pay for even seriously studying such a pie-in-the-sky idea?"

"Your Department," retorted Duncan, "which has spent more than sixteen million dollars on it already."

"Well, I know what I'm going to do about *that,*" said Eunice tartly. "Are there other kinds of solar electricity that *don't* make sense?"

"Probably," said Duncan. "I have mixed feelings, for example, about what they call OTEC—ocean thermal energy conversion."

"Is that some sort of sea-going energy religion?" asked Eunice.

"No, no," Duncan laughed. "The idea is to use the temperature difference between warm surface water in the tropical oceans and the deeper, cooler seawater to run an enormous, low-temperature turbine to make electricity. Not unlike solar salt ponds, but much less efficient. The resulting electricity is then sent ashore by underwater cables. OTEC has lots of tough engineering problems, not the least of which is how to keep barnacles and other critters from growing on the huge metal surfaces of the heat exchangers. You see, unless those surfaces stay completely clean, they can't transfer heat very well. Anyway, my basic conclusion about it is that it'd be a heroic engineering job that looks rather misdirected. After all, if I wanted to get warm water, I could get a lot of it more easily from my neighborhood power plant than by floating a huge platform out into the ocean in the middle of the hurricane belt."

"I suppose," Eunice inquired wearily, "that this nifty little gadget was my Department's baby, too?"

"Sure was," Duncan said cheerily, "and we haven't even talked about the biggest turkey on the farm."

"What's that?" Eunice asked. "It seems hard to be a bigger waste of money than zillions of mirrors in the desert, or, well, most of those other ways you mentioned to try to gather all that naturally distributed solar energy into one place so we can pay to distribute it back to the users again."

"Unfortunately," said Duncan, "in 1985 your Department spent about four hundred forty million dollars to promote nuclear fusion, which would try to reproduce in a power plant the nuclear processes that light the sun."

"Why not leave them right where they are?" asked Eunice. "It sounds like we have plenty of ways to use the energy we already get from the sun without needing to build artificial suns in our own backyards."

"That's rather my feeling," said Duncan. "Also, if we can get fusion to work, it'll be a much greater engineering achievement than putting people on the moon—which, of course, is why many engineers start drooling when they think about it. It's a vast and virtually permanent welfare program for unemployed nuclear-fission technologists. Worse, though, it would also have nuclear waste problems, and safety problems, and would tend to spread nuclear bombs—not as much as regular nuclear fission reactors, but still enough to be nasty. But the basic conclusion I came to a long time ago is that fusion is a very clever way to do something we don't really want to do."

"What's that?" asked Eunice.

"To make more big blocks of very expensive electricity," Duncan replied. "Remember, most of our energy problem is getting heat and liquid fuels to use in a highly dispersed way—a little bit here and there. Since we already have a lot more electricity than we can get our money's worth out of, what fusion can do, if it works and if we can live with it, is a fascinating, extraordinarily challenging solution to a problem we don't have. So I feel, as you said, that nuclear fusion ought to be very remotely sited. Ninety-three million miles away, like the fusion reactor we have, is just about where we want it."

Eunice listened quietly, then, as Duncan finished, she turned and gazed out the window at the golden sunlight slanting across the buildings beyond.

"Hmmm," Eunice pondered, her back still turned to Duncan. "If renewables are cheaper than or as cheap as oil and gas and coal, why aren't more people using them?"

"You do keep coming back to that," said Duncan, chuckling, "and it is hard to answer. But basically, it boils down to the same reasons people don't use energy as efficiently as would be economically sensible for them: The renewables got off to a slower start in the Industrial Revolution because nonrenewable energy sources were so easy to find at first. Now, the tax system and government policies are set up to encourage people to mine and burn depletable fuels faster instead of using energy wisely and sustainably. And many of the reliable, cost-effective renewables are still so new that people don't yet know where to get them.

"Again," added Duncan, "it really comes down to price. If you buy electricity, you aren't charged the actual price of the power that comes out of a new coal or nuclear plant or, perish the thought, fusion plant; you're charged an average price that 'rolls in' the old, cheap electricity with the new, expensive power. So you never really see the full cost of that new power plant. But, if you install solar panels, you, the consumer, pay the full cost of that system. The same is true when you install efficiency or any other energy system for your own needs: there is no big backlog of 'old, cheap solar energy' to 'roll in' with the full price of new sustainable investments. They look fully as expensive as they really are, but their depletable competitors look cheaper than they really are —and are often more heavily subsidized, too, even compared with solar tax credits.

"The renewable energy revolution," he continued, "is happening in so many little pieces—most of them left out of this Department's statistics—that few people realize what it all adds up to. You've seen a solar panel here and there, but how could you know that over a million American homes now use solar space or water heating? Those solar uses didn't exist five years ago, and I haven't even counted solar pool heaters. Close to a tenth of all the *new* houses being built are designed to capture solar energy through their windows, and in some areas virtually all of them are, because home buyers have learned to settle for nothing less.

"Aha!" he exclaimed. "Have I never told you about the solar electricity being sold to the major California utilities?"

"No," said Eunice, "but it *would* be California. As you know, we in Iowa always suspect that California is like one of those funny cereals—full of nuts, fruits, and flakes—so it'd better be a convincing story."

"Well," said Duncan, wincing a bit, "let me tell you what entrepreneurs there have been doing, purely to make money. A few years ago the three big California utilities began to offer to pay people for electricity at a price a bit lower than it would have cost the utilities to make themselves. That way, they'd have money left over for their investors and rate payers. By

March 1985, they'd already been offered about twenty big power plants' worth of privately financed electric generation—more than ten plants' worth being renewable, and the rest fossil-fueled cogeneration."

"What sorts of sources were they offered?" asked Eunice, interested in spite of herself.

"Everything," said Duncan. "Three-fifths was cogeneration, of which about a third used biofuels. Twenty-odd percent was windpower, about six percent small hydro, a few percent geothermal, one percent solar-steam and photovoltaic, a fifth of a percent hybrids. All this solar electricity, by the way, is demonstrably cheaper than conventional coal or nuclear plants. Of all the offers, about a tenth was already in operation, most was under contract and being built, and the rest was in serious negotiation; mere gleams in the eye weren't included in the totals. And to top that, new offers have been coming in lately at a rate equivalent to nine big power plants *per year*—faster than the utilities know what to do with it! If that isn't an example of the readiness and economy of sustainable electricity sources, I don't know what is."

Eunice's widened eyes gave Duncan his satisfaction. "Wow," she finally managed, "that is a lot."

"Yeah," Duncan resumed, "by 1990, at least a fifth of all the electricity used in California will come from private, nonutility sources, most of them renewable. In fact, the hydro and geothermal capacity that the California utilities now own, plus the privately financed dispersed sources they've already been firmly offered, total over three-quarters of the state's present peak power needs. The renewable projects already on line or planned total more than half of California's current power needs. And that doesn't even count, for example, projects to use geothermal heat directly in buildings and industry, or to make liquid and gaseous fuels from biomass, or to make domestic and industrial heat from the sun. So the future I've described is already clearly taking shape, right there in a sophisticated state that accounts for about a tenth of our whole national economy—and it's happening, by the way, for purely economic reasons. It's not flakiness that generated more than half a billion kilowatt-hours of windpower in

California in 1985; it's the profit motive and sound, practical engineering."

"But you still leave me with my original problem," Eunice said finally. "Many of the technologies you've criticized do sound silly and uneconomical. But what if the sensible solar-electric technologies don't work, or aren't enough?"

"Eunice!" Duncan moaned. "Where've you been? Remember all that we've been talking about. If energy is priced rationally and its consumption isn't subsidized, the demand for it will decline to the point that the solar technologies that we already know will work at a reasonable price can cover it."

Silence filled the room. "Wait a minute," said Duncan suspiciously. "I think something just got past me. I think you believe that sustainable energy is a flop and that people aren't, in fact, buying it. Right?"

"Well," Eunice hesitated, "yes, now that you mention it. That's right. I mean, I see a solar panel here and there, and I see those newspaper articles about windfarms and the revival of small dams, and I suppose lots of people are burning wood; but surely that doesn't add up to much on a national scale, does it? Not just in California, but all over the country?"

"Wrong!" thundered Duncan. "And I should have made this clearer long ago. What percentage of the total energy supply of this country would you guess is coming from renewable sources right now?"

"Maybe one or two percent," Eunice ventured timidly. "At most."

"Nine or ten percent," trumped Duncan. "The reason I can't tell you which number is right is that nobody's keeping track of how much wood is being burned in homes and factories, and the two biggest sources of renewable energy right now are wood and big hydro plants."

"You mean about a tenth of all the energy we use already comes from the sun?" asked Eunice incredulously. "All those glossy ads said we couldn't get any meaningful amount of energy from the sun for decades, so we'd have to build all those coal and nuclear power plants meanwhile!"

"You got it," said Duncan. "Do you know what's been the fastest-growing source of energy in this country since 1979?"

"Nuclear power?" Eunice guessed. "Or coal?"

"Wrong on both," Duncan chortled. "Since '79, we've gotten more new energy from sun, wind, water, and wood than from oil, gas, coal, and uranium. Half of all American utilities now buy surplus power from independent power producers, many—perhaps most—of them using renewable sources. Since 1979, too, more new electric-generating capacity has been ordered from small hydro plants and windpower than from coal or nuclear plants or both, not even counting the cancellation of more than a hundred of those plants. In fact, the scorecard for 1980–84, in thousands of megawatts, is something like this: nuclear orders and letters of intent, zero; coal orders and letters of intent, twelve—only one of them since 1981; nuclear and coal cancellations, seventy-seven; cogeneration orders and letters of intent, about twenty-five; renewable ditto, more than twenty; cogeneration and renewable cancellations, about five. Look who's winning.

"And as I think I said—but let me emphasize its significance—the delivered energy we're getting now from wood and wood wastes, in both homes and industry, is about twice as much as the delivered energy we're getting from nuclear power, which had a head start of thirty years and direct subsidies totaling more than seventy billion dollars—more than three hundred dollars for every American.

"Sure, the pricing structure, tax system, and incentives that people see—all these matter a lot in how fast this can happen. But you simply can't doubt, anymore, that we've got enough sensible technologies to do the job. The only question now is which ones in which locations will be the winners." Duncan "humphed" and fell silent.

Eunice smiled encouragingly, if a bit sheepishly, and nodded. "Yes, I guess when you put all the pieces together it does sound more reasonable. But it's hard," she explained, "to feel that it's all real when all the average person hears is how impractical sustainable sources are. Shouldn't this Department be telling people the other side of the story?"

"Right!" said Duncan. "If only you'd write our budget that way!"

"Hmm," Eunice thought for a moment, then brightened. "Well, okay, I will. From now on a technology is going to have to stand on its merits. It's stupid to spend most of our money trying to develop devices that'll never pay for themselves, and then not have money left to buy the things that we know will give us the most energy at the lowest cost. I suppose it's just the problem you mentioned earlier—that fancy billion-dollar gadgets are glamorous for the technologists, but simple and cheap ones, such as better windows, aren't?"

"Precisely," said Duncan. "But what you're asking for is a wholesale re-education of half the scientists and engineers in the country."

"Well," said Eunice firmly, "let it begin here. If those technologists want to do things for fun, let them pay for it themselves, just like they pay to go to the movies. If the big high-tech companies think it would be a nifty idea to build some kind of far-out billion-dollar device that, if it worked, would make energy at prices nobody can afford, then let them put up their own money. It's my job to figure out how to spend the taxpayers' money—and that's the little people, like old Mr. McFarland who lives in a tumble-down house down on Elm Street. From now on I'm going to help Americans get the most energy services for their dollar." She looked defiantly at Duncan, but he offered no argument at all.

"Of course," she continued more gently, "I hope the technologists will have fun doing that, too, and from your description it sounds like there's no end of exciting things to invent and discover."

"More than enough challenges to occupy all our technologists for generations," Duncan reassured her.

"But if they don't enjoy doing what people are willing to pay for," Eunice concluded, "it seems to me that they need job counseling, not more handouts. This Department may have misspent a lot of money, which may not in itself be bad; because if we don't make mistakes, we won't learn anything. But as long as I'm here, I'm not going to run it like a charity for distressed technological gentlefolk. I'm going to run it just like I ran that bake sale: I'll do my best to satisfy my customers with good buys."

"Do I take it, then," said Duncan, his admiration beginning to show, "that you *do* now feel somewhat reassured about the adequacy of sustainable energy sources at reasonable prices—if, of course, we use energy with proper efficiency?"

"Yes," said Eunice carefully. "I must say," she continued with growing confidence, "I started out quite skeptical about all this. But, if I think back over all you've said, it does seem that you've figured out costs and quantities. Adding up what you've said"— she rifled back through her notes—"it seems to me that if you're right, we can get enough heat, liquid fuels for transportation, and electricity from sustainable sources that are now available, at a price not substantially higher—and, in fact, probably lower—than we're paying now."

"And certainly lower than the price we'd otherwise have to pay to build the coal and nuclear plants, synfuel plants, Arctic pipelines, and so forth that we'd eventually need, without those sustainable replacements, as today's oil and gas supplies dwindled," added Duncan.

"Yes. Yes. I'm convinced," said Eunice. "But I'm also afraid," she continued with a tinge of weariness, "that I've had enough of numbers for just now. I feel as though I've been sucked into a calculator and sped past the screen again and again. So can we please do something else for a bit?"

"Why, Madam Secretary," Duncan said, grinning, as he looked at his watch, "do you realize we've talked the day away? A break is indeed in order. Would you like a final cup for the road? Good. Let me brew some fresh."

Duncan rose gracefully and headed to the next room, while Eunice wondered again whether this job wasn't more than she'd bargained for.

13 There's Work to Do

THE NEXT DAY was Friday, the end of Eunice's first week as Secretary of Energy. As her official limo conveyed her to the Forrestal Building for the fifth time, she actually began to feel as though she had a right to be there, even if she didn't belong to all the proper clubs. Thanks to her tutorials from Duncan, she realized she probably knew a fair bit more about the Big Picture than most of the people who worked for her. "Comforting feeling," she thought. "I wonder if it's realistic." She got out of the limousine unassisted and headed inside. It still threw off her driver, who was accustomed to passengers feigning helplessness. Why, one time, James told her, he had unaccountably forgotten about the Very Important Person in the back seat and gotten out for a smoke when he arrived at their destination. It wasn't until he flicked the butt of his cigarette away that he heard the knocking on the window and, flustered, opened the door for the disgruntled VIP.

As had become her habit, Eunice made a beeline for her meeting with Barb, her secretary. "No problem today," Barb drawled. "It's Friday. Nobody will expect any substance out of you until after the weekend. I'll tell them you left early to go to lunch at the Old Executive Office Building."

So it was off to another session with Duncan. And, as she made her way down the hallway, she could already taste his good coffee.

"You know," Eunice began brightly as she walked into Duncan's office, "this sustainable energy business is intriguing, but what about all the people who work in the industries you say are on the way out? Do they just start collecting welfare?"

"Wait a minute," protested Duncan. "Whatever gave you the idea that jobs will be lost when we switch to sustainable energy?"

"Well, there's my brother-in-law, who works for an oil company. And back in Illinois, where they're still building big nuclear plants, thousands of construction workers are worried about losing their jobs if those plants are canceled."

"Sure, I can see why you'd worry about that," said Duncan. "When a firm starts building a large energy facility, hundreds of very visible jobs are created. Yet, per dollar spent, efficiency and renewables create at least as many jobs at the time of construction, and often even more afterward. But the jobs aren't concentrated at just one site. In the long run, that makes a healthier local and national economy. There won't be a net job loss because of the shift to renewables, but you are right—there will be a shift to different jobs. Some of the displaced workers can make a direct transition. The metalworker who can weld together the cooling pipes for a nuclear reactor can also learn to plumb a solar water-heating system. Of course, if the joints aren't quite perfect, the consequences are much easier to handle in the solar case—they're annoying to a family rather than deadly to a whole city—but that's another subject."

Now it was Eunice's turn to hold up her hand. "Hang on," she said. "I want to see some solid numbers on this one. If my brother-in-law ends up unemployed because of one of my policies, I'll never hear the end of it."

"Ah, Eunice, you do seem to want the whole story," said Duncan. "It's not that complicated, really, but there are ins and outs and misleading statistics. Take an argument that's a favorite of many hard energy types: We have to have ever more energy or the economy can't expand and people won't have jobs. There's a simple analogy that disproves this argument. For the first three decades after World War II, the economy was expanding; employment and energy use grew, seemingly hand in hand. But, although those two trends were simultaneous, one was not the cause of the other. Over the same period, the consumption of Coca-Cola also grew; but that doesn't mean we necessarily need to drink more Coke to make the economy grow. Now that the real price of energy is much higher than it was in the 1960s, it makes sense for efficiency to grow faster than the economy, and hence for energy use to *shrink* while the economy grows. Improvements in energy efficiency will simply improve the economic performance of firms with enough common sense to use energy more productively. If those firms can keep their operating costs down by not wasting energy, they stand a better chance of prospering and keeping their employees well paid. In fact, using energy efficiently can *reduce* the percentage of GNP needed to buy energy services—and thus make the energy sector *de*flationary, a net exporter of capital and jobs to the rest of the economy.

"Take the people of Red Wing, Minnesota," he continued. "It's a town of about fourteen thousand, some fifty miles south of the Twin Cities. When the town built a plant to convert its municipal garbage into energy, making a profit for the town was only one of the aims. The seventy-odd tons of garbage that they burn every day also translates into stable energy costs for a tannery, which, with four hundred jobs, is a principal employer in town. Incidentally, the garbage-to-energy plant also has a payroll of more than one hundred fifty thousand dollars a year, brings in about that much in net income, and saves the town the expense of doing something else with the trash."

"Well, that's just one town," said Eunice. "I want you to explain what's really going on with energy and jobs."

"Okay, okay, I'm getting there," said Duncan. "You sure are lively for a Friday morning. Anyway, there are three basic employment effects that we'll look at.

"First, we have to examine the direct employment of people to build and operate an energy facility. We can compare how many people must be hired to supply a particular energy service using renewable energy, efficiency, or depletable energy sources.

"Second, we need to see what effect is caused by the ongoing costs of operating an energy system. I'm going to argue that the less it costs to operate, the more money will be available to buy other products—and the more jobs will be created in the businesses that people will patronize with the money they have left over.

"Third, we need to consider the other effects on the local and national economies. One issue is the type and location of jobs created by a new energy project. We may judge the effects differently if the new jobs are in the same place as the people who use the energy, or if the jobs are long-lasting instead of being part of a boom-and-bust cycle. Another angle is how the energy system affects the other industries in the city or community. Let's look at each of these in turn."

"All right, fire away," said Eunice, flipping to a new page on her legal pad.

"Hang on, let me get Hobart in on this one," said Duncan. He rose and moved to the doorway. "Hobart!" he hollered, "can you bring the energy and employment file?"

Hurried sounds of rummaging came from across the hall, and soon Duncan's assistant scampered in, pulled up a chair, and perched himself on it, crossing his legs Indian-style. Duncan grinned and shot a quick glance at Eunice. "The numbers from *Energy and Jobs,* please," Duncan prompted. He reached for the sheet that Hobart passed him, glanced at it, and looked up.

"Ah, yes," he resumed, "the very fact that you install solar energy equipment instead of building a power plant or other large energy facility will lead to the employment of more people. According to a study by the congressional Office of Technology Assessment, an eight-hundred-megawatt coal plant provides an average of about eight hundred jobs during the plant's lifetime, while it is under construction or in use. But supplying the same energy through the use of solar collectors would create thirteen hundred to two thousand jobs, without costing the consumers of the energy a penny more. The reason is simple: For every dollar spent on solar energy, a higher portion goes to pay for labor, thus providing meaningful work for more people. In addition, solar installations can be completed more quickly—in months—while large conventional plants have lead times upwards of a decade. So more of the cost of the power plant represents interest paid out during construction, an expense that lines the pockets of bankers and stockholders instead of benefiting many tradespeople."

"That's easy enough to understand," said Eunice.

"Now, even more jobs are created when existing buildings are retrofitted," said Duncan, "since the process of putting insulation into an existing ceiling is even more labor-intensive than installing it in a new house. That is, of the thousand dollars or so that insulating a roof may cost, a very high percentage—typically sixty to seventy percent—goes to pay for the labor of the installers. A correspondingly low percentage—thirty to forty percent—is spent on materials. Since a lot of the energy action in the next couple of decades is going to revolve around bringing the current housing and commercial stock up to snuff, that's a rosy prospect for the building trades."

"Run that past me one more time," said Eunice. "How is it that these renewables are cheaper *and* give more people jobs?"

"It's simple," said Duncan. "The extra money spent for labor to build, say, a solar collector is more than balanced by the lower cost of materials—there's less of them, especially the expensive kinds—and of the necessary production machinery compared to, say, a nuclear plant. Intuitively, we can see that even a very large amount of glass-fiber insulation will be a cheaper way to provide a given unit of energy service than its nuclear competitor, a rein-forced concrete-and-steel dome a hundred yards in diameter."

"Some people make the argument," Hobart chimed in, "that solar employees are paid lower wages than others. This, however, is not generally true. In fact, since most solar energy companies were founded within the past ten years, many of them offer such added benefits as worker ownership and control."

"Of course, we need to look at the flip side of the coin," said Duncan. "Will the shift to renewables reduce employment in the depletable energy business? Let's take the utility industry, for instance." Duncan looked down at the sheet in his lap. "Between 1961 and 1973, electric utilities more than doubled their output, more than tripled their revenues, and more than quadrupled the amount they spent on construction. Nonetheless, employment in the utility industry rose by barely twenty percent during that period. In fact, fossil fuels and electric power are two of the industries that create the fewest jobs per million dollars invested in them: about ten jobs per million dollars, compared with fifty-five jobs in food and related products or ninety in textile production. And it's not hard to see why—a huge power plant is so automated that it can be staffed by just a handful of people once construction is completed. Furthermore, that statistic of ten jobs per million bucks counts the construction work as though it were spread out evenly over the lifetime of the plant. In fact, building power plants is a boom-bust business, done essentially by skilled migrant work-ers."

"Actually," Hobart's eyes glittered as he broke in again, "the net effect is worse than that. Building a one-gigawatt power station . . ."

"Such as a big reactor," translated Duncan.

". . . loses the economy, directly and indirectly, more than four thousand net jobs. That's because the heavy cost of construction," he answered Eunice's surprised look, "starves the rest of the economy of capital that could be used to build other, more labor-intensive goods. Actually," he corrected himself, "almost anything you can possibly build is more labor-intensive, per dollar invested, than power plants."

"I think I understand these numbers," said Eunice. "Let's go on."

"Very well," Duncan chortled. "I hope you realize that you just understood in twenty minutes what has taken some economists years to figure out. But at least you didn't have the disadvantage of an economics degree to overcome.

"The next effect, known as the 'respending effect,' is most significant in terms of the number of jobs that it affects. Here's how it works: When homeowners improve their energy efficiency, they have more money left over to buy other things. For example, after you install insulation in your attic, you'll pay a lower monthly utility bill. If you pay a lower utility bill, you can spend at least part of the money you save on different goods. In other words, you'll probably buy a new rug or stick a few more toys under your Christmas tree. It's not likely that you'll buy a barrel of oil. Since you're buying other goods, your dollars are creating jobs in other sectors of the economy. And since the utility and fossil-fuel industries are among the least labor-intensive around, the money you spend on other goods produces more jobs than spending an equivalent amount on depletable energy. It certainly gives America more jobs than sending that money to an oil-exporting country in the Middle East or Latin America."

"Excuse me," said Eunice, "but how do you know that?"

A slightly hurt look flashed across Duncan's face but vanished as quickly as it had appeared; she *had* been questioning his facts all week. "Well," he said, "I'm glad you're keeping me on my toes. You're right to call people on their numbers in this business. The conclusions I mentioned have been supported by reams of research, by groups such as CONEG—that's the Coalition of Northeast Governors—and the U.S. General Accounting Office. To quote from all of them would constitute a book in itself, but I'll mention a few typical findings. One of the most recent such studies—called *Energy and Jobs*—was assembled by CONEG and published in 1983. It concluded that appropriate, cost-effective use of solar energy in the Northeast alone would create some forty thousand jobs, that increased use of wood would bring with it another thirty to forty thousand jobs, and that efficiency would weigh in with more than sixty-two thousand jobs. Remember, these numbers are just for the Northeast."

"And a Wisconsin study, 'How Low-Income Energy Conservation Affects the State Economy,' done by David Hewitt in 1982, said pretty much the same thing," said Hobart. "People in Wisconsin spend a billion dollars a year keeping their homes warm in the winter. If, say, three thousand dollars were invested per home to cut those bills by forty percent—that's a pretty conservative estimate; for that much money they should do lots better—a total of twelve thousand jobs would be created, counting both the jobs involved in the retrofits and those created by people spending the extra disposable income they would have. That's enough to knock, uh, let's see, half a percentage point off the state's unemployment rate." Hobart lost himself in shepherding imaginary decimal points across his lap as he recalculated his assumptions, beaming gnomishly as the number checked out.

"Good example," said Duncan. "Now, the next . . ."

"Wait, wait," Hobart insisted. "I have another one—a really good one."

"By all means," Duncan yielded with a wave of his hand.

"It's about Austin, Texas, see," Hobart said, "where matters were more urgent than in Wisconsin. They have a municipal utility there, and the city had to decide whether to invest more than three-quarters of a billion dollars in a piece of a nuclear power plant to provide their electricity. Not only was the price tag staggering, but the plant was being built more than three hours away; so it wouldn't even have employed any of the city's residents. The money to pay for it would have gone to bondholders in Dallas and

New York, turbine makers and uranium processors out-of-state, and so forth. Instead, city leaders realized that they could simply put money into efficiency and solar water heating, and create more than seventeen thousand job-years in Austin itself. In fact, the process of building a 'conservation power plant' for Austin is proceeding almost twice as fast as they expected."

"That's a lot of jobs," mused Eunice.

"Yup," said Duncan, "and it points out one of the most important effects of efficiency and renewables. In general, sustainable energy investments will create jobs where the buyers of that sustainable energy are. Large energy facilities, on the other hand, because they supply power for so many people, are typically built far from most of the eventual users of the energy."

"Donuts. . . ," interrupted Hobart.

"That's a nickname for me," Duncan explained to Eunice's look of confusion.

". . . the real effect of out-of-town energy is worse. Take Wooster, Ohio, a city of ninety-six thousand. In 1980, energy costs there totaled about three-and-a-half thousand dollars per household for energy used in homes and the commercial sector. That was about average for the United States. And about nine-tenths of that money flowed right out of Wooster—the equivalent of the loss of some seven thousand jobs. On a national scale, that adds up to a United States energy bill of more than nine percent of the Gross National Product. And Wooster is fairly typical. Communities as diverse as Springfield, Illinois; Santa Cruz, California; and Franklin County, Massachusetts, have conducted their own studies and obtained similar results. Typically, eighty to ninety percent of the money a community spends on energy leaves that town right away. That compares poorly with an average of sixty percent for all trade."

"Where does all the money go?" asked Eunice.

"Some of it goes to Mexico—and then back to New York banks," said Duncan, "some to Venezuela, some to the Middle East and other OPEC countries. Some goes to Alaska, some to the oil barons of Texas and Oklahoma, but very little stays and circulates in the city or town where the energy was finally bought. That money drains away, and with it our economic lifeblood; it becomes unavailable for more permanent or productive investment. In contrast, sustainable energy draws on local, often underemployed talent—carpenters, plumbers, welders—who typically can install insulation or solar water heaters with little additional training. And many of the materials can be made in the area where they are used. As money circulates in a region, it creates economic activity and employment every time it changes hands. The state of Nebraska, for instance, found that a dollar spent on depletable energy would only return seventy cents in economic benefit to the community where the energy was bought. But the same dollar, spent on energy efficiency or renewables, would return two dollars and fifty cents in regional economic activity."

"How can it create more than a dollar's worth of activity?" puzzled Eunice.

"No sleight of hand," Duncan said, grinning. "It comes from the fact that money can circulate several times in a community before it leaves. The plumber who installs your hot water system can buy a meal at a local restaurant, passing some money on to waiters and cooks, who then spend some portion of their incomes at the supermarket and the hairdresser, and so on."

"Okay, I see," said Eunice. "If you buy depletable energy, it's like a game of Monopoly where money gets pulled out of the game instead of being passed back and forth between the players."

"Right, except that this is *real* money." Duncan continued. "One more advantage in the employment created by sustainable energy is that it causes less dislocation than the fossil-fuel business. That's a result of the relatively small scale of most of the sustainable projects. When a centralized energy plant is built, workers flock to remote areas, live there for a few years, and leave ghost towns behind them when the work is done. Prime examples of this are the boom towns that sprang up in Colorado when oil shale looked like the next Gold Rush. Suddenly, villages such as Parachute and Rifle swelled with boom-town drifters and construction workers all hoping to land jobs on the projects. When people started using less oil and the price of crude dropped, Exxon and Arco realized that oil shale would amount to nothing but a millstone about their necks. So the projects collapsed, leaving a network of roads that aimlessly crisscross the Rockies, hard-hats who moved on in search of the next boom, vacant stores and office buildings, and bars whose patrons have left in search of greener pastures. Logic, economic realities, and human needs would have been better served if the workers had stayed where they originally lived and been hired to weatherize houses, retool automobile assembly lines for better fuel efficiency, and install solar collectors. Because we didn't do that, we have busted shale-oil boom towns in the West *and* unemployed people in Detroit.

"In fact," added Duncan, "by my best estimates, energy efficiency and renewable sources just in Colorado have *already* grown to the point where they're producing more than twice as much energy as we could ever have gotten from the Colony oil-shale project—which would have been the biggest construction project in history, dwarfing the Panama Canal. But the Colony energy, assuming the project ever worked, would have come far later, at ten times the cost, and would have disrupted the fragile Western Slope economy—*destroying* the sustainable ranching and small businesses there through inflation and job competition while building up unsustainable boom towns. The efficiency and renewables, on the other hand, have created lasting, high-quality jobs spread throughout the state. In fact, efficiency and renewables are already at least a quarter-of-a-billion-dollar-a-year business in Colorado."

"Why, then," asked Eunice suspiciously, "haven't I heard of it? It should be as famous as Silicon Valley."

"Because," Duncan explained, "it's not shown in state economic statistics as 'efficiency and renewables'; it's shown instead under headings such as 'hardware stores,' 'lumberyards,' 'construction and contracting,' 'window manufacture,' and 'home renovation.' "

Eunice relaxed and nodded.

"And incidentally," added Duncan, "another manifestation worth noting is the number of students in Colorado and a lot of other states enrolled in special efficiency-and-renewables programs, becoming solar technicians and designers, house doctors, and superinsulators. Colleges in some states, including Michigan and Washington, have entire departments devoted to the science and art of saving energy. In fact, when a friend of mine at San Jose State—a physicist named Don Aitken—taught his students how to solarize their dorms so everyone could take solar showers, it really changed their lives. Those students discovered they could take charge of their energy use, let the sun into their lives, and learn the skills to capture solar energy—and every one of them went on to a responsible job in solar policy or technology.

"You see," Duncan added, "sustainable energy can come in many sizes, not just Extra Large. In other words, enterprising folks can easily launch their own efficiency business. But ordinary people can't start their own oil refinery, because that business must be big to succeed. Sustainable energy sources are more conducive to the entrepreneurship that is part of our American heritage. And the benefits don't just accrue to the owners of the businesses. In terms of new jobs, small businesses are where the action is. Two-thirds of all new jobs are created in businesses that employ twenty people or fewer. If you count new jobs created versus old jobs abolished in recent years, the Fortune 500 companies have created *no* additional net jobs. And for all the reasons we have already seen, renewable energy and energy efficiency are better bargains than depletable fuels."

"Hmm, it does sound like efficiency and solar energy are good for employment, then," Eunice said. "How about that."

"That's not all they're good for," said Duncan. "Since energy costs are a substantial portion of the operating costs of many businesses, keeping those costs down will help all businesses stay afloat, like the tannery we started off talking about. Also, there are a number of secondary benefits for the environment, the poor and elderly, and national security—besides just our pocketbooks. Let's talk about all these secondary benefits today. What do you say?"

"I'll drink to that," said Eunice, "and I'll bet if we pour it soon, the rest of the morning pot won't have turned to oily black goo yet."

14 *Energy for Equity*

YEAH, BOSS," said Hobart in parting, "I'll look over those new forecasts from Exxon and Shell and see if any pattern emerges. Maybe they've scaled back their year 2000 estimates of energy use. Give you a new line for the matrix." He winked and scooted, reminding Eunice of a small, furry, amiable animal— maybe a chinchilla. Duncan shut the door behind his assistant and sat back down.

"You know, Duncan," Eunice began, "it's funny that you should say that sustainable energy is good for the poor. I've always thought of it as a toy of the rich. You know, even buying a solar heating system would have been a lot of money to shell out for any of us Middle America people."

"I can sure see why it would seem that way," agreed Duncan. "Many of the early solar installations were put up on the homes of the well-to-do, often to heat their swimming pools or spas. With all the price distortions in the market, that was one of the first places it was clearly economical to put them. And, of course, the high up-front cost of fancy solar equipment, which often makes it hard for individuals or families to raise the money for solar improvements, hinders the rich less. But solar has long passed the point of being a plaything for the wealthy. In fact, since it's a cheaper way of providing the same energy services than conventional energy, it is especially well suited to the needs of the less affluent."

"Yes, that's what I would have expected, based on what you've explained over the past few days," said Eunice. "But I just haven't heard of any instances where that has actually happened."

"Well, by all means, let me give you a few," Duncan said. "In general, many of the circumstances that have led poor people to turn to renewables are cases in which they are too poor to do anything else. Take the case of Colorado's San Luis Valley, the world's largest alpine valley—it's the size of Delaware, extremely cold, quite sunny, and has some of the poorest people in the country. For decades, the Hispanic residents of this region cut firewood on what they considered to be communal property that dated back to centuries-old Spanish land grants. However, over time the land had actually been lost to taxes—part of the sordid history of Anglo land grabs," Duncan said, scowling. "Anyway, a few years ago the new corporate landowner fenced off the forest and started shooting at people who tried to gather firewood the way they had done all their lives. You might say the folks had an instant energy crisis. Being poor, they couldn't afford the propane- or oil-fired heating systems that were the conventional alternatives to wood. One couple tells how it got so cold in their house one winter that the toothpaste and the eggs froze."

"I guess efficient refrigerators weren't what they needed," quipped Eunice.

"Easy for us to joke about now," Duncan said, "but it was a real crisis for them. Obviously, they couldn't buy fancy solar systems either. But they were able to employ versions of solar energy that were much more practical for them. A few people in the community knew how to build solar greenhouses and solar air collectors. These cost a couple of hundred dollars and used mostly scavenged materials. Soon, the people with the know-how held workshops to teach their neighbors how to build these solar systems. And in barn-raising style, homes all over the valley became solar heated. In just a few years, the valley went from fewer than half a dozen to *thousands* of solar structures. One out of every four or five homes in the valley is now heated by the sun. Solar buildings include trailers, the post office, and an ice cream parlor. They even have a solar mortuary. The people who sparked the movement now take pride in noting solar greenhouses attached to the homes of people who did not take part in the original program, who have learned the technology second- or third-hand. The program cost four to five million dollars. But that money was spent in local hardware stores and lumberyards. And now the energy savings are that much *each year*. Other renewable energy projects have sprouted, too, including a number of wind machines and a plant to produce ethanol from cull potatoes. Besides saving money, the shift to energy self-reliance has boosted the citizens' self-esteem and initiative. Emboldened by their success in the field of energy, two of the people who spearheaded the greenhouse project have branched out into health care and have started a local ambulance and paramedic service—crucial in their county, which doesn't have a single physician."

"That's tremendous," said Eunice. "Oh, I like that. Is a lot of that happening?"

"Quite a bit, actually," Duncan said. "Here, take another example. This one comes from Cheyenne, Wyoming, where a community greenhouse was built with mostly volunteer labor in 1977. Since then, the solar-heated greenhouse has supplied fresh produce for the local Meals-on-Wheels program, for the volunteer staff who tend the vegetable beds, and for sale to the public. The greenhouse has been completely solar heated, even in record-breaking cold winters, thanks to the black fifty-five-gallon barrels filled with water that soak up heat when the sun shines. Even more remarkable is the way the greenhouse is staffed. Senior citizens from the area work in it in exchange for the fruits and vegetables of their labor, as do some physically handicapped people and youth offenders working off court fines."

Eunice's eyes widened. "Another success story!" she said. "How many of them do you have up your sleeve?"

"Lots, actually," Duncan replied. "But before I go rattling off more examples, let me have a crack at explaining some of the theory behind this stuff. If you think the average American has had a hard time with the price of energy—which has risen twice as fast as inflation since 1978—consider how hard it is for people on lower incomes. Many of the poor live on fixed incomes that have fallen behind inflation. For many, heating bills have grown to equal the payments on their mortgages. For others—often senior citizens who are already paying as much as they can for housing, and for whom moving would be difficult if not impossible—the high cost of fossil fuels means they must choose between heating and eating. Let me put these costs in perspective. A seventy-year-old living on social security payments of four hundred dollars per month could expect to spend as much as half of that in the winter to heat a typical 1960s-vintage home in Chicago. For those living on Aid to Families with Dependent Children, AFDC, energy costs can total an even higher percentage of their monthly stipend. Nearly five million low-income people each year face a cutoff of natural gas because they can't afford to pay their fuel bills. And even for the average Chicago renter, energy costs in 1983 were typically a third of the monthly rent, compared to twenty-three percent in 1975 and a measly eighth in 1961."

"That's terrible," said Eunice. "To have to choose between being cold or being hungry."

"It sure is," Duncan said. "You've probably noticed in the news that whenever a severe cold spell sets in, a few people die of the cold—inside their own homes. In a characteristic Band-Aid approach, the federal government has provided a couple of billion dollars per year in fuel assistance to the poor and about a tenth that amount to help the poor weatherize their homes. In effect, the system is simply providing a subsidy to the companies that sell electricity, gas, and oil; the poor end up having to pay it immediately to their fuel supplier. In fact, some government housing projects are so energy-inefficient that tenants in one Chicago building faced three-hundred-dollar-a-month heating bills, even though they were keeping the temperature below fifty degrees. As one of the saner federal studies of the issue found, 'Poor people are poor in part because they lack the resources to be self-reliant.' "

"That does sound like a pretty sane study," Eunice said. "So they probably suggested that poor people be given the resources to become more self-reliant. Were their recommendations put into effect?"

"Of course not," said Duncan grimly. "This is Washington. But that hasn't stopped a considerable number of the poor from solving their problems on their own. That's not to say that it hasn't been difficult. Poor people face tremendous obstacles: lack of capital, lack of expertise, and despair. But when energy becomes an issue of survival and no one else will help them, people can often muster the resources to take care of themselves.

"There's a great example from a Black community in southern California," Duncan added. "It's called the West Side Community Development Corporation, and it was launched by a group of welfare-rights women. It has two aims: to offer low-cost renewable energy and efficiency to a poor section of San Bernardino that needs that kind of help, and to train people in energy skills. Many of the students, who are paid at minimum wage while in the program, go on to other jobs in energy and construction. The firm has cut its costs in half over the years and has pioneered a low-cost, high-performance solar water heater. What's more, participants have expanded the program to include the renovation of some thirty properties in the poor section of the city in which they live. They've installed solar systems in low-income housing, senior citizens centers, and farm labor housing."

"Renovating housing?" mused Eunice. "That's probably a pretty important part of helping the poor save energy. I mean, insulation won't do much good if the house is falling apart and half the windows are broken."

"True enough," said Duncan. "In fact, there's a builder in rural eastern Kentucky who has been renovating dilapidated homes to include superinsulation. The cost for the *entire* rehab project—house, lot and rehab costs—was just twenty-seven thousand dollars. That worked out to a monthly payment of one hundred dollars and an *annual* heating bill of a bit over eighty dollars. And energy retrofits can keep inner-city housing from being abandoned by landlords. A group in Chicago that helps people fix up housing, run food coops, and generally get organized did a neighborhood study that showed that a typical, economically sound

Chicago apartment building would become unprofitable by 1990 because of rising energy costs—unless it were fitted with appropriate, cost-effective weatherization. Pretty impressive, eh?"

"Indeed it is," said Eunice. "But can we take a break now? I feel like I'm in need of one of your stretches."

"Sure can," said Duncan. "But just remember: I stretch muscles, not facts."

15 Energy for Development

*A*H, SIGHED EUNICE, that feels better. The muscle knot that had been starting to form in her shoulders seemed looser, and she even felt less harried now that she had limbered up a bit. As Duncan unlocked the conference room door and grinned conspiratorily at her, Eunice worked out the last of her nervous energy with a couple of ceiling reaches. She followed Duncan back to his office with a demure air that vanished as soon as she was once more settled into her chair.

"Duncan," she began, her renewed enthusiasm showing, "I can see why the poor in this country are better served by sustainable energy than the depletable kind, although it seems that current government energy programs aren't helping them very much. But what about the poor of the world? You know, all those poor, starving children I always see in the magazine ads. Are they facing an energy crisis, too?"

Duncan frowned. "That's a pretty complicated question," he answered. "The Third World is a really diverse bunch of peoples and nations. Some people in the less developed countries are pretty self-sufficient. A few are even rich. But most are not. For example, the per capita use of commercial energy—fuels and power that are sold and shown in government stats—in the United States is nearly fifty times what it is for a billion and a half people in the developing world. Although," he amended, "most of the energy used in most developing countries is noncommercial, so people actually use more energy there than the official statistics indicate. Still, many developing nations are facing an energy crisis even more severe than the United States or many other industrialized countries, even though their people typically obtain far fewer energy services than Americans do."

Eunice wrinkled her brow in thought. "Why is that?" she asked.

Duncan pulled a bulky file marked "Third World—Basics" from one of his cabinets, sank into his chair, and let the file fall open at random on his lap. "Well," he said, "developing nations often import more oil than they can afford, and they use those supplies very inefficiently. Very few of them make much use of their sustainable resources even though many Third World countries have rich renewable resources and abundant opportunities to use energy more efficiently. However, before I go any further, please bear in mind that it can be dangerous to generalize about the matter. You can't picture the entire Third World as confronting a uniform energy crisis any more than . . ."

"Any more than Maine and Texas have the same energy problems," concluded Eunice.

"Uh . . . yeah, that's right, in fact," Duncan said. "Or any more than people in a Navajo hogan have the same energy problems as rich people in Taos or Santa Fe, even though they're both supposedly within the boundaries of New Mexico. So I'm going to generalize, but cautiously. Also, I'll try to mention exceptions to the general rule.

"The most widespread energy problem in the Third World is a shortage of fuel wood—most severe in such countries as India, Nepal, Indonesia, the Sahel on the edge of the Sahara, and East Africa. In rural Kenya, for instance, fuel wood provides almost all of the energy consumed—ninety-five percent or so. But as the population has grown—and at present rates it will double in less than twenty years—the villagers have stripped the land of trees. In many African regions people now have to walk dozens of miles to find wood with which to cook their food. After they gather the wood, they typically burn it in three-stone fireplaces, at an efficiency of only five to ten percent. At that rate, people in, say, West Africa use more than five times as much energy per capita to cook their food than do people in the developed nations, even though they eat less and get less actual cooking accomplished. As the demand for firewood grows, the environment is severely affected. The overharvesting of fuel wood has contributed to deforestation, soil erosion, and the conversion of farmland into desert. A related effect is that as wood becomes scarcer, the poor burn animal dung for heating and cooking. Thus, the nutrients in the manure that should refertilize the soil go up in smoke instead."

Eunice fingered her pendant uncomfortably.

"No," said Duncan, "it doesn't smell as nice as mesquite, either." He grinned a bit grimly. "Worse, the smoke is real unpleasant stuff. Many of the women who hunker over those fires get eye and lung infections. Some even go blind."

"Oh!" Eunice gasped. "But that's terrible . . ."

"The crisis is bad in the cities, too," Duncan continued. "Just because people live in cities, mind you, doesn't mean they have Julia Child-type kitchens. In fact, only six percent of the residents of Nairobi, Kenya, have electricity at all; most of them cook over charcoal burners called *jikos*. And charcoal isn't cheap, either— fully one-third of the income of the average urban laborer in Mali, West Africa, goes to pay for cooking fuel. It is circumstances like those that spawned the African proverb: 'It costs as much to heat a pot as it does to fill it.' And as more people move to the cities, the tree situation worsens. When charcoal is made, a lot of the wood is wasted; each meal cooked on charcoal thus requires twice the wood that a meal cooked on wood demands."

"Why, then, do people use charcoal?" Eunice asked. "Goodness," she added, "I don't think I'll ever be able to enjoy a backyard barbecue again."

Duncan smiled sympathetically, but chided, "Oh, come on. Remember, there are vast differences between your cookouts and an African villager's struggle for survival. But even in Third World charcoal uses there are important differences. In many cases charcoal makes good sense. It is easier to ship and handle than wood;

it can burn cleaner and better; and in applications where the char-coal process isn't stripping away the forest, it can be a sensible energy source if it's used efficiently with the right kind of stove and pot.

"And I don't mean to paint too gloomy a picture," he added. "There are solutions to most of the problems facing us. New stoves have been developed that are three to six times more efficient than the old three-stone fireplaces. Programs are under way to insulate charcoal stoves, doubling their efficiency at an extra cost of one dollar each—half the price of a traditional *jiko*. Still, because of cultural factors, it's often hard for these fuel-saving innovations to become established. Often, for example, the fireplace is more than just a food-cooker—it's the hearth, a social center, a space heater, a food-smoker—and efforts to improve efficiency must be balanced against their social acceptability."

"Oh, yes," Eunice brightened, "I know what you mean. My father fought like the dickens to keep our old wood-fired cast-iron kitchen stove, even when everyone else was getting gas ranges. And it was because he liked to come home, sit down in the rocking chair next to the stove, and warm up while he read the Sears catalog or the *Saturday Evening Post*. But surely, development aid and industrialization must be helping the situation."

"Maybe I'm being too hard again," said Duncan, "but often aid just makes things worse. For example, during the 1960s, so-called experts from the Western world introduced what they called the Green Revolution, a system of agriculture that promised vastly increased harvests. But that increase was to come from the use of tractors and petrochemical fertilizers. Let's put aside the social dislocations brought about by these innovations and look just at the energy effects. The nations that had been given these new technologies came to be tied to the continuing availability of cheap oil for machines, pumps, fertilizers, and pesticides. But soon after this change the bubble of cheap oil burst, and countries were faced with growing oil-import bills. Their petroleum-fueled in-dustrialization led to the same problem. India, for example, now must earmark about half of its export earnings to pay for oil imports. This need for hard currency forced farmers to grow such cash crops as coffee, cocoa, and sugar cane instead of food crops designed to meet the nation's own food needs. As a consequence, the self-reliance of the Third World countries was further eroded.

"Another consequence of the oil price shocks," Duncan said, "was to slow real economic growth in the West to one or two percent per year. That slowdown happened despite the fact that OPEC members were reinvesting most of their oil earnings in industrialized countries. In the Third World the effect was disastrous. Some developing economies were able to borrow more to keep their rates of economic growth high, but the economies of the poorer countries actually shrank during those years. Even those countries that had borrowed to keep growing found that when their growth slowed, they couldn't make payments on their loans from Western banks. Now, Western banks and governments may be stuck with the bill for the unwise development that they promoted."

"That sounds serious," said Eunice. "What can they do?"

"First," Duncan said, "we all have to realize that, even more than developed countries, the nations of the Third World cannot afford their petroleum addictions; they are badly in need of truly sustainable options. The crisis in firewood use is a classic example of an otherwise renewable resource—wood—being used faster than nature can sustain. But trying to switch to commercial fuels such as kerosene is ruinous. The results of OPEC dependency show that depletable resources are not the answer, and besides, commercial fuels are not even an option for most people suffering from the crisis—they are just too poor.

"Here, as in other cases we've already seen, efficiency improvements are the first necessary step. The firewood problems can be resolved only by reducing the amount of wood that each household requires. Greater efficiency can do that, or alternative fuels can do it. Of course, not all such initiatives will work. For one thing, these programs must be geared toward women, who have the responsibility for cooking and fuel-gathering in the Third World. Instead, many aid agencies just latch on to a favorite technology and call it the solution. For example, attempts to import such technologies as solar cookers have produced heat stroke or burned arms for some of the people who have tried them, but no ongoing solutions to the fuel wood problem. Besides, those technologies again ignore that the cultural roles of a cookstove transcend the simple heating of food."

"It would be like trying to replace all cars with public transit," interjected Eunice, "and not realizing the pleasure our family gets from a Sunday afternoon drive."

"Yeah," Duncan chuckled, "and I'll wager your teenage son would rather take a young lady to the drive-in in a Chevy than cuddle on a subway platform. But here, let me tell you about a few of the more outrageous examples of poor development planning, and perhaps we can reach some conclusions about energy aid to foreign nations in general. Development programs are often conceived more to benefit the donor country than the recipient. For instance, the market for photovoltaic cells in developing countries is largely a function of developed nations' aid policies to their former colonies. Eighty percent of all French solar collectors are exported to the Third World and are typically bought with foreign aid money that came from France in the first place. Yet these foreign transplants often don't work well. And take a look at these pictures on the wall."

Eunice had already noticed them. One was of a very sophisticated-looking solar water heater atop an African-looking building. The other was not nearly so pretty; in fact, it looked like it was held together with chewing gum and baling wire, Eunice thought to herself.

"I keep these pictures here as a constant reminder about what works and what doesn't," said Duncan. "These two water heaters are in the same Kenyan village, within sight of each other. One of my international development spies sent them to me. What do you think?"

"Well," Eunice said, "that one on the right looks like a refugee from the scrap heap. Why, I'd be surprised if it lasted through the first good wind."

"Yeah, that's the funny thing about it," said Duncan, grinning. "The one on the left is foreign-made, supposedly with very-high-performance panels and all. The other was put together locally, jury-rigged from scavenged materials, just as you suspected. But the flashy one broke down soon after it was installed, whereas the locally built system has produced hot water much more consistently." Noting Eunice's look of noncomprehension, he explained, "Local people built it, they understood it, and they could fix it. You know, the standard story in the Third World can be summarized in three words: 'No spare parts.' Such examples abound.

"Reforestation programs, too—one of the greatest needs in the Third World, along with efficient stoves and clean water—are not nearly as attractive for the developed nations, such as France or the United States, to fund. Tree planting is a very simple endeavor, requiring much more labor than capital equipment. Actually, there is real hope for reforestation and slowing the spread of the deserts in the Third World. In Kenya, for instance, women's groups have spearheaded the Greenbelt Movement, which has founded hundreds of public tree-lots and nurseries around the country. And new species such as the *leucena* are being introduced—a drought-resistant tree that fertilizes the soil and can come to maturity in as little as two or three years. If the United States gave an African nation four million dollars for tree planting, much less of that money would make it back to the United States than if the money were given to buy industrial products such as flashy collectors or backhoes that aren't made locally. It comes down to whether we should help less-developed countries acquire what we want them to buy, or to acquire what they really need.

"And even food aid, which makes our missionaries feel so good about themselves, often does more harm than good. I'm not talking," he hastened to add in response to Eunice's shocked look, "about feeding people in refugee camps when some disaster has resulted in mass hunger. But your average everyday grain shipments are often of much greater benefit to American farmers, from whom the U.S. government buys the grain to ship abroad, than to a developing country's future. You see, the free grain undercuts whatever local market may have existed, bankrupting local farmers. It can also divert a country's attention from building real rural self-reliance.

"But, again, it's really important to look carefully at each situation. None of these generalizations is going to be universally applicable. Many aid programs have been carefully developed; the Western workers have known the local culture, asked the people what *they* needed, used the appropriate technology, enhanced local control and decision making, and . . ."

"I remember an old proverb," interrupted Eunice, "about how if you give a man a fish you've fed him for a day; if you teach him how to fish you've fed him for a lifetime."

"Right on, Eunice!" Duncan agreed. "And maybe other people already know more about fishing than we do. Remember, many traditional societies have deep wisdom about sustainable agriculture, coherent cultural tradition, and technologies that stand lightly on the earth. These, combined with the best modern knowledge, can work wonders.

"And, indeed, there are many success stories. People in India and Nepal have built biogas digesters that use cow and pig dung to produce gas for cooking and lighting. The sludge left over after gas production can then be spread on the fields as fertilizer—and the digestion process will have killed most or all of the disease-causing organisms in the manure. China, by the way, promotes such digesters partly as a public health measure, providing disease-free fertilizer. Now, biogas isn't going to be appropriate everywhere. For instance, many Hindis believe that anything cooked over dung products is ritually polluted, so they can only use biogas for lighting and cooking animal food. And other social factors—such as availability of building materials, whether someone will stock and maintain the digester, and how the gas is distributed in the village—are critically important.

"Heh," Duncan chuckled, "you'll enjoy this. It illustrates how important an awareness of local cultural factors can be. In Nepal an aid agency built a biogas digester. The dung inside had to be stirred periodically to keep the bacteria on the job, devouring the sewage. But because of local taboos, no one wanted to take on that task." He grinned at Eunice, who was nodding in complete sympathy. "However, the extension worker built a Buddhist prayer wheel onto the stirring handle. Now, when villagers walk past the digester, they turn the wheel, send out a prayer to the universe—and speed the bacteria on their way."

"Oh my, that's terrific," said Eunice. "Can you tell another success story or two?"

"Some of the nicest successes come from using the ancient wisdom of local builders," said Duncan. "For example, people from Afghanistan to Persia to Mexico long ago discovered the principles of passive solar cooling. On the Mediterranean there were naturally air-conditioned cities two thousand years ago. More recently, the Egyptian architect Hessan Fathy showed his people how to build elegant but very cheap, efficient domed houses using ancient mud-brick technology. I've described the passive solar towns of the Anasazi in our own American Southwest, whose millenia-old buildings still stay within four degrees of sixty-eight degrees Fahrenheit year-round while the outdoor temperature ranges over a hundred degrees. They also invented drip irrigation. And to deal with a modern version of that problem, some farmers in India recently pioneered water wells cased with bamboo when they couldn't get steel well casings—and the bamboo was free, locally available, and worked better.

"Besides these already-tangible successes," Duncan continued, "there's tremendous potential for renewables in the Third World. Many of the new technologies offer sensitive development workers great opportunities. Carefully fitted into a local culture, cheap photovoltaics, for example, can help to electrify most of the developing world. Their use will save countries the impossible expense of running transmission lines over long distances. And small hydropower makes a lot of sense in many places, too, since the equatorial parts of the Third World have plenty of running water that could easily be diverted into small turbines without damaging river systems. In fact, as I've mentioned, in China there's often a tiny turbine—some even have wooden blades—picking off a kilowatt every fifty yards or so along an irrigation ditch.

Eunice heaved a sigh and relaxed. "It doesn't seem so hopeless, then," she offered.

"Well," Duncan replied, "it's a real race. Much of the world remains in crisis. The knowledge and resources exist in the world to meet everyone's energy and food needs; it rankles me to fall asleep each night knowing so little is being done."

Eunice caught Duncan's troubled look. "But what would you do?" she asked.

"First, I'd make sure that all proposed solutions were closely scrutinized from a broader perspective than simply whether the technology works on the test bench. Next," Duncan said determinedly, "we have to give up the dam-it-all approach to development."

"I beg your pardon? Damn it all?" Eunice asked.

"No, dams, as in beavers," Duncan said. "We send engineers to the Third World to help a country develop its resources. A lot of the engineers are frustrated 'beavers' from the Army Corps of Engineers—they can't stand the sight of running water, you know —who have run out of good rivers to dam in this country. So they build huge dams on huge rivers like the Amazon or the Nile and then try to find a way to sell the electricity. These dams may wipe out native peoples or, as in Egypt, stop the river from carrying silt to keep farmlands fertile, while creating stagnant water that causes dreadful diseases for millions of people. The dam builders also forget that these days it can make a lot more sense to develop lighter industries than heavier ones. Why, in Brazil, they've built a dam that generates as much electricity as twelve large nuclear plants, and they don't have anyone to sell the energy to. But the engineers think it's a beautiful dam. And the problem isn't limited to Western technotwits. Often the technical elite in a developing country believes passionately in the 'bigger is better' model. Many ministers want a big project, especially a nuclear one, for the prestige they think it gives them. Many use the excuse of 'rural electrification' to justify power plants for which no grid exists, or could be affordably built. And when a Western nation's aid agencies—for example, our Export-Import Bank—will pay a developing country to haul away one of, say, Westinghouse's nuclear plants, why that's almost too sweet for some Third World power brokers to resist.

"So what am I leading up to?" posed Duncan. "Simply that the Third World's energy crisis will not be solved with massive infusions of foreign aid. Often, when we try to help, we just make things worse. At best, we can provide technical advice on what we know can work and also information on what we have found doesn't work. But while we do, we must be open to learning from those we're trying to teach, because they have longer experience and often even better ideas than we do. Most important, the people in the Third World nations, the ones who will be affected by and supplied with the energy services, must pick the technologies they want. They will have a better idea of what will work culturally for them. If they need technical advice, they can always ask for it. But the Western specialists shouldn't try to sell them on a technology. That's a question they must resolve in their own minds."

"Can an Iowa bumpkin ask you for some advice, then?" Eunice said with a tentative smile. "Where can we get a bite to eat? And, this time, I've made a cultural decision. No international chef's specials, okay?"

"Sure, boss," Duncan replied, grinning. "We'll minimize the culture shock this time."

16 Cleaning Up Our Act

Just as Duncan was handing Eunice her coat to go to lunch, the phone rang. It was Barb, Eunice's secretary, calling to warn them that the Assistant Secretaries were heading off for lunch, so they had better lie low for a while until the pack of them was safely out of the building. So Eunice stifled a midday yawn and stood looking out the window over the Mall. A lavish autumn wind was snapping the flags and the grass was starting to look wintry. Her daydreaming centered on what Duncan had just said. She tried to picture spending half her days wandering through her Dubuque neighborhood, or even out beyond the city limits, scrounging for firewood so that she could cook dinner for her family. It was a difficult thing to imagine. And certainly the alternative—burning animal manure—made her nose wrinkle. Anyway, the tabbies and collies in the neighborhood didn't produce enough to make dung burning seem possible, let alone polite. She wondered, though, whether there was any connection between the Third World and the policies she should pursue as Secretary of Energy. After all, there were hardly any direct aid programs in her budget.

"Tell me, Duncan," she began, "what lessons can we apply to the United States from the energy problems of the Third World? Any of them?"

Duncan, already settled in his chair, leaned back and hooked his thumbs through his belt. "You remember what we were saying about deforestation and the march of the deserts a few minutes ago?" Eunice nodded earnestly. "Well, bad energy policy affects the environment in the industrialized world, too. The effects are somewhat different, but let me argue that efficiency improvements and judicious use of renewable sources can not only relieve some of the problems but also can help clean up our environment and even permit the natural systems of our planet to begin to restore themselves to health.

"You see," Duncan continued, "every pound of coal that we use, every gallon of gasoline, every gram of uranium—each of those represents some degree of insult to the environment. Fuel that we burn sends soot into the air along with noxious chemicals that help cause smog and acid rain. The fuels burned in the United States each year total some two billion tons—more than the combined weight of all the food and timber, iron and steel, copper and aluminum, cement and concrete, that we grow, mine, and use. Nearly all that fuel ends up in the air. A house heated with electricity from a coal-fired plant, for example, is responsible for the release into the air every year of a couple hundred pounds of nitrogen oxides and as much as four or five hundred pounds of sulfur oxides."

Eunice gasped. "But all the ads say how clean electricity is!"

"Sure," Duncan shrugged, "for you. But not at the power-plant end of the transmission lines. Anyway, in the atmosphere, all of these gases mix with clouds, rain, and snow and come down as a witches' brew of acids that has already decimated aquatic life throughout the Northeast and is spreading to the Great Lakes and the Rockies and the Pacific Coast. Such acids are also well on the way to wiping out the famous forests of Germany and Czechoslovakia. Just in America, each house heated with coal-fired electricity engenders enough sulfur oxides each year to fill three times its own volume with acid rain. And anyone who has been to a city dominated by cars—such as Los Angeles, Denver, or Phoenix—knows what kind of an eye-watering, throat-scratching brown pall hangs over those cities.

"When people mine coal and uranium," Duncan went on, "they leave mountains of tailings behind that actually leach poisons into the local streams—a third of a ton of uranium mill tailings every year, plus more than eight tons of other dirt moved to get at the uranium per year—all a result of producing power for one house heated with nuclear electricity. Of course, the mining brings all this material to the surface. Then something has to be done with the land. In several western towns, houses were even built on or out of tailings from uranium mines, which, although very low-grade, still had considerable radioactivity in them. Now, years later, the occupants of those houses are threatened with lung cancer. Coal is often strip-mined, with enormous machines tearing the tops off entire mountain ridges for miles, or eating away whole ranching valleys. Even if some effort is then made to replant the vegetation, mountains and underground aquifers do not easily recover from being skinned and turned upside-down. Coal and uranium miners suffer as well. Hundreds of Navajo uranium miners, for example, have gotten or will get lung cancer from their exposure to radioactive gas in mines that weren't properly vented. Coal miners often suffer 'black lung' from breathing so much coal dust. Many miners have died from these diseases. Many more are crippled. Then, when there is a downturn in electricity demand, the local mining economy is devastated, too.

"Oil is also an ecological culprit. Offshore oil drilling and crude oil shipping are responsible for dumping six million tons of petroleum into the oceans every year. Jacques Cousteau reports that it's hard now to find any part of the world's oceans without oil floating on the surface. Who knows what that is doing, say, to the phytoplankton?" Duncan grinned at Eunice's puzzled look. "They're the tiny plants, floating near the ocean surface, that begin the food chain of the oceans and give the world most of its oxygen.

"Perhaps worst of all, the burning of fossil fuels has raised the amount of carbon dioxide in the atmosphere. That accumulation of carbon dioxide threatens to bring on a phenomenon known as the 'greenhouse effect.' Just as the glass in a greenhouse lets light and heat in but keeps much of the heat from escaping, the carbon dioxide in the atmosphere does the same for the earth. Scientists fear that this effect could raise the temperature worldwide by as much as ten degrees Fahrenheit over the next several decades. Such a warming trend could turn temperate climates into deserts and melt large parts of the polar ice caps, raising the level of the oceans and flooding the coasts of every country in the world."

While Duncan was speaking, Eunice became gradually more and more upset. "That's terrible," she finally burst out. "Isn't there anything we can do to stop all this from happening?"

"Of course there is," said Duncan. "We've known for years how we can stop it. But we have been unwilling, as a country, to take steps to stop these problems. And, outrageously, some people say such things as, 'Well, that's the price we have to pay to have what we want.' Or even 'There's no proof the damage is all that bad.' They claim, for example, that the evidence isn't all in on the accumulation of carbon dioxide in the atmosphere. 'It's just a risk,' they say. Of course, if we wait for all the evidence to be in," Duncan added dryly, "New York will be under ten feet of water. Then the utility scientists will say, 'Oh, dear, you were right; it *was* the fault of the fossil fuel we were burning.' 'No kidding,' the New Yorkers will say as they don their scuba gear. Actually, by then, if you don't like it, you'll be able to get in your rowboat and row up to the Capitol steps to gripe to Congress about it."

Eunice snickered.

"In fact, I'm serious," said Duncan. "But the real point that ought to be driven home to everyone is that we have been ignoring the best way of solving these problem. For acid rain, the experts all talk about draconian worldwide regulation of who can burn how much coal or oil, or having to switch completely to nuclear —you can guess who's pushing that—or 'emission control,' which, naturally, costs money. Like putting scrubbers on factory and electric power plant smokestacks, for instance. But the fact is that if you get more work out of the same amount of electricity, you can burn less coal in the power plants and provide the same energy services—and both problems vastly diminish.

"The first thing we need to do is to start using energy more efficiently. If we insulate our houses, we'll need to burn less fuel to keep them warm; so we won't release as much pollution into the atmosphere, nor will we need to tear up as much land to get the fuels we need. Then the same would be true of all kinds of efficiency improvements—more efficient light bulbs, better-made appliances and motors, and so on. It's just like common sense would tell you—if you use less, you cause less environmental damage."

Suddenly Eunice frowned. "But I remember that car manufacturers always said they couldn't improve gas mileage *and* reduce emissions at the same time. Were they wrong?"

Duncan sighed. "Yes, they were wrong. They even had President Ford snowed. He accepted that argument when he formulated his energy policy in 1975. But now we know better. After all, we now have cars that adhere to the emission standards set by the Clean Air Act *and* get twice the mileage of their ten-year-old predecessors. The car makers were just being lazy and looking for an excuse to evade the pollution regulations. All it took was some Yankee or Japanese or European ingenuity to solve both problems at once. You see, unlike the Big Three in Detroit, Datsun and Honda and Volvo couldn't count on their powerful Washington lobbies to have the rules bent for them."

"Okay," said Eunice, "I see how energy efficiency can benefit the environment. But doesn't doing *anything* cause some pollution? What about manufacturing solar panels?"

"Sure, they're responsible for some pollution, too," said Duncan, "but less than depletable energy sources. And, when you think about it, that's not too surprising. Some kinds of solar panels, for instance, *may* generate a bit more pollution in their manufacture than does, say, a piece of coal plant to produce the equivalent amount of heat. That's mainly because the more materials-intensive—and therefore often the least economical—panels can require a slightly greater bulk of material to build, per unit energy provided. But better-designed panels use *less* material than their hard-tech competitors and offer a very wide range of choice among those materials. Moreover, solar panels don't belch smoke when you operate them. You can go on getting clean heat from them for years. Any extra pollution in the manufacture is far outweighed by what is saved in operating the collectors. In fact, after fewer than eight months of operation, solar panels will represent a smaller environmental impact for all pollutants than a coal plant equipped with scrubbers. And at the end of their lifetime the metal in the collectors can be recycled more easily than, say, concrete in a power plant.

"It boils down," he continued, "to the difference between a technology like solar that requires no further fuel after it is constructed, and a technology like a coal plant that has to be fed fuel every day that it operates. The advantages are even more remarkable for simpler technologies, such as passive solar heating, which just requires a bit more window glass or plastic film. Glass, which is made out of sand, one of the most plentiful materials around, is less pollution-intensive right from the start than comparable depletable energy sources."

"That's great," said Eunice. "Does that mean that *any* efficiency gain or renewable technology will be less polluting than a fossil fuel plant?"

"Well," hedged Duncan, "you know that there are fools out there who can screw up any good thing. Take the wood-burning stove, for example—one of the most ancient technologies for heating. Count Cronstedt developed efficient ceramic stoves for the king of Sweden centuries ago during a Swedish firewood shortage. The king ordered everyone to use them, and soon the stoves spread throughout northern Europe. Some great strides were made more recently, too, with the development of the airtight iron stove, which burns wood much more efficiently. But the slow fires that burn in that type of stove tend to give off some nasty pollutants because the flames are relatively cool, especially if you try to burn softwood overnight, without much air, in a stove designed for hardwood. In fact, wood stoves have become such serious polluters that some American communities were living under a pall of bluish smoke all winter and have had to enact laws restricting wood burning. But, once again, Yankee ingenuity came to the rescue. Dow Corning now offers a hundred-dollar 'catalytic combuster' very much like the catalytic converters that are standard on new cars. Not only does this little gadget burn the toxic exhaust gases; it also increases the efficiency of the stove by twenty to thirty percent."

"But if you had a well-insulated house . . ." began Eunice.

"Ah, right again, my dear," Duncan finished, "then you'd burn much less wood and put out much less smoke.

"However," he went on, "other technologies are not as easily redeemed. Plants that burn garbage to make electricity aren't just burning paper; they're taking in plastics, chemicals, and coatings of various kinds. Some have even been known to send such dangerous chemicals as dioxin up the smokestack. On an even more basic level, though, it may make little sense to build a waste-to-energy plant that demands a hundred tons of garbage a day, when it's becoming increasingly attractive to recycle or even compost much of that garbage. In fact, there's a fellow in Madisonville, Kentucky, who converts paper-rich garbage into a kind of papier-mâché that he uses to revegetate and reclaim intractable spoil heaps from coal mining.

"Also," Duncan cautioned, "with much of the heat content of garbage coming from the paper and paper products, a dependence on garbage for fuel in the name of energy saving may harm the ecological ends served by recycling. Now, you certainly won't get me to take a stand for or against garbage-to-energy plants. But we do need to figure out an energy balance and a cost-effectiveness for each case. If the wastes would have to be transported a hundred fifty miles to a recycling plant, it will likely be a net energy loss to recycle them; but if there's a recycling plant right next door, well, the answer will be quite different."

"Fine," said Eunice. "But can we generalize about the environmental effects of different energy sources?"

"You've probably already learned," Duncan said, smiling, "how dangerous it is to generalize about anything in this field. But let me take a stab at a rule of thumb or two. First of all, one characteristic of sustainable energy is that the technology is often located quite near the point of use—solar panels atop the roof, for instance, or windows that let the sunshine in. This feature eliminates the dislocation that comes with the transportation of energy from place to place. Electric transmission lines in this country already cover an area the size of New Jersey—eight thousand square miles. Oil is shipped halfway around the world, imperiling marine life along those arteries.

"Using energy sources that are local can not only cut out the impacts of moving the energy over long distances, it can also be fairer. Poorer, rural people are often told that their home must be the next national sacrifice area, having their mountains strip-mined, their fisheries polluted, their valley filled with a power plant, or such, for the benefit of more politically powerful people many hundreds of miles away in a city. If, instead, the same people who get the benefits of the energy also get the costs, both environmental and social—because the energy comes from their own locality—everyone is in a better position to judge how much is enough. It seems only fair, and it would go a long way to eliminate many of the environmental effects of energy. For example, a technology that's quite popular in Europe is 'block heating' plants. These produce all the heat and electricity used by, for example, an apartment building. In one such plant I saw in Heidenheim, West Germany, the generator was too quiet to measure—in fact, so quiet that the noise of its operation was quieter than the noise of water running underground in the sewers at midnight. The residents insisted that the plant *had* to be that quiet because there was an apartment six feet from the exhaust pipe. But the extra saving from capturing what would otherwise have been waste heat from electricity generation more than made up the cost of that sound-proofing."

"But wouldn't there be a lot of pollution if everyone had his or her own power plant?" Eunice asked a bit skeptically.

"That can be a problem," Duncan acknowledged. "It's the same case as lots of wood stoves, each putting out only a little smoke—until you have a valley full of them. And it's true, regulating thousands of small pollution sources can be a real treat," he added dryly. "But again, if the valley where the stoves are burning, or the neighborhood with all the little block plants starts getting unlivable, people will act. They see the consequences of their acts. It's very different from a giant power plant in the Ohio Valley quietly causing acid rain in New England. Often, even one big plant or refinery can have so much political clout that regulators quail before it rather than clean it up.

"Another important feature of sustainable energy systems," said Duncan, "is that the scale of the energy project is matched to the end use. Conventional energy plants tend to be big, like the thousand-megawatt electric power stations that are now the industry standard. But since most end uses are of relatively small scale, most sustainable energy sources are likewise small. And the smaller the energy facility, the less the cost of failure, and the lower the cost of keeping it clean, or preventing failure. Large failures, such as the breakup of huge oil tankers, hold great danger for the natural systems in which they occur. Take the proposal to put huge panels of photovoltaic cells in outer space and beam the energy back to Earth—those microwave beams, if their aim drifted, could fry people." He shrugged and added, "That, may, though, account for military interest in such nutty projects. However, no matter what the fuel, increasing the size raises the stakes. And high stakes are usually not compatible with protection of the environment."

"Is that what you meant before about risk?" prompted Eunice.

"Oh, right," Duncan said. "Forgive me; I start to lose my memory on an empty stomach. Risk. An obvious element of risk is that the failures of large power plants tend to be dramatic and possibly dangerous. That's true whether we're talking about a nuclear meltdown, a global warming caused by the greenhouse effect, or the death of lakes due to acid rain. Now, there may be a low probability that a particular event like that will come to pass, but the consequences if it does will be dire. That makes it hard to evaluate those risks. Different people will tend to put widely different price tags on a low probability of high damage. Folks who are 'risk-averse' will want to stay away from those kinds of situations. People of the Las Vegas mentality may want to roll the dice. But who's choosing to roll which dice, at what odds, for whom? Who decides? How? If you choose to rely on big energy technologies, especially such things as nuclear power, the society will have to make those evaluations by whatever legitimate political processes it has. If, however, it is cheaper to choose a less risky technology, such as sustainable sources, then the society can avoid the messy sorts of debates of risk versus benefit, and risk for whom versus benefit for whom. In those circumstances, it seems to me, the choice is pretty clear."

"But how do you know that?" asked Eunice.

"Huh . . . know what?" Duncan blinked, caught woolgathering.

"That sustainables have a lower total risk," Eunice persisted.

"Because Dr. John Holdren, a physicist at the University of California at Berkeley, and a team at the National Audubon Society, and Congress's Office of Technology Assessment, and the Solar Energy Research Institute, and a whole bunch of other folks have carefully studied the problem," replied Duncan. "They found, in brief, that sustainable sources generally have much smaller, briefer, and more manageable impacts on the environment and on human health and safety than depletable sources do. For example, you could be killed in a coal-mining explosion or cave-in, or from emphysema caused by breathing air polluted by burning coal, or you could be killed falling off your roof while cleaning a solar collector. But the latter risk is smaller and can be avoided by a 'technical fix'—for example, putting a sponge mop on the end of a long pole and staying on the ground.

"In fact," Duncan added, "there was a hilariously erroneous report published a few years ago by one Herbert Inhaber, who then worked for the Atomic Energy Control Board of Canada and later migrated to Oak Ridge. Inhaber claimed to have calculated that nuclear energy was very safe, other depletable sources were fairly safe, and sustainable sources were terribly dangerous. Naturally, lots of people in the nuclear industry started trumpeting his results from the housetops. But Dr. Holdren, one of the leading authorities on these matters, thought he smelled a rat and turned his graduate students loose to check Inhaber's calculations. They found layer upon layer of bloopers—methodological blunders, arithmetic mistakes, misinterpretation of sources, including Holdren's own work. Meanwhile Inhaber kept issuing new, revised reports and claiming he'd never said what was in the old ones. Holdren was professionally outraged about that—especially because some well-known scientific journals had published Inhaber's work without the usual checks, such as independent review. Holdren, in fact, concluded that the report was the most incompetent one he'd ever known to have been distributed by grown-ups. Holdren got some flak for using such strong words as 'incompetent' and 'dishonest'—words that were clearly meant for just such a situation—but eventually the Inhaber report was officially declared out of print, and Holdren received the Public Service Award of the Federation of American Scientists for exposing the scandal and upholding the integrity of the scientific process.

"Still, despite a lot of argument and research, many of the risks aren't well quantified," said Duncan. "For example, it's true that we don't know what the exact probability is that the greenhouse effect will cause serious climatic change at current levels of fuel use. And such climatic change—one of the two biggest energy risks (the other being nuclear war caused by the spread of nuclear bombs as a result of using nuclear power)—could dwarf even such impacts as acid rain or oil spills. In general, though, there are two points of view on questions like these . . ."

"Only two?" asked Eunice.

"Well, of course, there are actually lots more," Duncan amended. "But the two main views are either that a technology should be proven *safe* beyond a reasonable doubt before it is used, or that it should be proven *unsafe* beyond a reasonable doubt before it is banned or limited in some way. Now, that's a value choice that no amount of economic, scientific, or engineering analysis can make for you. Analysis can be used to calculate or guess various probabilities that may or may not be anywhere near right, but it can't tell you what *your* values should be. Now, suppose you happen to be of the school that the burden of proof lies on the technology and its proponents. The fact that a failure in a solar heating system is going to cause less damage than the meltdown of a nuclear power plant ought to make that solar heater seem more attractive to you. A nuclear power plant, on the other hand, is a very complex piece of machinery with different subsystems that can go wrong, and have gone wrong, in unexpected ways. That makes many folks kind of wary about them. Now the technotwits say—incorrectly, incidentally—that nuclear power has never killed anyone; therefore it is safe. Some of us, however, look at the big accidents and all the near misses and wonder how we've been so lucky as to escape a disaster so far."

"Near misses?" Eunice looked concerned.

"Oh, there've been partial meltdowns of the core, such as occurred at Three Mile Island and Fermi, and accidents that could have caused meltdowns but didn't, as at Browns Ferry and Salem. In the Fermi accident we may have been about thirty minutes away from contaminating all of Detroit. And there've been worse accidents at nuclear plants overseas: plutonium spills, sodium fires, even people killed. But my point is actually not so much the serious close calls as the stupid mistakes, made with frightening regularity in the normal course of running reactors. I guess my favorite is the time some workers at a plant hooked up the low-level radioactive waste tank to the drinking fountain."

"What!" Eunice's eyes bugged.

"Yeah, and there're lots more: reading blueprints backwards, leaving a wedding ring and bits of old pipe stuck inside pumps and valves. . . . You know, it's the kind of stupid things you'd expect an incompetent plumber to do. Though for what they pay those guys, they really ought to do better."

"How did you find out all that?" Eunice asked, a little horrified. "Surely people who do things like that don't go around telling about them."

"No, not if they have any choice in the matter. Sometimes, however, they get caught. There are inspectors at nuclear plants and all sorts of reporting requirements for such 'unusual' events."

"They certainly sound 'unusual' to me," Eunice observed.

"Well, it seems a senior safety official at the Nuclear Regulatory Commission was keeping a personal file of especially 'unusual' events. The existence of this file was discovered by the Union of Concerned Scientists. That's a group," he answered Eunice's raised eyebrow, "of scientists, engineers, and such, concerned with public policy. They're especially good on matters of nuclear power and nuclear bombs. Anyway, they sued the NRC under the Freedom of Information Act and got this official's so-called 'Nugget File,' which they then published. It's truly a gold mine of screw-ups. I'll get you a copy. Makes great bedtime reading, especially if you don't live anywhere near a nuclear plant."

Duncan made a note to himself.

Eunice sighed mightily. "With all of these uncertainties lurking," she said, "I think I'm rather grateful that sustainable energy sources are less risky. I'd hate to have to make a decision between safety and needed power. But," she brightened, "speaking of probability, what do you think the chances are that we could sneak by my Keystone Kounselors?"

"I'll risk it," said Duncan, his eyes twinkling. "After all, the alternative seems to be starvation. 'Cabinet Secretary found emaciated, dead, in subordinate's office.' What a scandal!"

"Oh, get your coat and come on," teased Eunice. "Enough talk, let's do something about it!"

17 Energy and Food

As THEY LEFT Forrestal, Eunice told Duncan about the excuse Barb had given for her—that she was going to lunch at the Old Executive Office Building. A twinkle entered Duncan's eye, and he responded, "Oh, then I know just the place for us to eat." It turned out to be a newly opened restaurant near Capitol Hill called OEOB. As Duncan put it, a little redefinition beats straight lying anytime.

Whatever the excuse, the restaurant pleased Eunice mightily. A simple place, it served plain fare—"real food," Eunice called it. It didn't intimidate her like some of the foreign bistros she had passed downtown. And when the check came, it was Duncan who picked up the tab. But not out of any chivalrous tradition, he explained. She should be able, he cautioned, to deny any social contact with him. So she winked as he put her down on his credit-card slip as a "high-ranking administration source." Then he grinned and offered her his arm.

"You know," Eunice said as they rode the back elevator up to Duncan's office, "I wonder if there isn't a connection between the food we eat and the energy issues we've been talking about."

"Without a doubt," said Duncan, politely stifling a postprandial yawn. "But then just about every industry or area of human activity is tied to energy. The trick in pinpointing the connections is to step back and look for a bigger picture.

"Take any memo we circulate," he continued, seizing upon an example at the same moment he turned the door handle and let them into his office. "It requires a lot more energy than you might think. Not only does it take kilowatt-hours to run the photocopiers, but it took a significant amount of energy to harvest the timber, to get the logs to the paper mill, to reduce the logs to wood pulp and then to paper, and to transport the paper here from, I guess, Maine. Then consider the energy inputs in fertilizer and petrochemical pesticides and herbicides that were applied to the trees as they were growing. Given the kind of intensive forestry now practiced, there is a large soil erosion problem in forests already known for low fertility. But rather than reform, the industry just pours on more energy-intensive chemicals. And that even neglects all of the fixed overheads—the uses of energy that are not directly increased by the circulation of our memo—such as the lights and air conditioning in this building, the energy it took the copier operators and repair technicians and lawyers who write the service contracts to get to work, and so forth. Even the photocopier toner is incredibly energy-intensive; it takes many kilowatt-hours per pound to grind it to such a fine powder."

"Phew!" said Eunice. "How do you come up with all those connections?"

"It's really not that hard," Duncan replied modestly. "Just adopt a 'systems approach'; then define the system. And remember to include all its parts—not just the one piece of paper, but the whole chain of connections. When you look at the memo, for example, it's obvious that the system is not just what happens in this building. The paper has to come from somewhere, the energy from somewhere, etc. Also, don't ignore the back end. Some folks who get the memo will file it away and never look at it again—that's energy-cheap, but it does take up floor space in this energy-intensive building. Some people are going to chuck it right in their circular files—that will take more energy, because then the garbage trucks will have to haul it away to the dump, and so on."

"Unless," teased Eunice, "it gets burned in a garbage-to-energy plant, in which case it would provide some useful energy in turn, right? Or couldn't it be composted, saving fertilizer that's made of natural gas?"

"Ah," said Duncan, "you're getting it. So why don't *you* take a stab at applying this systems approach to the nation's food system?"

"Well, I guess we should start with the farm and then work forward and backward," Eunice ventured. Encouraged by Duncan's nod, she continued. "Farmers use energy in their farm machinery to plow, plant, harvest, and to apply pesticides and pump water and so on. Maybe they have milk chillers or grain dryers. They transport the food to market, often in refrigerated trucks or boxcars, and the supermarkets—which have all those lights and freezer chests—sell it to consumers. Of course, a lot of food gets processed along the way, and that takes energy, too. Then I cook the food at home. No, wait; I drive to the supermarket and get it, then drive back home. Then the food that we don't eat and all the packaging gets thrown out and taken to the dump. And let's see, working backward from the farmer, it must take energy to produce the pesticides and the petrochemical fertilizers and maybe even the fancy hybrid seeds. Anything else I've left out?"

"Oh, lots of details, but broadly that covers it pretty well," said Duncan. "Definitely still a farm woman at heart." He smiled.

"Now, clearly, all of those steps require energy," said Eunice. "But exactly how much? And how can we make that energy use more efficient?"

"Well, before we delve into specific suggestions," said Duncan, "let me make a few comments about how farm energy fits into the overall U.S. energy picture. For starters, our food system accounts for about one-sixth of total U.S. energy consumption. That's the equivalent of about nine barrels of oil per year for every woman, man, and child in this country. You should bear in mind, too, that the cost of energy is quite significant for farmers. For instance, one study showed that owners of small farms in Nebraska with an average net income of thirty-seven hundred dollars per year had to spend even more than that amount in energy costs. And if that seems high, remember that twice as much energy is used in food processing and distribution as is used on the farm. So the solutions we seek should include energy use on the farm, but will also have to follow the food off the farm all the way to your table if not beyond. Of course, food is wrapped up with a host of other resource areas, such as water and topsoil. Just to give you a preview of some of the juicy stuff, get this: Every pound of hamburger you eat represents an energy input of a gallon of gasoline or the equivalent, about two hundred bathtubs-full of water, and forty to a hundred pounds of lost, eroded topsoil."

"Gracious. That's a lot of topsoil for one hamburger," said Eunice, startled. "It's a good thing it doesn't taste gritty."

"Uh, right," said Duncan, derailing briefly, but recovering. "So," he continued, "let's divide our discussion, for the purposes of simplicity, into two categories: on-farm and off-farm activities. Take irrigation, for instance. California's largest use of electricity is pumping water over the mountains. Eighty-five percent of the state's pumped water goes to agriculture. In general, irrigation demands about an eighth of the energy used on farms, but that's just an average. In the arid western states, where irrigation accounts for eighty-five percent of all water used in the whole country, the power requirement is much higher. This substantial chunk of energy use can be reduced in a number of ways."

"Hang on, let me think," Eunice interrupted. "First, you would want to improve the efficiency with which you use water. You'd want to obtain the same, uh, 'irrigation services' but use less water and money, the same as we try to do with energy. And only then would you want to explore new supplies of water that cost more. And you'd want to make sure that those new sources of supply would be sustainable, right?"

"Terrific!" said Duncan. "How would you like to be Secretary of Agriculture, too? Indeed, there's a host of ways—ranging from ditch linings and drip irrigation to better scheduling and different choices of crops—that can dramatically cut the amount of water that a farmer needs. And as far as sustainability goes, the reasons to become efficient with water use go beyond the energy field. Groundwater is an increasingly scarce resource, with two-thirds of the groundwater now used for irrigation coming from areas that have been critically depleted of water. In some areas of heavy pumping, the land has sunk as much as thirty feet. Parts of the Ogallala Aquifer beneath the High Plains are being used up two hundred times faster than they're being recharged. Throughout the area underlain by the Ogallala, twenty million acre-feet a year are being used for irrigation—more water than the Missouri River conveys past Kansas City during the irrigation season. Bear in mind that an acre-foot is enough water to cover an acre to the depth of one foot." Eunice nodded; she knew. "At this rate of consumption," Duncan continued, "the water in many parts of the Ogallala will be exhausted by the year 2000. At the same time, the high energy cost of pumping that water out of the ground is a factor in the financial troubles now besetting many farmers.

"One possibility," Duncan proposed, "is to improve the efficiency of water use while returning to the traditional methods of water pumping, using modern versions of the wind machines that were once seen all over the Midwest and still exist in many places. For those to be cost-effective, of course, the amount of water needed on those farms would have to drop. But then there's no point in setting up a sustainable energy system if the farm is going to dry up in ten years anyway."

Eunice nodded earnestly. Farm survival was a topic near to her heart. It also reminded her of other concerns. "Wouldn't," she asked, "such a reduction also ease the danger that salting up now poses to irrigated croplands? I've even read about areas—I think one was in California's Central Valley—where so much salt from the slightly saline irrigation water has soaked into the earth that it now threatens to make the land useless for farming by the mid-1990s."

"Right you are, of course," Duncan agreed.

"Okay," said Eunice, "But what about other energy uses on the farm?"

"Well," said Duncan, "take crop drying, for example. Now most of it is done with propane. But some farmers in Nebraska have built a six-thousand-bushel grain dryer that uses the heat of the sun to dry their corn. Not only does the five-hundred-dollar device save more than half its initial cost each year, but it doesn't harm the grain the way gas-fired dryers do."

"Well, now, I like that," Eunice replied.

"Another on-farm energy user," said Duncan, "is the chemicals that are applied to crops. Pesticides and fertilizers are typically made of oil and gas. Together they account for more than a third of the energy that goes into food production. For example, a sixth of all the interruptible natural gas in the country has lately gone into nitrogen fertilizer. More than a billion pounds of pesticides and about a hundred billion pounds of chemical fertilizers are applied to U.S. crops each year. Chemical fertilizers, by the way, are the fourth biggest manufacturing industry in the United States, right after oil, steel, and cement. Here, as with irrigation, many possibilities exist to reduce the amount of chemicals that must be applied to the fields."

"Like what?" Now Eunice was really interested.

"Well, one option that is much more practical than commonly imagined is to turn to organic methods of cultivation."

Eunice raised her eyebrows sharply.

"Now, give me a chance," Duncan protested. "I know that organic farming conjures up visions of bearded hippies picking over insect-eaten fruit, but it's really not like that at all. It's actually quite a sound commercial practice. When the Department of Agriculture compared fourteen pairs of farms in 1980, it found that organic farms required only three percent more labor per acre than conventional ones. Even more exciting, a study by the National Science Foundation showed that organic farmers' expenses were more than a third lower than those of conventional farmers; thus, when the lower yields for organic farms were taken into account, the net dollar return on organic farms was within two percent of that obtained on nonorganic farms. Some do much better than that.

"Nor are organic farms only practical in small sizes," he went on. "There are thirty thousand organic farms in the United States, ranging in size up to fifteen hundred acres. They require, on average, only forty to fifty percent as much energy per unit output as chemical farms; what's more, they can sustain those yields much longer. Chemical fertilizers, you see, actually hurt the soil in the medium and long run. They can cut the ability of the soil to absorb water. The crops then require more irrigation, which leads to severe topsoil erosion. They also harm the plants' and soil's ability to cycle their own nutrients. In contrast, a net increase of just one percent in the organic content of the soil through organic farming can reduce the loss of topsoil by as much as ten percent per year. Frankly, I think it's pretty clear that organic farming is a more sustainable endeavor than chemical farming. Organic farmers might be able to pass their farms on to their grandchildren. Chemical farmers probably won't, however; they'll have burned out their soil."

"You know," Eunice said, "I should tell my brother about all this. He's the one who stayed on the family farm, and he's having a really hard time making it from one harvest to the next."

"Well, let me give you some more ammunition," said Duncan. "Similar points can be made about pesticides. Even though pesticide applications per acre have mushroomed twelvefold from the late forties to the late seventies, losses to pests still grew from seven to thirteen percent of preharvest crops. We can hardly claim a victory over the insects that eat our crops when they have so dramatically increased the percentage of the crops that they get. About all that our poisons have done is simply to breed a more resistant, durable kind of pest—one that is more likely to cause serious infestations and that is increasingly difficult to control by any means. And although pesticides themselves are a relatively small component of the embodied energy used on farms, that share is increased by the energy it takes to apply the pesticides and the kerosene that is often used to dilute them. Worse, both pesticides and chemical fertilizers degrade water quality where they are applied, since the runoff from fields that have undergone this chemotherapy contains residues of those chemicals. This runoff then contaminates the streams, rivers, and lakes nearby. Really, when you look at it, our pesticide policy is loco. And energy isn't really the core of the issue. More important is that we're poisoning ourselves and destroying the ability of our land to support us."

Eunice shook her head in wonderment. "Do you have any of this in writing?"

"Yes, but just a minute," said Duncan. "As long as we're on the problems of agriculture, there's one more ingredient, if you will, that we should talk about. That's the way the food system is so heavily weighted toward meat production. Nearly seventy-five percent of on-farm energy and eighty-eight percent of all vegetable protein produced goes into livestock. But then it takes five to seven pounds of corn or soybeans to produce a single pound of live weight gain on a feedlot steer; so that shouldn't be a surprise. The protein conversation ratios for fowl are slightly better—and even better for eggs and dairy. But in effect, we're running a gigantic welfare program for cattle, chickens, and pigs. We're maintaining a livestock population that weighs four times as much as the human population it feeds. You know, if we were feeding all the grain to the equivalent number of people, the United States could support a population as big as or bigger than that of China."

"But I like beef!" Eunice's meat-and-potatoes background brought her up in arms.

"I do, too," soothed Duncan. "But there are better ways of raising meat. For instance, I buy a side of beef every so often from a rancher friend. But what I buy is range beef. It hasn't been fattened on grain."

"Oh," Eunice dismissed that with a flip of her hand, "I've heard of that. But everyone knows that beef with no finishing is tough."

"Actually, I prefer it," countered Duncan. "It's tastier. And much leaner. But you know, you don't have to be 'either/or'; I'm told that some big grocery chains are now buying beef that's been kept at the feedlot for a much shorter time. They call it extra-lean health beef."

Eunice pursed her lips, considering.

"But my beef is even better. You might say it's the natural critter right off the hoof. And it is more natural, too. My friend doesn't add hormones or antibiotics to his feed. That stuff is really nasty. The antibiotics in animal feed can even make germs resistant to antibiotics we might need to fight an illness. You know, the more I learn about the effects of all the various food additives on health, the more I think those organic guys are really onto something. Even Ronald Reagan special-orders additive-free beef."

"Hmpf," was Eunice's only comment. She reckoned she'd just have to think about all this. Duncan seemed really to be going too far. Maybe he just liked confronting the established order. Well, she thought that her world was quite all right. Although . . .

Duncan ignored her petulance and continued. "In general," he said, "what we see is that farms are beset by a resource crisis that goes beyond just energy. It includes water and water quality, soil fertility, and pest resistance. And all of this shows up in the economics. Partly as a result of production gains from cheap energy, the value of farmland rose dramatically. Many farmers borrowed heavily against that value. But then to pay the loans, they had to grow more; so they invested more in very expensive machinery and farmed more intensively. Now energy is no longer cheap, and the costs of their farming practices are catching up with them. As a result, a record number of farmers are facing bankruptcy. Back in 1984, one in six Colorado farmers intended to quit the business within the year, and more than one in three intended to quit before the end of the decade. All of these farm problems —water, environment, sustainability, energy, rural cultures, and economics—are intertwined. And there are very few simple answers. But many of the technologies that can help decrease the amount of energy the farms need also increase the viability of farms, such as organic farming, which saves at least one-third of the energy input, or farming that is better tailored to the climate and available rainfall of an area."

"Boy, it's no wonder my brother is thinking about selling the farm," Eunice said. "Things sure have changed since I was growing up on the land. But aren't we getting away from what we were talking about originally?"

"Oh yeah," winced Duncan. "Right, back to the big picture. Although the problems facing the nation's breadbaskets are so serious that I could spend days and days talking about them and exploring solutions to the messes that we've gotten into. But first let's finish our discussion of food and energy by at least mentioning the rest of the food web."

"Food web?" asked Eunice. She had a sudden vision of Hobart sitting at the center of a net woven of half-cooked spaghetti.

"Yes, web," said Duncan. "There is the whole network of getting food from the farm to, um, the OEOB." He grinned. "Anyway, our food system is hopelessly inefficient, especially off the farm. The average molecule of food in this country travels thirteen hundred miles from the time it is grown to the time it is eaten. Railroads use only a third as much fuel per ton-mile as trucks; yet trains carry less than a quarter of U.S. food shipments. And while fossil fuels and transportation were cheap, long-distance truck shipments boomed. That cheap transportation had an unfortunate effect on a lot of local agriculture. During the 1960s, for example, broccoli production in New York and New Jersey plummeted from . . ." Duncan finally gave up and reached behind him for a folder. "As you may have guessed, this area's a hobby of mine, but some of these numbers still elude me," he confessed as he rifled the file. "Yeah, here . . . from more than sixteen thousand tons per year to less than a thousand tons annually. Meanwhile, production in California zoomed from seventy-eight thousand tons to a hundred seventy-three thousand tons. A lot of that change was due to various subsidies that made it possible for centralized broccoli production in California to appear cheaper than local East Coast farming. And the change brought not just a decline in production, but the conversion of farmland in the urbanized East to suburban tracts, as well as the dismantling of greenhouses that had been used to grow lettuce, broccoli, and the like.

"Whoa!" Duncan sidetracked as he found another number. "If you think those other energy figures are crazy, consider this one. A head of lettuce contains some forty-seven calories; yet it takes about twenty-five times as much energy as that to transport it from California to New York. Overall, the food industry consumes about ten times as much energy as is contained in the food we eat."

"Oh, dear me," said Eunice—the first time she had used that expression in days. She had become a bit callous to the ridiculous way things were done, but all of this was sinking in and making her feel a bit at a loss.

"So what can we do about all this?" Eunice asked plaintively. "I know a lot of people who grow their own food, and it seems that having your own garden would cut down a lot on the cost of moving the food back and forth. And it's a lot better for your stomach—and your head—to eat fresh food you've grown than to get the stuff the big farms manufacture. I mean . . . but . . ." She stopped suddenly as she realized she was starting to echo Duncan's earlier point.

"How true," agreed Duncan, ignoring her confusion. "As a matter of fact, according to a 1983 Gallup poll, thirty-five million households in America had backyard or community gardens— more than forty percent of the total. Add to that the seven million who had herb gardens or window boxes, and that's about half the households in the country. Care to take a guess at the value of their harvest?" He grinned at Eunice, who merely blinked. "Some fourteen billion dollars per year—as much as the entire California agriculture industry. And do you know why most people said they gardened? Not to save money, but to have fresh food of better taste and quality than they could get in the store. We're talking about a pretty fundamental change in values and preferences, and one, I think, that is likely to last a while.

"The community gardens that I mentioned are one of the more exciting developments. The all-passive-solar greenhouse in Cheyenne, Wyoming, that I described before provides a hundred volunteer gardeners with ten tons of fresh produce a year and has expanded to include a farmers' market and a beekeeping project. Another attractive option is to build greenhouses near electric power plants and use the plants' waste heat to keep, say, tomato plants warm. Elegant, no?"

"But don't all of these take away from the farmers' incomes?" asked Eunice.

"To some extent, they certainly can," replied Duncan. "But farmers need to heed these trends and move more in accord with them, although I really doubt that city or even suburban dwellers will ever grow *all* their own food. Actually, in the long run, farmers are hurt far more by federal subsidy policies and programs that promote overplanting than they are by people growing more of their own food. Besides, a lot of the innovations that would make energy sense would help both the farmer and the consumer. For instance, farmers' markets, which bring farmers into direct contact with their customers, can cut out the middlemen, who take some sixty-nine cents of every food dollar that Americans spend. Consumers end up saving about twenty cents on the dollar, compared to what they would pay in supermarkets, and farmers make much more than they would by selling to a supermarket or a canning plant. Also, farmers' markets are sociable and lots of fun. So you see, there's some hope."

"You know," said Eunice, "I've been thinking about starting a garden again myself. If I did, of course, I'd start saving my kitchen scraps to mulch into my garden. Not only would that

make my plants grow better and make chemical fertilizers unnecessary, but it would mean a lot less garbage to haul off to the
dump. And that would save energy, too, right?"

"Bravo!" said Duncan. "There's someone with a good systems
mind."

"Systems mind?" scoffed Eunice. "You can compost that one
right here."

18 *Energy for Democracy*

MOVING RIGHT ALONG . . ." Duncan began, as he opened another file folder. But Eunice cut him off.

"Stop!" she ordered. Then added, "Please. I need some time to catch up on my note taking."

"Uh, sure," Duncan replied. He looked puzzled for a moment, but turned and picked up a report to read from the foot-and-a-half-tall stack on his desk.

Eunice began to shuffle the pages of her yellow pad. But there was more than note taking on her mind. During the discussion of food, a prickly thought had occurred to her. Something had been bothering her for a while—a nagging doubt about Duncan—and it finally started to crystallize as she doodled on her legal pad. He did look very proper and all, and he seemed to know what he was talking about. But there was one more piece to the puzzle that she wasn't sure about. There was an opinion about alternative energy and the like that she had read a long time ago, or was it something her cousin Jake had said? Something about solar being a hobby of people from the left end of the political spectrum. Yes, it was Cousin Jake. She didn't remember what he had called them—some kind of 'ist.' Leftist? Ecologist? Anarchist? All she was sure of was that he had seemed to disapprove of them. But Duncan didn't look anything like that—whatever "that" was. Still, she wondered. Those "ists," she decided, can be pretty insidious. Duncan certainly didn't seem too fond of the big utilities. On the other hand, he also seemed pretty skeptical of Big Government, even if he was a part of it. Hmm, she fretted. How could she bring it up tactfully? She couldn't just ask Duncan if he was one of those political agitator types; besides, he clearly didn't seem to be that. Well, she resolved, maybe she could avoid the topic of *his* politics but bring up a discussion of the programs and philosophies he had proposed.

Eunice set her pad on her lap and looked up at Duncan, who was quietly reading. "Tell me, Duncan," she asked, almost sternly, "what would your energy suggestions mean politically? I mean," her assurance lessened as she groped a bit, "is sustainable energy Democratic or Republican? Is it liberal or conservative? Is it on the right or the left?"

"Mmm," Duncan pondered, closing the report he held. "I'm tempted to say that it is neither. It's not right or left; it's in front," he said, grinning. "That's a bit too ambiguous an answer, though, isn't it? And even a bit too flip. But then it's hard not to be. Sustainable energy just doesn't fit on the political spectrum as people usually think of it—you know, leftist to liberal to middle-of-the-road to conservative and so on. In fact, political labels have played a fairly small role in energy policy so far."

"Really?" asked Eunice, her brow furrowing. "But weren't liberals outraged at Reagan's energy programs? And conservatives didn't like Carter's plans, either."

"Yes, Eunice," Duncan replied, "but that was just so much smoke. You see, the energy projects that Nixon, Ford, Carter, and Reagan supported have really all been pretty much the same. All of the infighting every few years, whenever a new president takes office, is mostly partisan hullaballoo. You remember what we talked about the very first day we met? How all of the energy plans that those four presidents proposed depended heavily on depletable fuels, nuclear power, and converting coal into electricity and synthetic liquid fuels. The window dressing was a bit different, I'll grant you. But whether Carter proposed the Energy Security Corporation to provide capital for large energy projects and the Energy Mobilization Board to ram them through, or Reagan chose to provide similar but subtler benefits through tax breaks, the results and built-in biases were very much the same. I'll admit, under

Reagan, with the budget cuts and the firings at SERI—that's the Solar Energy Research Institute—it became more difficult for people to get information about sustainable technologies and for scientists to get funding for research on, say, cheap photovoltaic cells. But those programs themselves were ripples on an otherwise unruffled surface of support for large, nonrenewable, inefficient projects. Small change in Uncle Sam's pockets."

"Okay," said Eunice, "I guess you really couldn't call one program Republican and one Democratic, at least not in terms of favorite technologies. And there hasn't been an administration yet to propose an end-use-based national energy plan, right?"

Duncan nodded his head. "Right."

"Well, if we can't come to any overwhelming conclusions about the relative merits of the two parties when it comes to energy," said Eunice, "perhaps we could get back to my original question. What are the political repercussions of a shift to efficiency and sustainable energy?"

Duncan leaned back in his chair and tossed the report he had been holding back onto the leaning stack. "I guess," he said, "the best way of characterizing them would be to say that sustainable energy increases the degree of choice we have about the political system we want. It doesn't lock us into a particular kind of government and business decision-making, the way hard energy does. You can get your power from a wind turbine whether you live under our current system of government or under a system that is oriented more toward individual and states' rights, or under communism, or even under no government. The technology doesn't care; it can be set up, installed, and operated under any kind of political system. Likewise, you can insulate your house and put in windows for passive solar heating under a variety of different systems. Actually, it might be most difficult under communism, at least as it is currently manifested. Lenin, you know, defined communism as collectives plus electrification. And by that he meant big, centrally run electric generators. The Soviets are still very skeptical of small, decentralized generation because they think it will lessen the Party's control.

"However," he continued, "let's consider the much narrower spectrum of political situations likely in the United States in the near future. Let's assume, as I think likely, that our political system will remain pretty much the same as what exists now. Laws might become looser or more restrictive, but we'll still have the sort of government that we all learned about in civics class—three branches, checks and balances, and so on. The refinements, I think, will involve small changes about which level of government— state, local, or federal—will have the authority to make what decisions, and about how much power will be left to the individual."

Eunice blinked and fingered the tumbled agate hanging from her neck. High school civics was a long way behind her. Still, she nodded for Duncan to continue.

So he did. "Now, suppose everyone decides that what we should do is to adopt a sustainable energy strategy for the country," said Duncan. "You can imagine a central government providing everyone with the materials they need to insulate their houses. Or you can imagine the government legislating certain minimum standards that every house must meet, as many cities and states have already done in building codes and appliance efficiency standards. Or you could imagine the government providing an incentive for people to save energy and use renewable instead of depletable sources. Or perhaps the government would see itself as the helping hand for the free market, trying to provide the right conditions for the proper functioning of the free market, so that people would see which options really were cheaper and decide if they wanted to choose them. All of these approaches are grounded in different political philosophies and justifications. But all are compatible with sustainable energy. It's just another example of the flexibility and adaptability of that kind of energy approach."

"Wait," said Eunice, "does that mean that what you've called 'hard' energy won't adapt to that variety as well?"

"Exactly right," said Duncan. "Just look at some of the plans that have been proposed to get the supposedly essential hard technologies built. Carter claimed an 'emergency.' He said that it required the suspension of normal democratic processes. Let's ignore for the moment that most of his proposals led the country away from an efficient, cost-effective energy path. Worse, they simply were not justified by the severity of the energy problem at the time, and they included a number of provisions that flew in the face of values that many Americans hold dear—such as a voice in what happens in one's own county or state. Take the multi-billion-dollar plants that Carter eventually proposed to build to convert shale or coal into liquid fuel. The people of the Rocky Mountains were to have no political power to decide whether the synfuels plants should be built. That was to be up to the oil companies that had bought mining and water rights in the area. And under Carter's Energy Mobilization Board, local opponents wouldn't have had a hillside to stand on and no way to intervene legally to object to the building of a plant or get the need for one seriously examined. Instead, the Board would have been authorized to steamroller their objections.

"You know," Duncan added, "we should have known better, because we'd already tried that approach. We steamrollered the Trans-Alaska Pipeline—remember, it passed on Spiro Agnew's tie-breaking vote after he deceived the Senate about the Canadian position on alternative routes—over the objections of critics who said the pipeline would produce an oil glut on the West Coast and should be built instead—or better still, built in the form of a railroad—through Canada to the Midwest. As it turned out, they were exactly right. Or again, for many years the Atomic Energy Commission was able to ram through reactor licenses while brushing aside all questions about the wisdom or safety of nuclear power. As a result of that arrogance, we've committed hundreds of billions of dollars to a mistake that's harmed energy policy more than any other single federal action, except maybe regulating the price of natural gas. And yet we keep hearing calls to 'streamline' nuclear regulation—even today, after the critics have been so richly vindicated."

"That would be a shame," said Eunice. "People at least should get a chance to raise questions and have their day in court. Why, if they tried to do something like that in my neighborhood in Dubuque . . . But wait, do you mean to say that it would be impossible for a hard energy path to be locally controlled?"

"Let's put it this way," said Duncan, "it would be about as likely as Exxon giving you the right to vote on where it drills for oil. You see, the hard energy path depends on very large energy facilities, such as power plants that churn out hundreds of megawatts or huge oil refineries. They then sell the product over a large area. So the people who will be getting the energy benefits are often not the ones who suffer the consequences. It's the same problem we discussed earlier, and it leads to a basic political imbalance. Take the case of the Four Corners coal plants in northern New Mexico. They provide electricity to cities hundreds of miles away; yet the people who live there suffer the pollution, the coal mining, the desecration of sacred Indian lands, and so on. In fact, some impoverished Navajos living under the power lines don't even have electricity in their homes. And because people in cities tend to have more political power than those in areas like Four Corners, the locals' objections go up in smoke. In contrast, a town like Burlington, Vermont, can and did decide to build a wood-fired power plant to generate its electricity. The residents there are the ones whose homes will be lit up—and they are the ones who will be affected by the emissions, will have the incentive to demand that they be cleaned up, and so forth. That, I think, is the sort of technology that is politically responsible, even if it is a waste to use a potential liquid-fuel feedstock such as wood to make electricity.

"Let me give you another example," continued Duncan. "Take the nuclear industry, which depends on a series of very large, very complex facilities for its fuel cycle to function properly. From the uranium mines to the enrichment plants and the fuel fabrication factories, each link is crucial for the operation of the nation's reactors. The back end of the fuel cycle is just as important, with waste handling and the possibility of reprocessing. The fear that nuclear material could be stolen and made into a nuclear bomb raises the stakes even further. As these stakes rise, so does the nervousness of law-enforcement authorities. Soon, far-reaching measures begin to be used to protect these plants in the name of national security, such as police infiltration of legitimate political groups and interference with our cherished rights of free assembly, speech, and the press. When the stakes get that high, some people in government find it easy to justify what we would consider illegal actions, such as wiretap authorization on flimsy evidence, or arresting people on scanty suspicion. In fact, the United States has been pushing a little-known international treaty so loosely phrased that it would arguably make it an international crime, comparable to piracy or genocide, for you and me even to discuss whether to take part in a nonviolent demonstration that might delay a shipment of nuclear fuel for five minutes.

"The hard energy path is simply incompatible with many democratic institutions. In fact, one nuclear proponent, Alvin Weinberg—sometimes called the father of the nuclear program—acknowledges that many of the issues of nuclear power are simply too complex for nontechnical people. They ought to instead, he says, be settled by experts, whose pronouncements should then be accepted on faith by the public. He even called for the official creation of a 'technological priesthood' to run the nuclear business. It seems to me that any technology that can't be governed by an informed citizenry is inherently a nondemocratic technology."

"Dear me," said Eunice. "But how can sustainable energy avoid the same problems? Does it actually foster a more pleasant political environment?"

"A fair question," acknowledged Duncan. "Consider, for instance, the town of Springfield, Illinois, where citizens from all walks of life spent a year and a half charting their energy future. Their discussions centered around projects that the city itself could undertake, since the city happened to own its own electric utility. The act of planning drew many members of the community into the political process who otherwise would have remained on the sidelines, and the public exposure that came with the eighteen-month process helped educate many Springfield citizens about energy. In the 1982 election, shortly after the plan was completed, all the candidates who supported the plan's recommendations were elected to the city council. The simple act of local energy planning—which could not, for example, be geared toward planning a local nuclear plant—strengthened democratic institutions, such as citizen participation, that are central to our political heritage."

Eunice was leaning forward in her chair by this point. "Really?" she asked. "It sounds just like the town meetings my grandfather used to tell us about, from the time when he was growing up in Vermont. These days, so many people don't vote, don't care about politics; they don't see any relevance in it for them. I wonder if a local planning process like that couldn't cut through some of this apathy that everybody keeps talking about."

"In fact, that's just what's happened in hundreds, um, actually thousands, of communities across the country. Remember the example I mentioned from the San Luis Valley in Colorado? Where they put all those low-cost solar systems on poor people's houses? That process not only helped people stay warm; it also gave the community a real sense of its own power and the confidence to begin tackling such other problems as health care. And it's probably that sense of empowerment that's simultaneously reduced alcoholism, crime, family abuse, and other signs of stress in the Valley—people just feel more able to solve their own problems."

Duncan rocked back and folded his hands behind his head. "You know," he said, "I've seen a fair bit of political history from my desk in Washington, and I'm not sure anymore that I blame people for not getting involved in national politics. Seems to me, maybe this new movement of bioregional politics might just make more sense. But that," he said, rocking forward, "is another discussion for another time. Let's see, what's next on the list of topics I drew up this morning on the Metro?"

19 *Building Real Security*

*A*H, RIGHT," Duncan said, looking over the back of a theater program on which he had scribbled a number of topics. "Here's an interesting problem for you, Eunice. Do you know what the federal government spends more than a third of its revenues on? We've talked about new and different ways of providing energy services, food, jobs, a clean environment, and a fair and free political system. But what area would get such a big chunk of money?"

"Welfare?" Eunice guessed.

"Welfare?" Duncan repeated, chuckling. "Oh, no, my friend. Welfare costs the federal government only a couple of dozen paltry billions—small change by our Washington standards. No, the answer is warfare, which, at some two hundred fifty billion dollars a year, weighs in at about nine times the combined costs of food stamps, Aid to Families with Dependent Children, and federal housing subsidies to the poor. What I'm getting at is this: As long as we're looking at providing energy, food, and political liberty in new ways and at the least cost, we should probably look at the military, too. So," he winked, "what are we trying to get from the military?"

"Um . . . well . . . I'm not entirely sure," said Eunice. "I mean, I know what I get, and that's a confidence that someone is out there making sure that no one invades America. It's a feeling of security, I suppose."

"Ah, security," Duncan said grandiosely. "And, my dear Eunice, how secure do you feel?"

"Well, I don't know, you know. I've never really thought about how I felt. But isn't the United States the strongest country in the world?"

"By some measures, it certainly is," Duncan replied. "It has more nuclear bombs and more sophisticated weapons systems than any other country. We now spend ten thousand dollars a second on the military. American influence, both military and economic, is felt around the globe. Truly, we are a superpower. On the other hand, . . ." he paused thoughtfully, ". . . in 1945 we were militarily invulnerable; whereas today, with about thirty thousand more nuclear bombs than we had then, we could all be blown up at any moment. So whatever we've been buying with all that military money, it hasn't really made us secure. In fact, Eunice, let me propose to you an unusual thesis: that there is no significant military threat to the United States that can be defended against."

Eunice sputtered, "But what about an invasion by the Russians? Or maybe the Chinese?"

"They're a rather long way away," replied Duncan calmly. "Because of our nation's shielding geography, we really don't need to worry about armadas of Soviets in rowboats. Anyway, our country is not only too isolated but also too big and too independent to be taken over physically. Can you imagine a Red Army squad marching into a holler in Kentucky or a town in Montana and announcing that they're taking over? They wouldn't last five minutes." Eunice nodded with a feeling of pride. "No, I can think of only three kinds of substantial military threats to American territory: minor border incursions of the kinds the Coast Guard is supposed to take care of; terrorism, against which a free society has no really effective defense, although we could make our society both less tense and less vulnerable; and nuclear attack, against which there's no defense, although, if you believe in deterrence and don't believe in nuclear winter, you might be able to deter it. Can you think of any more significant military threats I've left out?"

"No," said Eunice slowly. "Our allies—in Europe, for example —are closer to the Soviets and *could* be physically invaded. But you *did* say the United States, and to that extent I guess I have to agree with you. Odd, I never thought about that before."

"That thesis," continued Duncan, "was put forth by the Boston Study Group in its 1979 book *The Price of Defense*, a book so simple and clear that hardly anyone read it. And the Group's conclusion, logically enough, was that only about two or three percent of today's military budget is actually needed for defense of our homeland—enough to fund, say, the Coast Guard and some antiterrorist measures and a handful of Poseidon submarines. Those few subs are plenty, because *each* such submarine—and we have thirty-one of them—has the capacity to carry about enough warheads to land the equivalent of three Hiroshima bombs on *each* of the two-hundred-odd Soviet cities of more than a hundred thousand people. If that's not a deterrent, I don't know what is. The other ninety-eight or so percent of our military budget is for general-purpose forces. Their mission is to project American power into disputes in other countries where the President perceives the United States has an interest—to put it as neutrally as I can."

"So maybe," Eunice reflected, "the Department of Defense really ought to be split up. The tiny part of it that's really for defense could keep that name, and the rest could be called something else—maybe the Department of Foreign Military Intervention."

"Good idea," said Duncan. "It'd be a step in the right direction, away from Orwell. Of course, we haven't discussed whether that foreign-intervention mission is necessary or desirable, and if we got into that now, we'd be here at least all night. But if we're going to have this enormous military strength, and keep close to half of all the scientists and engineers in this country busy devising new ways to kill people, at least we ought to think about what it's all for.

"Anyway," he continued, "awesome though our military strength is, it has a soft underbelly. Our country is in the same position as someone who puts lots of locks and bolts on the front door while leaving the back door open. We have armed ourselves against conventional military threats, and we can send showers of incredibly lethal missiles in almost any direction. But the energy systems in this country, as well as many of the other vital links —food, water, data processing, electronic financial transactions, and telecommunications, for example—could be very easily disrupted by anyone with a bit of coordination and diabolical common sense. For example, in one evening, a small group of people could shut off, for about a year, three-fourths of the oil and natural gas that normally flows to the eastern states. And they could do that without even leaving Louisiana. The electric system is so vulnerable that people with a decent knowledge of the electric grid could probably black out most of the country. A couple of saboteurs in rubber dinghies or a couple of Iranian jets could destroy the Saudi oil terminals at Ras Tanura and Ju'aymah. That would cut off five-sixths of Saudi oil exports for up to three years, which is how long it would take to rebuild those terminals."

Eunice's eyes bugged as she listened to this litany.

"Pipelines, tankers, and oil refineries are all quite vulnerable to disruption," Duncan went on. "Whether the oil comes from abroad or not, the pipelines, tankers, and oil refineries are part of a long, slender line of supply that is necessary if we are to stay warm, well lit, mobile, and comfortable. Consider the Trans-Alaska Pipeline. It spans nearly eight hundred miles of rough country and carries a seventh of the oil fed into all U.S. refineries. Having it shut down would cost about four hundred dollars per *second*. If it failed in the winter, the nine million barrels of hot oil in transit would congeal in about three weeks into the world's biggest Chapstick. Damage to 'Hollywood and Vine'—the maze of four-foot-diameter pipe at the system's northern end—or to certain vulnerable parts of the pipeline itself, could take many months, even a year or more, to repair. With luck, the pumps would be powerful enough to start the congealed oil flowing again, but no one knows for sure."

"Wait a minute," interrupted Eunice. "Of course, long pipelines must be vulnerable, but I don't see how they could be bombed or blown up. Surely our military planners have thought of all that. I mean, aren't the pipelines and so forth so well guarded that terrorists could never get near them?"

"You'd think so," answered Duncan, "but in fact, those military planners, who are well aware of the problem, haven't been able to influence the design of civilian energy systems. That's why we have, for example, that eight-hundred-mile pipeline across Alaska. The army knows it's indefensible—they proved that to themselves with a test ten years ago—but what are they supposed to do, place GIs shoulder-to-shoulder along it? It's so accessible by road, river, and bush plane that it's already been shot at repeatedly and even bombed—incompetently—twice. The company that runs it, though, says there's no security problem. And that's only one pipeline. All the major oil and gas pipelines in this country, placed end to end, would stretch a dozen times around the Equator. The overhead electric transmission lines would go fifteen times around the earth. With all those strung-out arteries, we depend on luck and social tranquillity, not on guards or alarms."

Eunice shuddered.

"However, my confidence in that dependence has been pretty shaken," Duncan went on, "by the many instances of sabotage that have already happened. In 1982 that couple I mentioned, the Lovinses, prepared for the Pentagon a catalogue of recent attacks on centralized energy facilities. Well, I tell you, that really rang some bells in Congress, because nobody had realized before how fragile our entire energy system is. It turns out that most energy control and distribution centers are protected by chain-link fences, Keep Out signs, or nothing at all. Many of our most critical facilities are so wide open that some, for example, have been broken into by juveniles—fortunately, to hold beer parties inside, steal pencils, and scrawl graffiti, not to do real damage. Meanwhile, there are, on average, two incidents of terrorism every day somewhere in the world. At least once a week an energy system is attacked. In some countries, such as El Salvador, it happens once a day. Energy systems have *already* been attacked in more than half of the United States and in more than fifty foreign countries. That doesn't even count thousands of minor incidents, such as the ranchers who don't like the power lines crossing their rangeland, so they shoot out the insulators that separate the wires from the towers. Our Navy worries about how to protect oil shipments in the event of war, but pirates in small boats regularly board and rob

supertankers off Singapore and Nigeria. One of those tankers was even hijacked and never found again.

"Besides, sabotage isn't the only cause of massive failures in the nation's energy systems. Natural disasters—floods, earthquakes, ice storms, droughts—all disrupt the conventional supply of energy services, or vastly worsen existing disruptions. And different aspects of harsh weather can interact in unexpected ways that intensify the disruption, as they did during the winter of 1976–77, for instance, in the Midwest. Not only did the cold weather increase the need for fuel oil and coal, but it also froze the Ohio River from bank to bank, blocking the movement of barges carrying those very fuels. Coal, which had been wetted at the mine to suppress dust, froze solid en route to its destination and in some cases had to be blasted out of the railcars. So at the very time when the energy was most needed, it was unavailable.

"But even beyond natural disasters and sabotage," Duncan continued, "complex energy systems are often their own worst enemy. Within most of the complicated ones are the seeds of their undoing. That is, they're so complex that no one—not even the designers—can know what will go wrong or under what circumstances failures are likely. All they know is that such failures will occur. Three cases in point are pretty significant. When a federally sponsored study of nuclear accidents was written in the early seventies, the authors discounted many possibilities as being so highly improbable that they weren't even worth considering. Yet the fire at the Browns Ferry reactor, the near meltdown at Three Mile Island, and the failure of the Salem reactor's emergency shutdown system—the three most dangerous recent nuclear accidents in the United States—happened in ways that were dismissed by the authors of that report."

"I don't understand. How could they have missed something like that?" Eunice asked, deeply troubled.

"Maybe it really wasn't their fault," Duncan said, "except that they were so damned confident. You see, nuclear reactors are so large and have so many separate subsystems, each affecting others, that no one could know how the various components would interact to cause an unforeseen kind of failure with unknowable consequences. In the Apollo space program, the same thing happened. The complexity of the technology outstripped our ability to predict its performance; so failures occurred far more often than the engineers' meticulous analyses had projected. And rare events *do* happen. In the Oak Ridge Research Reactor in 1969, a safety system failed because *seven* layers of backup devices, each with three redundant channels, all failed simultaneously. That twenty-one-fold failure is about as unlikely as having the proverbial roomful of chimpanzees type out *King Lear*.

"But an even better example comes from the electric grid," he continued. "On July 10, 1977, the chairman of Consolidated Edison Company in New York said that a repetition of the blackout that had hit the Northeast in 1965 was remote. Three days later, most of New York City was blacked out for twenty-five hours. Much to the chairman's embarrassment, a situation came up that no one had foreseen. It was then magnified by the flawed response of the system's operators. Another hard lesson in the unexpected."

"It doesn't sound like these complicated systems make much sense, then, does it?" Eunice said.

"I don't know if I'd go that far," said Duncan. "I mean, I'm not suggesting we try to build backyard-sized blast furnaces as they do in China. But these issues of scale, complexity, and vulnerability are important ones that don't get nearly enough attention when energy plans are made. When you deal with an energy system that is very big and fragile—vulnerable to disruption by accident, sabotage, or natural disaster—a lot of costs creep in that you might not expect."

"Oh, you mean to provide spare power or refining capacity in case a couple of the generating units are disabled?" Eunice said.

"Well, that's one," agreed Duncan. "Take nuclear plants. A lot of utilities claim they will be cost-effective. But that claim assumes, among other things, that the plants will be in service, say, two-thirds or three-quarters of the time. The actual average for big nuclear plants is a fifty-four percent 'capacity factor.' Those two numbers may sound close, but the economic difference is worth several hundred million dollars a year per plant. And when that thousand-megawatt nuclear plant is down for repairs or routine maintenance, it's producing no power at all. That means that a huge chunk of the utility's generating capacity—enough to provide power to nearly a million people—will just have vanished. Either the power customers have to reconcile themselves to periodic blackouts, or the utility has to have enough backup capacity available to replace that plant. And that's expensive. The instant availability of the backup power to replace the failed plant also depends on an enormously complicated control and transmission system that can fail, and has failed, time and again."

"So, as we agreed, we should design energy systems to be smaller than we do now?" asked Eunice.

"That's true, although I'm less concerned about size," Duncan demurred, "than about something I would call 'resilience.' That's the ability of a system to absorb unexpected shocks and tolerate surprises with the minimum disruption for the people it's supposed to serve. A large power plant that must have all of its valves and pumps and control rods in the proper position to be useful at all—and which otherwise is a useless three-billion-dollar hunk of machinery—is hardly resilient. Many big transmission lines rely on transformers, switches, and controls that are all special-order. They take a year or two to make, and spares for them aren't kept in stock anywhere. Pipelines can be cut easily by well-placed charges of dynamite or by unlucky combinations of leaks and sparks. The transformers and power lines that feed the oil pumps are often easily accessible to saboteurs. So are the highly specialized control centers. In fact, the two biggest pipeline systems in the country are controlled from the same building, and until recently there was no backup control room. Once a pipeline is crippled, chances are that it will take a long time to mend. Also, there are usually few if any parallel pipelines through which fuel can be routed, few trained people who can swarm over the countryside turning valves by hand if the controls fail, and few experts skilled enough to mend or rebuild the controls.

"Refineries are similarly fragile and unsuited to improvisation. Each refinery is designed to handle specific kinds of crude oil and may be crippled if those particular flavors are unavailable. And, like pipelines, they're virtually accidents waiting to happen. There are more than two hundred sources of flame in an average refinery; so uncontained gases are readily ignited. And, if that's scary, liquefied-natural-gas facilities are even worse. Some are in the middle of such city harbors as Tokyo, London, and Boston, and a major fire could destroy the city about as effectively as a multi-megaton hydrogen bomb. Remember the disaster in Mexico in 1984? That was liquefied gas in action."

Eunice was aghast. "It sounds almost as though the designers of our energy systems didn't even think about what they were doing," she said. "How could they ignore those dangers?"

"I know that with 20/20 hindsight it's tough to understand why, but engineers ignore stuff like this all the time," replied Duncan. "Let's step back for a moment from the specifics I was rattling off and look at some general principles. Most engineers look only at the details of the project they are working on. They don't generally think much about how their piece will fit into the whole."

"They don't," ventured Eunice, "do systems thinking."

"Right!" Duncan was genuinely pleased. "Now," he continued, "that might not be so bad if they designed each piece to stand alone, and to be not just technically reliable in the face of predictable trouble, but also to be actively resilient. But they don't. Instead, many major energy facilities are near each other; so an accident to one can disable others. And many of these systems are interlinked, or mutually dependent; so failures can spread. Half of our oil is extracted by electric pumps. Most refineries need outside power and electrically pumped water. Oil is often delivered in oil-powered trucks. Some power plants can't start without power from other plants, and then they need oil for backup power and lubrication. Most coal mines flood if their electric pumps stop. Nearly all our coal is moved by diesel fuel. Even home furnaces can't burn their oil or gas without electric pumps and ignition; so in a power failure, that big tank of oil in the basement does you little good. Almost no thought has been given to how the whole energy system will behave if its interconnected pieces start to fail."

"Heh," Duncan chuckled, "you know what's really needed?"

Eunice shook her head.

"People with nasty, evil, suspicious minds," he answered, his blue eyes glinting. "The types who fall asleep at night thinking of all the ways something could go wrong. Those are the kinds of people I would like to have designing our really essential national systems."

"But isn't that being a little paranoid?" Eunice asked uncomfortably.

"No. Realistic," Duncan corrected. "Until now we've been designing energy systems as though we lived in a time of social tranquillity. Unfortunately, that's not the sort of world we have.

"The design philosophy I would like to see used," continued Duncan, "would seek to establish an energy system based on things that have already shown that they can withstand unexpected shocks. Like nature. For example, the strategy of a tree is never to rely on only one leaf. And each leaf has a varied network of veins. Even if the random nibblings of a caterpillar chew through a couple of those veins, there are many other ways of getting nutrition to and from virtually the entire leaf. A resilient system, like a treeful of leaves, has many small components that can be swapped around or easily replaced in case one fails. And they shouldn't all be connected to one central hub, but should instead have many short, sturdy links between them. An energy system designed this way could accommodate many failures, instead of amplifying small failures into large catastrophic ones."

"That's fine as a philosophy, Duncan," Eunice said. "But has anyone ever done that with an energy system? What would a resilient system actually look like? Or what does an *un*resilient one look like?"

"I can give you a couple of examples. In fact, I already did. Remember how, in World War II, Japan's small, dispersed hydro plants were more than a thousand times less susceptible to bombing damage than the centralized thermal power plants?" Eunice nodded. "Well, similarly, senior Nazi officials said after World War II that if the Allies had bombed Germany's centralized power plants early, we could have shortened the war by at least two years. The only reason we didn't do that is that our experts thought, wrongly, that the German grid was so well interconnected that damaged plants could easily be replaced by others. Now, unfortunately, terrorists know better, and major energy facilities top the list of their targets worldwide. Oil depots are attacked by the CIA in Nicaragua just as they are by leftist guerrillas in some other Latin American countries. One attack on Rhodesia's oil depot raised that country's national budget deficit eighteen percent in a few minutes. Seeing this risk, such countries as Israel and China have wisely and deliberately decentralized their energy systems as a security precaution, and Sweden is doing the same thing. Even the Russian army wants to follow suit; but the Politburo won't let them do it, because decentralization would reduce the Party's political control. Sound familiar?"

"Yes," said Eunice, grinning, "although our own bureaucrats would claim other reasons. But is there anything communities can do to increase our resilience?"

"Sure," replied Duncan. "In fact, that's probably the best level at which to work. One of my favorite examples comes from the town of Holyoke, Massachusetts, which had its own gas-turbine electricity generator. Ordinarily the town used it only for peaking power, since it was expensive to run. However, when Holyoke's power engineer saw the 1965 Northeast blackout rolling toward him, he cut the town loose from the regional grid and fired up the local generator. The money he saved by not having to shut down the town paid off the entire cost of the power plant in the first four hours. In Coronado, California, a few years ago, they didn't even realize that surrounding San Diego was blacked out, because their own power came from a local industrial cogeneration plant. Or look at Israel, where almost all the homes have natural gas. But it isn't delivered by pipeline; instead, each home has its own bottled supply. Presto—one less big target for terrorists to attack. Or take the case of the West Chicago gas station powered by photovolta- ics. On opening day a violent thunderstorm blacked out the rest of the city. The solar-powered pumps were the only ones in the city pumping gasoline. The resilience there came from the fact that there was more than one energy source powering the city's gas pumps—and one that couldn't be cut off."

"You know, Duncan," Eunice said, "all this sounds like so much common sense. Why don't engineers just design systems this way as a matter of course?"

"Right," scoffed Duncan. "You know, most engineers aren't trained that way anymore. Elegant, rugged simplicity seems to be a virtue of the past, and civilian systems are seldom designed with potential disruptions in mind. Let me give you an example. Con- sider a refinery in which the oil must go through several processes in succession. If one of the stages is shut down, the only way the others can keep on working is if there is some 'buffer' storage between the stages—some partly refined oil stored so that a failure in one unit won't make all the rest grind to a halt. But putting in those intermediate holding tanks costs money; it means that extra product must be kept on hand, eating interest, rather than being sold immediately. Skimping on such buffer storage looks like an economy—just the kind that accountants love. But when failures *do* happen, the design turns out to have been penny-wise and pound-foolish. Hundreds of millions of dollars are tied up in a plant that can't work at all because any failure leaves the later stages of processing with nothing to work on. Refineries that have a 'looser fit,' or more 'graceful' failure, fail more slowly and hence work more of the time. Similarly, by law, new boilers in Sweden, even if they will normally burn oil or gas, must also be designed to burn coal or wood, and their proprietors must keep about a nine or ten months' fuel stockpile on hand. On the other hand, most American boilers are very finicky about what they burn. Such stockpiles as the Strategic Petroleum Reserve that are supposed to solve this are also so centralized that in a real emergency they probably couldn't be processed and delivered."

"Well, what you're saying," concluded Eunice, "is that designers shouldn't spend their time cooking up new, sophisticated, and technologically complex ways to make things work. Instead, they should design devices that do the job as simply as possible. The more complicated a mechanism, the more likely it is to break down. And the more understandable a technology, the easier it is for common people to be able to repair it; and the more easily people can repair it, the more likely it is to stay in service for a long time."

"Ah, the wisdom of housewives," said Duncan with undisguised admiration. "I can tell you've dealt with some not-so-good plumbers before. And here's what an energy system designed along those lines would look like. Let's take resilience as the criterion. As it happens, renewable energy sources tend to be among the most resilient around, for the obvious reasons. Renewables tend to be well dispersed—on a rooftop or neighborhood level— instead of being collected together in one power plant big enough to serve a million people. So when things do go wrong, it's only one house, one neighborhood, or one factory that's affected—not entire cities, counties, and regions. And since sustainable energy tends to be available at least regionally, the lines of supply are much shorter than for centralized electrical generation or for the supply of oil and natural gas. Shorter lines of supply make for fewer disruptions. Also, the sun doesn't go on strike the way coal miners or transportation workers sometimes do."

"And," Eunice chimed in, "the rain and wind won't form a cartel to raise prices the way oil exporters do."

Duncan nodded. "The design of sustainable energy systems, too, predisposes them to be less vulnerable to widespread disruption than depletable resources are. The only moving parts in a passive solar heating system are the sun, the earth, and the air that carries the heat around your house. There's not much that can go wrong, and no attractive targets for explosives or the like. Or suppose you drive a sixty-five-mpg car—which is a good deal less than has already been tested. Such a car would run for hundreds of miles on a half-full gas tank. If the entire U.S. vehicle fleet were that efficient, it could run for about a year just on the oil already stored at gas stations and in pipelines, refineries, and other parts of the delivery system. By using energy efficiently, we'd use up our fuel stocks more slowly and thereby buy the precious time needed to mend what's broken or to improvise new supplies. In contrast, if a pipeline stops feeding crude oil to a modern refinery, that refinery generally runs out and has to shut down in a matter of *days.*

"What's more, renewables tend to be relatively easy to understand. I'll bet I couldn't have explained the inner workings of the petroleum industry to you in the same detail as I did for solar and other sustainable technologies. You can build a working solar collector from a *Popular Science* or *Mother Earth News* article, but not a working refinery or reactor. If a solar system fails, it's usually pretty obvious what's wrong, and anyone with a minimal degree of plumbing or electrical knowledge can fix it. And since there would be thousands of pretty much identical, interchangeable parts in these systems—mostly things you can buy at the local hardware store—it'd be far easier to replace faulty parts than if they had to be specially made and took years to manufacture. There's lots of room to improvise if systems are simple enough to fix and make locally.

"When more houses use solar cells to generate their electricity, too, they'll have an immediate source of short-term emergency power. Since the cells produce the same kind of low-voltage direct current as your car battery uses, you'll simply be able to plug your house into your car!"

"My car?" Eunice asked skeptically. "That can't give me very much power."

Duncan grinned. "More than you think," he replied. "It'll give you enough power to keep your refrigerator and radio going for days. In fact, the generating capacity in the generators and alternators of America's cars and trucks is about a sixth that of all the power stations in the whole country!

"In summary," concluded Duncan, "if we move toward a more efficient, diverse, dispersed, renewable energy system, our energy system could become so resilient that major failures of energy supply would no longer be possible. And such real energy security, far from costing extra, would cut our energy bills—that is, the premium for our 'energy insurance policy' would be *negative.*"

"Well, I just have one more question," Eunice said. "You know, we started out talking about the army. But if our energy systems are so vulnerable that an army can't keep us secure, what do we have one for anyway?"

"Watch out, Eunice, the room might be bugged," Duncan said, grinning. "Thirty-five years ago, they would have hauled you before Senator McCarthy for asking that." Eunice gave a little gasp. "However, it's a valid question," Duncan went on, "and you don't really need to worry about bugs. I have the room electronically 'swept' for them fairly often."

As he spoke, Duncan's watch beeped softly. Eunice jumped visibly. Duncan only laughed. "Not to worry. However, perhaps this is the appropriate time, with the sun now setting over the Pentagon, to look at the relationship between energy and armies."

20 *Toward a Durable Peace*

N<small>OWADAYS</small>," D<small>UNCAN BEGAN</small> matter-of-factly, "the entire firepower of World War II can be packaged to fit neatly beneath your bed. Powerful nuclear bombs can even be made small enough to fit in an athletic bag or a shopping bag. What does that suggest to you?"

"No . . ." Eunice's mouth was agape. "Do you mean that if I felt like it I could wheel a nuclear bomb around the supermarket?" She gasped and tried to block out the sudden vision of herself and all the check-out clerks frozen in terror as under her paper towels and frozen peas she found a nuclear bomb gently beeping.

"Which means," said Duncan, answering his own question, "that there are lots of ways to deliver them."

Eunice puzzled over that one. "You mean . . ."

"I mean nuclear warheads don't have to arrive by missiles, whose radar tracks reveal where they come from. Instead, they can arrive anonymously via rental vans and parcel services. They can be left in the trunk of a parked car, or checked at Union Station in a duffel bag, or brought into New York Harbor by a cabin cruiser or a tramp freighter. And what do you suppose would happen if Manhattan disappeared in a bright flash at eight o'clock tomorrow morning . . ."

Eunice's face registered her growing horror.

". . . but nobody said," Duncan played out his scenario, " 'We did it.' Against whom, then, would we retaliate? Colonel Qadaffi on general principles? Of course, retaliation couldn't put New York back together again. But it might make us feel better. Or suppose someone called the media and said: '*We* did it. We're the Thirtieth of February Liberation Army. And you'll hear from us again.' Suppose we didn't have a clue as to who or where they were. What would we do then?"

The look of horror remained on Eunice's face.

"Now, nuclear terrorism," Duncan continued, "sponsored either by foreign countries or by groups acting on their own, is a pretty extreme notion, although there have already been such threats, and there are clearly groups with the kind of hatred that could push them to try it again. But it's a dramatic example of how our security is undermined by the spread of bombs to even more countries, to groups that aren't countries at all, and even perhaps to individuals. You see, if other groups get access to nuclear bombs or even bomb material, it completely undermines the reason we say *we* have nuclear bombs. Even if you think nuclear deterrence is effective and moral, and not just mutual suicide, stray nuclear bombs destroy whatever theoretical basis there ever was for deterrence. You simply can't deter people from attacking you unless you know who they are and how to retaliate against them.

"And by the way," Duncan added somberly, "remember that a credible *threat* of nuclear violence, especially if publicized, can achieve the same political goals as an actual attack. Can you imagine the panic if someone announced that a nuclear bomb will go off in two hours in Wall Street? Since hundreds of bombs' worth of nuclear material used by American government and industry labs can't be accounted for—some of it might be missing and some of it is suspected to be missing—any threat that's technically knowledgeable is automatically credible. As I said, our government has *already* received credible threats of nuclear terrorism and has sent out specially equipped technical teams to search for hidden atomic bombs. As far as is publicly known, those threats were all bluffs. Although, if one weren't a bluff, but the bomb didn't go off or were found and inactivated first, you can be sure that fact wouldn't be publicly known—in fact, it'd be highly classified. It's even conceivable that our own government is already secretly making concessions of some kind under a nuclear blackmail threat, and we don't even know it. That's a consequence of living in the nuclear age."

"Oh, me," whimpered Eunice, "you make societies out to sound like armed camps. It bothers me to have to think about this at all. I'm starting to feel like checking under my bed every night for terrorists—who knows what they could be plotting?"

Eunice sat and stared sadly past Duncan and out the window. And he let her. These were disturbing matters, and, as the Cabinet member officially responsible for building the bombs, she did need to come to grips with the issue. However, Duncan was pleased when Eunice shook herself and stated firmly, "But I won't let my life be governed by those kinds of fears."

"And you don't really mean what you just said about looking under your bed?" he asked gently.

"Well, maybe not," conceded Eunice. "But it's the whole principle of it," she said disgustedly. "Why do we need to be afraid of those kinds of disruptions at all?"

"Because," said Duncan, "terrorism is basically theater, and there are few ways to get people to pay closer attention to your cause than to threaten them with nuclear attack. That's especially true of the United States, with our uncensored media and with lots of people around the world nursing real or imagined grievances against everything our country stands for. All our military might can't deter or prevent a terrorist nuclear attack; in fact, it may even invite one by making us look like bullies. And just look at the countries known or suspected to have secret nuclear-bomb programs: Israel, South Africa, India, Pakistan, Argentina, Iraq, Iran, Libya, Taiwan, South Korea—"

"Wait a minute!" interrupted Eunice. "Do you mean those countries are on their way to joining the Nuclear Club, too?"

"Yes," replied Duncan, "our government acknowledges that they and others are moving that way, although some are moving faster than others. For example, Israel, South Africa, and India almost certainly have bombs already; I believe Pakistan does, Argentina might be close, and the others are trying to get them. Then there are such later possible candidates as Brazil, the Philippines, Nigeria, Turkey, Spain, Egypt—"

"But that's terrible!" cried Eunice. "I mean, *we* have lots of bombs, and so do the Soviets, and the Chinese, and the British and French; but we're all *responsible* nations, not like some of those unstable ones you mentioned."

"What about Germany?" asked Duncan dryly. "Remember that we're now best friends with some countries that, only a couple of generations ago, were being run by mad dictators. Both Germany and Japan have so much pure nuclear bomb material now—some we've given them and some they've made themselves —that they could both have world-class nuclear arsenals very quickly if they chose to. Worse, a 'stable' country—maybe even our own—easily could have an unstable leader sometime in the future. The kind of political responsibility you spoke of had better be more solid than anything in the history of the world, because once you make nuclear bomb materials, they stay explosive for *billions* of years."

"Stop," said Eunice firmly. "Let's go back a few steps. I want to know what it takes to build nuclear bombs and how all these countries are getting their hands on those ingredients, so that I can understand whether there's a way any of us can stop all this."

"Okay," said Duncan, "I can do that simply enough if I leave out the technical details. Building an atomic bomb requires basically five things. The most important is a small amount of concentrated fissionable material, such as plutonium or highly enriched uranium 235—typically a piece about the size of a lemon or a grapefruit, depending on what kind of material you have, how pure it is, and how well you design bombs."

"And that little," marveled Eunice, "can blow up a city?"

"Yes, indeed," replied Duncan. "Destroying Hiroshima took the fissioning of just twenty-six ounces of uranium. The amount of mass converted into pure energy was only a gram—a sliver of metal smaller than a stick of chewing gum."

Eunice's jaw dropped. "And where does one get such materials?"

"Oh, lots of places," said Duncan breezily. "From nuclear research labs, university research reactors, nuclear submarine fuel, government stockpiles or shipments of actual bombs and parts, some civilian nuclear fuel factories, the black market. In fact, there are already *tons* of bomb material that nobody can account for, and some of it may be on the black market already. After all, it's worth more than heroin. And other countries keep track of their inventories even more sloppily than we do. The most prolific source of bomb material, though, is nuclear power plants."

"I thought the kind of fuel they use is so weak, so diluted," said Eunice, "that it couldn't possibly cause a nuclear explosion. That's what all the ads say: 'Nuclear plants can't blow up.' "

"That's mostly true," confirmed Duncan. "You aren't worried about the reactors themselves becoming bombs—although reactors may blow up in non-nuclear explosions caused by hydrogen or steam, and external bombs can blow up reactors and spread the radioactive inventory in the core all over. And, indeed, the *fuel* used in most reactors is *not* directly bomb-usable.

"Although," he added, "that's not true for fast-breeder reactors or many research reactors or naval reactors or high-temperature gas-cooled reactors. But that's not the point. The point is that every reactor *makes* a powerful bomb material, plutonium, as it burns up its fuel. And that plutonium can be extracted from the highly radioactive spent fuel. In fact, our government wants that extraction to become a general practice worldwide, to help the nuclear industry, they say. But once the plutonium is extracted, it's directly usable for bombs in a matter of minutes to days. We used to think that the particular kind of plutonium made in power reactors couldn't make powerful or reliable bombs—it doesn't have the ideal composition. But it turned out that though not ideal, 'reactor-grade' plutonium is perfectly usable, and its technical shortcomings can be largely or wholly overcome by designing the bomb differently. So it's important to know that one typical big reactor makes close to a hundred bombs' worth of plutonium every year. Also, that the nonexplosive nuclear fuel that goes into the reactor can be converted into plutonium in your basement, and that the equipment used to make slightly enriched reactor fuel can be misused to make highly enriched uranium instead—an ideal bomb material."

"But even if you had the fissionable material," said Eunice, "wouldn't you need a whole lot more resources than that? In fact, your own little Manhattan Project?"

"No," said Duncan, "because practically everything you'd need to know is in the technical libraries of any sizable university. That knowledge is the second ingredient of bombs. And it's already published—too late to stop it. In fact, many of the data that are secret in the bomb business are openly published in technical papers on civilian nuclear reactors.

"Then the third ingredient," he continued, "is technical skills. Those, too, are widespread. Tens of thousands of people, some of whom were fired and are disgruntled, have actually made bombs for governments, and hundreds of thousands have the needed skills from other lines of work—metallurgy, electronics, explosives, and so on. In fact, terrorists needn't bother with all that fancy stuff; they can just throw together a crude, simple design that would work. It would be clumsier and less powerful than a professionally designed bomb, but it would still be likely to kill an awful lot of people."

"Wouldn't making a bomb require special equipment?" persisted Eunice.

"Not necessarily," said Duncan. "Simple designs wouldn't need any to speak of. More complex designs could be made with an ordinary machine shop and the kind of chemical equipment you can buy from any lab-supply catalog. To the extent that a really fancy design could benefit from specialized nuclear equipment, all that is available over-the-counter too. That's the fourth ingredient. And the fifth one, *non*-nuclear components—such as high explosives and special fuses to fire them at the right time—are commercially available too. In fact, probably every significant part of our military nuclear bombs, other than the fissionable material itself, can be openly bought under some other name."

"Why on earth—" began Eunice.

"Because, dear lady, the manufacturers want to make more money by creating other markets for their products. Even the high-explosive lenses used to compress the fissionable material to cause a professional, military nuclear explosion are readily available as tools for commercial metal forming."

Eunice stared at him in amazement. "But doesn't that mean," she said, "that so long as we keep on running nuclear power plants, and expanding the businesses and the kinds of research and development that support them, we'll supply more and more of the one missing ingredient—the plutonium or other bomb material —and thus continue to spread bomb kits all over the world?"

"Yes," said Duncan. There was a long pause. "It means just exactly that. But . . ."

"But what?" asked Eunice grimly. "Surely that's all there is to say. It's too late. All we can do now is pray."

"No," replied Duncan, "there's a way out. It's absolutely true, as you say, that the nuclear and other materials, the knowledge, the skills, and the equipment that nuclear power puts into circulation are dual-purpose and already widely available. And we might as well add to that list the big, technical organizations needed for an enterprise as complex as nuclear power—although you don't need them to build just a few bombs. Such groups tend to spawn bomb programs, too, as several countries discovered when their 'civilian' nuclear teams ended up building bombs. But some of those ingredients wouldn't be available *without* nuclear power to drive them."

"Aha!" exclaimed Eunice. "So better light bulbs can help avoid bomb building!"

"Huh!" Duncan exhaled in surprise. She caught onto this stuff faster than the experts. "That's exactly right. Suppose nuclear power no longer existed. Just imagine it for the moment—we'll come back to that assumption later. In such a world, all those bomb ingredients would no longer be items of commerce. A few of them could still be used for special tasks, mainly in medicine. But the amounts needed would be very small and fairly easy to monitor. On the whole, you simply wouldn't be able to buy anymore the most important of the bomb ingredients that nuclear power makes available and for which it creates a market. So it would be harder to get those things. You'd have to shop around more for them, and you'd be more likely to be noticed doing so.

And then, if you were caught, it would be a lot more embarrassing, both for you and for your supplier, because for the first time your motive in wanting such things would be *unambiguously military*. Right now, you can buy a bomb kit under an innocent-looking civilian disguise: you can say, as Pakistan does, that it's all part of a civilian nuclear power program to make electricity vital for development. But without that excuse, it would be clear that what you are really after is bombs, and you'd have to justify your program accordingly before the world. This wouldn't make the spread of bombs impossible, but it would make it much more difficult. For most of the countries I named before, it would make it prohibitively difficult.

"In fact," continued Duncan, "that's a flaw in the argument that the nuclear industry often makes. They say that if a country wanted to build bombs, it wouldn't use the less-than-ideal plutonium from power reactors, but would instead build special, dedicated, military plants exclusively to make the special type of plutonium that's ideal for bombs. But, if, as the industry also says, such a country would feel inhibited in using civilian reactors as bomb factories, because it might get caught, surely it would feel even more inhibited in building special plutonium-production reactors that have *only* military uses. If it were caught with those plants, it would have no civilian excuse or 'cover' for what it was doing. Furthermore, such military plants would have to be paid for out of the nation's own budget, just for military purposes, whereas the civilian plant also makes saleable electricity and gets subsidies from the exporting country so generous that they sometimes amount to paying the customer country to haul the reactor away."

"Do you mean," asked Eunice, "that the sales of nuclear plants to developing countries are subsidized?"

"Of course," said Duncan, "nobody would be foolish enough to buy such a plant if not subsidized and, indeed, often bribed to do so. There hasn't been a single sale of a nuclear plant to a developing country on normal commercial terms. And as far as I can see, none of the companies making nuclear plants has ever made a nickel on reactor sales either, although some of them show a net profit because they make so much on repairs and fuel after the plant is built."

"Aren't there rules or police of some kind," asked Eunice, "to make sure that nuclear equipment and materials are used only peacefully?"

"In principle, yes," said Duncan, "but they don't work. You see, the rules were written, not to make the world safe from nuclear bombs, but to avoid getting in the way of nuclear commerce. They're therefore so full of loopholes that about all that's left is a *belief* that we have achieved security. But that's a false belief. Any country that really wants to make bombs can do so with little fear of detection or sanction. Any country, without violating any treaty, can make a whole arsenal of devices that aren't quite bombs, but can become bombs in five minutes by turning the last screw. In fact, our country's recent policy has actually been to make it easier for countries to have secret bomb programs, by increasing their access to nuclear technology or military aid."

"Huh?" Eunice looked at Duncan as if he'd lost his mind.

"It's true," he explained. "South Korea, Taiwan, and Pakistan have all used the threat of creating bomb programs to extort military concessions from the United States. That approach is rationalized in part by something called Article IV of the Non-Proliferation Treaty, which we promoted in the late sixties. It says that if a country *promises*, unenforceably and quite revocably, not to make bombs, then countries like ours that have nuclear technology promise to enhance their access to that technology for exclusively peaceful purposes. Now, I can't readily imagine an *exclusively* peaceful use of nuclear technology; we've learned too much since the sixties to remain naive on that score.

"But it seems to me that we really blew it with that section of the treaty, because it was written by nuclear experts in a narrowly nuclear context, at a time when nuclear power was generally believed to be cheap, safe, and indispensable. So not surprisingly, Article IV was framed solely in terms of transferring nuclear technology. But the underlying purpose of that part of the treaty is not to provide nuclear technology for its own sake, but rather the secure and affordable energy that nuclear power was supposed to provide for global development. Now, suppose we took that legitimate *purpose* seriously. Then, if countries like ours, instead of exporting reactors, simply helped other countries to use new energy-saving technologies and nonviolent, sustainable energy sources, that should satisfy the purpose of the treaty at least as well. We could even call it a Sunbeams for Peace program, though that seems redundant, since as far as I know sunbeams haven't been used for war since the Battle of Syracuse."

"But surely," objected Eunice, "we couldn't preach efficiency and sustainable energy for other countries unless we practiced them ourselves. They'll watch what we do, not what we say."

"Bravo!" exclaimed Duncan. "Clearly, the example we set is our most powerful source of influence in the nuclear arena. If a country like ours, which has lots of fuel and wealth and technical skill, says we must have nuclear power and a plutonium economy, how can we expect other countries without our advantages to draw a different conclusion for themselves? Indeed, it's the bad example we set that's propping up the teetering nuclear programs in Europe and Japan. Our example is supporting the export of reactors to developing countries that, but for our example, could choose to build a really modern energy system from scratch.

"And don't forget," he continued, "that our military policy sets a vivid example, too. Our nation is the only one to have used nuclear bombs in warfare, the only one that refuses to promise not to use them first again, and the primary one that bases its whole position in the world on threats of nuclear violence."

"No!" Eunice gasped. "Our bombs are just to . . . what was it you said . . .deter? . . . other countries from using theirs. Surely if the Russians weren't threatening us we would be happy to agree not to use our bombs. . . ."

"I wish that were true," Duncan replied. "Actually, this country is the one threatening to use its bombs on other people, and we've made such threats, on average, about once a year since 1945." Eunice looked both dumbfounded and ashamed. "If we set that kind of example for the world," he shrugged, "how can we expect other countries not to want the same bullying capacities for themselves? They'll want to 'succeed' in the way in which we define success. The Soviets have repeatedly offered to agree, if we will also, not to be the first to use nuclear bombs. But we have steadfastly maintained our right to use nuclear bombs against any

non-nuclear attack they might make. Now don't get me wrong,"
Duncan warned. "The Soviet military scares me a lot, and I don't
trust them at all. Although their record of upholding treaties is just
about as good as ours. Which is to say both sides fudge just as far
as they think they can get away with. Actually the biggest treaty
violation is our proposed 'Star Wars' space defense system—it's
a clear and blatant violation," Duncan concluded, shaking
his head.

Eunice reflected on this. "It seems to me," she said, ignoring
his diversions, "that the key to your argument is that you assumed
a non-nuclear future. But if your least-cost energy strategy—
choosing the best buys first—will do the same things we were
promised that nuclear power could do, only faster and cheaper,
then nuclear power is simply unnecessary and uneconomic."

"Exactly," said Duncan. "And that's even more true for developing countries—short of capital, with highly dispersed village-
scale uses for energy, with no electric grid, without a modern
technical infrastructure—than it is for us. But again, it's our example that's crucial. If we continue to extol nuclear means of providing energy and security as worthy of admiration and imitation,
and to treat non-nuclear sources of energy and security as second-
class and unworthy of a modern people, we can expect others to
continue behaving in exactly the way that ultimately does the
greatest harm to their—and our—security. Frankly, we're being
utter fools. The marketplace is providing us now with a wonderful
opportunity to straighten out both our energy policy and our
concept of security. Nuclear power is dying of an incurable attack
of market forces, throughout the world's market economies,
and—"

"Isn't it doing well in France?" Eunice interrupted. "That's
what I always see in the papers."

"France, remember," intoned Duncan, "has a centrally
planned economy and a flair for the grand folly. Nuclear power is
no exception. The French nuclear/electric industry is in the most
serious kind of economic as well as technical and political trouble.
In fact, its reprocessing plant doesn't work right, plants are more
often sited by decree than by consent, the 'solution' to the nuclear-
waste problem is still speculative, and the reactors are cracking.

On the financial front, the industry is geared up to make far more reactors than anyone will buy, and the national utility—unable to sell all that electricity—is essentially broke, with more than ten billion dollars in unrepayable debt. I suspect they're worse off today than if they'd kept on burning oil! Not, of course, that oil was the alternative to nuclear power. The French nuclear program has, in fact, been outpaced by more than three to one by energy savings, which had only a tiny fraction as much support from the French government. Anyway, looking at all the economic and technical problems of nuclear power in France, I don't see how that program can survive another decade.

"Interestingly," he continued, "the pattern of the collapse of nuclear expectations is identical in countries with widely varying conditions. It's the same in Canada, where there are no regulatory obstacles to building nuclear plants, and in West Germany, where the price of electricity isn't regulated, as it is here in the United States. If you look at any of the market economies, nuclear power is in deep trouble, with costs rising almost as fast as ours and no prospect of selling the electricity. It's only in the centrally planned economies with their bureaucratic momentum that nuclear forecasts remain high.

"Nuclear power is collapsing, then, for basic *economic* reasons. But that gives us a great opportunity. In order to get out of the nuclear power business, our government needn't be antinuclear. In fact, it can protest that it loves nuclear power, but loves the market more. All we need to do is recognize and abide by the verdict of the marketplace, rather than resorting to heroic measures to bail out a failed technology." Duncan sat with his arms outstretched, as if orchestrating all those crocodile tears; then he stopped and looked thoughtful. "I suppose," he admitted, "nuclear power deserves an orderly terminal phase—a kind of hospice—and a decent burial, and we should certainly help the nuclear technologists to recycle themselves into more promising lines of work. But you'd be amazed, if we did all that, how quickly the nuclear programs abroad would be abandoned, too, for lack of economic viability and domestic political support. In fact, did you know that one advanced industrial country has already embarked on this course?"

"Which one?" asked Eunice.

"Sweden," replied Duncan. "Seventy-eight percent of Swedes voted in 1980 to abandon nuclear power by 2010 in favor of efficiency and renewables—and that's just what they're doing."

"I thought," said Eunice, "I vaguely heard something about that vote, but the other way around. I thought they voted to *endorse* nuclear power."

"The 'big lie' technique," said Duncan, his annoyance show-ing. "A lot of people were told that, and believed it. But I was there at the time, and I can assure you that the pronuclear plank only got eighteen percent of the vote. The only real debate was over whether to phase out nuclear power immediately or slowly, and whether to abandon or to complete and temporarily operate the plants they already had built or were building.

"In fact," he concluded, "that really makes my point about the political power of example. The U.S. nuclear industry was so terri-bly afraid you might find out about the Swedish example that they actually distorted the result. It's just like the way they try to sell nuclear power here by saying how well it works in France, and in France by saying how well it works here. All of us here know that nuclear has terrible problems here, but, gee, if the French can do it, maybe we ought to stick with it. And the French public gets the same argument, the other way around. If the industry is that scared of the political power of the Swedish example, imagine the power of the American example. We're still the world leader in many kinds of technology, you know. If we simply admitted that the nuclear experiment hadn't worked, but that we had lots of other options that we were going to pursue because they did work and cost far less, that statement would reverberate around the world. And for that matter, if we really got serious about stopping our nuclear arms race, we'd find it a lot easier to get other countries not to start making bombs for themselves. Right now, it's hard to explain why, if bombs are so bad, we're making several more of them every day—another Hiroshima's worth every hour or two—and why, if we have about thirty thousand of them, other coun-tries shouldn't make even one."

"And then," added Eunice excitedly, "other countries would have neither the means to make bombs easily—because bomb kits would no longer be available for civilian purchase—nor the mo-tive, because we'd have set a better example. So we'd have slowed or maybe even stopped the spread of nuclear bombs. And the same energy choices that made this possible would also give us the more direct security benefits you talked about."

"That's it; that's exactly right," Duncan agreed, his eyes glow-ing. "You see, if we choose the cheapest energy buys, we won't care nearly so much if Mideast oil—or for that matter, our own oil —is flowing or not. And if our allies do the same thing, neither will they. And for that matter, if the Soviet Union does the same thing, neither will they. Then we won't need to try so hard to control the affairs of other countries, and we also won't invite terrorist attacks on ourselves for any of those reasons."

Duncan was infected with Eunice's excitement. It all seemed so possible. He cooled, though, and admitted, "Actually, I can't claim that simply cutting our dependence on other countries' resources will, by itself, eliminate U.S. intervention around the world. The sources of that intervention are much more complex. Part of the reason for those policies is the values choice that has been made under some administrations that the United States should be the world's policeman. We've poured a lot of money and political prestige into supporting unpopular governments friendly to our corporations. And that support has made us a lot of enemies and has made American targets more attractive to nationalist terrorists. However, without the pressure of the U.S. need for Mexican and Venezuelan petroleum, African uranium, and so on, these decisions just might be based a bit more on our political ideals."

"Well, okay," mused Eunice, "but how do we move toward that kind of self-reliance?"

"Part of the answer," said Duncan, "lies in transformations that are happening within our society already. As we shift toward an economy of information and services, and away from an economy of heavy industry and mass production, our need for raw materials is declining. And as we begin to recycle aluminum cans, for instance, we lose our dependence on Jamaican bauxite from which fresh aluminum is made. When New York's telephone company replaces hundreds of miles of copper cable under Manhattan with optical fiber, our need for Chilean copper suddenly takes a nose dive. And some of the richest metal mines in this country are in the municipal dumps, landfills, and junkyards of this country."

"But what will those countries do if we're not buying their exports? Won't this just make them poorer?" Eunice asked.

"It could," Duncan admitted, "especially if we don't start helping developing countries to build sustainable economies that take care of their people, rather than clinging to an economy that depends on being continuously ripped off by Western nations taking their primary resources, which we then make into manufactured goods and sell back to them at unaffordable prices. That's great for a few big corporations, but it leads to a pretty unstable world."

"It seems to me," Eunice said in annoyance, "that our government would buy more security and goodwill for its aid dollars if it simply tried to decrease world inequities and tensions rather than to help those corporate interests."

Duncan grinned his agreement.

"But aren't those economic shifts helping to force the kinds of changes that will be fairer for everyone?" Eunice asked hopefully.

"Not quite, I'm afraid," answered Duncan. "Certainly part of the solution is under way. But there are other causes of international instability besides interventionism and competition for natural resources. What a friend of mine punfully calls 'the din of inequity'—the rising discontent among the less developed nations —comes from many sources. Those countries still face terrible problems of food scarcity, overpopulation, sudden urbanization, and so on. On the other hand, if we help those nations achieve a sufficiency of material resources—in part through energy efficiency and renewables—we'll reduce the tensions and make ourselves, too, more secure in the process. The more secure and well-provided-for that your neighbors feel, the more secure you can feel, knowing that they will not need to steal any of your possessions to keep themselves alive. And their leaders won't have to start wars with their neighbors to distract their people from poverty. An end-use approach to the needs of the less developed nations might also mean that they can gain abundance without having to waste millions of barrels of valuable, nonrenewable energy sources in the process. And it'll be cheaper for them, too, as we saw earlier today."

"Oh, I see," said Eunice. "If we ask ourselves what they really need to improve their standard of living, we can help them meet their real needs, such as adequate food, shelter, health care, and education—just what I seek for *my* family. And if we help them become efficient to start with, they won't have to go through the phase of squandering resources as we did. Why, just think of the opportunity—to do it right the first time. It almost makes me wish I were Secretary of Energy in a country like Bolivia or Pakistan."

Duncan chuckled at the notion of Eunice going off to La Paz or Islamabad to make energy policy. "Um, maybe," he stalled. "But before you buy a one-way ticket to South America"—he chuckled again—" . . . I think a couple of your predecessors have actually considered it . . . let me add that good energy policy is only one of many steps on the road to peace. Indeed, the world has gotten to such a dangerous place that it's long past time to rethink fundamentally how we're relating to one another. We have too many hair-trigger weapons to keep on calling each other names and acting like little boys on a playground." Duncan imitated a youthful swagger. " 'I'm tougher than you are . . . My daddy'— read, my missile fleet—'can whip your daddy.' Frankly, it's high time we started communicating directly with the people we perceive to be the Enemy and trying to straighten out our differences. We might find, for instance, that the Ukraine in the Soviet Union is a lot like the plains of Nebraska, and that the farmers there have a lot in common with the farmers here. Also, the more like human beings we seem to each other, the less likely we are to want to push the button and blow our opponent and very likely the world to smithereens."

"Has anyone ever," ventured Eunice, "taken an end-use look at war and peace? Have we ever really asked what we'd *get* out of going to war? Maybe there are easier—not to mention nicer— ways to get what we need. If what we really want to be secure is life, liberty, and the pursuit of happiness, as I learned a long time ago in school, maybe there are better ways to get those things than arming ourselves to the teeth. Certainly, that's the way we're headed, with baby bombs under every terrorist's arm. And I must say, that doesn't increase my feeling of security. And if *we* didn't put so much emphasis on nuclear weapons, maybe the Soviets wouldn't feel they had to. Do you think we could convince them of that? Have we ever really tried? In fact, Duncan, if we helped them adopt a sensible energy path, *neither* of us would need to project our military power so far into the rest of the world, and our countries could *both* sleep easier. Don't you think?" Eunice asked him hopefully.

"You know," said Duncan, "Hobart came up with a number the other day so incredible that I didn't believe it; so I checked it, and he's right. You know that Rapid Deployment Force we have poised to take over the Mideast oil fields—and maybe start World War III in the process?"

"Yes," said Eunice uneasily. "Although, if pipelines and refineries are as easy to blow up as you say, there might only be a smoldering ruin for them to occupy."

"Well," Duncan said triumphantly, "Hobart calculated that one year's budget for the Rapid Deployment Force, if invested in weatherizing houses, would about eliminate American dependence on Mideast oil once and for all—and save American householders about eight billion dollars every year thereafter as long as the buildings remain standing."

"Yes . . ." Eunice said hesitantly, ". . . yes, you said that before. But that just reinforces my point," she exclaimed. "Because the Soviets could fix up *their* buildings, too, and do other things to gain more security in energy, in food, and in all the ways we're talking about. If we even helped the Soviets to feel more secure—if we helped *everyone* to feel more secure so that we wouldn't worry about them coming to take what we have and they don't— wouldn't we be making ourselves much more secure, too? What do you think?"

Duncan grinned, knowing he couldn't begin to answer Eunice's questions. But those were the questions to be asked, weren't they? So he grinned again and said, "You know, Eunice, perhaps Secretary of Energy isn't a high enough position for you. But on that note, let's do call it a day. I think we have quite enough to sleep on.

"Oh, and Boss," Duncan called as he pulled his coat off the hook and watched Eunice trundle off down the hall, "have a good weekend."

21 Freeing the Market

*I*T WAS A GREY MONDAY MORNING in Washington as Eunice returned to her office. The weekend had been magnificent. She and her husband Joe had taken an autumn foliage trip into the Virginia hill country and had caught the trees at the peak of their color. As her limousine purred along and she relived the trip, what stuck in her mind was not the beauty of the Appalachian countryside. Instead, it was the way energy had kept coming back to haunt her on the trip. The times they had stopped to fill up their car, she had surprised Joe by wanting to keep track of the miles they had driven and the number of gallons of gas they put into the car. "Only twenty miles to the gallon," she had grumbled. "Duncan talks about cars that do three times as well. Do you realize, Joe, that we could have made this trip without ever stopping to get gas if we had one of those cars?"

Then they had stayed at a motel with the usual paper-thin walls and single-pane windows, and she spent several minutes telling Joe about how much better the place could be insulated. The icing on the cake was that the motel was electrically heated, with the baseboard heaters along the *outside* walls. The managers of the motel hadn't wanted to hear about the improvements they could make, but she still felt a strong tinge of pride at the back-of-the-envelope calculations she had done to try to persuade them that she was right.

Suddenly, a thought dawned on her. "James," she called out to her driver, "what sort of mileage does this limo get?"

"Huh? Uh, well, I don't know, ma'am," he said. "Probably somewhere between fifteen and twenty."

"Between fifteen and twenty?" Eunice repeated. "And this is the official car of the Secretary of Energy?"

"Yes, ma'am. But you know, the last one we had got about eight or ten. This is one of the new, efficient big cars."

"But isn't this ridiculous?" she argued. "The least we at the Department could do is set a good example."

"Well, ma'am," James replied drolly, "I could pick you up in a little teeny car tomorrow." He grinned into the rear-view mirror.

"No. No," Eunice said thoughtfully, "I wouldn't want to imply that status shouldn't be recognized. I just want to have the most efficient, appropriately sized car that can be had." Eunice made a mental note to ask Duncan sometime about efficient limousines. He had said there needn't be lifestyle changes, although, she mused, she really didn't need a car big enough to play rugby in. She'd have to think more about the symbolism of all this. But maybe some example-setting by executives was in order. She thought again about the weekend. What had Joe kept asking? "If all this makes so much sense, honey, why don't we see more of it around?" She could quote Duncan's statistics about how fast sustainable energy and efficiency were taking over the market—sustainables accounting for more than nine percent of all U.S. energy consumption, and energy use per dollar of GNP having dropped by twenty-five percent in ten years—but she really had no answer for Joe about why if it was *so* much cheaper, it wasn't happening even faster. "Gosh," he had said, "if there was a place where you could get beer for a quarter of the price that most stores charge, no one would buy it anywhere else. So why does everyone buy electricity instead of all the efficiency they can get?" She really hadn't known what to say, and the issue was uppermost on her mind as she walked down the wide corridor to her office.

After her usual early session with Barb, disposing of Friday's questions and quibbles, Eunice headed for Duncan's office. As she neared his hall, she was greeted by the rich smell of coffee brewing. "If I ever forget where his office is," she mused as she walked down the hall, "I can always find it by that smell." It was a wonder more people didn't pester him for a cup now and then. But he was alone, waiting for her, reading the morning papers and energy newsletters while their morning cups trickled down into the pot. "So how was *your* weekend?" she asked.

"Oh, not too bad," Duncan replied. "One of my friends over in Transportation took me up in his light plane—what a view! We took off in the Virginia suburbs and headed out toward the real country to see some foliage. Great stuff. How about you?"

"Joe and I saw the foliage, too, but without ever leaving the ground, thank you. And I found," she looked at Duncan dolefully, "it very hard to leave energy behind."

Duncan grinned. "You'll get over it. Any new insights?"

"No," Eunice replied, "but I had a lot of trouble explaining some things to Joe."

"What's that?" asked Duncan, grinning. "That we're really just friends?"

Eunice pursed her lips. "Come on, now. No. No, I just can't explain why efficiency and sustainable energy options generally aren't more popular and widespread than they are. I mean, I quote him your statistics about sustainable energy really being here already, but it doesn't carry the weight I want it to. He still wants to know why everybody hasn't bought these fancy light bulbs or wrapped their houses in seventeen layers of insulation."

"Actually, it's a subject we've been circling around for a while now, and one I keep promising to explain later. But you impatient young people," Duncan said, smiling, "you just want to know everything at once. However, this does seem a good time to tackle it. So . . . why haven't efficiency and sustainables been employed on a large scale already?"

Duncan rocked back in his chair as he mentally shifted gears. "The truth is," he began, "there are a lot of impediments to the advent of sustainable energy use; so many, in fact, that I am continually surprised at how quickly changes *are* happening. To really understand the situation," he continued, "you have to realize that when we make comparisons between the costs of, say, electric heat and insulation, we make a number of assumptions. The biggest of those assumptions are bundled together under the heading of a 'free market.' It's a term we use pretty casually. But you should realize that there really is no such thing as a 'free market.' "

"There isn't?" Eunice questioned. "But everyone talks about America having a free market. Isn't it the American Way that we can choose what we want to buy in a free market?"

"Right, and people are free to choose between Pepsi and Coke," said Duncan patiently. "But the term 'free market' means a great deal more. It comes from formal economic theory, and it means a specific state of affairs characterized by conditions that probably can never exist in reality. At least, no country in the world has them. Now, don't get me wrong, there are degrees of freedom in markets; ours is certainly freer than, say, Great Britain's or Poland's. But let me explain a few of the conditions that are necessary for a true free market. I think you'll see right off why we don't really have one. For one thing, for a free market to operate, consumers must have perfectly complete, perfectly accurate information about all the different products available to them. They must know the full range of products and services they can obtain, how much each will cost, how reliable each is likely to be, and so forth. So, for instance, if you don't know that insulating your attic will pay for itself in a single year and thereafter save you money, you will likely continue to buy heating energy instead of putting in the insulation. If you don't know that eighteen-watt light bulbs are on the market that give off as much light as a seventy-five-watt incandescent, you're obviously not going to buy one. And, if you don't know that you can cut your heating bill in half by adding a solar greenhouse onto the south side of your house, you won't build one."

"That makes sense," acknowledged Eunice, "although I wouldn't have guessed that freedom had much to do with knowledge. But I guess you can't make a decent choice without knowing what you're choosing between. And I certainly didn't know much about energy before I took this job."

"Yeah," Duncan chuckled, "there are a lot of folks who could do with a bit more knowledge. And in that regard we'll always be dealing with a somewhat imperfect market. But market theory goes even farther. It assumes that everyone has the same access to capital—money, if you will. That means that you should be able to get a loan to insulate your attic as easily as your utility can get money to build its next power plant or gas pipeline—*more* easily if your investment is less risky. If the investments are equally risky, you should pay the same rates of interest; if one investment is riskier, then the person making it should be charged a *higher* rate of interest. In fact, however, because of government subsidies, and because the structure of the capital marketplace favors big investments, utilities building nuclear power plants that may never be completed and that run barely half of the time if they *are* finished, are often getting money at lower effective rates of interest than people who want home-improvement loans. Through tax subsidies, you and I are in effect financing new nuclear plants at *negative* net interest rates! Or take the superefficient light bulbs we've talked about. They last thirteen times longer than a standard bulb, but they retail for more than fifteen dollars a piece. They are a much better investment than a power plant in terms of how much energy service gets delivered per dollar invested, and they offer a much higher return than a money-market account, but very few people are going to walk into their local bank and ask for a three-hundred-dollar loan to replace the main light bulbs in their house. And, if they did, the bank would probably give them a hard time."

"Even when Joe and I were planning nothing stranger than another kid's room, the bank made it very difficult for us to get any money out of them," Eunice nodded.

"Too bad you're not a utility," Duncan commented, "then you could have borrowed millions." To Eunice's horrified look he added, "Sure, almost any utility building a nuclear plant will be borrowing tens of millions every month, even though it's likely many of them will never be able to pay it back.

"Further, for a real free market to exist, there must be perfect competition. There can be no monopoly, which is exactly what utilities are. And no monopsony, which is the opposite—only one buyer. Free-market theory also assumes that everyone competes fully and fairly. There can be no antitrust problem with a few big industries dominating sales of a product. There also can be no governmental barriers to foreign competition, such as more efficient Japanese cars or appliances. But, as you know, our government erects all sorts of trade barriers to protect our inefficient domestic manufacturers. For that matter," Duncan shrugged, "there would be no regulated prices. Oil would not have been so artificially cheap for so long, as natural gas and electricity still are. Wind and solar electricity would have looked competitive long ago if consumers saw the real cost of building, say, nuclear plants reflected in their utility rates. And in a free market anyone is free to go into—or drop out of—any business. Utilities wouldn't have to keep your lights on anymore, nor would they keep their monopoly on serving you."

"Wait, wait," Eunice interjected. "How are utilities a monopoly?"

"You try to go out, build a little hydro dam, and sell power to your friends," Duncan challenged. "You know what would happen? Until 1978, when Congress passed the Public Utility Regulatory Policies Act, or PURPA as it's now known, you could have been ordered by the state to stop operating. You would have been infringing on the service monopoly of your local utility. It has, by state law, the right to be the only company selling, for example, electricity. In return, it is regulated by a state or federal bureaucracy, which is supposed to guarantee that the utility charges a fair rate and gets a fair return on its investment. Now, under PURPA, your utility is supposed to buy back whatever surplus power you want to sell it and to pay you its 'avoided cost'—how much your generation saves the utility. And, if your utility offers you a derisory price, or makes you post a million-dollar bond before you interconnect, or otherwise puts unreasonable barriers in your way, at least you now have the right to sue for as much justice as you can afford. But you still can't sell to your friends."

"What would happen now if you fought for the right to make and sell electricity?" Eunice asked, fascinated.

"To tell you the truth, I don't completely know," Duncan admitted. "PURPA says that the regulated utility either has to buy your power and pay you a 'fair' price—set by the same regulators that tell the utility how much it can charge—or has to transmit or 'wheel' your power at a fair price to someone else who wants to buy it. The Supreme Court has upheld PURPA; so at least now you can go into business. But, if you want to have more than that one customer, then you become a utility yourself, subject to a nightmare world of regulations. No sensible entrepreneur would dream of doing that."

"So the new rule has turned it from monopoly to mon . . . ?" Eunice couldn't pull up the word.

"Monopsony," Duncan finished for her. "Right. But whatever you call it, it's hardly free, unfettered competition. Now, from a policy standpoint, one of the reasons many utilities are in such trouble is that they've never had to compete. They don't know how. And as some of their customers, especially the big ones, try to drop off the grid and make their own power or buy it from someone else, as under a free market they should be able to, some utilities are asking the federal government to tell their customers that they *have* to keep buying costly utility power. Public Service of New Hampshire has done that with some of the municipalities it serves, for instance."

"But that sounds like . . ." Eunice searched for the right word. Duncan's concern about defining terms had left her a little unsure. "Communism . . . ?"

"Well, totalitarianism of some sort," agreed Duncan.

"But what will the utilities do if lots of people find out about efficiency?" Eunice persisted.

"Hold that thought, Eunice," Duncan raised his hand judiciously. "I promise we'll come back to the perils utilities face in a free market. For now, though, suffice it to say, they do not operate within one today."

"I'll say," huffed Eunice.

"Let's see," Duncan rewound his thoughts. "We've said that in a free market there are no barriers to market entry or exit. Uh, what else? Oh, yes. Market theory assumes no transaction costs; that is, it should cost a bank as little to do the marketing, credit checks, and paperwork to loan money to a million customers as to one. Which is just ignoring reality, if you ask me, but that's what the theory assumes. Also, it assumes no unemployment or underemployment of any resources, such as people.

"The really important conditions are what market theory does *not* cover," he went on. "It assumes, for instance, that all costs will exist within, and be counted by, the market. Anything that isn't, the theory says, isn't important." He grinned and shook his head.

Eunice shrugged. "What's wrong with that?" she asked.

"Nothing, except history," Duncan replied. "You see, there are in fact a lot of costs that nobody noticed or directly paid for for a long time. For example, air and water pollution. Historically, air and water were thought to be 'free goods,' available to us all. But, if what you do with the air is breathe it, and what a utility does is dump its wastes into it, the utility gets to use your lungs as a scrubber for free rather than paying to put scrubbers on its plants. Acid rain, radioactive uranium mill tailings, oil spills—all the environmental costs of energy extraction were never counted in the free-market theory."

"But isn't that why we have a government?" asked Eunice.

"That's exactly the debate," said Duncan. "But you see, in a free market, a company would be free to do all it can get away with profitably. Since most of us recognize the need for limits on the pollution and hazards imposed on others the market has slowly come to be regulated. The issue for the political system is how far to limit the market. The only point I'm making here is that the market is incapable of doing that itself.

"Similarly," Duncan continued, "markets were never designed to be fair. Equity, caring for people less fortunate than ourselves, is just not a part of the market agenda. Distributing resources to different people over a long time—say, between generations—is also strictly outside what a market can do."

"But that's awful," Eunice protested. "How hardhearted! In my family we've always helped the less fortunate . . ."

"Whoa! Hold on a second!" Duncan stopped her run. "That's exactly why our government has developed as it has—to cover the many areas that free markets don't. Now some people argue that it has gone too far. And others want to see it completely control economics. But what I think is needed is a clearer understanding of what markets do well, and where our values might be better served by the political process. For example, what a free market does really well is to be efficient—to allocate resources so that the greatest possible number of people at more or less the same times benefit at least cost. To the extent that this is what we want, we should keep restraints off the market.

"And even though there will likely never be a truly free market, there clearly are strong market forces. Frankly, in energy, at least, I think we'd be much better off with a freer market. Energy is a commodity, just like any other, and will be most efficiently allocated through the free play of market forces. If people had not perfect but at least adequate knowledge of what energy costs really are, and had to pay them, they would have a pretty good incentive to make efficient choices. Then, if they had the opportunity to act on that incentive, their choices would reflect what is best for them. Finally, if the whole process were bounded and guided by the political process, making sure that we protect those values that we care about but that markets simply aren't equipped to cope with, such as environmental protection and equity, well, I think the American people would soon show that energy just isn't a problem anymore."

"But why doesn't it work that way?" Eunice persisted. "I guess that's sort of the question I started with—why isn't it happening?"

"Okay," Duncan replied, "let's look at that specifically: how the energy marketplace differs from a free one, especially in how energy is priced. But, first, let's take a quick stretch."

"Well, I don't know, Duncan," Eunice teased. "Are there any other entrepreneurs offering stretches this morning? Maybe someone will pay me more for stretching with them?"

Duncan just rose and grinned in mock disgust.

22 *Prices that Tell the Truth*

$W_{\text{HAT A DIFFERENCE}}$ from the first time she had stretched with Duncan, Eunice thought. After stretching just a few times, she could now touch the floor not just with her fingertips but with her knuckles, too. Why, a few more weeks with Duncan, and she'd probably be able to do all those body twists that Indian yoga masters perform. Wait, she thought, a few more weeks? At some point she was going to have to start being Secretary of Energy and stop coming here every day. The thought was at once troubling and exciting—she wasn't quite sure she could handle the job, but she knew that these tutorials with Duncan were only the beginning of her work here.

So it was with a sigh that she trooped back to Duncan's office with him. Duncan noticed her downcast eyes. "What's the matter?" he asked.

"Oh, nothing important," she said. "I just know that pretty soon I'm going to have to stop taking classes from you and start being your boss. I am, after all," she said with some trepidation, "the Secretary of Energy, and I'm not sure I'm ready for that."

"You're much readier than you may think," Duncan said, smiling with real warmth. "Anyway," he added, "we're getting close to the end of what I can teach you. Beyond that, it's just detail and updates for which you can always call on Hobart or me. In fact, even if you had never run into me, I'll bet your common sense would have taken you a long way." He waved down her attempt to disagree. "But before I do turn you loose on an unsuspecting Department," Duncan cowered in mock terror, "let's finish up our syllabus. We were talking about how unfree the actual market is. The first type of unfreedom I want to explore is the kind that comes from false prices."

"False prices?" Eunice said. "Are those the times people try to jack up the price on you when you're not paying attention?"

"No, no," said Duncan. "Under free-market theory all the costs of a product are supposedly reflected in the price a consumer is charged. The price is what tells people what is easy to produce and what isn't. It's perhaps the most important means of communicating information to buyers. The easier it is to produce something, the cheaper it should be. By 'easy' I mean a product that requires relatively little investment, labor, skill, and/or natural resources. If prices are inaccurate, then people have the wrong information about the relative costs of different commodities. Here, let me get Hobart to help us with the numbers. He keeps track of a lot of the stuff I haven't had time for." Duncan rose, opened his door, and bellowed into the hall. "Hobart!" he called and waited for Hobart to poke his wispy head into the corridor. "Would you come in here and bring your subsidies file, please?" Duncan sat back down, leaving the door ajar for his gnome-in-residence.

"So . . . prices," he began, leaning back in his chair. "Since price is about the biggest factor in people's choices of what to buy, what we really care about is not so much the *absolute* price, as the price of one product *relative* to another. So in looking for 'prices that tell the truth,' we want to look at the different forms of energy and see if any forms receive preferences over the others.

"Ah, Hobart, come on in. Just in time, too. We're beginning to talk about differential subsidies." As Hobart pulled up a chair, Duncan turned back to Eunice and continued, "One place to look is at government policies: Are they helping or hindering various energy providers? Which ones are getting the sweetheart deals, and which are at a disadvantage because their competitors are getting favored treatment? It's not easy to get that information, but fortunately researchers out at Battelle Pacific Northwest Labs have compiled some figures on what the subsidies were, at least until 1977. The subsidies have in general gotten a lot bigger since then. The Battelle researchers found that the government has provided a tremendous amount of subsidy to conventional energy producers. Take the oil industry, for instance. Historically they've gotten hundreds of billions of dollars. They even got a 'depletion allowance' for oil they extracted, a subsidy called 'intangible drilling allowances' that likewise reduces the amount of profit they must report to the Internal Revenue Service . . . How much does that come to already, Hobart?"

"Um, a bit over seventy-six billion 1982 dollars," Hobart said. "And that just counts up through 1978."

"Seventy-six *billion?*" asked Eunice, her mouth agape.

"Yes, billion," Duncan said. "But that's just the beginning. Add incentives that the government handed out to people who found and extracted 'new oil,' add the tax benefits that the feds set up for owners of small wells, and add the subsidies for pipeline construction."

"Another seventy-nine billion," intoned Hobart.

"Now add in the federally supported dredging of waterways to accommodate giant oil tankers and the maintenance of port facilities."

"That's nine billion more," said Hobart, "and don't forget the two-and-a-half billion for research and development, which brings us to one hundred sixty-six billion dollars."

"And remember," Duncan said, "that's just through 1978. In fiscal year 1978, subsidies to oil were increasing at the rate of more than two billion 1982 dollars per year. By fiscal 1984, when Rocky Mountain Institute totaled the subsidies for just that year, oil was getting eight point six billion a year and gas, four point six billion. And even beyond the subsidies we've covered so far, there are other government expenses that are partially a subsidy for the oil industry. Take the enormous amounts of money spent on highways, for instance, without which the oil industry could not sell its product."

"But that would be a subsidy for fuel alcohol producers, too, wouldn't it?" countered Eunice.

"True enough," said Duncan, "but the construction of super-highways was a big factor in the shift from railroads to trucks, cars, and buses. This, in turn, increased the consumption of gasoline and diesel fuel, because it takes several times as much fuel to move a ton of freight by truck, for example, as by rail."

"Subsidies have played an even more important role in the development of nuclear power," Hobart chimed in eagerly.

"The total amount the government has spent is less than for oil because nuclear power is a newer technology and less widespread than oil," Duncan added more soberly, "so there have been fewer companies able to gorge themselves at the federal trough. However, without the subsidies, the industry would never have gotten off the ground. The government has spent most of its nuclear budget to develop various nuclear technologies, including some flavors that have proven to be rather large white elephants. What are the numbers on those, Hobart?"

"Got 'em right here," he said. "Let's see, for fiscal 1984, nearly sixteen billion dollars for fission. Before that, through 1978, they spent a bit over seventeen billion dollars for standard reactors and another six billion for fast-breeder reactors."

"Fast-breather reactor?" blinked Eunice. "Now I've heard everything. What's it panting about?"

"Fast *breeder*," said Duncan between chuckles. "It's a scheme to get more fuel out of a reactor than you put in. Not a bad idea on the face of it. The problem is that breeders are very expensive, they're probably unsafe, and worst of all, they facilitate the spread of plutonium for terrorists and other nations to make into nuclear bombs. They were expected to provide all the energy the world would need, fueled by a seemingly inexhaustible supply of uranium. But as people began to discover efficiency improvements, it turned out that we didn't need all of that new energy, especially in the form of electricity, and that we could get by much more easily, cheaply, safely, and reliably on sustainable sources and efficiency. So Congress eventually canceled the Clinch River Breeder Reactor, which was tough to do, because it was in the Senate Majority Leader's home state. In fact, that 'first demonstration breeder reactor' was actually, depending on what you count, anywhere from the second to the fifth one in this country; but all

the previous ones had demonstrated was economic and safety problems. In fact, Clinch River was getting so expensive that, if completed, the electricity it would have produced couldn't ever have competed with today's expensive solar cells stuck on your roof. And, if we'd spent the Clinch River money on those solar cells, they'd have been in cheap mass production by now."

"Hmmm," said Eunice, "so how much is the government spending on renewable energy?"

"I suppose we should use data from the last ten years for that comparison," Duncan said, "since solar didn't get a lot of press and political attention until then. What figures do you have, Hobart?"

"For 1978, I have nearly eight billion 1982 dollars being spent on nuclear, and about half a billion on solar and all the other renewables. That was under President Carter, who at least paid lip service to solar. Since then, the renewables budget—for both research and subsidies—has been slashed almost to the vanishing point. President Reagan's request for renewable-energy research funds in fiscal year 1986, for example, was only $174 million, seventy-three percent less than Congress had appropriated in 1981. That doesn't count tax breaks for renewable energy, but those are tiny compared to the tax breaks for power plants, synthetic fuels, oil and gas, and other competitors. On the best estimates I've seen for, say, 1984, renewables and efficiency are getting only about eleven percent of all subsidies to the energy system—even though they provide eighteen percent of the total energy services. Meanwhile, nuclear was getting over a third of the subsidies for delivering one and a half percent of the energy.

"Before we leave nuclear, there are several more forms of subsidy to that industry that we should look at," Duncan said. "For one, the federal government invested close to three billion dollars, and is now investing another eight to ten billion dollars, in uranium enrichment plants that process uranium into usable fuel. They also subsidized uranium mining and exploration, but it's hard to pin an accurate number on that because a lot of the uranium was originally sought for making bombs. The feds also spent more than two billion dollars regulating the nuclear industry and establishing safety practices for nuclear power plants. Last, there's the matter of insurance."

"You're not going to tell me that the federal government is in the insurance business, too," protested Eunice.

"Actually, I am," Duncan said. "Back in the fifties, when the nuclear business was just getting started, the federal government passed a law called the Price-Anderson Act. Its purpose was to guarantee that the nuclear utilities would never have to pay more than a token amount in the event of an accident. You see, no one knew what the risks associated with nuclear power would be; in fact, they still don't. The utilities made it very clear that they wouldn't build reactors unless they had some shield from the extremely high liabilities that could result; so the feds said that the utilities would not have to pay any damages caused by any nuclear accident that exceeded five hundred sixty million dollars."

"You mean that if a nuclear accident happens that causes more damage than that, taxpayers will foot the bill?" Eunice asked.

"Only if Congress agrees to pay out of the goodness of its heart," said Duncan. "The way the law reads, a combination of federal and private insurance—by now it's about all private—will pay damages up to that five-hundred-sixty-million-dollar ceiling, and above that level, *nobody* is liable. There's nobody you can sue, because the law shields them from liability. Further, the fine print in your household insurance policy says your company won't cover you for nuclear accidents either, so you're just out of luck. Imagine the federal government's offering to insure anyone who put a solar collector on his or her roof against the collector's blowing off and hitting someone on the head. The whole idea is pretty absurd."

"So why did the federal government make the offer?" Eunice asked.

"Well, it was a time not long after the atomic bombings of Hiroshima and Nagasaki, and American leaders were anxious to show that the power of the atom they had unleashed could be a positive force. 'Atoms for Peace,' they called it. It was an important political idea, and besides, everyone—except the insurance companies—thought the benefits of nuclear power would far outweigh the risks. The power was going to be 'too cheap to meter.' "

"Now it looks like it's 'too expensive to buy,' " said Eunice, raising an eyebrow. "Is that where these subsidies have gotten us?"

"In a sense, that's right," said Duncan. "The subsidies enabled people to escape the true costs of their actions; so they went on trying to produce nuclear electricity as if it were much cheaper—nowadays at least seventy percent cheaper—than it really is. Of course, if the subsidies allow the power companies to keep the prices of the resulting electricity low, people will go on buying more electricity under the same false assumptions."

"It's worse than that," Hobart broke in, "because the subsidies go much further than the specific amounts spent by the government on this technology or that oil well. There are also some basic mechanisms set up in the tax structure to make it much easier and more attractive for large companies to invest in big energy-producing devices than for the small homeowner to insulate or use solar. For instance, a company can take an investment tax credit on the money it spends to build an energy facility. It can then depreciate the cost of that plant over a period far shorter than the facility's actual lifetime . . ."

"Investment tax . . . depreciate . . . ?" asked Eunice, enfolding her pendant in her right hand.

"Oh, yes, sorry," said Duncan. " 'Depreciate, verb, to lessen the value of.' It's an accounting practice that lets companies claim as an expense the decline in the value of their equipment from one year to the next as it wears out. Now, anything that a company can claim as an expense reduces the amount of income tax it has to pay. And the quicker it can claim depreciation, the better a company's cash flow looks. For example, a utility can depreciate a nuclear plant, which is supposed to last for thirty or forty years, in just ten years. If a company keeps building more and more plants, it can escape paying taxes on just about all of its income, because it will be able to keep claiming 'accelerated' depreciation. And investment tax credit means that a tenth of the cost of just about any productive asset that a corporation buys—such as a power plant—is paid for by the Treasury, simply by deducting ten percent of that asset's cost from the tax that the corporation owes. And then there's the special tax break that lets utility stockholders exclude from their taxable income the first seven hundred fifty dollars a year—twice that for couples—of utility stock dividends that they reinvest in more utility stock. That little break has brought the utilities billions of dollars in new tax-free capital while raising everyone else's taxes. Then, too, utilities, which borrow many billions of dollars every year, deduct the interest charges from the taxes they owe. And now that they've persuaded the IRS that equipment to prevent release of radioactivity is preventing pollution, they're using tax-exempt Pollution Control Bonds to finance a growing proportion of nuclear plants—twenty-seven percent of the latest Georgia Power Company plant, for example. And they're also using lots of cheap federal money, meant for electrifying rural areas, to bail out private utilities' faltering nuclear construction.

"Now, the reason all this makes a difference is that when an individual buys a solar hot-water system or an efficient light bulb, those are not treated as business expenses; so they cannot be depreciated and do not qualify for the investment tax credit. That makes investments in power plants and refineries seem more attractive—and enables the energy services they provide to be priced lower than they should be—compared to other possible supplies of energy services. That's one reason that some of the greatest success stories in sustainable energy are cases in which firms have been formed to take advantage of the kinds of tax benefits that are freely available to other energy producers. Just in the few years since Congress passed the solar tax credits there has been a rush of third-party financers to build renewable energy systems for other entities—for example, an office building. The investors then collect money for the energy services provided or lease the system back to the owners of the building at a price that works out to a good deal for everyone concerned."

"But Duncan," Eunice asked, "isn't the solar tax credit a loophole, too?"

"It's a subsidy," he said, "without a doubt. But look at it this way. Nuclear plants benefit from accelerated depreciation, investment tax credits, interest deductions on the massive amounts of debt they depend on, and the dividend reinvestment exclusion—you name it; they've got it. When you add them all up, they cover two-thirds of the cost of a nuclear plant. That doesn't even count the research and development, the uranium enrichment, the federally guaranteed waste disposal, the limited accident liability, and so on. The solar tax credit, at forty percent, pales by comparison. Moreover, a business that buys electricity or fossil fuel can deduct its cost from taxable income as a business expense, but individual taxpayers can neither do that nor deduct the cost of solar or energy-saving equipment in their homes. And solar or energy-saving investments by a business save taxes much more slowly than buying the fuels or power that they replace. Every way you look at it, the tax scales are weighted against the best buys."

"So if we make sure all the energy sources are treated the same," said Eunice, "does that make the practice of subsidy all right?"

"Umm, not exactly," Duncan replied, "for a simple reason. Subsidies of any sort make energy supplies seem less expensive than they are compared with other goods and services, such as food, entertainment, clothing, and so forth. This means that people will in general spend more on energy than would be wise, and less on eating out, going to the movies, or a new pair of pants. Now, saying that energy prices are too low may not sit well with people like us who still remember twenty-five-cent-a-gallon gasoline and twenty-dollar monthly heating bills. But those were unusual times, fueled by an abundance of cheap oil and gas at home at prices that were artificially held down. In fact, a similar situation prevails now, especially in electricity. Electricity is sold not at the cost of producing the most expensive kilowatt-hour or even what it costs to produce a kilowatt-hour to replace the one you just used, but at the average cost of all electricity generated —'rolling in' costly new electricity with cheap old electricity."

"Wait a minute," Eunice said. "Why should it all be sold at the cost of producing the most expensive electricity—say, ten cents a kilowatt-hour—if the utility happens to be paying only a nickel for most of it?" She hesitated. "Are those numbers reasonable? Does my question make sense?"

"Oh, yes, very much. All your questions make sense," Duncan said, smiling. "Just remember what we were saying before about price being an important way of communicating information to consumers. If the price is set at the average cost of producing the electricity, then people will think it's cheaper than it really is and use more of it than is worthwhile. Consider this situation. A utility has a cheap source of hydropower that costs it only a few cents per kilowatt-hour, but present demand uses up all of that available cheap power. If demand increases, the utility will have to build a power plant that supplies more expensive electricity—eight to twenty cents, say. Now, suppose you have an electrically heated house. If you conserve, then you will be saving your utility at least eight cents for every kilowatt-hour you do not use. But if you're paying the average price of three cents per kilowatt-hour, you have very little incentive to conserve. So the three cents that you pay may tell you the truth about what it *used* to cost to provide you with power, but it doesn't tell you anything about the true *replacement* cost, which is several times larger."

"But what about all the people who can't afford energy even at those prices that you say are too low?" Eunice protested.

"You're quite right," said Duncan, "there are many people who are suffering from the climb in energy prices. But the way to address that problem is to help the people who need help—not to give everyone a break on their energy prices and thus encourage more use of electricity, or any other form of energy, than is economically rational. That may sound like an academic argument, but failure to follow economics—or, in this case, kidding ourselves about what the future really costs—commits us to pay later the full costs of that power plant the utility was encouraged to build. It's especially distressing when we could have avoided it if we'd signaled the true costs early on, and so encouraged people to choose the more cost-effective route of energy savings."

"Yes," Eunice conceded, "I can see that. But I still worry about the elderly and the poor. What will they do?"

"It's a tough problem," Duncan agreed. "But I think we should be honest about it. Using energy subsidies to try to achieve distributional equity in society will just mess up both policies. The rich will be subsidized and the poor will stay poor. Instead, I would like to see us address these problems head on. The people who can pay should pay. As for the people who can't, the society and its government should help them become less poor. The sad truth is that the government has often been pretty clumsy at trying to help people solve all sorts of problems. Maybe if we look at how some of these programs have failed we can be better prepared to implement some that will work."

23 *But the Government Won't Let Me Do It!*

W‍HY WOULD A GOVERNMENT," Eunice asked, "that is supposed to be helping people, do such a clumsy job of it? Although," she reconsidered, "thinking back to my first meeting with my Assistant Secretaries, I can't say I'm all that surprised."

"Oh, no, Eunice, have Hobart and I made a cynic out of you?" Duncan winced in mock horror.

"I think my advisers did a good enough job of that, thank you," she replied. "You know, one of these days I'll have to go back in front of them and tell them what *I* think should be done. I've learned so much so quickly—but I'm not sure I'm ready to put it all together. In fact, that meeting is scheduled for Tuesday. Wait, what day is this?" Eunice paled, losing her composure. "That's tomorrow! What am I going to do? There's no way I can have it all figured out by then."

"Yeah," said Duncan thoughtfully, "tomorrow would be pushing it." He thought a moment. "Well, just tell Barb to delay the meeting. It's standard practice around Washington—one of the reasons nothing gets done on time."

"I hate to do that, and so early on the job," Eunice fretted. Soon, though, her housewifely determination took over. "However, I don't think I have much choice."

Duncan grinned and handed her his phone.

Dialing her office, Eunice waited, then said, "Hello, Barb? This is Mrs. Bunnyhut . . . uh, yes, Eunice. Can you call up my Assistant Secretaries—yes, the ones I'm supposed to meet with tomorrow—yes, call them and say that we're postponing the meeting by a week? Super. Terrific. What, a reason? Do I have to give one? Oh, dear. Well, say I'm still learning. No, that won't do, will it? Tell them . . . well, just figure out something that isn't too incriminating. I trust you. You're a dear. Thanks again. 'Bye."

"Decks clear again?" Duncan grinned at Eunice's visible relief. "Well, back to the government and how often it gets in the way —unintentionally or on purpose—of people's taking care of their own energy needs. Here's a classic example of federal bungling, which might help you understand some of the problems with keeping energy prices low so as not to hurt the poor." Duncan check-glanced at Eunice to make sure she was following. "When President Carter proposed his energy plan back in 1977, he recommended a two-part plan to help the poor. First, the government was to provide them with assistance to help pay their energy bills. Second, the government was to provide money to help insulate and caulk their dwellings so they would use less energy. But the vagaries of the political process took their usual toll on Carter's proposals. By the time the proposals emerged from Congress, the section that would have helped poor people weatherize their homes had almost disappeared. What survived as a more-or-less permanent expedient was a program to pay the energy bills that low-income people ran up—in effect, passing tax money straight to the oil and electric companies. In 1979, the federal government spent more than three billion dollars to help the poor stay warm, all of which went to energy companies like Exxon and Consolidated Edison. But the programs did almost nothing to help the poor stay warm without heavy subsidy. One research arm of the federal government even articulated a program that would have fixed up some sixteen million homes over a five-year period, saving the federal government billions of dollars over the medium and long term. But that was too sensible to be enacted."

"Oh, that's just silly," Eunice reacted angrily. "What a wasted opportunity! What happened? Was it a case of the right hand not knowing what the left was doing?"

"More like the liberal hand not knowing what the conservative one was up to," Duncan said. "Most of those programs were killed by right-wingers trying to cut welfare handouts. I do wish that these so-called fiscal conservatives would design programs based on cost-effectiveness." This was obviously a long-standing grudge of Duncan's. "Here, let me give you another example. One of the things we talked about earlier was that people need information about the options available to them so that they can make intelligent choices among them. In the field of energy, such information doesn't always make it to consumers. I think one of the best roles for the government is to help the market work better by providing that kind of data for appliances, insulation, and all manner of new energy technologies, in much the same manner as the Environmental Protection Agency tests the mileage of cars that come on the market, or the Consumer Product Safety Commission tests the fire retardant in children's pajamas.

"In fact," Duncan went on, "this Department *was* doing a lot of those things. The Solar Energy Research Institute, operating under our contract, was testing and reporting on many different sustainable technologies and energy-saving devices. The Department published a magazine called *Energy Consumer* that was aimed at giving people the tools, confidence, and expertise to solve their own energy problems. Partly as a result, dozens of networks of community energy groups were formed. We also published thousands of reports on how to use energy more intelligently. Then came Ronald Reagan and his appointees, supposedly such great believers in the free market. But what did they do? They halted the publication of *Energy Consumer*. They withdrew other publications that were similarly helpful to consumers. They tried to block the release of a report commissioned by our Department that said that, if we did the cheapest things first, the United States should need less energy in the year 2000 than we use now, and that we could obtain more than a third of the energy we will need from renewable sources. The report, the best document of its kind at that time, detailed the technologies that supported its conclusions."

Eunice leaned forward in her chair. "Was it finally released?" she asked.

"Ah, this story is true cloak-and-dagger," Duncan said, grinning and stretching back in his chair. "Who says the life of a government bureaucrat has to be dull? The director of the Solar Energy Research Institute, a fellow by the name of Denis Hayes, came to Washington for a meeting with his superior. Not long before he was to walk into the meeting, one of his colleagues beckoned him aside. He warned him that his new boss was about to order him to destroy the report. Immediately, the story goes, Denis walked back to his motel. He phoned his boss, explaining that he 'had the flu' and couldn't make the meeting. You see, it's been done before." Duncan grinned again at Eunice. "Anyway, Denis then called his deputy back in Colorado and instructed him to get several dozen copies of the report—several hundred pages long—out in the mail that day, come hell or high water. A week later, when he had the meeting that he had put off, he could honestly say that the mailbags had passed the point of no return, so to speak. The report was later published both by the Ottinger Committee in Congress and by Brick House Publishing Company under the title *A New Prosperity*. It's become a basic reference for people working in the sustainable energy field."

"Why, that's a great story!" Eunice clapped her hands in delight. "One of the legends of the energy field, I suppose."

"Pretty close to it, anyway," said Duncan. "At least, the understandable haste certainly made a good excuse for all the typos in the book. But let it also serve as a lesson for you, Ms. Administrator—that sort of attempt to suppress information is not considered cricket in free markets."

"Well, destroying a study that's already been completed seems like a terrible waste," said Eunice. "And I think the government should put out lots of information. It gives people a source that they can trust. Or at least it should. Keeping information from people reminds me a bit of the book bannings that some people in our town used to ask the school board for. You know, keeping subversive books like *Huckleberry Finn* and *Little Women* out of the schools."

"It's not at all different," agreed Duncan. "You know, now the librarians at some government energy libraries are being ordered to throw books away—generally books about sustainables. And they're told not to send them to other libraries or state agencies that might be able to use them. Sounds to me like those 'free-marketeers' are trying to impose their own ideas of what people should and shouldn't know, instead of just letting people make their own choices based on all the available facts."

"Just like little kids who are sore losers," murmured Eunice.

"But enough of these James Bond stories," said Duncan. "I promised to list ways the government is interfering with the direction the energy sector wants to take. One of my favorite stupidities goes back to subsidies and how they are administered. After letting the nuclear boys get away with murder, the Internal Revenue Service puts the screws to people claiming solar and insulation credits. For example, the IRS has ruled that you can't take the forty percent solar tax credit on a greenhouse if you also use it for anything besides solar heat—like, say, growing vegetables."

"You mean I can't even have a geranium in it?" Eunice asked, incredulous.

"Nope," said Duncan. "And sometimes tax credits are written so that people are rewarded for the money they spend, not for whether they save any energy. It would be far better for the tax credit to depend on the predicted or measured performance of the system instead.

"Other times," continued Duncan, "the problem the government poses is not one of law but of attitude. When President Carter presented energy conservation as a sacrifice, he instantly turned many people off to the idea. As one astute friend of mine from an Arkansas utility says, 'Better to tie conservation to people's pocketbooks than to wrap it in the flag.' In this country, self-denial just doesn't sell."

"No, the idea of shivering in service to my country sounds a little silly, especially with what I know now," said Eunice.

Duncan paused, then said, "Actually, in all fairness, I should point out that the federal government doesn't have a monopoly on silly regulations that get in the way of smart energy and smart energy users. Local governments do a lot of harm, too. For instance, the building codes they pass and enforce are almost always obsolete. Many actively get in the way of the proper use of energy. In 1975, for example, the American Society of Heating, Refrigeration, and Air-conditioning Engineers—ASHRAE, for short—came up with a 'model' code that suggested certain levels of insulation for new buildings. But by the time the code was publicized and adopted by local governments, new energy prices and technologies had made it obsolete. The levels of insulation that it encouraged were far too meager to be cost-effective. But many builders followed the recommendations religiously and even called the more stringent superinsulation technologies unworkable.

"What's more," Duncan went on, "ASHRAE tried to limit the amount of windows a house could have because windows were seen as net losers of heat. But then solar builders proved they could heat a house using solar energy with south-facing windows. So some codes were altered to encourage large areas of south glazing and restrict glazing on other sides. But, as soon as the ink was dry on *those* revisions, new insulation materials came along that made it possible to heat a house with an ordinary amount of south-facing windows, or even with windows facing in other directions. So many counties and cities again had to scrap the codes, or at least those codes calling for houses to be oriented with their broad side toward the south. And so it goes. As fast as local elders change their codes, the state of the art leapfrogs ahead of them. As you can see, nobody is being a bad guy, but the regulations have the effect of hindering people who want to do what the rising prices of energy encourage them to do. Worse, many people look at the standards set out in the codes and assume that they are recommendations—an optimum—instead of a bare minimum."

"So what's a county to do?" asked Eunice. "We can't abolish all regulations . . ."

"It's a tough question," said Duncan. "Part of the solution is to write the codes, if any, so that they allow for innovation. The best codes don't tell you how to do it; instead, they set a performance standard of how well a building should do, or how little nonrenewable energy it should require. Such standards can be changed easily, and they give builders and architects the most flexibility in figuring out how to comply. One of the best of the current building codes—Title 24—is in effect in California. The code allows builders to follow a choice of prepackaged efficiency options; to use a simple point system to see if their own designs would pass muster; or, for the energy-savvy architects, to calculate the amount of externally supplied energy the house would require. Buildings that meet the standard use a third to a fifth or less of the energy that a typical 1975 house would have used. By and large, the building community has found the code pleasant to live with, even though the state keeps making it tougher."

"That sounds very good," Eunice said, "even if it's not exactly free market." Duncan winked and nodded. "But those codes only affect new buildings. What do you do with existing buildings?"

"Ah, very good point," Duncan approved. "Something like eighty percent of the buildings that are going to be here in 2000 are already built. Clearly, retrofitting—fixing up older buildings— is the name of the game. This will switch our topic a bit—from the sins of government to how it can help—but if you don't mind . . ." Eunice motioned him to continue. "Various communities have passed laws requiring that existing housing stock be retrofitted with basic, sensible efficiency measures, such as attic insulation, weather-stripping, water-heater blankets, and so forth. Eugene, Oregon, for example, gave its property owners four years to bring their housing up to snuff, with compliance to be checked whenever there is a change in electrical service. And these codes turn out not to be a great enforcement burden. They are typically simpler than the electrical and plumbing check-offs already common whenever a house is resold. The Davis, California, inspection, for instance, takes just fifteen minutes to complete.

"In fact, let me expand a bit on Davis," said Duncan, "since it has become something of an inspiration to other cities. That's a town that has really taken its energy duties seriously. The town passed an ordinance saying their streets were to be laid out with cul-de-sacs linked by bike paths, so that the bicycle became the easiest way to get around town. The city converted its car and truck fleet to the smallest, most efficient models that could still get the job done. Ordinances direct that old, poorly insulated houses be retrofitted upon resale and that new buildings not shade existing solar collectors. Recently, when the utility in that region offered towns a hundred-thousand-dollar prize if they shaved their summer peak electrical demand, Davis, even though it was the most energy-efficient of the competing towns to start with, was able to win it hands down—because people already were conscious of how to use energy wisely. Not a bad model, eh? Of course, towns are not all as sensible as this."

At this point, Hobart, who had been sitting quietly following the conversation, bounced in his chair and requested, "Tell her about the baseboard heaters."

"No, you tell her," Duncan replied, smiling at his assistant.

Hobart licked his lips conspiratorially. "Well, there's a town in New England," he began, "that requires that every house have a furnace or other heating system. You see, no one told the code people that a solar greenhouse can warm a home just as well and as reliably as an electric heater. Your house could be superinsulated and all south-facing glass, and your name be 'Ole Sol,' but you still have to have a 'real' heater. Well, suddenly a set of electric baseboard heaters started circulating among solar builders in the town. Whoever finished a house and was awaiting inspection simply borrowed the heaters, plugged them in, and made the inspector happy. The heaters then passed on to whoever needed them next."

Eunice clapped her hands. "Why, that's great!" she said. "I guess people will find a way around anything. But actually," she reconsidered, "it's not so great. Governments should be in the business of helping people, not getting in their way."

"Yeah, but you have your work cut out for you," said Hobart. "Wait till you tackle the communities that ban clotheslines or wind machines, outright, or that ban wind machines indirectly via height restrictions—which, however, doesn't apply to TV antennas, so folks simply put a TV antenna on top of their wind machine. Or the bank that wouldn't finance a passive solar house; so the owner-builder, when asked how it would be heated, said 'forced hot air'—and he got his loan. Or the municipality that wouldn't let a friend of mine build his underground greenhouse, because, they said, that was an agricultural use in a residential zone; so he built it anyway, called it a 'cold-frame,' and now has a four-hundred-square-foot walk-in cold-frame. You can find an awful lot of places where various silly rules and habits left over from the cheap-oil era are actively *preventing* people from using energy in a way that saves money."

"Actually," added Duncan, "an amazing number of local governments have put together good programs. The city of Fitchburg, Massachusetts, for example, organized five hundred volunteers to teach residents how to weatherize their houses. Workshops were held six days a week for six weeks, with three out of five households taking part. Residents learned how to weatherize their homes and were offered cheap weatherization kits for sale at the end of the workshops. Those who couldn't pay got them for free. Participants cut their energy bills by a seventh—worth an average of nearly a hundred fifty dollars per home in the winter of 1979 alone.

"Or take a case from the opposite coast. In Oceanside, California, the city has set up a 'municipal solar utility,' which licenses dealers to lease solar water heating in the city. Customers pay a small deposit and a monthly fee on which they can take the fifty-five percent state solar tax credit. The advantage of the city's participation is that homeowners can be sure that the companies are legitimate; in fact, the city places demands on the firms involved—for example, that they must guarantee full maintenance and repair. There are now three firms licensed. Perhaps most exciting, private investors have ponied up twenty million dollars toward installing solar systems in the city. As the director of the program says, 'If most people had three thousand dollars, they would probably go on a vacation' instead of buying a solar heater. The leasing scheme means that people can have the vacation *and* the solar system.'"

"Now that's really clever," said Eunice.

"Sure," said Duncan, "so dozens of other cities and counties have copied it. Actually, you could consider the whole program a special case of 'quality control.' You see, some states now require that solar collectors be inspected and tested by a state agency. Some maintain lists of licensed contractors, with a hotline number that one can call to find out if there are any complaints on record against a contractor. Elsewhere, similar lists are kept by utilities. Some states actually had consumer education programs to increase people's sophistication when they had energy work done on their houses. Unfortunately, most of those programs died when the Reagan administration cut energy funding to the states, and community groups have seldom found the small funding they need to do the job, say, by publishing periodic reviews of how various contractors and equipment vendors have performed.

"Happily, though, some states or cities have picked up some of the slack. For example, St. Paul, Minnesota, has done a remarkable amount to promote renewable energy. A few years back the mayor even called for a mass energy mobilization. The objectives were twofold: to get people more informed about energy and to collect city data on energy use. The city mailed surveys to some one hundred thousand residents and small businesses, but that was just the beginning. The mayor then closed the city hall for three days while three thousand volunteers, city employees and others, hit the streets, contacting people door-to-door. Businesses donated energy information kits and prizes, staffed energy hotline telephone banks, donated vans to transport the volunteers, and even fed the hungry troops. In the end, volunteers had contacted all but eight percent of the target households and companies, and now St. Paul has perhaps the most complete energy profile in the nation. A year later, a roving 'caulkmobile' was still on the streets offering free caulk and instruction in its use. Zoning ordinances have been changed to promote energy efficiency and renewables. The city created a City Energy Resource Center that has offered more than a million and a half dollars in low-interest weatherization loans that need not be repaid until a house is sold."

"That's impressive," Eunice conceded.

"Hang on, it gets better," said Duncan. "The city and Control Data Corporation, one of the largest local employers, are cooperating on a new hundred-fifty-five-acre 'energy park' development to include residential, industrial, and commercial uses. It is intended as a model of an energy-efficient neighborhood and will draw on energy management, daylighting, earth sheltering, and superinsulation, as well as active and passive solar systems and district heating. The park is expected to attract energy-related firms and to help create six thousand jobs. It even demonstrates a good way of keeping transportation needs down. With the retail stores, offices, and housing all in one place, people can live and work in the same neighborhood and not have to subject themselves to long commutes.

"Actually," Duncan was on a roll now, "transportation in general is an area that local governments can have a lot of control over. For example, four-fifths of the communities in California are putting bike paths and lanes into their traffic plans; three-fifths are synchronizing traffic signals and setting up dial-a-ride systems. And many localities have established special freeway lanes for carpools and buses that enable energy-efficient commuters to cut through nasty traffic snarls."

"Yeah," teased Hobart, "but I hear that in some places people even built dummies for their back seats to make it look as though they had enough people to count as a carpool."

"Like you say," said Duncan, tipping an imaginary hat to Eunice, "people will find a way around anything. No, actually that was only a couple of people out in California. And they got caught."

"Duncan," Eunice exclaimed suddenly, "this is silly! I *am* the government now. At least I'm a part of it," she added, blushing just a bit. "I'll just stop all this nonsense. I mean," she hesitated, "at least I'll try. But what should I do first?"

Duncan grinned broadly. "No way. I don't want to spoil your fun in coming up with your own energy policy," he said merrily. "I have a hunch that when the time comes you'll do just fine in drawing one up. In fact, I'm looking forward to it." He rocked back and regarded Eunice with a broad grin, his blue eyes twinkling delightedly.

24 *Where Will I Get the Money?*

ALL RIGHT, DUNCAN, no more on that for now," said Eunice. She glanced at Hobart and found herself with an unexpected and uncomfortable thought. "Will he serve me as faithfully as he does Duncan?" she wondered to herself. "Will my policies capture his loyalty, and more, the loyalty of the American people?" Eunice's eyes pleaded momentarily for some sign. Hobart, however, merely blinked blandly behind his Coke-bottle lenses and waited like a placid tree frog for the conversation to include him.

Eunice shook off her thoughts and refound her place. "Um," she began, "there are still a few blank spots left from the list of failings of the free market that you gave me. So far," she consulted the notes in her lap, "you've explained about consumers not having the right information about the energy services they buy, and you've explained government interference in the market with subsidies and regulations. There was something else, though, about its being hard for individuals to get into the energy business themselves on a small scale, wasn't there?"

"Yes, 'imperfect access to capital' it's called," said Duncan. "What that means is a family can't raise the four thousand dollars to put a solar water heater on its roof as easily and at as low an interest rate as an oil company can raise forty million dollars to add on to one of its refineries, or a utility can get several billion to finish a power plant. You see, corporations are set up as capital-raising machines. They can issue millions of dollars in commercial bonds and get millions more from issuing new shares of stock. They can even obtain seven- or eight-figure lines of credit from banks. They already have large assets, so they can use those as collateral for their loans, and investors see them as good risks, however shaky they may really be and however nonsensical those investments may be. But when your average family walks into a bank to get a loan, they just don't have the same financial standing.

"The odd thing is," Duncan went on, "that there is much *less* risk, per dollar invested, in putting a solar water heater on a house than in building a new oil pipeline or nuclear power plant. If you install solar water heating, you know that there will be a demand for the hot water. In fact, you put it there because you know you'll keep taking showers and washing your dishes. But you can't nec-essarily draw that conclusion if you build a new oil pipeline or shale-oil plant. People are using less and less oil all the time, and there may just not be a need for that new facility. What's more, if a power plant malfunctions, the replacement parts will probably have to be custom-made, a process that may take months, whereas solar systems are made of off-the-shelf components. And the sun will continue shining free for billions of years, whereas we don't know if the price of oil next year will be fifteen dollars a barrel or fifty. Indeed, the sun may be such a good investment that a new power plant will never be needed, because before it's finished, its competition may have already displaced the need for it."

"Wait," said Eunice, "if the refinery, say, is less of a sure thing, why is it easier for the oil company to raise money for it?"

"Ah," Duncan nodded, "that's the basic paradox. According to conventional economic wisdom, the riskier investments should be harder to find money for. But banks are used to investing in oil companies and not in solar collectors. Also, most investors don't realize how profoundly the economic climate for oil companies has changed since the 1973 oil embargo. So banks—and pension funds and other major investors—continue to put money into oil compa-nies and utilities."

"But how could they do otherwise?" asked Eunice. "No pension fund is going to say to me, 'Do you want to borrow a few thousand dollars to install a solar hot-water system?'"

"Oh, yes they are," disputed Hobart. "At least the smart ones. And on some solar systems," he said, retreating slightly. "In California, anyway, the sheet-metal workers' pension fund will third-party-finance putting a solar system on, say, a school or hospital. The fund hires out-of-work sheet-metal workers to do the installation, pays them union wages, and then takes its payback out of the energy savings the system generates. The school gets the system for free, too."

Eunice blinked, working her way through all the terms and concepts. Finally she nodded and smiled. "So everyone wins," she said. Hobart beamed and nodded.

"There are some other mechanisms in place, too," added Duncan. "Continental Savings and Loan in San Francisco offered what it called 'Solar T-Bill' accounts. They paid the same rate of interest as regular Treasury bills, but the money invested in them was earmarked for loans to people who were solarizing their homes. Indeed, banks are changing their lending attitudes in many places. Although," Duncan noted, "that process takes a long time in an industry as conservative as banking. In the San Luis Valley of Colorado, bankers were initially very skeptical about loans for solar improvements. But now they're eager to make solar loans to families who owe mortgage payments, simply because the solar addition will reduce the family's household costs and make it more likely that they can repay their larger home loans on time."

"It sounds like banking is another place where good information is important for the system to work—for the, er, 'proper functioning of the market.' Right?" asked Eunice, tentatively testing out some of Duncan's terms.

"Yes, precisely." Duncan nodded, pleased.

"Oh, Donuts, can I tell about the Seattle bank?" asked Hobart.

"Sure," Duncan said, smiling. "go ahead."

"Well, say you want a loan from Seattle Trust and Savings Bank," said Hobart. "You might be able to get a better deal under their Conservation Loan Program if the house you're buying meets certain efficiency standards, or if the car you're buying meets certain EPA mileage ratings. And if you're buying a boat, you can get the good deal if it's a sailboat or if the engine is especially efficient. Why? Because the less you pay for fuel, the likelier you are to meet your loan payments."

"Do a lot of banks do that?" Eunice asked.

"More and more all the time," Duncan replied. "And you're right, getting information to bankers is real important in bringing about the solar transition. But that's not the whole answer. There are a number of other problems that information won't solve. Take split incentives, for instance."

"Is that like splitting wood or splitting atoms?" Eunice asked, smiling.

"Neither," said Duncan, "it's more like splitting hairs. For example, take an apartment house in which tenants pay their own utility bills. Tenants don't know how long they're going to be living in a place, so they have no reason to make major improvements to the building, even if those energy-saving improvements will save them money. Who knows, they might be gone by the next winter. Besides, as renters, they probably have less income and a less robust credit rating than an owner. Thus the most they might do is to put a few bucks into energy-efficient devices they can take with them when they leave, such as an efficient shower-head or an insulating blanket for the water heater. The landlord, in turn, has no incentive to put money in because he isn't paying the utility bills. The incentive to do something is thoroughly split. So where can the money come from to weather-strip the windows and doors, to insulate the attic, and to add storm windows?"

"I don't know," said Eunice. "Is this a trick question?"

"No, seriously," he persisted. "Take a stab at it."

"Well," she began, fingering her pendant, "perhaps if the landlord installed those energy-saving measures, the apartments would fetch a higher rent on the market because tenants would have lower energy bills."

"Not a bad plan, if the market really worked," Duncan said. "That's how things should operate. However, who has even adequate, let alone perfect, information about how much they will save in one apartment compared to another? And few prospective tenants can evaluate a landlord's claims about how much this or that gadget will save. The rental market is a good example of an area where the market needs some help to reach the goal of allocating resources most efficiently. But the notion that the landlord can recoup energy-saving costs has led some local governments to mandate 'energy labels' on rental units. Then people have accurate information to work from. It's rather like the energy ratings that now appear on all major appliances. And, in theory, landlords will have an incentive to fix up their places so as to compete better. This doesn't work, though, in a tight rental market."

"What about a law to make property owners bring their buildings up to some standard, the way we have electrical and plumbing codes?" Eunice ventured.

"Another good idea," said Duncan. "And some cities have done it. However, like many codes, these are hard to enforce except when a building is sold. Worse, mandatory retrofit ordinances put a burden on landlords, many of whom are small-business people with limited access to capital. But," he encouraged, "try again. You're on the right track."

"Maybe someone else could come up with the money," said Eunice, "and whoever happened to be renting the apartment at the time would be responsible for paying the loan back? No," she corrected herself, "those tenants might be too hard to trace. And no one would pay to just install the stuff outright, as a gift."

"Actually, it's not impossible," Duncan teased. "There are a couple of utilities that are paying outright to install conservation equipment in people's houses. And that's got to be a good deal. Ah!" he said to Eunice's look of disbelief, "I'll fill in that one when we talk about utilities. But, here, here's a neat one. A nonprofit group, Citizens Energy Corporation in Boston—run by young Joe Kennedy—took a pot of money that it got from an oil company refund on overcharging folks for oil. The state allowed them to be the trustee for this money, which they put in a bank as collateral for loans that the bank then made to landlords so they could fix up their rental properties. The tenants kept paying the same utility bill, but they paid it to Citizens Energy. They, in turn, paid the lower utility bill, met payments on the loans, and took some of the rest of the saved money and gave it back to the tenants to do other low-cost energy-saving measures. Eventually, when the loans are paid off, the tenants' bills will go down and stay down. It's another 'everyone wins' situation. The money to fix up the building comes from the money saved on energy once the building is fixed up. But the best thing is that it deals effectively with the split-incentive problem, which is about the toughest kind of market failure to deal with.

"Take this other kind of split incentive, for example. When contractors build a house, there is little reason for them to care how much energy the place will use and great incentive for them to keep costs down. Many work on very small profit margins and barely scrape by. But it's those same contractors who purchase most of the heating and cooling systems and the household appliances."

"So," Hobart chimed in, "they install the cheapest heating system they can—all-electric—and cheap, energy-wasting appliances. Home buyers are then stuck with energy bills as high as a couple of thousand dollars a year."

Eunice was getting frustrated. "But there are remedies," she insisted. "Duncan mentioned one of them before—builders who agree to pay the first three years' utility bills on the houses they sell you, as a gesture of good faith and confidence in their efficiency measures. And don't appliance standards keep the absolutely outrageous refrigerator models off the market and out of the new houses?"

Hobart was momentarily taken aback. "Yeah, but these problems don't solve easy," he insisted.

"Well, let me cheer you both up with a couple of success stories," said Duncan. "And actually they're coming to play a large role in the energy market. One of them is the third-party financing we've mentioned several times. Sometimes it's used for energy-saving investments; it's even more attractive with the renewable-energy investments that receive tax breaks. The theory is that certain people are more able to take advantage of the tax credits than others; for example, colleges, hospitals, and other nonprofits have no more use for a tax credit than for a shipment of promotional Smurfs. But the tax credits allow for-profit investors to pool their resources; fund the installation of a solar water heating system, or photovoltaics, or any renewables; take the tax credits to give themselves an immediate return; and then provide the energy produced to a host institution at a low fee. In these 'micro-utility' arrangements, the energy provided by the solar system can even be measured and billed for at a rate somewhat less than the regular utility would charge, ensuring that the institution will come out ahead."

"For that matter," said Hobart, "the fee can be based on the reduction in energy the institution must buy from the regular utility, adjusted for variations in the weather. These arrangements are especially useful if the installation involves energy management—efficiency as well as sustainable energy supply. Such third-party financing enabled the University of San Francisco, for instance, to install solar water heaters on its dormitories."

"But hang on," said Eunice. "Again it's tax credits. You're just giving solar investors the same kinds of tax benefits that you criticized the utilities for."

"Of course," said Duncan. "I admit it. And again I would prefer a free market, if I had my druthers. But until the leaders of this country have the political will—or backing—to cut *all* the energy industries loose from subsidies, the market isn't going to be free. And I figure if it's not free, the least it ought to be is fair. These third-party financing deals help provide that fairness— what some people call a 'level playing field.' Imperfect, I agree, but a way to make the best of a distorted situation.

"But," Duncan waived as if to dismiss the problems of subsidies, "my favorite arrangements have nothing to do with tax credits. Indeed, you might say they are even returning the worst subsidy hogs to the fold of entrepreneurship." Eunice blinked at Duncan's theatrics as he proclaimed, "Utilities!"

"Come again?" asked Eunice.

"Utilities," Duncan repeated. "Indeed, I think utilities are an important factor in getting to a sustainable energy path. For one thing, they have been in the energy business for a long time and have the respect and trust of many people who don't want to think too much about energy. Another reason is that they regularly make investments in power plants that they do not expect will pay back for twenty, thirty, or forty years, whereas homeowners typically demand a payback within a year or two and renters within a matter of months. With such a long payback horizon, financing renewables should be easy. And, as we've seen, utilities are well accustomed to raising a lot of money for major investments—they spend more than thirty billion dollars a year. So let's get a cup of coffee to tide us over the late-morning blahs, roll up our sleeves, and talk about utilities."

25 *The Care and Feeding of Your Utility*

*L*ET'S SEE IF I've got this right," recited Eunice. "Fresh-roasted, fresh-ground coffee in the filter. Two level tablespoons per six-ounce cup, yes? Then just-boiled water through the filter, and presto."

"By George, Hobart, I think she's got it," Duncan said as the three hovered over the coffee pot in his side office. "If I teach you everything, though, Madam Secretary, you have to promise not to fire me."

"Oh, Duncan, don't be silly," she said. "How could I get along without you?" Her concern showed. But then she brightened and added, "If I fired you, whom would I stretch with in the morning? You'll come visit me, won't you, when I've reinhabited the executive suite?"

"Now, that's a thought," Duncan said. "but let's get back to utilities. I want to run through this before we break for lunch.

"You've probably noticed that electric utilities have been in the news a lot lately. And unfortunately for them, the news items haven't been particularly good ones. A number of large utilities have canceled big, half-finished power plants. The Washington Public Power Supply System up in the Pacific Northwest lowered the boom on two nuclear plants and mothballed two more, and thereby touched off the largest municipal bond default in history.

Nuclear plants from Indiana's Zimmer and Michigan's Midland to New Hampshire's Seabrook and Middle South's Grand Gulf will probably stand as steel-and-concrete monuments to a future technology whose time has passed. Ten years ago all this would have seemed a utility executive's nightmare, but now news of another cancellation hardly makes the front page, even though it means a multibillion-dollar loss. How could this be?" he challenged.

"Because they don't make economic sense?" ventured Eunice.

"Good, that's a decent general explanation," replied Duncan. "But what is uneconomic about them? I mean, the utilities in question probably thought that the plants would be good investments when they broke ground. What changed?"

"Well, what about all of the energy-saving devices you keep talking about?" asked Eunice. "Didn't you say that a lot of those were recent inventions?"

"Yes, as a matter of fact I did," Duncan replied. "And you're right, that's a big part of the reason. Customers are getting too smart to buy expensive electricity; they've found other ways of obtaining the energy services they need. The plants that these utilities are now trying to complete were ordered ten or twelve years ago, but now, as it comes time to finish them, they're no longer needed or competitive. Again, that's one drawback of ordering large plants, which produce no electricity while they eat up a decade's worth of construction costs and interest."

"Hang on," interrupted Eunice. "How did they know ten years ago that we would need a plant today?"

"A key point, Eunice," said Duncan. "They used something called forecasting. Or if they were sophisticated, 'econometric forecasting,' which is just a fancy way of saying that they looked at how fast electricity demand had grown in the past, projected that ten years into the future, and concluded that people would keep on using ever more electricity, in much the way they had in the past. The forecasters noticed that, in the past, electricity and the Gross National Product had increased together; therefore, they said, since we want the GNP to increase, obviously we need more electricity if the economy is to grow. Therefore we'll need more power plants.

"But suddenly electricity began to get more expensive, and as a result people starting using less. The utilities then faced the same situation that confronted the energy forecasters we discussed a few days ago, but they blithely kept forecasting rapid growth in electricity demand anyway."

"Why did they make that assumption about people continuing to use more and more electricity?" asked Eunice.

"Well, because they didn't know any better," said Duncan. "Also, the historical period on which they were basing their forecasts was an era when energy had been getting ever cheaper. The fact that it has gotten more expensive and that we now have all the new efficiency devices rarely get plugged into the models. Relying on those models is not unlike trying to drive a car by looking in the rear-view mirror. And to stretch our analogy, the fact that the plants took so long to build meant that the car would zip along for a quarter-mile before any steering or braking could take effect. The utilities' problem was compounded by the fact that the power plants they were building were very capital-intensive. That meant that the electric companies had to pour billions of dollars into these plants before they could get any electricity out. It also meant, especially for the nuclear plants, that much of the cost of the electricity they would produce would depend on construction costs, not operating costs. So the electric companies were draining themselves of cash in trying to complete these plants. And, despite various subsidies, eventually the utilities began to run out of easily available money. Just like any other enterprise, a utility can only borrow so much money or sell so much new stock."

"That doesn't sound like a very good position to get into," sighed Eunice.

"No, it's not," Duncan agreed. "And some analysts who pointed this out a few years ago, before it was fashionable to do so, were roundly shouted down. 'Oh, no,' said the conventional wisdom of the financial community, 'the utilities will be fine. They just need to finish the plants and get rate relief.' By which was meant higher prices for utility customers. But the conventional wisdom was wrong. It assumed that despite construction delays the utilities would be able to get their money back and indeed make a tidy profit, because the regulators were mandated to charge people enough to guarantee the utilities a fair return. But there was one thing they hadn't counted on: price elasticity."

"Price elasticity?" Eunice repeated carefully.

"Yes," said Duncan. "But it has nothing to do with rubber, I assure you. It's a measure of how your consumption of any commodity will change as its price increases. An elasticity of zero means that no matter what the price you will continue to use the same amount. That, by the way, is about what most utility economists used to believe about electricity."

"But that's silly," Eunice protested. "What about all the energy-saving devices and other ways to get the same service while using less electricity? Why, if some stupid regulators jumped the prices on me, I'd just switch."

As Hobart bounced approvingly in his chair, Duncan grinned and agreed, "Yes, I believe you would. Now. But what about a week ago, when you hadn't heard of any of this stuff?"

"Mmm," Eunice conceded, "I see your point. But sooner or later I'd have heard, and by then I'd have been so mad I'd have bolted just as soon as I could."

"Aye," Duncan said distractedly, as he ran a quick calculation. "What you're saying is you have a pretty high long-run elasticity." He grinned at Eunice's sudden blush. "Now, an elasticity of minus one means that if the price rises by one percent, people will use one percent less of the commodity. The problem the utilities face is that when some of these new power plants go on line, the rates charged for electricity increase substantially. But when that happens, customers suffer what has come to be known as 'rate shock.'" Eunice nodded emphatically. "Well," he continued, "that's when folks start trying to find out how they can maintain their standard of living but use less electricity. In many instances, these rate shocks are serious; increases in electricity prices of thirty to eighty percent are not uncommon. Right now about a third of Americans are facing some sort of rate shock." Eunice gasped and covered her mouth. To which Duncan added, "But the utility has almost no choice. It is stuck with a new plant and bonds to pay off. It has to have higher rates. But if those rates trigger decreased demand, it will be back where it started, or worse. It will not have nearly enough income to cover its expenses. The moral of the story can be summed up in Miss Piggy's Fourth Law: 'Never try to eat more than you can lift.' The plants many utilities were building, aside from all their other drawbacks, were simply bigger than all their other assets."

"Would it help," asked Eunice, "if the rates increased more gradually? Or if the utility had some way of telling people while it was building the plant that the rates would have to go up—a kind of pay-as-you-go plan? Maybe then the utility would have realized sooner that the plant would be unnecessary."

"Perhaps," said Duncan. "It could have been like seeing a plane in their rear-view mirror."

"I beg your pardon?" Eunice said.

"You know, like the old joke. Suppose you're heading down the road in your hot new convertible. You look in your rear-view mirror and see a plane coming at you. What do you do?"

"What?"

"I don't know about you, Eunice," Duncan said, grinning coyly, "but I'd adjust my rear-view mirror."

"Now, that's not fair," she said. "That's a trick question."

"Well, electric power can be a tricky business," Duncan replied. "But to give you a straight answer—yes, it might have helped the utilities realize the folly in which they were engaged before they had quite sunk *all* of that money into the plant. And, indeed, many utilities would like to do just that—charge the rate payers for what is called CWIP, construction work in progress. However, that evades the discipline of the capital marketplace; it makes your customers finance something that Wall Street might, for good economic reasons, consider a bad risk. Also, CWIP only works if you then heed the response and cancel the plant as demand drops, but then you've sunk millions of dollars of your customers' money in an abandoned pile of concrete. And some utilities are notoriously resistant to reading the writing on the wall. Kansas Gas and Electric Company and Public Service Company of New Hampshire, for instance, even borrowed money at high interest rates to pay stockholder dividends—and even some interest on money they'd already borrowed—when all of their cash was tied up in the nuclear plants each was trying to finish. Several big industrial customers of such strapped utilities have even threatened to leave the grid and cogenerate their own power if the nuclear plant comes on line and the rates rise.

"The tragedy of it is," Duncan continued, "that so many electric companies have continued to throw good money after bad. About thirty billion dollars a year is being spent to build power plants that are uneconomical and uncompetitive. And since these plants must operate for thirty to fifty years to pay off, the utilities are really playing You Bet Your Company that customers will take that long to discover that efficiency costs a lot less than, but is just as convenient as, power from their wall sockets. Of course, these technical fixes are the same ones I've been harping on for days now: the eighteen-watt light bulbs, the superefficient refrigerators, the new ballasts for fluorescent lights that eliminate flicker, hum, and forty percent of the energy consumption. For industry, the breakthroughs include microcomputer controls for heavy machinery, efficient new processes in smelting and petrochemicals, improved heat-recovery devices, and better controls, sizing, and drivetrains for electric motors."

"But the utilities couldn't have known about these when they started the plants; so it's not really their fault, is it?" asked Eunice.

"You may be right," said Duncan. "I've been so busy trying to pull utilities out of the graves they've dug for themselves that I haven't had time to figure out who is to blame. Myself, I'm just working on how to get everyone out of the mess without anyone's going belly-up. However, if utility executives had really been thinking, they should have been worried about building anything with such a long lead time. It's just asking for trouble.

"But I've got to admit," he went on, "they weren't alone in bad forecasting. Take one of these Department of Energy reports," he said, gesturing to a shelf that sagged noticeably under the weight of numerous several-hundred-page typescripts. "It simply asserts that demand for electricity will increase by three percent per year between 1983 and the year 2000, give or take one percent.

Now, let's ignore the fact that building power plants to meet such an increase would require that one plant per week be ordered for the next ten years or so—in a country that only ordered one small coal plant in the four years 1981 through 1984. Let's just look at the uncertainty in the growth rate. That slack of a single percentage point in either direction represents an uncertainty of *three hundred billion dollars* in the investment that utilities would need to make in fifteen years. They simply can't run a business with that sort of risk overhang. They should see for themselves that they've got to change." As Duncan spoke, the phone rang. "Excuse me, please, will you, Eunice? Humpf," he said, "I thought I told the guys at the secretarial pool to hold my calls.

"Hello, Holt here," he said into the phone. "Oh, yes, George; sure, I remember you. You're the fellow in East Cupcake with Sweetland Power and Light. Right, yeah, you're the ones building the Mausoleum nuke. You're what? . . . advice about canceling it? Uh, yeah. Yeah, sure. I'll come, of course. You want me there when? Wednesday? The day after tomorrow? Ugh! Well, I suppose. Okay, I'll call you when I've found a flight. What? Oh yeah, I've got all the details. No. No, I won't tell any of the citizens' groups. Although you know you're going to have to work with them on developing a plan for implementing alternatives . . . Yeah, I can get you together with them when I'm there. Huh? Aw, c'mon. They're decent folk, just like you guys are. Right? Yeah. Oh, relax. It'll work out fine. Take it easy. 'Bye now." He turned to Hobart. "Get me the Mausoleum file and the financials on Sweetland Power and Light." As Hobart scuttled out, Duncan called after him, "Oh, and get me a flight, too. I've got to leave here in a day and a half."

Eunice, who had been listening in rising horror, couldn't contain herself any longer. "Wait, you can't leave," she said, her voice tense. "I still have lots to learn, and you have to help me get ready for the meeting next week."

"Well, I'm afraid I haven't any choice," Duncan told her. "I've been waiting for this to break for two years now. These guys are ripe for a least-cost abandonment and efficiency program. Anyway, I've really taught you just about all I can. And you know almost all of it already. I'm sure you'll do fine." He smiled reassuringly, then narrowed his eyes as if to find his place again and resumed his tutorial as though Eunice's concerns were settled. "Anyway," he continued, "if utilities are to survive, they have to reduce that uncertainty about how much electricity their customers will want to buy. At several thousand dollars per kilowatt of capacity, it is simply too expensive to build more plants just in case there is high demand. Utilities have a great deal of influence over what demand will actually be," he continued, "and they ought to be trying to move the market in the direction that is most favorable to them *and* to their rate payers: the direction of the best buys in energy services.

"Actually, all the utilities have to do is rethink their role in the energy marketplace and realize that they are not just supplying kilowatt-hours—they are supplying energy services. For years, utilities have been making investments on behalf of their customers. Those investments happen to have been in power plants. In this day and age, the cheapest way of providing more energy services is to invest in efficient refrigerators, light bulbs, motors, etcetera. Every kilowatt-hour that you save by using electricity more efficiently can then be sold to someone else. For instance, the Tennessee Valley Authority boasts that it has built the cheapest thousand-megawatt power plant around—by insulating thousands of attics throughout the Tennessee Valley.

"Now, either the utilities are somehow going to help customers make those investments, or the rate payers, just as you said, Eunice, are going to turn their backs on the utilities, make those investments without them, and let the utilities rot with their uselessly expensive power plants."

Eunice looked puzzled. "Well, why not let them suffer the consequences of their actions? Why are you so intent on playing the Lone Ranger with that utility?" Her own concerns gave a bit of testiness to her voice.

Duncan shrugged. "Well, that second option really would be a pity. The utilities are basically decent organizations with decent people working for them. If the utilities go broke, they'll take a lot of good people down with them, and conceivably even the whole financial system. Remember, these are billions we're talking about. On the other hand, if they get into the efficiency market, they can make their investments small, fast, and cheap, which seems like a good deal all around."

"Hmpf," said Eunice. "But how can utilities do that? Are they supposed to prowl the streets shouting 'New lamps for old'?"

"Actually, that's not far off. Here, let me give you a few examples of how this could work," Duncan said. "A lot of utilities already offer low-interest or no-interest loans to finance energy improvements. That's a step in the right direction, but it doesn't go far enough. Poor people are often reluctant to take on new debts, for instance. In fact, some surveys have found that loans will only reach roughly the upper middle class—the fiftieth to eightieth percentile of household income. That's a start, but utilities have a really strong incentive to get all their customers involved in saving. Remember, the alternative to the installation of an energy-efficient appliance is the utility's investment in an uneconomic power plant."

"Wait, are you suggesting that the utility might actually buy the customers' appliances for them?" said Eunice.

"Pretty close again," Duncan said. "Utilities serving more than half of all Americans are trying a rebate program that does roughly that. 'Buy an efficient appliance, get a check.' It's about that simple. And some of the rebates go much further. Several California utilities will pay you several hundred dollars for every kilowatt by which you reduce their peak load, and they don't care how you do it. For every kilowatt-hour that your new appliance or savings measure, whatever it is, will save in its first year of operation, the Snohomish Public Utility District will pay about thirty cents. And if you're lucky enough to live in Hood River County, Oregon, Pacific Power and Light will pay you a dollar and fifteen cents per kilowatt-hour for weatherization measures on an experimental basis. Say they did the same thing for appliances, and say you bought an energy-wise refrigerator that used a hundred kilowatt-hours per year. Pacific Power and Light would send you a check for about sixteen hundred dollars—more than enough to pay for the 'fridge and keep it stocked for a while. And the utility can afford to do that because the alternative for it is far more costly. In effect, by financing your electricity-saving refrigerators the utility is installing in your house a reliable, very cheap little hydro dam that will for decades save power for resale to someone else."

"That's incredible," gasped Eunice. "With that kind of rebate, it would be economical for everyone to throw out, er, recycle their old refrigerators right away and buy new, efficient ones."

"Yup, that's just the idea," said Duncan. "And utilities are catching on to these ideas. In Santa Monica, for instance, the city has taken over a federally mandated program called the Residential Conservation Service that requires utilities to offer energy advice and inspection to their customers. Instead of waiting for residents to contact *them,* city inspectors go door-to-door through the neighborhoods, offering energy advice to people. And instead of just recommending what people can buy, the inspectors actually install the basic conservation devices in the houses they visit —weather-stripping, water-heater insulation, efficient shower-heads, and so forth. It works especially well since three-quarters of the people in that area are renters who wouldn't want to pay to improve their landlords' buildings anyway."

"That's great," said Eunice. "But who pays the bill?"

"The utility pays the city for every audit that city people perform," said Duncan. "And the utility pays the forty- to fifty-dollar cost of the equipment installed. Nice, huh? But for utilities this sort of program is quite a bargain, considering how much money it saves a company in not having to build new power stations or find new natural gas, or even to fuel the plants it already has. Pacific Power and Light, again, is piloting a similar program in Hood River County. But instead of confining itself to the simple, easy-to-install measures like the ones in Santa Monica, Pacific Power and Light is installing as much insulation as is cost-effective. That means fifteen inches of glass-fiber in the ceiling, twelve inches under the floor, and four to six inches in the walls. The utility expects to bundle up the entire community of fifteen thousand people in a couple of years. Then it's going to track what happens, gathering some good data on exactly how much it's saving and at what price."

"I don't know about you, Duncan, but I'm moving to Hood River County," Eunice declared.

"Oh, I reckon you won't have to wait too long before your own utility decides to start a similar program," he said. "More and more of them are coming around all the time. Witness my phone call."

"Mmm," Eunice responded as she thought a bit. She cocked her head and thought some more before asking, "Okay, I can see that one of these rebate programs is better than building a nuclear power plant. But what about a utility that has just finished a five-billion-dollar monument to its own ignorance of energy-efficiency methods?" Eunice asked. "What does it do?"

"The incredible thing about efficiency is how cheap it is," Duncan replied. Eunice waited for this to make sense; so Duncan added, "Efficiency is cheaper than even the *operating* costs alone of a nuclear reactor, which has supposedly the lowest operating costs of any power plant. So even if you have just completed a reactor, it would be cheaper to write it off and buy efficiency instead than to generate electricity to try to sell for inefficient appliances. Of course, from the customers' point of view, this means lower bills and greater reliability. By the way, efficient appliances are also more reliable than nuclear plants, which typically have nearly twice the downtime predicted. So, by investing in efficiency, which costs less than running its existing power plants, a utility can cut its costs faster than its sales and revenues drop. It can save so much on operating costs that the savings can pay off the money already spent on an abandoned plant like Mausoleum—while *lowering*, not raising, everyone's electric bills.

"And that's about it," Duncan said. "It seems so simple when you just look at the theory . . ."

"But the implementation is what gets messy," Eunice finished for him.

Duncan nodded. "So that's why I'm off to work with that utility. It is going to be messy. It always is. All this talk is cheap, but getting these programs to work in the marketplace is always the real test. There are always a lot more barriers than you imagined. Oh," he said suddenly, "there is one such barrier I should caution you about. It's called the 'no losers' test. It tends to come from the people who were vocal proponents of large power plants and were proven wrong when efficiency turned out to be such a good buy. Sometimes I tease them by calling it the 'sore losers' test. A friend calls it the 'hardly-any-winners' test. They don't want utilities to spend anything on conservation unless it will lower the bills of everyone—participants and nonparticipants as well. But if some people refuse to accept the kinds of good deals that utilities are starting to offer, it seems to me that it's their own fault. Besides, for years, while utilities helped demand to grow, nonparticipants—that is, people whose demand was stable—shared in those costs. Now that the sound economic solution is to help people lower their demand, I think it's only fair that nonparticipants contribute—or, better yet, leap on board and improve their energy efficiency, too.

"Incidentally," added Duncan with an impish gleam in his eye, "you know all those billions of dollars that some utilities say it'll cost to clean up their dirty power plants to reduce the acid rain that's threatening the trees and lakes downwind?" Eunice nodded. "Well, efficiency can pay for that cleanup, too. Rather than raising everyone's electric bills to put scrubbers on dirty coal plants, we can use loans, rebates, purchases of savings, and similar incentives to install superefficient lights, motors, and appliances. Then we'll use less electricity, burn less coal, emit less sulphur, but *lower* everyone's electric bills, because efficiency costs less than coal. And then we can reinvest some of the savings in whatever combination of fuel-switching, stack-gas cleanup, fluidized-bed conversion—that's a remarkably clean way to burn almost anything—or other cleanup measures you happen to favor. And when we're through, we'll have reduced sulphur emissions several times as much as Congress is considering, but at the same time everyone's electric bills will have gone down, not up."

"Do all of these nifty programs apply just to efficiency improvements," asked Eunice, "or can sustainable energy production get into the act, too?"

"Sure, sustainables and other good competitors, such as cogenerating power in factories, are welcome," Duncan said. "In fact, ideally, they should be treated the same way. A few utilities are even proposing that. These utilities want to hold an auction for efficiency and privately generated sources of supply. For example, a utility will start out at a penny per kilowatt-hour, say, and offer ten-year contracts to people who will either supply electricity at that price or will save it at that price. That would work out to the utility's paying you fifty-seven dollars a year to keep a fifteen-dollar superefficient light bulb in a socket in your house that you use an average of twenty hours a week—and to agree to do that for ten years. After everyone who liked that price had signed up, the utility would raise its offer to two cents per kilowatt-hour, then three cents, and so on, until it had signed up enough capacity to offset the electricity demand that it anticipated. If 'supplies' ever ran low, it could always hold another auction. And if the technologies changed, the people who had signed the contracts could always bargain among themselves, as long as all of their commitments continued to be covered."

"What about the plants the utility operates?" asked Eunice.

"They could enter the auction, too," said Duncan. "They would simply offer their power at the price per kilowatt-hour that it costs to operate them. So hydro plants could bid at a penny a kilowatt-hour, but oil plants probably couldn't bid until seven or eight cents a kilowatt-hour. The auction, however, would never get that high. It would probably meet everyone's needs at around four cents a kilowatt-hour."

"But what would happen to the oil or coal plants that wouldn't have gotten a chance to bid?" Eunice asked.

"They would just sit idle," said Duncan. "Or be retired. We want to do the cheapest things first, remember; so the most expensive tools will probably not be used very much. In effect, the utility's role would shift to that of a broker, keeping track of who was producing power and who was saving it, and making sure that all the energy services that people wanted to pay for could be provided, but not necessarily providing those services itself. The utility could, if it wished to keep power plants around, be a supplier of last resort, perhaps, but it would rarely need to step in."

"Boy," said Eunice. She paused then, and a mischievous look came over her face.

"This is really a change in what I thought utilities were all about. But can we have another kind of auction now?" she asked. "Who'll bid a dollar for the privilege of taking me to lunch, Dutch treat? Two dollars? Sold to the gentleman in the sports coat sitting in the government-issue chair. Let's go."

26 Community Energy Studies: Crunching the Numbers

DUNCAN PLOPPED DOWN in his chair, leaned back, and stretched. "Was that better?" he asked. "See, exotic cuisine's not really so bad."

"Mmm," Eunice fairly purred. She'd liked the little crêpe wagon Duncan had taken her to this time.

"Now, Madam Secretary," Duncan gestured expansively, "what would you like to hear?"

Eunice thought for a moment. "Actually, I'd like to have you talk about how one would go about *doing* all this. I mean, theory is all right, but how can I mobilize people? I can't just snap my fingers and make everyone energy-self-reliant. Lord knows, I don't even know what to say to those Assistant Secretaries." She grimaced.

"Well, you know," Duncan said, furrowing his brow, "one of the best ways to show the need for action is to bring it home, so to speak—to do a community energy study."

"What's that?" Eunice asked.

"It's a way of determining how much energy your community is using, what it is costing, what local sustainable sources are available, and what you can do to implement a more sensible energy policy," said Duncan. "There have been studies like this done in literally thousands of communities. Megastudies have even been done for the world, for the United States, Canada, England, West Germany, France, Sweden, Denmark, other European countries, and many Third World nations. Basically, they all show the same thing: that present energy supplies are costly and insecure; that energy efficiency is the best buy and sustainable sources are next best; and that such a common-sense energy policy is best—and sufficient—for whichever region has been studied. The tough part now is knowing where to start. To tell you about all the studies would take months. And, while I've come to enjoy those sessions," Duncan grinned with mock wistfulness, "pretty soon you'll have to stop joining me for coffee and assume the helm of this errant ship. After all, it's up to you to chart the energy course for the nation," he teased. "And as for myself, I must be off to East Cupcake. But not immediately," he soothed, noting that Eunice was looking panicky. "We've a bit more to cover before you're on your own.

"So let me give you an example that shows the persuasive power of these studies. In 1977 a group of citizens in Franklin County, Massachusetts, decided to take a look at their energy situation. Franklin County is an area of tenuous farms and depressed mill towns with many people out of work. It's also the poorest county in Massachusetts. The citizen study group found that every household in this cold, cloudy area spent an average of more than thirteen hundred dollars per year to buy electricity, bottled gas, and oil. That amounted to twenty-three million dollars a year leaving Franklin County for Venezuela and elsewhere. It was also the same amount as the total payroll of the county's ten largest employers. Under the most optimistic of future forecasts, by the year 2000 a typical household would send out fifty-three hundred dollars to buy energy, without even counting inflation. Just to generate enough extra money in the county to pay for home energy, the single largest employer would have to duplicate itself every couple of years until the turn of the century."

"My gracious!" Eunice gasped. "That's terrible . . . why, the future's hardly possible for them! What can they do?"

"Actually," Duncan agreed, "it's really worse than that. The total county energy import bill for all sectors was about forty-eight million dollars in 1975. By 1980 it had risen to one hundred eight million current dollars, of which fifty-two million dollars was just for households."

Eunice shook her head in disbelief. "But what can they do?" she repeated.

"Well," Duncan continued, "the broad-based study group held an informal sort of town meeting and presented these results. Of course the people from the chamber of commerce turned white. Which is just what the citizens' group wanted—they had people's attention. And the study group had worked out what could be done instead: making the buildings heat-tight, using passive and active solar heat, running vehicles on methanol from the sustained yield of some unallocated public wood lots, and meeting electrical needs with wind or microhydro within the county. Local machine shops, with skilled workers unemployed, could make all the equipment. The cost of all these projects would be about the same as what the county was then paying for household energy—about twenty-three million dollars per year. But the leaky bucket—the hemorrhage of dollars—would thereby be plugged up. The money, the jobs, and the economic multiplier effects would stay in Franklin County, not go to Venezuela.

"You know," Duncan digressed, "before the 1973 oil embargo, a dollar used to circulate within the county some twenty-six times before going outside to buy an import; today, it circulates fewer than ten times. Franklin County, like practically all counties in the country, is bleeding money. A fair consensus developed, as a result of the citizens' analysis, that the only hope for economic development would be to stop the bleeding by promoting local energy efficiency and self-reliant renewable supply. As a result, what was a paper study became the Franklin County Energy Project."

Eunice's eyes sparkled. "What happened, did they do it?" she asked eagerly.

"Some," Duncan said. "More than ninety percent of county residents polled in 1980 said they had reduced their energy use since 1974; nearly half used or planned to use locally abundant wood for heating. Weatherization projects had cut energy use in half in more than two hundred homes, and energy checkups saved an average of five hundred sixty dollars per surveyed home per year. Total energy use in the county actually didn't grow during

1976–78. Once the energy problem was presented so that people could see it as *their* problem, and one not just of convenience but of economic survival, they were motivated to start solving that problem on their own. This is in the best tradition of local self-help and self-determinism. Even Ronald Reagan remarked in a nationally syndicated 1979 newspaper column"—Duncan's eyes twinkled as he smiled, picked up a copy of *Brittle Power,* and thumbed to a page—"the study found that . . . a carefully planned transition to renewable energy sources would not be difficult, would probably yield actual increases in the local standard of living and would cut back sharply on air and water pollution . . . I suspect quite a few communities and counties across the country are going to undertake the kind of study that the people in Franklin County have pioneered . . . They can act in their own communities to take charge of their own future. That's a spirit worth bottling and spreading around."

"He said *that!"* Eunice choked, hardly believing her ears.

"Yes, and it's even true," Duncan said. "Economically, the people of Franklin County achieved the equivalent of bringing in a new multimillion-dollar business. They did it by making least-cost purchases of energy, which in turn strengthened existing businesses as well as the financial condition of individual residents."

"Oh, my!" Eunice clapped her hands in pleasure. "How wonderful."

"Well, yes—as far as it goes." Duncan turned more serious. "But there is also another, more somber lesson to be learned from Franklin County. Although many individuals there are still seeking ways to save energy and money, the citizens' steering group disbanded long before accomplishing all of its goals. They chose an implementation plan that required new state legislation, and many members burned out chasing that elusive goal. At the same time, the group lost its Department of Energy funding in the change of administrations. Some group leaders accepted jobs elsewhere teaching others how to do such a study. And with the passing of energy as a crisis issue for most people, the formal effort was much reduced. Thus, the example of Franklin County provides two lessons: the magnitude of the opportunity at hand and the message that any energy mobilization must continually be recreated. Individuals come and go, and new ideas bring bursts of excitement and dedication; but in time those grow old. A community that makes the commitment to invest in itself must continue to do just that, to seek out new ways to plug leaks and new technologies to employ. The experience of Franklin County should give us all hope, but it also shows that it's not easy.

"But," Duncan brightened, "it also shows the sorts of numbers available from doing a community energy study."

"How," Eunice asked, somewhat intimidated, "does one do that?"

"First," said Duncan, "you find someone, or a few people, with an aptitude for numbers. You know, some people are good with dogs and some with cars and some with computers; well, some people have a knack for arithmetic. Don't assume it has to be someone with a particular background, either. It could be a smart high-school kid, or a retired businessperson, or a mechanic, or a farmer. Then, when you have your lead analyst, you assemble a broadly based group of citizens who are willing to guide your number-crunchers' assumptions and goals, review their work as it goes along, and finally give it greater legitimacy when it's finished."

"But what exactly do these number-crunchers *do?*" persisted Eunice. "What do they try to calculate, and what do they start with?"

"Ideally, if their time permits, they go through a simple series of steps," replied Duncan, "to figure out what their community's energy system could look like in the long term on various assumptions that I'll describe in a moment. Then they work backward to see what would have to be done when to get there. What assumptions? Well, first they should probably look at a future that might be called the 'Past Writ Large'—what'll happen if nothing changes. This assumes that everything that is already happening—the outflow of dollars from the community, the risk of supply interruptions, the risks to the environment and to local social cohesion, the likelihood of rate hikes—will go on happening, only more so. By the way," he added mischievously, "that's the place to work out that paying the local energy bills in 2010 will require the payroll from seven hundred new jobs every year from now till then—say, a new General Chemicals plant every year—or whatever example will be locally vivid and concrete. Then, if people don't like the way that future works out, they can examine one or more futures you will have provided that move purposefully in another direction, such as one emphasizing the cheapest options first—mainly efficiency and perhaps some local sustainable sources."

"What do you mean by 'one or more futures'?" asked Eunice. "Isn't one enough?"

"One will be enough ultimately," agreed Duncan, "but the range and the effects of choices may be clearer if the group is able to calculate several alternatives. You're painting various scenarios, various 'what if's.' Then people can try on the alternatives and see which they think they like. For example, a 'technical fix' or 'economic efficiency' scenario could show the power of energy-saving technologies that don't affect lifestyles. Then the group might want to consider another scenario in which people also try some mild lifestyle changes of the kinds they're already practicing, such as driving not just more efficient cars but perhaps also smaller ones, or growing more food at home, or doing other things that Americans weren't expected to do in 1973 but that, in fact, many of them have done enthusiastically since. Finally, the group might even want to include a 'conserver society' future in which the community actually limits the amount and kind of economic activity it really wants—a subject that was off-limits in the other scenarios. By separating these kinds of alternative futures, the study group can make it unambiguously clear which savings result from better technologies and which from shifts in how we live."

"Okay," said Eunice thoughtfully, "so the group assumes certain directions of future evolution for the community and explores in each case what the energy system would look like, how it would work, and what it would cost. But how far into the future."

"Typically about fifty years," Duncan replied. "That may seem like a long time, but actually it's only about the time a power plant or other major energy plant ordered now would be expected to retire. Historically, major changes in the energy system—such as the shifts from wood to coal, coal to oil, and oil to gas—have taken about a half-century, simply because so much old equipment has to be fixed up or retired and replaced. The efficiency/solar transition actually appears to be happening faster than that; but it's still convenient to look far enough into the future so that enough time has elapsed to change or replace today's old, obsolete energy-using devices. And remember, we're not trying to say definitively what *will* happen in fifty years, but only what *could* happen. We're trying to delineate futures that are somewhere between a forecast and a fantasy, or between the unavoidable and the miraculous."

"Hmm." Eunice considered that. "And what does the group calculate, in what order?" she asked.

"First it figures out, for some recent year, how much energy of what types the community actually used for each main task. The three end uses are evaluated: heat, liquid fuels for transportation, and electricity. Some analysts also separate out 'mechanical work at fixed sites'—normally done by electric motors—from other electrical applications. Heat is normally classified as low-temperature, under the boiling point of water; medium-temperature, up to a few hundred degrees, for, say, cooking; and high-temperature, for such industrial uses as blast furnaces and cement ovens. Electricity used to provide heat or, usually, cooling is classified as heat."

"But where do people get all this information?" asked Eunice. "I'm sure I wouldn't have any idea where to start."

"Take it one sector at a time," said Duncan, "and it's not really so hard. Transportation fuels are virtually all liquids—mostly gasoline, diesel, and aviation fuel—and you get the data either from such official sources as the Energy Information Administration—which has state and, often, county data—and the state or municipal energy office, or from companies that sell the fuel. If fuel and utility companies are represented in the advisory group and understand why the analysis will be important to the community and to their business, they're usually glad to cooperate. In some cases, people have simply done a survey of all the gas stations, oil dealers, etc., promising not to publish the disaggregated data, then added up the total. Then all you have to do is decide how you want to count, say, gasoline bought outside your study area by people who live inside it and vice versa. It doesn't matter how you count it, as long as you are explicit.

"Electricity is the next easiest kind of energy use on which to get data," Duncan continued. "Most utilities have both sales and market-analysis data on how many appliances people have, how many homes use electric heat and air conditioning and water heaters, and so on. In some cases in which the electric utility hasn't wanted to help, the gas utility—its main competitor—has offered the data instead. Or the state utility commission may be able to help, since the utility can hardly refuse a data request from its own regulators. If all else fails, you can use data for another utility whose customers have similar incomes, habits, and climates to those of your community—it'll probably be close enough. All you do," Duncan explained, "no matter whose data you use, is take the total use of electricity and subtract the amount used for space conditioning, water heating, and perhaps, depending on your definition, refrigeration and freezing. With luck, you'll also be able to get enough data from the chief engineers of the main local industries to estimate how much electricity is being used for motors, electrolysis, electric furnaces—which you should count as heat—and other uses, such as lighting. What you want to know is the tasks using electricity that are really electricity-specific, and how much they use.

"Then all you're left with is heat. The only difficult kind to estimate is industrial heat. Again, the fuel suppliers or the industries themselves should be able to tell you about how much fuel is burned for what processes. Then you can just ask the person who runs each process what temperature is needed to make the process work. If you want to be fancy, there's a report from Inter-Technology written for the Energy Research and Development Administration—the predecessor of this Department—that analyzes the temperature required for practically every industrial process in the country. What's not industrial heat is either the low-temperature kinds I just mentioned—basically for buildings, domestic hot water, and clothes drying—or for cooking. So now you know how much of what kinds of energy you're using. That by itself will be a real eye-opener—especially how little of your energy is required in the form of electricity."

"But all those numbers are for past energy usage, and I suppose you pick the most recent year for which you can get the numbers," said Eunice. Duncan nodded. "But then how do you figure out how much of what kinds of energy you're going to need in the future?"

"Again," Duncan explained, "it's not that complicated. You need to make two kinds of assumptions: how much each kind of economic activity will grow, or shrink, by your 'end point' or 'target' year, perhaps around 2035; and how much more efficiently people will be using energy by then to provide each product or service. Projecting economic activity is kind of fun, because you have to be explicit about who's going to be using how much of what: how many houses and offices with so much floor space, how many schools and hospitals, how many person-miles and ton-miles of transportation, how many widgets and tons of steel and board-feet of lumber produced. If you just extrapolated a community's present economic growth rate, you might end up with enormous projections that are hard to tie to any physical reality. But if you work in *physical* terms, it's much harder to project more economic activity than people will have the time or inclination to pursue. That is, you'll identify 'saturations,' such as people's difficulty in figuring out what to do with more than one or two houses per family, or their inability to drive more than one car at the same time, or the unlikelihood of their washing clothes and dishes that are already clean simply because someone forgot that each family will need to wash only so much and no more."

"But how do you know," Eunice continued, "how efficiently each energy service can or will be provided decades from now?"

"You don't *know*," replied Duncan, "but you can and should *assume*. The way I do it is just to ask how much efficiency, for each use, is worth buying with today's efficiency-improving technologies, either at today's energy prices or at those that I can reasonably expect to prevail in the long term. Naturally, the lower the energy price, the less efficiency will be worth buying. But on any reasonable assumptions there will be so much savings that long-term energy demands will be much smaller than today's. That is, I simply assume that fifty years or so is long enough to have implemented the best of today's cost-effective energy-saving measures *completely*. If you think that's not long enough to do the whole job, then consider a somewhat longer period—long enough to finish implementation. And remember, if we improve our energy efficiency at only, say, three percent every year for fifty years, we'll then use only twenty-two percent as much energy per task as we use today."

"The idea being, I suppose," said Eunice slowly, "that once you see how efficient we *could* and, economically speaking, *should* become in the long term, you can then figure out how fast you'd have to improve your efficiency to achieve that goal in that time?"

"Precisely!" exclaimed Duncan. "And that's the next step. After seeing what you can do with energy efficiency by, say, 2035, you then estimate how efficient you'd have to become by, say, 1990, or 2010, or other years in between, in order to achieve your long-term goal on time. It's simplest to assume just that you'll improve your efficiency at a constant rate, although you might reasonably suppose that in a rapidly growing community, you can become efficient even faster by designing new buildings and factories to be efficient in the first place."

Eunice nodded and thought, then nodded again. "So you've now calculated various levels of activity," she said, "traffic, home occupancy, industrial production, and so on—for a series of 'snapshot' years from now to about a half-century from now, and for each of those years, you calculate about how much of what kinds of energy would be needed to do those tasks?"

"You see how logical the process is?" said Duncan with delight. "And once you know all that, it's time to look at where your community can get the right amounts of those various forms of energy—heat, liquid fuels, and electricity. To be conservative, I usually do this step only with technologies that are cost-effective practically everywhere right now, although some newcomers, such as solar cells, are becoming competitive so quickly and with such virtual certainty that you might want to include them as supply options, too. But the basic task is again quite simple: to estimate, for each of your 'snapshot' years, what mix of energy sources—conventional fuels and power and all the alternatives you can think of—will do each task in the cheapest way. You use as much of the cheapest option as you think you'll have available, then as much as you can of the next cheapest, and so on, until you have all the required energy of that type."

"Would you do this starting at your long-term, 'end point' year and then work backward toward the present, just as you did for end-use patterns," asked Eunice, "so as to see how much of what kinds of energy supply you'd need to build by what years to meet your needs?"

"Yes, exactly," said Duncan. "And by estimating how long it takes to build each kind of energy-supply system, you'll be able to figure out when you'll have to start building each system in order to have it working in time. Don't worry about where to get this kind of information. Many state utility commissions and energy offices do their own elaborate analyses of energy-supply options, and some, such as those of the California Energy Commission, are especially detailed and authoritative. And all the companies that make energy-supplying technologies will be glad to give you more data on cost and construction time than you can possibly digest."

"No doubt," said Eunice with a wry smile. "Now, so far you've only told me about the kinds of things engineers consider: how much insulation could or should be in my roof, how many power plants and oil refineries—or solar panels and biofuel plants —I'm going to need by a given year, etcetera. When do I start considering what all these technical choices are going to *do* to the community whose future I'm concerned about?"

"Right now," replied Duncan. "You've hit on the very next step: evaluating, as best you can, what the impacts of your proposed energy system are going to be. And not only how the system you propose will take up land, use water, and affect air and aesthetics and how people relate to each other. You should also look at the policy instruments that you propose to use to encourage people to buy the energy-saving and -supplying devices you've proposed. These will have subtle social and economic impacts, too, and this is just the time to start trying to anticipate them. Then the next step, as you might expect, is to see whether your advisory group likes the sound of all those impacts. Do they appear to add up to a future you like and that you think your neighbors would like to live with? Is there anything disagreeable or even intolerable about them? If so, now's the time to go back and look at ways to soften or eliminate whatever impacts you don't like. You can do that by pushing harder on energy efficiency, by changing your mix of technologies—perhaps using slightly costlier ones because they're more attractive in other ways not counted in their price— or even by changing your assumptions about long-term economic activity. After all, there's nothing sacred about anyone's guess of what your town will look like in fifty years, and the whole point of this process is to try to envision and choose several possible versions of what people might want for themselves, rather than just drifting toward what someone else might want for them."

"But once you've come up with a future that looks feasible and pleasant," said Eunice, "what do you do with it?"

"Ah, that's the most important point of all," said Duncan. "Your group should plan from the beginning to devote at least half its total effort to presenting its work to others in a form they can understand and to organizing the community to take the next steps. After all, the goal is to help people realize their opportunities and start to grasp them, not just to write a report that sits on a shelf." He gestured at the papers spilling from his shelves. "Once people start analyzing their energy future," he warned, "they often get so caught up in the seductive details of the assumptions and numbers that they forget why they started. Then they tend to put all their effort into the analysis and not leave themselves nearly enough time and money to tell others what they did and why."

"What are some other common mistakes people make in this kind of work?" asked Eunice. "There must be lots that you've found. I want to know what people do wrong, because then we all can stop repeating the same old dumb mistakes."

"And start making interesting new mistakes," Duncan said with a laugh. "Good for you," he added. "I wish everyone else in this business were as sensible. I think you might want my lists that, Chinese-style, I've called the Eight Mistakes and Six Methodological Blunders. Ah," he grinned and made a note to himself, "I know where we should go for lunch next time. A great Hunan place—they have a dish called Four Delights Chicken that is out of this world."

Eunice looked at him with some trepidation.

"Anyway," resumed Duncan, "the First Mistake is to put most of your effort into analyzing energy supply. Everyone does it. We're all hung up on what kind of power plant to build, or what kind of solar gadget to put on the roof. But about ninety percent of our effort in analyzing our community's energy opportunities should be put into efficiency improvements, not supply. Then we'll find so much efficiency that the supply problems usually become almost trivial.

"The Second Mistake," he continued, "is to start doing your analysis right away without doing a scoping calculation first."

"What on earth," asked Eunice, "is a scoping calculation? Is it anything to do with telescopes?"

"More like kaleidoscopes," replied Duncan, laughing. "It's a simple estimate of the broadest outlines of your community's energy problem: what the main terms of demand will be and what the problem terms of supply will be. In other words, before analyzing anything in detail, you should sit down with a pocket calculator and the back of a large envelope and do *very* rough estimates of which end uses are probably going to account for the largest parts of local energy demand and which uses obviously aren't going to be easy to meet with local resources. You may often find, for example, that by the time you count cogeneration, small hydro, wind, and so forth, your community is likely to end up with a lot more sustainable electricity supply than the small amount of electricity it will need, but that there's no obvious local source of sustainable liquid fuels for transportation. Or you might find that there's a local biofuel source that will give you a surplus of liquids but that you may well be short of high-temperature heat for the local glass factory. By identifying these terms early, you can devote extra effort to analyzing them. For example, if you're likely to be short on liquid fuels but long on low-temperature solar heat, then you can work harder on car efficiency and not so hard on superinsulation."

"Seems obvious enough," said Eunice. "You mean people don't do it that way?"

"No," said Duncan sadly. "Even though we all know we should, it takes a conscious effort, and often even the best of us still forget. Which brings me to the Third Mistake: getting hung up on a number. Many's the time I've spent days or weeks hunting all over," his hands circumscribed the paper overflowing his office shelves, "for a particular number needed for my analysis. The more I couldn't find it, the harder I tried. What I should have done was to guess."

"Wait a minute," objected Eunice. "Are we doing analysis or guesswork?"

"We're talking precision guesswork," said Duncan mischievously. "Or what my military friends call SWAG, Scientific Wild-Assed Guess. Remember, there's no such thing as exactitude in projecting for 2035 anyway. We do the best we can, but, in the end, this is all guesswork. The physicist Niels Bohr said it best: 'It is difficult to make predictions, especially about the future.' "

Eunice frowned a moment, then smiled as she got his point.

"Anyway, if you guess a number," Duncan advised, "then put a big star on it to remind yourself that it's only a guess. Once a Pentagon analyst forgot to do that in calculating the military value of the antiballistic missile. His guess eventually got passed all the way up to the Joint Chiefs of Staff, with each layer of the bureaucracy assuming their subordinates had checked it. When it became controversial—practically the centerpiece in the ABM debate— and was traced back down to its origin, some poor lieutenant had to admit, 'They told me they needed this number by three o'clock, and I looked all over for it but couldn't find it; so I guessed.' There were lots of red faces over that one.

"Often, however, in the energy business, you'll come back to the number later in your analysis and find that it doesn't really matter whether it's the right number, because the energy demand you calculated with it is only a tiny part of the total demand.

"And the Fourth Mistake," he continued, "is closely related: being overprecise. Did one of your kids ever make a map for a Scouts merit badge?"

"He surely did," said Eunice sternly. "It took me days to get the mud out of his socks."

"They probably didn't tell him, but what he should have done first," said Duncan, "was to calculate, at the scale of his map, what distance on the ground corresponded to the thickness of a pencil line on his sketch."

"A pencil line?" said Eunice in puzzlement. "Oh, of course! Because if he measured more accurately than that, he couldn't draw it anyway; so there'd be no point in measuring that exactly. Oh, wait till I tell him that! I remember how he struggled over whether something came out to four or five inches. In the middle of a swamp, no doubt. Oh, the mud on those jeans!"

"Well, that same mistake," said Duncan, "is common in energy analyses. It is, as Aristotle once remarked, 'the mark of educated people, and a proof of their culture, that in every subject they look for only so much precision as its nature permits or its solution requires.' "

"I like that," said Eunice. "I must remember to tell that to those Assistant Secretaries who put in their briefing books ever so exactly how much energy we're going to need in the year 2000, when I'll bet they don't know within five percent how much energy we're using right now."

"Absolutely right," said Duncan. "Although none of them will admit it. But all those imposing columns of computer-generated statistics with lots of decimal places *look* so convincing that few people would guess that major sources of historic energy statistics often disagree with each other by as much as tens of percent. We seem to know a great deal more about the future than about the present or the past."

"What's the Fifth Mistake?" asked Eunice curiously. "I rather like these Mistakes, even though I don't want to meet them in dark committee rooms."

"The Fifth Mistake is multiplying alternatives."

"Why not?" asked Eunice. "You said to do various scenarios."

"Yes," said Duncan, "but the point of building energy scenarios isn't to show how many futures are possible; it's to help your audience focus on what general kinds of futures they'd prefer and why they differ. And you can best help them by choosing internally consistent sets of assumptions, at least one of which will pretty closely fit their own view of the future, so they'll say, 'Yes, that's about what I think will—or should—happen; now this scenario lets me see the consequences of proceeding in that way.'

"Consider the more usual way of presenting energy choices. You can't decide how many people will live in your town in 2035;

so you choose a high, medium, and low population case. Then you can't decide about economic growth; so you have three cases of that. Then three more for world oil prices, and already you have twenty-seven alternatives. Why, that's enough choices to keep people undecided indefinitely!"

"And the Sixth Mistake?" asked Eunice, a little chastened. The notion of twenty-seven alternatives was a bit frightening and, on reflection, a bit silly.

"Inconsistency," intoned Duncan gravely. "For example, describing an energy future in which solar energy will make zillions of jobs but solar energy will be very cheap. For that to happen, all those solar workers will have to be earning way below the minimum wage. Or describing an economy that exports vastly more widgets than it needs to sell in order to make enough money to buy what it needs. Or employing more people than will actually be living in your town. And so on. There are innumerable kinds of futures that just can't happen because the numbers won't add up right.

"The Seventh Mistake is more subtle: supposing that your own analytic work will be linear and predictable—cut and dried according to a preset pattern. It may sound as though I've described it that way, but, in fact, you'll need to improvise a lot as you go along, because only once you're in the middle of the analysis will you find what problems are really important. Therefore your analysis has to be modular and recursive." Eunice wrinkled her nose in noncomprehension. So Duncan explained, "Modular means your chain of calculations is so designed that you can unplug a number, massage it, refine it, plug it back in, and go on to the next weakest number. Recursive means you keep looping back to earlier parts of the calculation to refine assumptions and thus to solve problems you discovered later."

"Massage a number?" said Eunice as though it had slightly risqué connotations.

"Sure," Duncan replied, grinning. "A term of the trade. It means, for instance, to run various calculations to see if it is the right number, and to try by different means or by using more refined data to calculate it more exactly."

"Oh," Eunice replied.

"And the Eighth Mistake," concluded Duncan, "is among the most common: producing an opaque, unreadable, technotwitese report that sounds like you made it all up from whole cloth. It is of utmost importance that your group's work should be scrutable, documented, and transparent. Scrutable means a professional reader can get your results from your stated data and methods. Documented means you say where your assumptions came from so that people can check them. And transparent means that a lay reader can grasp the general outlines of what you did even though he or she may not know enough to reproduce the details of the calculation."

"Great! All that makes sense. But now you've got me wondering about the Six Methodological Blunders," said Eunice.

"Which, in the best policy restaurants, even come without MSG," Duncan joked. "The First Blunder is to try to Analyze By Committee. Sure, the steering group should certainly have people with different skills and perspectives and kinds of knowledge. And various of these people can and should work on different areas of the analysis. But there has to be at least one person in the middle—preferably two, in case the first one leaves town or falls under a bus—who *knows* the numbers—what they are, where they came from, which ones need to worked on next. Otherwise the whole exercise will dissolve into incoherence.

"The Second Blunder is Not Writing It Down. I mean recording your assumptions—it's surprisingly easy to forget what on earth you assumed in order to get a certain result. Also, always write down your bibliographic sources. So many times, if I'd done that, I could have saved myself no end of frustration trying to find that little scrap of paper on which I wrote where a number came from, or trying to reconstruct some result that no longer made sense six months later. It's vital, in fact, to start writing your eventual report early, too. That'll make weak points more obvious while there's still time to give them the emphasis they deserve.

"And the Third Blunder"—Duncan grinned, moving quickly —"is Asymmetry. If you apply a certain criterion to energy sources —price, or safety, or whatever—apply it to *all* sources and *all* efficiency improvements, not just to the ones you don't like. Don't assess some options at their historic costs—the old, cheap stuff—

and others at their marginal cost—the new, expensive stuff; instead, compare marginal with marginal and historic with historic. If you value some kinds of energy at their true market value, do the same for competing sources, too, rather than comparing some free-market costs with some heavily subsidized costs. And so on."

"Again, excuse me," said Eunice in bewilderment, "but does all this really need saying?"

"I dare say," said Duncan dryly, "that you'd be hard pressed to find a significant policy document ever published by this Department that obeys these simple principles." Eunice looked shocked. "Bureaucracies often think their job isn't to speak the truth; it's to support the boss's position, however irrational. Remember, this Department has a branch called Policy, Planning, and Analysis, and that exactly states its priorities—policy first, analysis afterward."

"I sometimes feel as though I've wandered into *Alice In Wonderland,*" said Eunice in dismay.

"You have," Duncan confirmed, "and you won't wake up. Don't worry, though—you're the White Queen, and you can do whatever you want. Actually, I don't suppose you can behead people, but otherwise . . ."

"If I can do whatever I want," said Eunice primly, "I think I want to find out about the remaining three Blunders."

"Yes, Your Highness," said Duncan with a little bow. "The Fourth Blunder is Supposing That Your Community Is Like Every Other One."

"But didn't you say," asked Eunice, "that energy choices are pretty much the same in communities more or less everywhere? And that if you can't get your real data, take someone else's?"

"Yes," admitted Duncan, "but I should also have emphasized that every place has real, unique quirks. No two places are *exactly* alike. And we need to be careful about those local peculiarities. For example, is energy use in Denmark like that of, say, rural northern Germany? Sort of, but watch out! Denmark has an enormously disproportionate use of jet fuel. Why? Because the transatlantic flights of SAS all tend to tank up last in Copenhagen. Likewise, you can get really fouled up calculating oil use in Norway, because the merchant fleet that flies the Norwegian flag—and whose oil use therefore shows up in Norwegian statistics for energy use—uses about as much oil as all the rest of Norway. Or if you live in a place like Switzerland, which imports lots of food and raw materials and fertilizer—all containing energy—but which exports mainly bank accounts and watches and pharmaceuticals, you can actually end up using, directly *and* indirectly, a lot more energy than you're buying directly. The Swiss, for example, import a lot more energy embodied in goods and services than they export, and that net import—what they call 'grey' energy—is about a third as big as all their direct purchases of energy put together."

Eunice was feeling completely bewildered. It was already a lot to undertake studying Dubuque. But to take on a part of the world she'd never been in . . . ? However, once more she smiled gallantly.

"Then there's the Fifth Blunder," Duncan said, "which is really a whole garden of Blunders: making your report too dry and abstract rather than spicing it up with precedents, analogies, vivid examples, and concrete local case studies; not making clear whether you're claiming that your results only illustrate possibilities or are in some way optimal; just stating your results without saying which assumptions are important or insignificant to those results, and why; writing just one report when your diverse audiences really need several reports—some popular, some technical, some short, some long—plus video briefings, specialized pamphlets, filmstrips, radio talk shows, even comic books; speaking to your audiences in your language rather than theirs; implying that your energy future will solve everyone's problems; not telling people what they should do next to start achieving the future you describe; ignoring whatever you can't put in numbers; being patronizing; in short, Not Telling People What They Most Want And Need To Find Out from your work.

"And finally," he concluded grandly, "the Sixth and worst Blunder is Lack of Process. Lots of little groups decide they are the fount of all energy wisdom. They go off in a corner and beaver away for months. Then, with great fanfare and greater expectations, they deliver a report as if it were graven on stone tablets. Yet their press releases are ignored, their meetings unattended. They elicit a giant 'ho-hum.' They become puzzled, embittered, or burned out, and nothing happens. What went wrong? Well, what they should have done is to design in real community participation from the beginning. And participation doesn't mean sending a fancy review committee a copy of the report that your experts just wrote in their name; it means continuously seeking, honoring, and using the ideas of a diverse group of thoughtful people. It means nurturing the kind of relationship with those people that makes them stakeholders in the result, so that they really care about not what *you* find, but what you *and they* together find. Then they will care, too, about spreading the word and making it happen."

"You know," said Eunice, "what you're describing isn't really all that different from the way I organize a bake sale, or the way I have to work if I want something to happen in my church or the PTA. If I put on a hoity-toity expert act, nobody'll listen. But if I speak to their concerns, in terms they're familiar with, then they open up. I have to listen more than I talk. I have to build relationships of trust and affection in the community. And when I do all that—just caring about other people, I suppose—it's amazing how fast things do happen once we all put our minds to it."

Duncan nodded. It occurred to him suddenly that he had all the theory, but this woman had actually done it. "That," he said, "is how America's energy problem will actually be solved. It'll happen from the bottom up, not from the top down, and your Department will be the last to know. Or at least it was going to be the last. I think maybe," he said, nodding admiringly, "that you're going to change all that."

"In as much of a hurry as I can," declared Eunice, "without violating the principles we just laid out. I suppose in its own way this Department is a community, too, however artificial; and if I want to change things around here, I'm going to have to pay attention not just to our official mission, but also to people's career goals and feelings and even their personal identities. Some of the more senior people may be too entrenched to be flexible enough for a retread, but I'm sure lots of people lower down in the Department still have the capacity to flower in new directions. Oh, dear! I'm beginning to think I've just become a kind of den mother to umpteen thousand threatened bureaucrats, most of whom I've never even met . . . But if some of them are like you," she concluded gratefully, "maybe there's hope for the organization yet."

27 *Getting Organized*

*I*T WAS GETTING TOWARD the end of a long day. Eunice crossed her arms and hugged herself. Duncan agreed by stifling a yawn. Eunice shook her head gently, as though musing. Actually her thoughts were already stealing away to wonder whether she could talk Joe into trying out that little cafe in Georgetown she'd been driving past each day.

"Well, Boss," Duncan said, smiling, "let's call it . . ."

"Um," Eunice nodded, somewhat distracted. She gazed across the Smithsonian's red stone towers into the gathering gloom of a D.C. evening. As she thought, her dinner plans warred with her worries about Duncan's departure. But then even this concern was overridden by a thought that had been quietly bothering her all day. "You know, Duncan," she ventured, "that was a nice talk about how to do a community energy study. You've taught me a great deal since we first met. And I think I have a pretty good idea about what people, and indeed the country, ought to be doing. But the question that keeps coming back to me is *how* to do it. And telling me how to crunch numbers didn't really answer my question."

"Ma'am?" Duncan returned, startled, from his own culinary reveries.

"How do you do it? How does one actually get started?" Eunice persisted. "For example," she explained, gathering steam, "what should *I* do first? Suppose I were just a housewife again," Eunice's eyes twinkled, "... *just* a housewife." She chuckled. "But, anyway, suppose . . . How would *I* begin? Not what—there are lots of whats: a study, weather-stripping, better appliances, new industrial motors, solar panels, and all that. But *how?*" She frowned. "Who has to do what, and why will they want to do it?"

Duncan looked at her and resisted the temptation to look at his watch. He partly suppressed a groan, sighed, closed his eyes, rubbed them, then looked uncomfortably at Eunice. He sighed again and rose to pour a new cup of coffee. Can't it keep? he wanted to ask. But a glance at Eunice told him that it wouldn't; she was clearly pumped up now.

Duncan searched his thoughts. What to say? Actually, this wasn't his area. Implementation ought to be left as an exercise for the reader, he thought dourly. Instead, he looked at his superior a little helplessly and pleaded, "Eunice, what do *I* know about getting my hands dirty? I'm a bureaucrat, remember . . ." Then he grinned wanly, trying to find some of Eunice's determination to miss dinner, and teased, "You know how many Secretaries of Energy it takes to change a light bulb? None," he chuckled, in reply to her confusion. "The free market'll do it."

"But that's just the point," Eunice exclaimed. "It won't. Or not fast enough; or if it does, a lot of poor people will be hurt; or if everyone does save and the price drops, the oil companies and banks that finance them will go broke, and low prices will just encourage increased demand . . . I mean . . . oh, no, I sound just like my Assistant Secretaries did . . . We've got to get more organized than that," she announced in exasperation.

But, as Duncan prepared to groan again, Eunice stopped as though she'd just remembered where she'd left a lost earring. "Organize," she exclaimed softly. "But, of course. My gracious, energy's just like any other community challenge—you organize!"

Duncan pulled his head back like a disturbed turtle. "Uh? . . ."

"No, don't you see," Eunice continued excitedly, "this Department will never do it for us; it's up to each of us to get active in our own communities. Not like it was a crisis—yet—but just out of plain old common sense."

"Well," conceded Duncan, with a mixture of unsure anticipation and pride, "that *is* why the President hired you."

"Yes, and I think it's time I started helping the country to use more of its own common sense. This really is a job for each one of us: to look around our community and ask, 'Why are we using energy in these dumb ways?' and 'How can we save money by saving energy?' There ought to be lots of programs to help people. Locally based programs, giving information, helping small entrepreneurs become house doctors, identifying and clearing institutional barriers—you know, making the market really work." Eunice set her jaw in determination.

"Um, Madam Organizer," Duncan drawled, "just how do you propose to go about this here task?" His face, however, betrayed a growing interest.

The question brought Eunice back from her crusade. "Well, I don't really know," she admitted. "All I know is what we housewives did back in Dubuque." She continued a bit more timidly. "I mean, I'm not a professional or anything . . ."

"Heh, you are more than I am," Duncan reminded her. "I've never organized anything more than my desk." He grimaced, glancing at the teetering heaps of paper about him.

"I guess the most important thing is to realize that it isn't really organizing," Eunice began. "There isn't any such thing as an unorganized community, you know. People all have accustomed ways of doing things—habits, understandings, and the like. To come in on a group of people and start preaching, well, they're just not very likely to listen. They'll be polite, maybe, but they won't change. I guess the first thing is to respect them as people, as intelligent, capable people that you're going to work with, not some group of children that need parenting and talking down to. People don't like that," Eunice cautioned Duncan.

He nodded studiously—it made sense. He wondered, as he made a note to remember that with Sweetland Power and Light, how many of his fellow bureaucrats would have thought of that.

"And it's particularly important to talk to people in a way they can understand," continued Eunice, "using words they know and concepts they're used to. It's especially important to talk about the problems that specifically concern them. You know, if I were going to talk to a banker about giving loans to help people put solar collectors on their homes, I wouldn't talk about decentralization, or saving oil, or all that. I think I'd say that reduced utility bills give homeowners more money in their pockets and make them a better mortgage risk. You taught me that." Duncan continued to watch her in outright amazement. "I don't know; maybe it wouldn't work. But that's what I'd do.

"And I'd talk about comfort—how all this will increase quality of life. I think a lot of those young people who talk about appropriate technology are right—we *should* live more simply, or . . . no, not simply, necessarily, but more thriftily, so that things last, so that we don't run through all the oil and the trees and the copper in the world—and, well, it's what you've been saying: using the right tool for the job. But when they talk about it I always think of living on the frontier, clearing ground for a homestead, and, well, it's not very appealing . . ." Eunice shrugged as though a little embarrassed.

"It's true," Duncan hastened to relieve her uncertainty, "and lifestyle change isn't necessary. If you want to live in voluntary simplicity, that's one thing. And who knows," he joked, "some of us desk-bound bureaucrats would likely benefit from some lifestyle changes. But that's no basis on which to present an energy policy. Folks can be just as mobile, industrial, ordinary, and comfy as they like. But they'll save money if they do it efficiently and renewably."

"So you say," Eunice said, grinning.

Duncan's face lost its professorial air, and he looked at Eunice thoughtfully. "What you're saying, then, is that the first rule of organizing is to talk to people where they're at, not where you're at."

"Well, that," she agreed, "and to value people, to really care about *them*, not just the message you're pushing."

"Makes sense," said Duncan. "What you're after is to influence people, to encourage them to take some action. I know I'm a lot more interested in someone's teaching me new stuff if I think that person cares about me and is trying to make me better off." He looked at Eunice self-consciously. But she was lost in her thoughts of organizing.

"One of my friends in Dubuque used to say that to get some-one to do something you had to convey three things: something is happening, it's going to hurt you, and this is what you can do about it."

"Yeah," Duncan nodded, "that'd get my attention."

"It seems to me," Eunice continued thoughtfully, "that the most important thing we can do is to help people feel more power-ful, more able to solve their own problems. I think what matters far more than whether a community decides to do a big weatheri-zation program, or hire a city energy coordinator, or organize its local utility, is for that community to realize that this is *their* decision, whatever it is they decide to do. You know, so much of the time I used to feel helpless. All the 'experts' on TV told me to 'do this, buy this, eat that.' It seems like people used to know how to take care of themselves, and now we're being told to go to professionals for everything. You know, I think the 1980s could be called 'the age of disabling professionals', a time when 'experts' have turned citizens into clients. What we really need more of is a sense of our own self-worth, the sense of confidence that *we* can do it. And the leaders we need are ones who will help us decide what *we* want and need, what's important to us, ones who won't just bring out their pet programs to impose on us."

"How do you do it? Organize, I mean?" Duncan jumped in while Eunice caught her breath. "How did *you* organize?"

"Huh? How did *I* . . ." Eunice blinked a bit as she abandoned philosophy for pragmatics. "Well, I guess I talked to people first. I just told them what was bothering me and asked if they felt bothered, too. I remember once we really needed a park, a place where little Jimmy, that's my son, and all his friends could play. The city didn't seem to care, even though it had this perfect site. Well, first I talked to one person, then I talked to two people. I tried to hook people up to each other to form a network of people who cared. Then, when we had a little group together, we decided on our first task—nothing too hard—you know, it's really important not to lose at that first effort. And we picked a project whose results we could actually see and feel. In fact, we cleaned up the park site—got all the broken bottles and old cans out and hauled the trash off to the city dump. What was important wasn't anything we did; it was the working together, gaining a sense of our worth and strength—a sense of success.

"Then we put together a formal organization. We picked our president—no, not me . . ." Eunice shook her head at Duncan's grin. "We chose a woman who was really good at letting others take the credit. She was the wife of the local pastor, too, and everyone respected her. She said her job was just to be the facilitator, to help us reach an understanding we all could agree on. And she handled all the little details so that the volunteers, who only had a little time, could really get the job done."

Duncan nodded. Eunice was rapidly confirming his long-held suspicion that housewives could run the world anytime they put their minds to it.

". . . Wonderful woman, Mrs. Farley," mused Eunice. "She made sure we were careful not to take on too much at once. So we never suffered from . . . burnup?" she tried.

"Burnout," Duncan corrected her. "Very smart," he acknowledged. "But how did you really get things done?"

"Well, we taught ourselves how the system works. We made friends with a reporter at the paper, who showed us how to write press releases. And we attended city council meetings until we knew how to present an issue. And then we did it. We filled that hearing room. Even the local TV people were there.

"And, you know, the council was just as gracious and considerate as they could be." Eunice beamed proudly. "And now we have our park. You know, I still think it's the prettiest one in the whole city. And they—the council members—seemed to need to take credit for the park when they ran for reelection; so we let them."

Eunice lapsed into silence. Duncan waited. "It makes me think," she mused, "maybe what I should do is quit this Washington job and go home. I think I could get far more done as a local energy worker than trying to get anything out of all this," she motioned at the building surrounding her. "You know, Joe and I could open a one-stop energy shop. We'd hire someone like Hobart," she smiled motheringly, "to tell us all the latest and best technology. And we'd have an army of house doctors going door to door. Why . . ."

Duncan's jaw dropped in the triple horror of losing Hobart, losing Eunice's common-sense Secretaryship, and having all his tutorials be for naught. "Madam Secretary! Eunice, we need you!" he finally managed. "Look, by staying here you can develop and encourage and launch those same programs you spoke of. You can have the effect of getting *thousands* of energy shops going. And if *you* don't, they'll put someone in your place who might be dreadful," he pleaded. "We never know what the Secretary roulette will bring."

"Oh, Duncan, I didn't know you cared." Eunice felt genuinely touched. "But it's only been a week that I've been here . . ."

"Quality shows." Duncan managed, looking a bit sheepish. "I had my doubts," he admitted, ". . . but you're . . . just wonderful," he blurted, squashing a startling desire to envelop Eunice in a big, long hug.

They looked at each other suddenly embarrassed until Eunice broke the spell. "But back home," she said with some annoyance, "I'd know what to do. Here I feel so helpless. This is all such a big old bureaucracy that spends most of its money on big power plants and bombs."

"It's true that Washington will be the last to know about the changes happening in energy; but if you're here, maybe it'll find out a little faster," Duncan offered, begging just a little.

"But there's so much work to be done," Eunice lamented, "and the real action is out in the communities. Isn't that where I should be?"

"Dear, dear Eunice," Duncan murmured, feeling a deep tenderness toward this suddenly feisty woman who chafed to save the world. "But," he chided gently, "even you can't take on the problems of *all* the communities—and, remember, for it really to work, they'll have to do it themselves, won't they?

"But will it help," he tempted, "if we celebrate the end of your lessons over dinner? My dear Madam Secretary, you've graduated." He grinned his most engaging smile, then stood and offered his arm to his boss.

28 *"Leaders Are Best . . ."*

W<small>HAT A WEEK</small>," thought Eunice as she sat in her office, collecting herself before her meeting with the Assistant Secretaries. First, she had bid farewell to Duncan as he took off to save Sweetland Power and Light. She had found herself suddenly at a loss for words. But he just squeezed her hand, looked right at her with those keen blue eyes, and said, "Ah, Eunice, I know you can do it." Well, she had thought, as her eyes misted just a bit, maybe she could . . . maybe she just could.

So she'd cloistered herself behind the great walnut doors and hammered out what she thought was a rather decent policy, if she said so herself. From time to time, though, she worried that she was getting to be a bit too much of an expert. Was she losing the forest of real people in the trees of statistics? Well, happily, she had someone to keep her from losing touch. So she ran a few bits of her policy past Joe, and with considerable success. He liked most of it right off; as for the rest, she found that she had been able to explain herself and deflect his objections without too much trouble. And explaining it to a critic had taught her how to say it all more simply. Hobart had been a huge help, too, always coming up with the figures she needed, trotting up and down the corridors with precarious bundles of technical documents.

And it was simply unthinkable that she could have done it without Barb. Barb had managed to limit to an hour a day the time

Eunice had had to spend on the obligatory points of ceremony that came with being Secretary. Perhaps most importantly, Barb had been her conduit to the outside world. "You know, Eunice, the Assistant Secretaries are getting restless," she had warned. "They're a bit worried about your taking matters so thoroughly into your own hands."

"But isn't that what the President appointed me to do?" Eunice had asked pointedly.

And Barb had reassured her, saying, "Of course it is. But, you know, the Ay-Esses are always looking out for their own Ay-Esses-Esses. Or their pet programs, mostly. They're supposed to be on your side, but really each one is on his own side."

"Yes, I did notice that at my first meeting with them," Eunice had sighed. "I'm not sure what to do about it, though."

Barb had promised to think of something. And, by gosh, Eunice mused, that woman had come up with a brilliant plan. Eunice had been a trifle uneasy about it at first, but she trusted Barb's vast experience with Washington. And, indeed, every time she thought about their scheme, she chuckled slightly to herself.

But now it was time to go for broke. The gauntlet of the Assistants waited. Now it was up to her. So she summoned Barb, who picked up a large cardboard box, and together they marched down the corridor to the conference room. Eunice noted with a twinge of glee how much more confident she felt going into this meeting than she had in the last one. Perhaps, she thought, it was because now she knew her facts and had more than just a blank legal pad with which to defend herself. *I hope that's true,* she chided herself. She walked in, once again took her seat at the head of the table, and waited while the Assistant Secretaries grew silent.

"Good morning, gentlemen," she began. "It is a pleasure to be meeting with you again. This has been a most productive two weeks for me, as I trust it has been for you. And while I must apologize to those of you who have found me hard to reach, I'm sure you will understand that the transition has placed great time demands on me and my immediate staff."

The Assistant Secretary for Nuclear Power leaned over to one of his colleagues and stage-whispered, "Yeah, right, picking new draperies for her office."

Eunice ignored the interruption and continued speaking. "In this meeting, I will outline the basics of the energy policy I have developed. Please save your comments until you have heard me out. Then I will throw the floor open for discussion." She looked each one of the men in the eye, holding them all in silence until she had completed the circuit around the table. As she released them from her regard they stirred in unconscious discomfort. Her self-assurance had caught them unprepared.

"The basic premise underlying my policy," began Eunice—*my* policy, she thought, with pride—"is that energy is not just for the experts. If the people have accurate information, they will make the best decisions themselves. And that's not an original idea, of course; Thomas Jefferson, for instance, believed that. And I agree. When you come right down to it, people are really pretty smart."

"I beg to differ, Madam Secretary," said the Assistant Secretary for Policy. "These issues are horrendously complicated. Why, it has taken all of us experts many years to solidify our knowledge to the point that . . ."

"No doubt," said Eunice dryly. "But it's not clear to me that your kind of technical knowledge has gotten us anywhere. Besides, if I can come to grips with the *nation's* energy situation in two weeks, surely other common folks, given time, can understand *their own* circumstances." She fixed the group again with a firm look and reminded them, "Now, I will ask you all again to hold your comments—and applause—until the end of my remarks."

The Assistant Secretary for Synfuels's upper lip twitched as though he wanted to sneer, but after a glance at his colleagues he hunched his shoulders and held it.

With the room silent, Eunice continued. "The other pillar of my policy is the free market," she resumed, unruffled. "Simple points. For instance, from now on we will do the cheapest things first, and we will let people choose how they want to satisfy their needs for energy services. We will ensure that people have both incentive and opportunity to choose wisely for themselves. Of course, the only way they can make those choices is for the prices of different forms of energy to reflect their true costs. I know you all realize that, if people don't know what energy really costs, they won't know how much is enough, and will continue to spend less than they should on ways to use energy more efficiently. So my first set of policy decisions will be to do our level best to remove all subsidies from the energy sector. And that means everyone," she added, over the sudden hubbub of voices, "*all* technologies. Quiet, please. That also means that this Department—and the rest of the federal government, if I have anything to say about it—will no longer pay utilities to build power plants, will no longer limit liability for nuclear accidents under the Price-Anderson Act, and so on. It means that I will urge that the federal Synfuels Corporation be disbanded, and it means that such subsidies as fossil-fuel depletion allowances and intangible drilling deductions are out."

With the whole room astir, the Assistant Secretary for Coal and Petroleum groaned.

Eunice thought, "Just like cutting my *kids'* allowances." She smiled to herself and went on. "Of course, all of these subsidies will be phased out gradually, to give everyone time to adjust. And," she continued, looking directly at the Assistant Secretary for Nuclear Power, who was staring blankly, as though a bomb had gone off in his head, "solar tax credits will be eliminated, too. But with all the other subsidies gone, the various forms of solar won't need a tax credit to compete fairly. Gentlemen," she raised a hand and regained their attention, "I recognize that many energy subsidies are buried in other agencies or mandated by Congress, but it will be the policy of this Department to ferret them out wherever they exist and to take a hard line on their elimination."

"Oh, no," murmured the shell-shocked Assistant Secretary for Pricing to no one in particular, "a *real* free marketeer."

"Yes," Eunice answered him. "I believe that truthful energy prices, and freedom to act on them, will save this nation trillions of dollars just by the turn of the century, which is," Eunice went on, "more than enough to pay off the entire national debt. And we will strive with all our minds and hearts to achieve those savings." Again she fixed them all with her confident gaze.

"Let me speak now," she continued, "in more positive terms about what else I want us to achieve. It will be the primary mission of this Department to help people figure out for themselves what to do. We will be, not hucksters selling a predetermined future, but messengers and facilitators. We will seek to expand people's horizons of choice. We will look for obstacles to using energy in ways that save money—barriers to the normal progress of a market economy—and do our best to clear them away.

"One such obstacle is clearly ignorance. Until two weeks ago, I had no idea how much energy and money *I* could save just by using energy more efficiently . . ."

"Or about anything else," the Assistant Secretary for Policy groused in a stage whisper.

But Eunice smiled benignly at him and replied, "People should not have to become Secretary of Energy in order to learn about energy. So the consumer information programs of this Department will be revitalized and greatly expanded. Such services as directories of vehicles' and appliances' energy efficiencies will be taken out of suspended animation. The latest and best techniques for energy labeling of buildings and their components will be adopted. And all of our energy publications will be scrutinized by panels of citizens to make sure they are indeed written in English or Spanish or whatever else Americans prefer to read. By the way," she added, grinning, "you might want to have similar panels look over the briefing books you gave me.

"Now, in order to publish accurate information, we have to obtain it. This will mean revamping the research and development that is funded by the Department. Presently, about ninety-five percent of our research money goes for the least-needed form of energy, electricity, produced at the least economic scale—that of central power plants. I am convinced, however, that this country has more than enough electricity and power plants already if only we use that costly energy efficiently. We certainly don't need to make still more at even higher cost. Instead, we will refocus the Department's R&D on the best buys, and on the kinds of energy our citizens most need: heat and liquid fuels. Our programs, being based on 'best buys first,' will, I am sure, turn out to favor efficient use over increased supply. And we will maintain a fast-reacting national clearinghouse of data on the newest energy-saving methods. Of the research funds that still go for energy supply, almost all will go to those technologies that show substantive promise of cost-effectiveness—not such rat holes as the multibillion-dollar fusion program." The Secretary for Nuclear emitted an anguished squeal and then fell silent. "If the Russians, or the French, or anyone else," Eunice continued, "want to spend their money on follies, let them. If the corporations now benefiting from this Department's fusion research contracts really think fusion is such a great idea, let them put their own money into it, just as the solar entrepreneurs have had to do for years."

She paused and quickly consulted her notes. "Ah, yes," she resumed, "the Solar Energy Research Institute and this Department's regional offices, cut to the bone in 1981, will be restored to their former stature, and more, but their emphasis will be more on the social, institutional, and behavioral factors that influence people's purchase of the cheapest technologies. The Department will continue to gather and disseminate information on energy use in this country . . ."—here you go, Hobart, this is your part, she thought—". . . but will make a stronger effort to document and define the end uses to which energy is put, ways to increase the efficiency of those uses, and ways to document the extensive use of sustainable energy in this country."

Eunice paused for breath, looked around the room, and noticed that profound shock had settled on all the faces in the room except Barb's. And Barb, though fifteen years Eunice's junior, wore the look of a proud mother.

Well, Eunice thought, at least they're quiet. And you know, she admitted to herself, I'm enjoying this. So she smiled warmly and continued. "Another way of communicating information," she said, "is to demonstrate what can be done. As a friend of mine says, 'Whatever exists is possible.' So this Department will also strive to show off fine, practical energy technologies. By the time summer rolls around, this building, for instance, will have cut its energy use by at least two-thirds; I've already hired a house doctor for us, and indeed I expect that we will find we can do even better than the computer predictions. Just as importantly, I am going to give the top three echelons of this Department time off so that they can put into practice on their houses the most cost-effective, energy-efficient technologies we know of, and then, for any who want, we'll make a media event out of it. For starters, Joe—that's my husband—and I will be hosting the television networks and the press next weekend at our home in Dubuque. We'll have our caulk guns ready, and everything we'll need to build a nice sun-space, too. I figure it should be done by late Sunday afternoon.

"Which is all part of a more general point," Eunice said, shifting gears slightly. "I expect each of you and your deputies to spend at least a third of your time in the field, at least two hundred miles from Washington, although you may visit places like Baltimore by special dispensation." In response to the roomful of wide eyes, she explained, "You are to find out what people are doing there to solve their energy problems, what is getting in their way, and how we can help. This policy is effective Monday. My secretary, Barb, will be glad to put you in touch with worthwhile people and places you can visit. I suppose once you find out what people are doing and can do, you will even find that you have some skills and expertise to offer them yourselves, but only *after* you have listened to what their needs are. Washington may be the last to know how the energy problem is being solved, but I intend for you at least to try to find out.

"You see," she continued, "the place where progress on these issues really happens is not on the Capitol Mall," she gestured out the conference room window, "but in the village square. It happens in communities. And as a primer on what can be accomplished on a local level, I have a personal gift for each of you." Eunice reached into a box by her side and pulled out a stack of paperback books. This was an idea she had borrowed from Hobart, who had lent her his copy. For the past week, when she hadn't been cooking up her new policy, she'd been reading that book. "Here you go, gentlemen, your very own copies of *The Milagro Beanfield War,* by John Nichols. It's the story, as you'll see, of how change actually comes to a community. I'm sure you'll find it entertaining reading. Just multiply the story in that book by the hundreds of thousands of communities and neighborhoods in this country, and not just Hispanic, but Irish and Italian, Jewish and Native American, white and Black and Asian; you know, Americans of all sorts. I think you'll begin to get an idea of how real communities work, and how the energy problem is going to be solved from the bottom up if we simply let the people do it."

As Barb quickly handed out the books, Eunice watched her Assistant's faces wrinkle into puzzled looks. She was struck particularly by the hint of a bemused smile growing on the face of the Assistant Secretary for Emergency Planning. Hadn't he been in the Peace Corps? she asked herself.

"Which is not to say," she interrupted the examinations of the book, "that this Department can't help. But we must learn how best to do that, with grace and finesse. We will strongly support the establishment and early operations of autonomous, local energy offices, to be run in partnership with state and local governments. And I don't want to see more than three people in any of the offices; the staff should be out working with local residents, not playing bureaucratic games with each other. Their mission will be to help clear away barriers to the sensible use of energy—not unlike a small sustainable-energy cheerleading squad. The Department will also make available no-red-tape seed money in chunks of, at most, fifty thousand dollars to existing local groups with proven track records of community organizing, like the bunch of lively folks who worked with me to get the park we wanted in Dubuque. These grants will fund work in communities to foster people's energy self-reliance and their ability and confidence in organizing themselves."

Eunice consulted her notes again. "We will also greatly expand the grant program that gives up to ten thousand dollars to people and small groups to test out their promising ideas for appropriate energy technologies. The point will be to dole out what money we have in many small bits, so that we can get the most minds working on these issues and coming up with new concepts. The application forms will be simple, one page long, and judged by citizen juries in each region. The smallness of the grants will ensure that people work on these projects because they believe in their worth and possible future profitability, not just to live off the fat of government grants. We will take risks. We will make mistakes. And we will celebrate and learn from those mistakes. We will try many initiatives at once and see what works. We will make every effort to recapture the entrepreneurial spirit of a small business. So we will work with small-business people and learn from them.

"And," she spoke even more determinedly, "we will apply similar ideas to our work with other nations. We need much better exchanges with other industrialized countries that are ahead of us on energy efficiency. Why, Western Europe, you know, needs little more than half the energy we use, yet lives about as well. And we will also redirect the development money that we send to the less industrialized nations. It will be our policy to share our knowledge of modern energy-saving techniques and of appropriate, sustainable resources with these people. At the same time we will seek to adapt what we can from their already sound, traditional methods of energy use and from the ingenious, simple technologies many of them have invented. And we will call this two-way program Sunbeams for Peace." Eunice paused again and sized up the reaction. Well, she thought, I've certainly stirred things up. The room, however, was absolutely still. The Assistant Secretaries stared silently at the woman who stood before them.

"Moving back to our own country," she said, "we have an obligation to smooth the transition to a sustainable energy path. After all, we in this Department are in part responsible for a number of failed solutions. For example, people who have trained in energy specialties that we will no longer need, such as nuclear power, do deserve our help in training for new, more practical careers. The swift and orderly transition to an efficient auto fleet is worthy of our attention, as well. Thus, this Department will actively pursue a policy of getting gas-guzzlers off the roads as soon as possible; we will provide incentives for owners to scrap their petropigs . . ."—she allowed herself a quick grin; that had been her own term—". . . starting with the twelve thousand or so which this Department owns and operates.

"Similarly, we will help the poor get out from under the need to buy large quantities of energy. Instead of subsidizing their fuel bills forever, we will help them achieve energy self-reliance by encouraging and setting up third-party financing for community retrofit programs. Inefficient, obsolete factories that are relics of artificially low energy prices likewise deserve help in retooling and rebuilding to meet the challenges of the new era of efficient energy use that we are entering. It makes far more sense for construction workers to rehabilitate those industrial plants than for them to build, say, a huge oil-shale facility. What's more, our ambitious retrofit and scrap-and-build programs will continue to provide them employment in their chosen fields.

"Now, as far as I can tell," Eunice continued, "nuclear reactors are just a special kind of obsolete, inefficient factory. Therefore we will provide advice on the orderly replacement of these white elephants with cheaper efficiency improvements. We will also refocus our nuclear activities away from expanding unneeded enrichment capacity and promoting technologies that spread nuclear bombs, and toward sincere efforts to clean up the current nuclear mess rather than expanding it. I will urge Congress to proceed more carefully in resolving the issue of nuclear waste. But as we will shortly stop producing more of it, this will make it a less urgent and less open-ended problem. And although I have been amused at suggestions that the waste be mailed to utility stockholders as a compulsory dividend, or stored in utility boardrooms, I think it makes the most sense that it continue to be stored at the reactor sites to keep it from being transported dangerously and unnecessarily, until we succeed in our efforts to find a permanent solution without the geological risks that premature burial in unsuitable centralized sites would now present."

At this point, Eunice drew herself up to her full five feet two inches. Dear God, she prayed silently, give us the wisdom . . .

"We must also," she said aloud, "confront the unpleasant fact that this Department is responsible for designing, manufacturing, testing, and maintaining this country's nuclear bombs. I gravely doubt that our mountainous arsenal of bombs improves our security one bit; in fact, given the risk of accidental nuclear war, I think they may actually make us less secure. However that may be, I am quite sure that they have no place in this civilian Department. Therefore I have asked that this responsibility and related ones— such as the production of uranium fuel for nuclear submarines— be removed from our Department. In fact, I want all classified activities—all military secrets—out of here, so that citizens can visit a government office, not an armed camp, and so that our own employees can regain their freedoms of speech and association. Indeed, for too long, the civilian nuclear program has served as a cover for various military activities of whose necessity and wisdom I am not yet persuaded. Our entire national energy program has in turn been subtly distorted by those military missions. So long as this Department of Energy is mainly a bomb factory—to the tune of nearly two-thirds of its budget—whoever runs it—except, so far, me—seems bound to share certain preconceptions that are unsympathetic to the economically efficient energy policies, the emphasis on efficiency and sustainable sources, and the honoring of human diversity and democratic values that I have outlined. This long-standing prejudgment of the most basic premises of our national energy policy is an intolerable disservice to our nation, and I intend to put an end to it. By so doing, I pray that we shall be making a far greater contribution to true national and global security than these programs have done heretofore."

As Eunice paused to collect herself, the Assistant Secretary for Utilities elbowed the Assistant Secretary for Nuclear Power. "Hey," he asked, a little shaken, "I didn't know *we* still had the bombs."

"Shut up, you fool," hissed the nuclear man.

"Please," Eunice quieted them both, "I have only a little more. But it goes to the heart of all the work we do." She paused. "We must, from now on, all recognize that the problems of energy are closely related to problems of resource use in general—to urban decay and renewal, to our security, to transportation systems and education, to food and land and water. And to many other areas of national concern. Therefore I intend to sponsor working groups that will cut across departmental lines, whose mission is to make common-sense recommendations directly to me and to the other Cabinet officers. If we are to stop shuffling off our various problems onto each other—proving yet again that the cause of problems is prior solutions—we need . . ." she paused, ". . . a vision across boundaries." As that novel notion began to sink in, Eunice took a deep breath. "Now," she said, "I thank you all for your kind attention. And I invite your reactions to the program I have just laid out."

"Madam Secretary!" the Assistant Secretary for Nuclear Power practically shouted over a hubbub of voices. "You can't do any of this. Why, it will never fly in Congress or before the people, and it certainly will not make it in this Department." His breath came in gasps as he glared at Eunice.

Poor fellow, Eunice thought. But then I have rather demolished his fiefdom. Ah, well, she nodded to herself, his reactions weren't much worse than she'd handled in her kids a hundred times when they'd refused to face reality.

"My dear Mr. Assistant Secretary," she began in a deceptively placid tone, "please understand a few things. For one, I have, of course, discussed this plan with the President's Special Assistant. And he agreed that it is *exactly* the sort of common sense that I was hired to provide. So did certain key figures on the Hill with whom I have already had informal discussions. As to whether my policies will fly in this Department, you should know that it is not my plan that will fly or drop, but my staff."

She smiled gently and added, "Of course I have utmost confidence in your ability to change gears and adopt a more sensible, market-oriented, people-oriented attitude. But, if you doubt your ability to do so, please feel free to seek an interdepartmental transfer. I should warn you, though, that you may find more free-market administrators in high office, if the early reception this plan has received elsewhere is any indication.

"And as to whether the American people will accept this: I have issued a press release over my signature, outlining in detail the plan that I have explained to you and that, in the months and years ahead, you and I will carry out together. Couriers should be delivering that release to the *Post,* the *Times,* and the rest of the press," she paused and checked her wristwatch, "right about now. In fact, it's probably on the ten o'clock news already. And we'll all have the chance to find out on the editorial pages and in the mailbags whether the people want common sense or not— whether they want energy policy to be done *for* and *to* them, or *with* and *by* them. I do think that, if *I'm* ready for a policy like this, the general public will be pretty receptive, especially if we fulfill our responsibility to explain it to them fully and clearly. Of course, in the press release I expressed my complete confidence in the ability of my able and learned staff to implement a plan so critical to the national well-being."

In the silence that followed, the noise of the air-shuffling equipment sounded thunderous. The Assistant Secretaries suddenly looked drained. The Assistant Secretary for Emergency

Planning frowned speculatively, then as his colleagues watched, grinned thoughtfully. As Eunice stood in the solid silence, still facing her bewildered Assistants, Barb rose, walked over to her, and handed her a small, white envelope. The writing on the outside, Eunice noted with anticipation, was Duncan's. She tore it open and read:

> Hi, Boss. Great job! (Remember, I have my sources . . .)
> Here's a present for your office wall. You've earned it.
>
> Leaders are best when people scarcely know they exist,
> not so good when people obey and acclaim them,
> worst when people despise them.
> Fail to honor people, they fail to honor you.
> But of good leaders who talk little,
> when their work is done, their task fulfilled,
> the people will all say: 'We did this ourselves.'
> —LAO TSE
> *Chinese philosopher, ca. 550* B.C.

Bibliography

PRICES (in U.S. $) and availability current as of August 1985 but may change. Where ordering address given, price includes delivery within the United States. Prices separated by slashes denote cloth/paperbound prices. An asterisk (*) denotes an organization whose address is listed at the end of the bibliography.

Many of the basic entries are applicable to more than one section; however, we have listed some of them in only one place.

I: What Is Past Is Prologue
(Chapters 1 and 2)

Lovins, Amory B., "Energy Strategy: The Road Not Taken?", in *Foreign Affairs,* October 1976, Vol. 55, No. 1; available as a reprint from the Council on Foreign Relations*. 32 pp., $3. Republished and greatly expanded in *Soft Energy Paths,* Harper and Row Colophon, 1977. 231 pp., $4.95. Original posing of energy issues in terms of end-use. Suggests that nations must choose between "hard" and "soft" or sustainable energy path.

————, *World Energy Strategies,* Harper & Row Colophon, 1973. Out of print. Early but still useful discussion of constraints on global energy use and of associated values issues. Introductory material on numbers and concepts.

Sant, Roger W., *et al., Creating Abundance,* McGraw-Hill, 1984. 192 pp., $14.95. Chapter 8, "Some Myths About Energy," debunks several common misconceptions about the nature of the energy problem.

Stobaugh, Robert, and Yergin, Daniel, *Energy Future,* Random House, 1982 or latest edition. 368 pp., $6.95. Reviews main energy options, their problems and prospects.

II: How Much Energy Do We Need?
(Chapters 3 through 5)

GENERAL

Lovins, Amory B., *Least-Cost Electrical Services as an Alternative to the Braidwood Project,* Rocky Mountain Institute, 1985. 172 pp., $50 from RMI*. Extremely detailed account of electricity savings possible in all end-use sectors. Testimony before the Illinois Commerce Commission.

Lovins, Amory B. and L. Hunter, *et al., Least-Cost Energy: Solving the CO$_2$ Problem,* Brick House/Wiley, 1982. 192 pp., $21.95. Semi-technical discussion of the long-term potential for energy efficiency in West Germany and other industrialized nations.

Lovins on the Soft Path, award-winning 16 mm, 36-minute color film, explaining end-use concepts and renewable energy sources. For rent or sale (including VCR formats) from Bullfrog Films*.

Nash, Hugh, ed., *The Energy Controversy,* Brick House, 1979. 450 pp., $7.65, from Friends of the Earth*. Amory Lovins responds to sixteen of his critics; his responses are printed side-by-side with their allegations, and readers are invited to decide who is right.

Rocky Mountain Institute*. Publications list and description sent free. Focuses on efficient use of resources and building global security. Founded in 1982 by Amory and Hunter Lovins.

Sant, Roger W., *et al., Creating Abundance* (cited in Part I). How we can have as much energy as we need simply by using current supplies more efficiently. Updated survey of "least-cost" energy thesis. Leads up to two scenarios of energy use: "least-cost" and "business-as-usual".

RESIDENTIAL ENERGY USE

Energy Auditor & Retrofitter, bimonthly, $35/year from 2124 Kittredge, Suite 95, Berkeley, CA 94704. Covers energy-efficient products and techniques for existing homes.

Energy Design Update, monthly, review of residential energy efficiency technologies; oriented toward builders. $107/year from P.O. Box 716, Back Bay Annex, Boston, MA 02117.

Geller, Howard, *Energy-Efficient Appliances,* American Council for an Energy-Efficient Economy, 1983. 48 pp., $15 from ACEEE*. The performance and economics of efficient residential appliances, and how to speed their introduction. Updated semiannually in *The Most Energy-Efficient Appliances,* semiannual, $2 per copy, 17 pp., from ACEEE*. Lists the most efficient mass-produced gas and electric appliances on the market and their energy consumptions. Keep abreast of ACEEE's publications list.

Home Remedies, Mid-Atlantic Solar Energy Association, 1981. 253 pp., $10 from New England Solar Energy Association, P.O. Box 541, Brattleboro, VT 05301. How-to manual of first-aid and long-term therapies to diagnose and heal your home's chills and fevers.

Nisson, J.D. Ned, and Dutt, Gautam, *The Superinsulated Home Book,* Wiley, 1985. 316 pp., $19.95. Design and construction of homes that require under $100 worth of heating and cooling per year, in any climate. Coauthored by a former builder now editor of *Energy Design Update.*

Parks, Alexis, *People Heaters,* Brick House, 1980. 128 pp., $6.50. How to keep yourself warm instead of just heating the air in your house, using techniques of architecture, interior design, and clothing.

Sackett, James, *A Development Strategy for Superinsulated Housing,* Public Technology, Inc., 1985. 88 pp., $22 from PTI, 1301 Pennsylvania Ave., N.W., Washington, DC 20004. Strategies for introducing superinsulation to a city's existing housing stock. Thorough economic analysis.

What Works: Documenting Energy Conservation in Buildings, American Council for an Energy-Efficient Economy, 1984. 562 pp., $54.95/29.95 from ACEEE*. Proceedings of a 1982 national conference on how well energy-efficiency improvements to residential and commercial buildings actually worked, and how to implement such programs. Technical. *Doing Better,* proceedings of 1984 conference, 12 volumes, $100 from ACEEE*; table of contents free from same address. Subsequent proceedings, as they become available from ACEEE.

INDUSTRIAL ENERGY USE

Energy User News, weekly, review of developments in industrial and commercial energy savings and cogeneration. $49/year, from Fairchild Publications, 7 E. 12th St., New York, NY 10003.

Industrial Energy Use, U.S. Congress, Office of Technology Assessment, 1983. 174 pp., $6 from U.S. Government Printing Office, Washington, DC 20402, USA (Pub. No. 052-003-00915-3). Conservatively explores opportunities for gains in the efficiency with which industry uses energy. Compares likely effects of various policy instruments on that goal.

III: What Kinds of Energy Do We Need?
(Chapters 6 through 8)

Lovins, Amory B., "Reexamining the nature of the ECE energy problem, *Energy Policy* [U.K.], Sept. 1979, pp. 178–198. Survey of European and North American end-use structures and efficiency opportunities, ca. 1978.

Meier, Alan, *et al., Supplying Energy Through Greater Efficiency,* University of California Press, 1983. 200 pp., $19.95. The potential for energy saving in California's residential sector, including costs of various measures and their aggregate energy savings. Data several years old, but methodology useful.

A New Prosperity, Solar Energy Research Institute Solar/Conservation Study, Brick House, 1981. 454 pp., $39.95/19.95. The most comprehensive study of U.S. energy use ever undertaken. Focuses on relative cost of saving energy and supplying energy renewably, and on policies that could move the U.S. toward sustainable energy use.

Olivier, David, *et al., Energy-Efficient Futures: Opening the Solar Option,* Earth Resources Research, 1983. £43 in sterling from 258 Pentonville Road, London N1 9JY, United Kingdom. A study of British energy efficiency in about five thousand end-use sectors. Most detailed of any country ever surveyed.

Ross, Marc H. and Williams, Robert H., *Our Energy: Regaining Control,* McGraw-Hill, 1981. 354 pp., $22.95. Using energy efficiency as a springboard for economic growth and sustainable use of energy. Less technical than *A New Prosperity.* Good documentation.

Sampson, Anthony, *The Seven Sisters,* Bantam Books, 1976, updated 1980 or later. 384 pp., $4.95. The history of the domination of oil markets by seven multinational firms, and responses by OPEC nations.

IV: Where Can We Get the Energy We Need?
(Chapters 9 through 12)

GENERAL

Annual Review of Energy, $56/year from Annual Reviews, Inc., 4139 El Camino Way, Palo Alto, CA 94306. Covers technical advances, economics and sociology of putting energy to work. Global scope.

Butti, Ken, and Perlin, John, *A Golden Thread,* Van Nostrand Reinhold, 1980. 289 pp., $19.95/9.95. Fascinating account of the uses of solar energy from ancient Greece through the early Industrial Age to the present day.

Deudney, Daniel, and Flavin, Christopher, *Renewable Energy: The Power to Choose,* W.W. Norton, 1983. 431 pp., $18.95/8.95. Nontechnical description of the major renewable sources of energy, complete with ideas on implementing a transition and a vision of what a renewably fueled society might look like.

Leckie, Jim, Masters, Gil, *et al., More Other Homes and Garbage,* Sierra Club Books, 1981. 416 pp., $14.95. Excellent how-to manual. Explains the design of efficient and renewable energy systems —heat, electricity and biogas—clearly enough for the nontechnical reader to follow.

A New Prosperity, listed in Part III. Includes assessment of various renewable energy technologies; slightly out of date, but still a standard reference.

New Shelter, nine times annually, $11/year from Rodale*. General design hints include a healthy dose of energy efficiency and renewables—mostly heating, but also some electricity.

Renewable Energy at the Crossroads, Center for Renewable Resources, 1985. 20 pp., $5 from CRR*. A brief, non-technical summary of the principal forms of renewable energy, with up-to-date figures on their use, cost, and funding sources in the United States. See also new items as they appear on the Center's publications list.

Renewable Energy News, monthly, $28/year from SolarVision*. Leading trade journal for the application of renewable technologies. Covers policy and legal developments as well as hardware.

Sørensen, Bent, *Renewable Energy,* Academic Press, 1979. 683 pp., $55. Technical discussion of the physics, theory, and global distribution of renewable energy flows.

Solar Age, monthly, $32/year from SolarVision*. Latest developments in solar technology, focusing on commercially available equipment and information of use to contractors and installers.

Tools for the Soft Path, International Project for Soft Energy Paths, Friends of the Earth, 1982. 288 pp., out of print. Excellent compilation of articles from *Soft Energy Notes* (an excellent global newsletter published 1978–83) on efficient and renewable use of energy in all sectors of the economy and in both developed and developing nations.

Whole Earth Review*, quarterly, $18/year. Articles about sustainable and appropriate technologies, as well as the design of life and current events. Access information to books, periodicals, and products. By the publishers of *The Next Whole Earth Catalog, Second Edition*—similar focus, but in book form, 608 pp., $16.95 from Whole Earth Access, 2990 7th St., Berkeley, CA 94710.

Worldwatch Papers, about five times annually, $25/year includes other Worldwatch publications, from Worldwatch Institute, 1776 Massachusetts Ave., N.W., Washington, DC 20036. Issues of global concern, such as health, education, energy, and environment.

HEAT

Anderson, Bruce, *The Solar Home Book,* Cheshire Books, 1976. 297 pp., $12.95 from National Association of Home Builders, 15th & M St. N.W., Washington, DC 20005. Guide to design of passive solar systems, embracing the theory and practice behind such design elements as roof ponds, shading, and mass walls. If you use this book, remember to update the technologies described.

Littler, John, and Thomas, Randall, *Design With Energy,* Cambridge University Press, 1984. 366 pp., $49.50/19.95. The theory of passive solar design, energy efficiency and layout as applied to the cold, cloudy climate of Great Britain.

Reif, Daniel K., *Passive Solar Water Heaters,* Brick House, 1983. 208 pp., $12.95. Various types of batch heaters—their design, construction, and installation.

———, *Solar Retrofit,* Brick House, 1981. 200 pp., $11.95. How to design and build four types of passive solar heaters: direct gain, passive and active air collectors, and greenhouse. Again, remember to consider recent advances in the technology before following the plans here. Check for more recent Brick House* or Rodale* publications, reviewed in, for instance, *Solar Age.*

Yanda, Bill, and Fisher, Rick, *The Food and Heat Producing Solar Greenhouse,* John Muir Publications, 1980. 208 pp., $8 from Muir, P.O. Box 613, Santa Fe, NM 87501. Walks the reader through the design and construction of a solar greenhouse retrofit. Covers indoor gardening and examples of private and community greenhouses around the country.

LIQUIDS

Bernton, Hal, *et al., The Forbidden Fuel,* Boyd Griffin, 1982. 312 pp., $19.95. The history, politics and development of fuel alcohol in the twentieth century.

Energy from Biological Processes, U.S. Congress Office of Technology Assessment, 1980. Volume One: Overview of technology, fuel cycles and policies. Volume Two: Accompanying technical and environmental analyses. Vol. One (Pub. No. PB 80-211477, 195 pp.) $19; Vol. Two (Pub. No. PB81-134769, 234 pp.), $20.50; or $4.50 per volume on microfiche; from National Technical Information Service*.

Jackson, Wes *et al.,* editors, *Meeting the Expectations of the Land,* North Point Press, 1984. 320 pp., $22.50/12.50. Chapter Six: "Energy and Agriculture," includes a discussion of the feasibility of liquid fuels from crop and forestry wastes, and the conditions for sustainability.

ELECTRICITY

Hirshberg, Gary, *The New Alchemy Water-Pumping Windmill Book,* Brick House, 1982. Out of print. Excellent plans for a simple wind machine that will pump large volumes of water even in a slow wind. Also includes a good method for assessing whether windpower is suitable for you.

Lovins, Amory B., *Least-Cost Electrical Services as an Alternative to the Braidwood Project,* (cited in Part II), on the growing use and grid interchange of renewably generated electricity.

Maycock, Paul D., and Stirewalt, Edward N., *A Guide to the Photovoltaic Revolution,* Rodale Press, 1985. 288 pp., $9.95. The economics, recent technical developments, and politics of photovoltaics.

Munson, Richard, *Electricity: New Consumer Choices,* Center for Renewable Resources, 1985. 20 pp., $3 from CRR*. Brief examination of new sources of generation, changes in utility management, and current statistics on load management and renewable generation.

Naar, Jon, *The New Wind Power,* Penguin Books, 1982. 251 pp., $12.95. Contemporary advances in the design of wind machines and the inroads they are making to the generation of power in the United States.

Northwest Conservation and Electric Power Plan, Northwest Power Planning Council (interstate compact), 1985. Two volumes, ca. 150 to 200 pp. each, free from NWPPC, 850 SW Broadway, Suite 1100, Portland, OR 97205. Shows how a least-cost strategy can meet all needs for additional electric services from efficiency improvements and renewable sources, pushing the need for new power plants far into the future.

V. Sustainable Energy and . . .
(Chapters 13 through 20)

... JOBS

Grossman, Richard, and Daneker, Gail, *Energy, Jobs and the Economy,* Alyson Publications, 1979. 124 pp., $3.45 from Carrier Pigeon, 75 Kneeland St., Room 309, Boston, MA 02111. Basic reference on job creation from renewable energy and improved energy efficiency.

Scales, John K., and Popkin, James M., *Energy and Jobs,* Coalition of Northeastern Governors, 1983. 97 pp., $7.50 from CONEG Policy

Research Center, 400 North Capitol St., Suite 382, Washington, DC 20001. Detailed analysis of the employment effects of efficiency and sustainables in the Northeast. Most thorough regional analysis available.

. . . THE POOR

Creative Energy Conservation for Low-Income Households, Alliance to Save Energy, 1985. ca. 100 pp., $11 from ASE*. Analysis and case studies of federally supported programs to help poor people use energy more efficiently.

Energy and the Poor, National Center for Appropriate Technology, 1979. 33 pp., $2 from NCAT, P.O. Box 3838, Butte, MT 59701. Proposal for an energy strategy to help the poor become more self-reliant.

. . . THE THIRD WORLD

Brown, Lester R., *et al., State of the World 1985,* W.W. Norton, 1985. 301 pp., $18.95/8.95. Global perspective on problems of environment, health, energy, and population.

Darrow, Ken, *et al., Appropriate Technology Sourcebook,* Volunteers in Asia, 1981. Two volumes, 320 and 496 pp., $7 and $8 from VIA, P.O. Box 4543, Stanford, CA 94305. Thorough bibliography of ap-tech designs for energy, sanitation, water supply, agri-, aqua- and silviculture. Imbued with sensitivity to cultural concerns. Some 1,000 books reviewed in the *Sourcebook* are reproduced fully in a portable microfiche library.

Reddy, Amulya K.N., "Alternative Energy Policies for Developing Countries: A Case Study of India," pp. 289 to 351 in *World Energy Production and Productivity,* ed. R. Bohm *et al.,* Ballinger, 1981. 448 pp., $28.50. Reviews India's energy needs and shows that accepted forecasts of energy demand are impossible given India's resources. Recommends improved efficiency and use of renewables. New publications by Dr. Reddy available soon from Center for Energy and Environmental Studies, Princeton University, Princeton, NJ 08544.

TRANET Journal, quarterly, $30/year from P.O. Box 567, Rangeley, ME 04970. Abstracts of and access to developments in appropriate technology worldwide.

Organizations involved in these issues include Volunteers in Asia (above), Volunteers in Technical Assistance (VITA), 3706 Rhode Island Ave., Mt. Ranier, MD 20822, USA, and Intermediate Technology Development Group (ITDG), P.O. Box 337, Croton-on-Hudson, NY 10520.

. . . THE ENVIRONMENT

Brown, Lester R., *State of the World 1985,* described above. Environmental issues from a global viewpoint.

Christensen, John W., *Global Science,* Kendall/Hunt, 1984. 355 pp., $19.95, from K/H Publishing, 2460 Kerper Blvd., Dubuque, IA 52001; 30-day examination copies available. High school text covering population, food, energy, economics, and the finiteness of resources. Accompanying lab manual ($9.95) and teacher's guide ($19.95).

Gofman, John W., M.D., *Radiation and Human Health,* Sierra Club Books, 1981. 928 pp., $29.95. Voluminous, lucid work on the link between radiation (particularly at low levels) and cancer and other diseases.

Holdren, John P., *et al.,* "Environmental Aspects of Renewable Energy Sources," in *Annual Review of Energy,* 1980 (Volume 5), pp. 241–291. Rigorous analysis of the ecological effects of various renewable energy resources.

Inhaber, Herbert, *Risks of Energy Production,* Atomic Energy Control Board of Canada, 1978. ca. 120 pp. Withdrawn from distribution. Purports to show that risks of renewable energy sources are much greater than those from nuclear power. Concise rebuttal by Anne and Paul Ehrlich in *The Mother Earth News,* July/August and September/October 1979, pp. 116–117 in both issues, documenting the methodological flaws and inaccuracies surrounding the Inhaber report. Full demolition in *Risk of Renewable Energy Sources: A Critique of the Inhaber Report,* by

John Holdren *et al.*, 1979, Pub. No. ERG 79-3 from Energy Resources Group, Lawrence Berkeley Lab, Berkeley, CA 94720. See also Holdren's letter in *Science,* May 11, 1979, pp. 564–567.

Lovins, Amory B., "Cost-Risk-Benefit Assessments in Energy Policy," *45 George Washington Law Review,* 911–943 (August 1977). Pitfalls and fallacies of such comparisons.

Lovins, Amory B. and L. Hunter, *et al., Least-Cost Energy: Solving the CO_2 Problem,* described under Part II. Increasing energy efficiency to avoid the risks of the 'greenhouse effect.'

Lovins, Amory B., and Price, John H., *Non-Nuclear Futures,* Ballinger, 1975. Out of print. Examines fundamental problems of nuclear power, including entire fuel cycle and proliferation hazards. Part II analyzes net energy yield of nuclear power programs.

Not Man Apart, ten times annually, $18/year; $25/year includes membership in Friends of the Earth, from FOE*. (Student and low-income membership, $15/year.) Thorough environmental journal covering energy, toxics, wilderness, and peace issues.

Patterson, Walter C., *Nuclear Power,* Penguin, 1983. 256 pp., $4.95. Nuclear technology, how it works and sometimes doesn't, and associated policy issues.

Pawlick, Thomas, *Killing Rain,* Sierra Club Books, 1984. 224 pp., $14.95. Comprehensive treatment of acid precipitation in North America: causes, effects, and political ramifications.

Pollard, R., editor, *The Nugget File,* Union of Concerned Scientists, 1979. 95 pp., free from UCS, 1384 Massachusetts Ave., Cambridge, MA 02138. Documents obtained under the Freedom of Information Act that chronicle dozens of revealing mishaps at nuclear plants across the United States.

... WATER AND AGRICULTURE

Berry, Wendell, *The Unsettling of America,* 1977. 228 pp., Sierra Club Books $14.95/Avon $6.95. Collection of essays on stewardship of the land.

Empty Breadbasket, Cornucopia Project of Rodale Press, 1981. 170 pp., $4.95 from Rodale*. A review of the problems facing American agriculture and the growing threat of infertility and unsustainable farming.

Jackson, Wes, *et al.,* editors, *Meeting the Expectations of the Land,* described above (Part IV). Anthology on how to move toward a sustainable agricultural system.

Jackson, Wes, *New Roots for Agriculture,* Bison Books, Univ. of Nebraska Press, 1985 (orig. pub. 1980). 150 pp., $6.95. Argues against the soil-mining typical of current agribusiness and in favor of perennial farming in harmony with the land's natural systems.

Lappé, Frances Moore, and Collins, Joseph, *Food First,* Ballantine, 1978. 619 pp., $4.95 from Institute for Food and Development Policy, 1885 Mission St., San Francisco, CA 94103. Issues of equity, politics and distribution of food, with particular attention to problems of the Third World. Solid publications list from IFDP covering their further research on those issues.

Pimentel, David, and Terhune, Elinor Cruze, "Energy and Food" in *Annual Review of Energy,* 1977, pp. 171–195. Rigorous analysis of energy inputs to agriculture. Prof. Pimentel continues to publish and can be reached at Dept. of Entomology, Cornell University, Ithaca, NY 14583.

Sheaffer, John R., and Stevens, Leonard A., *Future Water,* William Morrow, 1983. 288 pp., $14.95. Halting the waste of water in America can do more to prevent a shortage than all the new supply options under consideration—and be cheaper to boot.

Organizations Pertaining to
Water and Agriculture

Ecology Action, 5798 Ridgewood Road, Willits, CA 95490; John & Betsy Jeavons. Agriculture on a household level.

The Land Institute, Route 3, Salina, KS 67401. Headed by Dana and Wes Jackson. Investigates prospects for sustainable, perennial agriculture.

New Alchemy Institute, 237 Hatchville Road, East Falmouth, MA 02536. Work on the integration of human shelter, aquaculture, and gardening blending low-cost food production with energy efficiency.

Rodale Press*. Good publications list, including periodicals.

The Small Farm Energy Project of the Center for Rural Affairs, Hartington, NE 68739. Focuses on more efficient uses of energy in farming.

... POLITICS

Anderson, Walter Truett, ed., *Rethinking Liberalism,* Avon Books, 1983. 296 pp., $4.95. Chapter 3, "Energy and Community," by Lovins *et al.* on political implications of sustainable energy.

The Four Corners: A National Sacrifice Area, Christopher McLeod, *et al.,* distributed by Bullfrog Films*. 1983, 58 min. The abuse of the American Southwest in the search for ever-more energy. Covers desecration of the region from the point of view of ecology, water, and Indian spiritual significance. Resource Guide, 24 pp., available for $3.50 from Four Corners Films, Box C-151, La Honda, CA 94020.

Lovins, Amory B., *Soft Energy Paths* (see Part I), on the political problems posed by the hard energy path and on how sustainable energy skirts them.

... SECURITY

Lovins, Amory B., and L. Hunter, *Brittle Power: Energy Strategy for National Security,* Brick House, 1982. 512 pp., $17.95/8.95. The vulnerability of centralized energy systems to accident, natural disaster, and sabotage; designing resilience into a system through the use of efficiency and renewables.

The Price of Defense, The Boston Study Group, New York Times Books, 1979, out of print. Analysis of the actual defense needs of the United States and how they could be best satisfied.

... PEACE

Bulletin of the Atomic Scientists, ten times annually, $22.50/year from BAS, 5801 S. Kenwood, Chicago, IL 60637. Covers the nuclear threat and possible solutions.

Cochran, Thomas B., *et al., Nuclear Weapons Databook,* Volume One, *U.S. Nuclear Forces and Capabilities,* Natural Resource Defense Council, Ballinger, 1984. 360 pp., $38.00/19.95. Technical detail on the significance of American strategic weaponry. Presented clearly enough for a lay audience to enter nuclear arms arguments. Volume Two: *U.S. Nuclear Weapons Production Complex,* 1984. 400 pp., $38.00/19.95. To be followed by six other volumes.

Foreign Affairs, five times annually, $25/year from the Council on Foreign Relations*. New thoughts on U.S. foreign policy and world role.

Lovins, Amory B. and L. Hunter, and Ross, Leonard, "Nuclear Power and Nuclear Bombs," in *Foreign Affairs,* Summer 1980, pp. 1137–1177. (Reprint available for $3 from Council on Foreign Relations*.) Demonstrates the link between nuclear power and the spread of nuclear weapons throughout the world. Expanded and republished as *Energy/War: Breaking the Nuclear Link,* Friends of the Earth/Ballinger, 1980, out of print.

McPhee, John, *The Curve of Binding Energy,* Farrar, Straus & Giroux, 1974. 232 pp., $10.95/4.95. Gripping story of Ted Taylor, a bomb designer who made proliferation a public issue.

Nakazawa, Keiji, *Barefoot Gen,* Project Gen, 1978. Two volumes, 284 pp. and 341 pp., $7.20 each from War Resisters' League, 339 Lafayette St., New York, NY 10012. Adult cartoon book recounting from a little boy's point of view the hell that resulted in Hiroshima when the atomic bomb was dropped. Next best thing to visiting the Peace Museum.

O'Heffernan, Patrick, Lovins, Amory B., and L. Hunter, *The First Nuclear World War,* William Morrow, 1983. 444 pp., $17.95. Scenario for a nuclear war and how to prevent one from happening.

Patterson, Walter C., *The Plutonium Business and the Spread of the Bomb*, Sierra Club Books, 1984. 288 pp., $16.95. Discussion of the perils of plutonium and proliferation that neatly connects technical and policy aspects of the issue.

Rocky Mountain Institute*, various publications, send for list.

Science, weekly, $60/year from the American Association for the Advancement of Science, 1515 Massachusetts Ave., N.W., Washington, DC 20005. Broad-ranging coverage of scientific policy issues and technical developments.

Sharp, Gene, *The Politics of Nonviolent Action*, Porter Sargent, 1974. Three volumes: *Power and Struggle*, 144 pp., $2.95; *The Methods of Nonviolent Action*, 368 pp., $4.95; *The Dynamics of Nonviolent Action*, 480 pp., $5.95. The theory and practice of nonviolence. Draws on examples from India under Mahatma Gandhi, civil rights struggles in the southern United States, resistance to the Nazi occupation of Europe, and others. Sharp continues to publish; he's at the Center for International Affairs, Harvard University, Cambridge, MA 02138.

Spector, Leonard S., *Nuclear Proliferation Today*, Vintage Books, 1984. 478 pp., $5.95. Country-by-country assessment of the spread of nuclear materials and bomb-making capability.

Sweeney, Duane, editor, *The Peace Catalog*, Press for Peace, 1984. 363 pp., $14 from Press for Peace, 5621 Seaview Ave., N.W., Seattle, WA 98107. Articles on working toward peace; resources for peace groups; directory of organizations in the United States.

VI: How Do We Get There From Here?
(Chapters 21 through 28)

SUBSIDIES

An Analysis of Federal Incentives Used to Stimulate Energy Consumption, Battelle Pacific Northwest Laboratory, 1981. ca. 200 pp., Pub. No. DE81-031928, $22 paper/$4.50 microfiche from National Technical Information Service*. Catalog of subsidies to the energy industries through 1978.

Heede, H. Richard, *Preliminary Assessment of Federal Energy Subsidies in Fiscal Year 1984,* Rocky Mountain Institute, 1985. 29 pp., $20 from RMI*. Counts subsidies to various energy sources and end-use efficiency. More detailed version scheduled for late 1985.

CODES AND LOCAL GOVERNMENT INITIATIVES

California Energy Commission, Title 24 Energy Standards, 1983 or most recent edition. Separate volumes on commercial buildings, apartment houses (four units or more), and other residential buildings, and for each of 16 climatic zones. Publications list and fact sheet free with self-addressed legal envelope from CEC, Attn: Publications Dept., 1516 9th St., Sacramento, CA 95814. Best state energy code currently in force.

Coates, Gary J., editor, *Resettling America,* Brick House, 1981. 555 pp., $27.50/17.95. Chapters 10 and 13 on bold action by local governments.

Conference on Alternative State and Local Policies, various publications, list from CASLP, 2000 Florida Ave., N.W., Washington, DC 20009.

Lovins, Amory B., and L. Hunter, *Review of Codes Regulating Energy Efficiency in Pitkin County* (Colorado), Rocky Mountain Institute, 1983. 82 pp., $15 from RMI*. The 1983 state of the art in building codes; what works, what doesn't.

CREATIVE FINANCING

Cogan, Douglas, and Williams, Susan, *Generating Energy Alternatives,* Investor Responsibility Research Center, 1983 updated summer 1985. 224 pp., inquire for price from IRRC, 1319 F St., N.W., Suite 900, Washington, DC 20004. For 120 major U.S. utilities, lists activities undertaken in energy efficiency, load management, and renewables.

Lovins, Amory B., *Least-Cost Electrical Services as an Alternative to the Braidwood Project* (cited in Part II). The increasing role of third-party financing in energy investments.

Munson, Richard, *The Power Makers,* Rodale Press, 1985. 320 pp., $16.95. Popular survey of the institutional revolution in the electric utility industry.

Powerline, six times annually, $15/year to individuals from Environmental Action Foundation, 1525 New Hampshire Ave., N.W., Washington, DC 20036. Citizen initiatives, rate battles, utility regulation. Other good publications (write for list).

Talbot, David, and Morgan, Richard E., *Power and Light,* Pilgrim Press, 1981. 262 pp., $6.95 from Environmental Action Foundation, cited above. Practical strategies for the transition to renewable energy sources.

Third-Party Financing, Alliance to Save Energy, 1982. 118 pp., out of print. 60-page summary for $4 from ASE*. Ways private investors can fund energy-efficiency investments in industry.

HOW TO DO A COMMUNITY ENERGY STUDY

Bott, Robert, *et al., Life After Oil,* Hurtig Publishers, 1983. 203 pp., $24.95/12.95 from Hurtig, 10560 105th St., Edmonton, AB T5H 2W7, Canada. Good example of calculating energy end-use needs on a province-by-province level.

Harte, John, *Consider a Spherical Cow,* William Kaufmann (Los Altos, CA), 1985. 283 pp., $24.95/12.95. Introduction to number-crunching. Harte leads the reader from simple calculations through more complex problems. Exercises with answers at the end of the book. Practical math and environmental analysis made fun.

Okagaki, Alan, *County Energy Plan Guidebook,* Institute for Ecological Policies, 1979. ca. 200 pp., $7.50, from IEP, 9208 Christopher St., Fairfax, VA 22031. How to study a community's energy use and devise a renewable energy plan. Includes worksheets.

Olivier, David, *Energy-Efficient Futures* (cited in Part III), good example of ascertaining end-use needs in great detail.

Romer, Robert H., *Energy Facts and Figures,* Spring Street Press, 1985. 72 pp., $8.95, from 104 Spring St., Amherst, MA 01002. Introduction to measurement and calculation of energy numbers.

ORGANIZING IN A COMMUNITY

Alinsky, Saul D., *Reveille for Radicals* and *Rules for Radicals,* Vintage Books, 1969 and 1972. 235 and 196 pp., $3.95 and $2.95. Basic community politics texts. How to organize in your community, build coalitions and exert pressure for change.

Coates, Gary J., editor, *Resettling America* (cited above). Chapters 6, 8, 9, 12, and 16 on communities organizing themselves toward a more sustainable society.

CoEvolution Quarterly, Winter 1981 (No. 32), issue on bioregions and organizing in naturally-bounded communities. $4.50 from Whole Earth Review*.

Community Energy Self-Reliance, Proceedings of the First Conference on Community Renewable Energy Systems, Solar Energy Research Institute, 1980. ca. 400 pp., $40 paper/$4.50 microfiche from National Technical Information Service*, Pub. No. SERI CP 354421. Reports by community activists on their projects.

Lovins, Amory B. and L. Hunter, *Brittle Power* (cited in Part V), Chapter 17, on community energy projects.

Nichols, John, *The Milagro Beanfield War,* Ballantine, 1974. 652 pp., $3.50. Fiction based on fact about a poor community in northern New Mexico, threatened by low self-esteem and water-grabbing, manages to hold onto its livelihood and character and to regain some of its pride. Hilarious as well as educational.

Schell, Orville, *The Town That Fought to Save Itself,* Pantheon Books, 1976. Out of print. How the residents of a small town near San Francisco successfully resisted pressures for growth and took control of their collective destiny.

Shining Examples, Center for Renewable Resources, 1980. 210 pp., $5 from CRR*. Summary of several dozen community renewable energy projects, including successes and lessons of each.

Publishers' Addresses

Alliance to Save Energy, 1925 K St. N.W., Suite 206, Washington, DC 20006.

American Council for an Energy-Efficient Economy, 1001 Connecticut Ave., N.W., Suite 530, Washington, DC 20036.

Brick House Publishing Company, 34 Essex St., Andover, MA 01810.

Bullfrog Films, Oley, PA 19547. (215) 779-8226.

Center for Renewable Resources, Suite 638, 1001 Connecticut Ave., N.W., Washington, DC 20036.

Council on Foreign Relations, 58 E 68th St., New York, NY 10021.

Friends of the Earth, 1045 Sansome St., San Francisco, CA 94111.

National Technical Information Service, 5285 Port Royal Road, Springfield, VA 22161; add $3 handling fee per order.

Rocky Mountain Institute, Drawer 248, Old Snowmass, CO 81654.

Rodale Publications, 33 E. Minor St., Emmaus, PA 18049.

SolarVision, 7 Church Hill, Harrisville, NH 03450.

Whole Earth Review, 27 Gate Five Road, Sausalito, CA 94965.

Index